The Trotman
Careers Directory

Edited by Ken Reynolds and John Mainstone

TROTMAN

The Trotman Careers Directory
This first edition published in 2002 by Trotman and Company Ltd
2 The Green, Richmond, Surrey TW9 1PL

© Cambridge Occupational Analysts Ltd 2002

The Job Classifications used in this Directory have been sourced from
the Careers Library Classification Index (CLCI) which is published by
the Department for Education and Skills (DfES).

British Library Cataloguing in Publication Data
A catalogue record for this book is available from the British Library

ISBN 0 85660 842 4

Design/Layout by Robin Mills
Printed and bound in Great Britain by Creative Print & Design (Wales) Ltd.

Contents

A few years ago, UCAS joined with the CSU and AGCAS in editing a publication called *What do Graduates do?* I was criticised by some people who said that UCAS was involved with getting students into university or college and had no locus in where they went to when they left. My response at the time was that, if they didn't understand that students went into Higher Education to work themselves into a job or career then I had to fall out with them.

These days the outstanding younger generation, with which UCAS deals, year after year, are focused on what they want to study and what they would like to do when they graduate. This book, *The Trotman Careers Directory,* gives huge advice on what young people might do whether they leave school at 16, or 18, or go on to Higher Education. Personally, I like the style of the book, which is addressed to the reader as 'You'. It is not one of those rather formal worthy books but treats the reader as an individual.

Trotman also publish a book called *From Learning to Earning,* which reviews employers' attitudes in various job areas and families to subjects studied and institutions attended by graduates. That book has a clever series of league tables, which I normally thoroughly dislike but could well be read in conjunction with this *Careers Directory.*

Despite the fact that we all now understand that there is no such thing as a job for life, we need to understand that there is a continuum through school, Higher Education and into employment and this book emphasises that and, in my view, is an invaluable contribution to the whole educational and careers advisory process.

Tony Higgins
Chief Executive
UCAS

Welcome to the *Trotman Careers Directory*. In this publication, we cover some 235 career ideas in 170 carefully chosen chapters, analysed under the unique WORKBRIEF headings. We cover a further 80 careers in the Additional Career Outlines Section.

Job Title

What is involved?	What sort of work would I be doing? What kind of responsibilities would I have to deal with in a typical day or week?
Opportunities for training	What sort of courses and qualifications are available? Do I need qualifications before I start? Can I work towards these on a part-time basis? Is there a choice of qualifications and/or routes?
Requirements	What exams would I have to pass in order to be considered for entry to this kind of course or work? Are there any other specific requirements?
Kind of Person	What personal qualities would help me succeed in this type of work? What skills are particularly important?
Broad Outlook	Is there likely to be a demand for this type of work in the future? What are the promotion prospects? Is there a chance of self-employment?
Related Occupations	Are there any similar careers for me to consider at this stage?
Impact	How would this type of work affect my overall lifestyle? Would my work limit my free time, especially in the evening or at weekends? Is it likely to be hot/cold, dirty/clean, noisy, active, dangerous or whatever? What levels of stress would be involved?
Earnings potential	How much would I be paid? Am I likely to be on salary/commission/bonus or whatever? Could this type of career give me an adequate or very good lifestyle? Are there any benefits apart from the salary?
Further information	Where can I obtain more detailed information about this type of work? (Especially in terms of website addresses)

Why Workbrief?

Well, the chapters are brief and they're about work! Much more than that, Workbrief allows us to brief you about a type of work by answering questions about both the 'hard' facts (What will I be doing? What entry qualifications do I need?) *and* the equally important 'soft' aspects (Will doing this job affect my family or social life? What personal qualities might be important?). With each title analysed under identical headings in a clear double-page format, you get a clear briefing about a specific occupational area and you should find it easy and beneficial to compare and contrast a number of different career options.

Create Your Own Fantasy Career!

If you want to research ideas a little more fully, you could write out the Workbrief headings on a separate sheet of paper and complete the spaces with details of your own ideal job. You could then check out our descriptions to see how closely they match your 'fantasy' Workbrief. You may not find a perfect match but you will learn a lot in the process about yourself and about how to make the most of your potential. If you don't come up with any reasonable matches, you might need to ask yourself if you are being realistic in your ideal assessment.

The WORKBRIEF Focus

The *Trotman Careers Directory* makes no claim to being fully comprehensive in its coverage of the world of work. It is aimed primarily at people who anticipate achieving or have already attained a range of GCSEs/S grades or equivalent at A-C/1-3, who hope to achieve A level/AVCE/Advanced Higher/Higher or equivalent qualifications and who are likely to progress to higher education, who are undergraduates or have already graduated. (See our comments below about equivalent qualifications.)

Our Workbrief analyses are listed in alphabetical order but you will see that we have also given a reference for the Careers Library Classification Index (CLCI), which is widely used in specialist libraries of careers information. We have added a separate index, showing groups of related career areas under the CLCI headings. We are most grateful to the CLCI authorities (COIC) for allowing us to use this Crown Copyright reference system

Equivalent Qualifications

While we are aware that the majority of our readers will progress from GCSEs/S grades to A level/AVCE/Advanced Higher/Higher examinations, we acknowledge that there are many equivalent qualifications – notably the Edexcel and SQA national certificates and diplomas, the International Baccalaureate (IB), the European Baccalaureate (EB), the Irish Leaving Certificate (ILC) and National Vocational Qualifications (NVQ) and Scottish Vocational Qualifications (SVQ). For certain types of work, moreover, the Modern Apprenticeship/Skillseekers route might be more appropriate than traditional full-time study. You might also find that an Access course could at some stage help you return to higher education opportunities after taking a break from your studies.

We have tried to adhere to a standard format, rather than fill each entry with lengthy and repetitive listings of every possible alternative qualification. Most professional bodies and higher education institutions go out of their way to be fair and flexible when considering entry qualifications and it is always worth making specific enquiries if you feel uncertain about matching the requirements for entry to a course or career.

We have deliberately not mentioned Advanced Subsidiary (AS) level qualifications in England, Wales and Northern Ireland because – while they add very useful breadth to post-16 studies – they are not normally specified as essential for progression to the training routes we describe in the Workbrief chapters. They *may*, however, prove valuable in contributing to the points total required for entry to higher education. (See information below on the UCAS points tariff.)

We include the current version of the national qualifications framework to show the official equivalence and progression routes of major qualifications. You should be aware that these levels are merely broad indicators of equivalence and that they do not guarantee automatic acceptance by a professional body or higher education institution. *You must always research options relevant to your individual circumstances.*

The National Qualifications Framework for England, Wales and Northern Ireland

Level of qualification	General		Vocationally –related	Occupational
5	Higher-level qualifications			Level 5 NVQ
4				Level 4 NVQ
3 Advanced level	GCE A level	Free-standing mathematics units level 3	Vocational A level or AVCE (Advanced GNVQ)	Level 3 NVQ
2 Intermediate level	GCSE grade A*- C	Free-standing mathematics units level 2	Intermediate GNVQ	Level 2 NVQ
1 Foundation level	GCSE grade D–G	Free-standing mathematics units level 1	Foundation GNVQ	Level 1 NVQ
Entry level	Certificate of (educational) achievement			

You can find out more about these qualifications and about the most recent changes by visiting the following websites:

Department for Education and Skills
Website: www.dfes.gov.uk

Qualifications and Curriculum Authority
Website: www.qca.org.uk

Learning and Skills Council
Website: www.lsc.gov.uk

QCA for Wales
Website: www.accac.org.uk

Northern Ireland Council for the Curriculum, Examinations and Assessment
Website: www.ccea.org.uk

Scottish Qualifications

There are similar developments within education and training in Scotland. The Scottish Credit and Qualification Framework brings together all the major Scottish qualifications, showing how they interrelate to open up career and personal development opportunities.

You can find out more from the Scottish Qualifications Authority.
Website: www.sqa.org.uk

UCAS and Higher Education

Many of the Workbrief chapters highlight the need for a degree or higher national certificate/diploma. We have refrained from repeating in virtually every chapter the procedure for applying to higher education but you can access a complete database of UK higher education provision and full details of how to apply through the Universities and Colleges Admissions Service (UCAS) at: www.ucas.com

UCAS operates a points system (the UCAS tariff) to recognise achievement in the exam routes outlined above. We have set out in the chart the main features of the system. You will find that some universities and colleges make offers in terms of points, while others ask for specific grades.

For example, you might be asked for BCC at A level or Advanced Higher, or BBCCC at Higher or simply for 260 tariff points. Qualifications such as the National Diploma or International Baccalaureate are not included in the present UCAS tariff. However, they are quoted on the UCAS website, under each individual HEI's entry requirements.

Universities and HE colleges make their own decisions on offers and have their own reasons for specifying certain subjects and grades. If you accept an offer of, say, BCC and then go on to achieve or exceed those grades, you would be guaranteed a place. However, if you achieve CCC and try to make up the equivalent number of tariff points by adding, say, a grade E for a different subject taken at AS, there is no guarantee that you would be accepted in every case.

You must ensure that you understand precisely the exact nature of each of the offers you receive.

You can work out your points score online, using the UCAS tariff calculator at the UCAS website address. You may also find it useful to visit www.highereducation.co.uk

The Open University is not part of UCAS but you can explore its enormous range of courses at: www.open.ac.uk

UCAS TARIFF
(Revised March 2002)

GCE/VCE AS	GCE/VCE A level	VCE Double Award	1-unit	Key Skills	Points	Adv. Higher	Higher	Int. 2	Standard Grade Credit	Core Skills
		AA			240					
		AB			220					
		BB			200					
		BC			180					
		CC			160					
		CD			140					
	A	DD			120	A				
	B	DE			100	B				
	C	EE			80	C				
					72		A			
A	D				60		B			
B					50					
					48		C			
					42			A	Band 1	
C	E				40					
					38			B		
					35					
D					30					
					28			C	Band 2	
E			A		20					Higher
			B		17					
			C		13					
			D		10					
			E		7					Int 2

You should note that points scores can be aggregated from different qualifications and that there is no ceiling to the number of points which can be accumulated, thereby recognising the full breadth and depth of your achievements. You cannot, however, count the same or similar qualifications twice, which means that AS scores are subsumed into A level scores in the same subject, Scottish Higher scores are subsumed into Advanced Higher scores in the same subject and so on. The tariff is still being developed to include other qualifications.
With grateful acknowledgement to UCAS.

England/Wales & N. Ireland
Typical Year 12 and 13 (Sixth Form) Subjects

GCE AS/A level
Accounting
Additional/Further Maths
Ancient History/Archaeology
Art/Design
Biology/Human Biology
Business Studies
Chemistry
Classical Civilisation
Computing
Design/Technology
Drama/Theatre
Economics
Electronics
English
English Literature
Environmental Science
French
German
General Studies
Geography
Geology
Government/Politics
Greek – Classical
History
History of Art
Home Economics
Information/Communication
  Technology
Latin – Classical
Law
Mathematics
Media/Communication/Film
Music
Physics
Psychology
Religious Studies/Philosophy
Social Studies
Spanish
Sport/PE

VCE A level/Double Award
Art/Design
Business
Construction/Built Environment
Engineering
Health & Social Care
Hospitality & Catering
Information & Communication
  Technology
Land & Environment
Leisure & Recreation
Leisure & Tourism
Manufacturing
Media: Communication & Production
Performing Arts
Retail/Distributive Services
Science
Travel & Tourism

Typical National Certificate/Diploma Programmes
Art & Design
Agriculture/Land-based
Business & Finance
Care/Health/Early Years
Computer Studies
Construction & Built Environment
Engineering – Electric & Electronic
Engineering – Mechanical &
  Manufacturing
Engineering – Motor Vehicle
Engineering – Other
Hotel & Catering/Hospitality
Housing
Language Units
Leisure/Travel & Tourism
Media
Performing Arts
Public Services
Science

Scotland
Typical Fifth and Sixth Year Subjects

SQA Higher & Advanced
Higher
Accounting & Finance
Administration
Art & Design
Biology
Business Management
Classical Studies
Computing Studies
Craft & Design
Drama
Economics
Engineering
English/English Communication
French
German
Geography
Geology
Graphic Communication
Greek – Classical
History
Home Economics
Latin
Mathematics
Modern Studies
Music
OIS
Physical Education
Physics
Politics
Psychology
Religious Moral & Philosophy Studies
Science
Spanish
Technological Studies

Scottish Group Awards
available at Higher & Advanced
Higher levels
Art & Design
Arts
Business
Care
Communication & Media
Computing & IT
Construction
Engineering
Hospitality/Catering
Land & Environment
Performing Arts
Science
Sport & Leisure
Technology
Travel & Tourism

Scottish National Certificate
Group Awards/Units/Modules
Admin, Business & Management
Agriculture/Horticulture/Animal Care
Built Environment
Care
Catering, Hospitality, Food & Drink
Communication/Media/Performing
  Arts
Computing & IT
Creative & Technological Arts
Distribution/Customer Services
Engineering & Manufacture
Environment Management
Financial Services
Hairdressing & Beauty Services
Languages
Leisure & Tourism
Personal & Social Development
Processing & Extraction
Public Services
Science & Mathematics
Transport Services

Republic of Ireland
Typical Leaving Certificate Subjects & NCVA Level 2 Certificates

Leaving Certificate – Higher & Ordinary

Accounting
Agricultural Economics
Agricultural Science
Applied Maths
Art
Biology
Business
Chemistry
Classical Studies
Construction Studies
Economic History
Economics
Engineering
English*
French
Geography
German
Greek
History*
Home Economics (General)
Home Economics (Soc & Science)
Irish*
Italian
Latin
Maths*
Music
Physics
Physics & Chemistry
Spanish
Technical Drawing

Also Foundation level

National Council for Vocational Awards Level 2 Certificates

Applied Science – Animal Care
Applied Science – Food
Applied Science – Horticulture
Applied Science – Lab. Techniques
Art/Art-Craft-Design/Craft
Business Studies
Business Studies – Administration
Business Studies –Bi-Lingual Secretary
Business Studies – Financial Services
Business Studies – Secretarial
Call Centre Operations
Community/Health Service – Childcare
Community/Health Service – Community Care
Community/Health Service – General
Community/Health Service – Nursing Studies
Computer Aided Design
Construction Technology
Control Technology
Cultural & Heritage Studies
Cultural Arts Practice
Design/Interior Design/Graphic Design
Engineering Technology
Fashion Design
Furniture Design
Green Keeping
Hairdressing
Horsemanship
Hotel & Catering
Information Processing
Information Technology
International Teleservices
Language & European Studies
Marketing
Media Engineering
Media/Multimedia Production
Motor Technology
Network & Software Systems
Performing Arts – inc Theatre/Admin/Music
Print Journalism
Retail Studies
Sport & Recreation
Tourism

Career guidance

Making career decisions is never easy and you should seek as much help as you can get. It often helps to talk things through with friends, family, teachers, lecturers, training providers, employers and – last but certainly not least – a professional careers or personal adviser. You should be able to book an interview in your school or college or, if that is not possible, your local careers or Connexions centre.

Disclaimer

While we have made every effort to ensure that the *Trotman Careers Directory* is accurate and up to date, we recognise that careers information is always changing and that broad descriptions cannot always cover every detail of every person's individual circumstances. We cannot, therefore, accept any liability for errors, omissions or apparently misleading statements.

As we go to press, the framework of National Training Organisations (NTOs) is changing to a smaller number of Sector Skills Councils (SSCs) but the process is by no means complete. We understand that remaining NTO website addresses will either remain current for some time to come or will automatically redirect you to the most relevant new SSC address.

We welcome comments and suggestions for improvement. Please email any observations to: info@coa.co.uk

Abbreviations

AH – Advanced Higher (Scotland)
A level – GCE Advanced level
AS – GCE or VCE Advanced Subsidiary level
AVCE – Advanced Vocational Certificate of Education (Advanced VCE A level or double award)
EB – European Baccalaureate
Edexcel – The Edexcel Foundation incorporating BTEC and London Examinations
GCE – General Certificate of Education (AS or A level)
GCSE – General Certificate of Secondary Education
GNVQ – General National Vocational Qualification
GSVQ – General Scottish Vocational Qualification
H – Higher (Scotland)
HEI – Higher Education Institution
HNC – Higher National Certificate
HND – Higher National Diploma
IB – International Baccalaureate
ILC – Irish Leaving Certificate
ICT – Information and Communication Technology
IT – Information Technology
NC – National Certificate
ND – National Diploma
NVQ – National Vocational Qualification
S Grade – Standard Grade (Scotland)
VCE – Vocational Certificate of Education (England, Wales & N. Ireland)

When covering engineering careers in this publication, we are concerned particularly with training and working as a professional engineer. There are many other valuable roles in engineering – at operative, craft and technician levels – but they are outside the immediate scope of this book. The professional level can be divided into two groups: chartered and incorporated.

As a *chartered* **engineer**, you would be involved with the processes of innovation, creativity and change that drive technological progress. You would develop and apply new technologies, promote advanced designs, improve production efficiency and pioneer new management methods. You could lead projects and work towards a senior management role in your organisation.

As an *incorporated* **engineer**, you would be more concerned with maintaining and managing applications of current technology, seeking to extract maximum efficiency from existing systems and processes. As with a chartered engineer, you could work towards a leading management role.

Aspects of the roles often overlap in practice and there is a corresponding closeness in the training routes available. The quickest route to either qualification is to obtain a degree accredited to Engineering Council standards by one of the professional engineering institutions. If you want to be a chartered engineer, you should select a four-year MEng course, for which you would need high grades at A level/Advanced Higher/Higher or equivalent. Maths is generally an essential requirement.

If you want to be an incorporated engineer, you should select a three-year BEng (or BSc or BTech) course. This would be more involved with practical applications than the more mathematical and theoretical syllabus of the MEng. Entry requirements for BEng courses are usually lower and more flexible.

You can convert your incorporated engineer qualification to chartered status by following an extra period of learning, known as a *matching section*, to bridge the gap between the BEng and MEng standard. You can do this over several years, while you are working, if you wish.

Whichever route you take, you could seek sponsorship for all or part of your course. You would gain industrial experience by working for your sponsor during the summer vacation and you would receive a salary to offset your student loan. You could also extend your course by a year in order to incorporate longer periods of industrial experience in a sandwich course.

When you have finished your degree, you would enter a period of *initial professional development* with an employer, during which you would apply your knowledge to solve real problems in a working environment. The final stage of this process is a professional review, in which you would have to show that you have the necessary competence and commitment. When this is successfully completed, you can call yourself a *chartered* or *incorporated* engineer and add the letters CEng or IEng after your name. Chartered status would also entitle you to register with the Fédération Européene d'Associations Nationales d'Ingénieurs and claim the title European Engineer (EurIng).

Further Information

The Campaign to Promote Engineering
Website: www.engineering.org.uk

The Royal Academy of Engineering
Website: www.raengbest.org.uk

The Engineering Careers Information Service
Website: www.enginuity.org.uk

The Year in Industry
Website: www.yini.org.uk

The Engineering and Technology Board
Website: www.etechb.co.uk

The Engineering Council, London WC2R 3ER
Website: www.engc.org.uk

The Careers Library Classification Index (CLCI) is used in most careers libraries to classify careers literature and leaflets. It is also used in Occupations (COIC). Its coding is used throughout this careers directory to facilitate the accessing of these reference sources.

B Armed Forces

BAB	Royal Navy/Royal Marines Officer
BAF	Army Officer
BAL	Royal Air Force Officer

C Administrative, Business, Clerical and Management

CAB	Civil Service Administrator
CAB	Diplomat
CAB	Patent Agent
CAB	Patent Examiner
CAG	Local Government Administrator
CAL	Health Service Manager
CAP	Chartered Secretary
CAS	Human Resources (Personnel) Officer/Manager
CAT	Office Manager
CAT	Secretary Linguist
CAT	Secretary/Personal Assistant
CAV	Software Engineer
CAV	Systems Analyst
CAV	Webmaster
COD	Management Consultant
COF	Operational Researcher
COP	Environmental Health Officer
COP	Trading Standards Officer
COT	Health and Safety Inspector

E Art & Design

ED	Artist/Illustrator
ED	Graphic Designer
EG	Industrial/Product Designer
EJ	Fashion Designer
EP	Textile Designer
ET	Interior Designer
EV	Photographer

F Teaching and Cultural

FAB	PE Teacher/Instructor
FAB	Teacher
FAC/FAD	Journalist
FAE	Museum /Art Gallery Keeper/Curator
FAF	Librarian/Information Professional
FAH	Archaeologist
FAL	Interpreter
FAL	Secretary Linguist
FAL	Translator

G Entertaining and Leisure

GAB	Actor
GAB	Dramatherapist

GAD	Musician
GAG	PE Teacher/Instructor
GAG	Professional Sportsperson
GAG	Sports Coach
GAJ	Leisure Services Manager
GAL	Broadcasting Researcher
GAL	Journalist
GAL	TV/Film Camera Operator
GAT	Stage Manager
GAX	Tour Operator
GAX	Travel Agent

I Hospitality, Catering and other Services

IB	Catering Manager
IB	Hotel Manager
IB	Restaurant Manager/Owner

J Health and Medical

JAB	Doctor
JAD	Midwife
JAD	Nurse
JAF	Dental Technician
JAF	Dentist
JAG	Pharmacist
JAL	Dispensing Optician
JAL	Optometrist (Ophthalmic Optician)
JAL	Orthoptist
JAN	Physiotherapist
JAP	Radiographer
JAR	Occupational Therapist
JAS	Speech and Language Therapist
JAT	Podiatrist/Chiropodist
JAV	Dietitian
JAX	Clinical Biochemist
JAX	Medical Physicist
JAX	Microbiologist
JOB	Medical Physicist
JOC	Ambulance Technician/Paramedic
JOD	Chiropractor
JOD	Dramatherapist
JOD	Homoeopath
JOD	Osteopath

K Social and Related Services

KEB	Probation Officer/Criminal Justice Social Worker
KEB	Residential Social Worker
KEB	Social Worker
KED/KEK	Careers/Personal Adviser
KEG	Youth Worker
KEL	Psychologist

L Law and Related

LAB	Advocate
LAB	Barrister
LAC	Solicitor
LAD	Legal Executive
LAK	Patent Agent

LAK	Patent Examiner
LAZ	Barristers'/Advocates' Clerk
LAZ	Licensed Conveyancer

M Security and Protective
| MAB | Police Officer |
| MAF | Fire Officer |

N Finance and related
NAB	Accountant (Professional)
NAB	Accounting Technician
NAD	Banking Executive
NAG	Insurance Broker
NAG	Insurance Underwriter
NAJ	Actuary
NAK	Financial Adviser
NAL	Investment Analyst
NAL	Stockbroker

O Buying and Selling
OB	Market Researcher
OB	Marketing Executive
OD	Advertising Executive
OE	Retail Manager
OE	Sales Executive
OG	Events and Conferences Manager
OG	Public Relations Officer
OM	Sales Executive
OP	Buying Executive

Q Science, Mathematics and related work
QOB	Chemistry Technician
QOB	Pharmacologist
QOB	Physicist
QOB	Research Chemist
QOD	Biochemist
QOD	Biology Technician
QOD	Biotechnologist
QOD	Marine Biologist
QOD	Microbiologist
QOD	Research Biologist
QOK	Economist
QOL	Geologist
QOL	Meteorologist
QOL	Oceanographer
QON	Food Scientist/Technologist
QOS	Materials Scientist
QOS	Metallurgist
QOT	Forensic Scientist
QOX	Biology Technician

R Engineering
RAC	Aeronautical Engineer
RAD	Agricultural Engineer
RAG	Chemical Engineer
RAK	Electrical Engineer
RAK/RAL	Electronics/Electronic Engineer

RAM	Biomedical Engineer
RAV	Marine Engineer
RAX	Automotive Engineer
RAX	Mechanical Engineer
ROB	Mining Engineer
ROD	Manufacturing Engineer
ROF	Naval Architect

S **Manufacturing**

SAS	Petroleum Engineer
SAV	Industrial Chemist

U **Construction and Land**

UB	Architect
UB	Architectural Technologist
UD	Building Technician
UD	Construction Manager
UJ	Building Services Engineer
UL	Golf Course Designer
UL	Landscape Architect
UM	Auctioneer/Valuer
UM	Building Surveying Technician
UM	Building Surveyor
UM	Estate Agent
UM	Hydrographic or Marine Surveyor
UM	Land Surveyor
UM	Quantity Surveying Technician
UM	Quantity Surveyor
UM	Rural Practice Surveyor
UM	Surveyor (Chartered)
UN	Civil Engineer
UN	Structural Engineer
US	Town Planner
US	Town Planning Support Worker
UT	Cartographer

W **Animal, Plants and the Environment**

WAB	Farm Manager
WAD	Horticultural Manager
WAF	Forest Manager
WAL	Veterinary Nurse
WAL	Veterinary Surgeon
WAR	Countryside Conservation Officer
WAR	Countryside Ranger/Warden

Y **Transport**

YAB	Air Traffic Controller
YAB	Airline Pilot
YAL	Merchant Navy Officer
YAS	Freight Forwarder
YAS	Logistics Manager
YAS	Shipbroker

Ken Reynolds is an experienced careers adviser, writer and consultant. He currently edits *Careers Adviser*, *School Leaver* and *Which Course* magazines for Independent Educational Publishing. He is a member of the Institute of Career Guidance Editorial Board and one of the judges for the annual National Career Awards.

John Mainstone is Managing Director of Cambridge Occupational Analysts, the higher education and careers consultancy.

Contributors

The entries in the *Trotman Careers Directory* are based on original articles supplied by:

Jennie Barnes

Annie Edgar

Sue Eynon

Graham Garrett

Jill Garrett

Bob Jackson

John Mainstone

Ken Reynolds

Jo Roberts

Godfrey Thomas

Note from The Editor

I would like to thank John Mainstone, Managing Director of Cambridge Occupational Analysts, for his unswerving commitment to this book and to Carol Mainstone for her encouragement and support throughout. We completed most of the editing, updating and final research shut away from the world in the Carbis Bay Hotel in West Cornwall. Not even the stunning coastline or the splendid restaurants of neighbouring St Ives could distract us for long from John's determination to get the job done to the highest possible standard.

Thanks too to all the team at Cambridge Occupational Analysts, especially Diane Lannon, Simon Foster and Joyce Lane; also to Rachel Lockhart and Tom Lee at Trotman.

Finally, my most grateful thanks to my partner, Sue Eynon, for selflessly sacrificing far too many evenings and weekends to my never-ending quest for the perfect Workbrief analysis.

Acknowledgements

We acknowledge the considerable help given by the following organisations:

UCAS
Qualifications and Curriculum Authority
Scottish Qualifications Authority
Association of Accounting Technicians
Institute of Actuaries
Institute of Practitioners in Advertising
Faculty of Advocates
Royal Aeronautical Society
Institution of Agricultural Engineers
Council for British Archaeology
Royal Institute of British Architects
British Institute of Architectural Technologists
Armed Services Careers Office, Norwich
Bar Council
Institute of Barristers' Clerks
Institute of Biology
Chartered Institute of Building
Institute of Chartered Secretaries and Administrators
Association of Clinical Biochemists
British Dental Association
Dental Technician Training and Advisory Board
College of Dispensing Opticians
British Medical Association
Institution of Electrical Engineers
Chartered Institute of Environmental Health
E Skills
Forensic Science Service
Hotel and Catering International Management Association
National Council for the Training of Journalists
Institute of Legal Executives
Chartered Institute of Librarians and Information Professionals
Institute of Management Consultants
Market Research Society
Institution of Mechanical Engineers
Meteorological Office
Society of General Microbiology
Institution of Mining and Metallurgy
Royal Institute of Naval Architects
College of Occupational Therapists
College of Optometrists
General Osteopathic Council
Chartered Institute of Personnel and Development
Royal Pharmaceutical Society
British Pharmacological Society
Chartered Society of Physiotherapy
Society of Chiropodists and Podiatrists
British Psychological Society
Institute of Public Relations
Society of Radiographers
Royal College of Speech and Language Therapists
Royal Institution of Chartered Surveyors
Royal Town Planning Institute

The Career Descriptions

What is Involved?

As a professionally qualified accountant (you might be known as a chartered or certified accountant), you would be working with financial and management information, using your specialist knowledge to advise a range of clients, from individuals to large organisations. There are several different professional bodies in accountancy and your initial employment could be linked to the specialist activities of the body you choose. There is considerable overlap between the various professional qualifications and you could easily move between sectors later in your career.

Major areas of work include private practice (also known as public practice, which is not terribly helpful), the public sector and industry/commerce. In the first of these, you would work in a specialist firm of accountants offering services ranging from basic bookkeeping to audit (independent assessment of your client's current financial position), taxation advice, management consultancy and corporate financial planning. Working in the public sector could see you handling very large budgets in local or central government, the National Health Service, colleges or universities. As an accountant in industry/ commerce, you could be involved in keeping financial records for a company, overseeing credit control systems and possibly participating in strategic planning for the organisation's future development.

Opportunities for Training

To gain recognition as a qualified accountant, you would need to spend several years pursuing the professional training route of one of the six main bodies, as listed under Further Information opposite.

There are many routes to professional qualification. Most take three to five years and usually involve work experience in an approved organisation, part-time study and lots of exams. You may be able to start as an accounting technician and then work your way towards professional status.

Requirements

As with training routes, entry requirements vary from one body to another. You would need at least two A level/AVCE/Advanced Higher, three Higher or equivalent qualifications, together with three GCSE/S Grade passes at A-C/1-3, including English and maths, to enter a training contract with ICAEW, ACCA, CIMA or CIPFA.

ICAS, on the other hand, would require a degree. In practice, the most common entry route to professional accountancy training is with a degree in any academic subject. If you choose an accountancy-related degree subject, you should gain exemption from some of the exams set by the professional bodies.

Kind of Person

You need to be very computer, figure and systems literate. You should enjoy working with figures, be diligent and accurate. Employers are looking for good academic results together with skills such as leadership, communication, numeracy, interest in finance and business, self-motivation and commitment.

B road Outlook

An accountancy qualification is a very useful tool and demand for accountants is currently growing in all sectors. As your career develops, you could choose to work for a very large organisation, you could become self-employed and work as a freelance consultant or you could take advantage of the worldwide recognition of UK accountancy qualifications and travel extensively.

R elated Occupations

You might also consider: banking executive, insurance underwriter, actuary, management consultant or financial adviser.

I mpact

Your lifestyle as an accountant would depend very much on the sort of organisation you join and the area of specialisation you choose. Audits can take you all over the country and a large international partnership would expect you to travel. High salaries are usually associated with increased stress and longer working hours.

E arnings Potential

Accountancy positions tend to pay well, although this can mean anything from a respectable salary to a huge one. Starting salaries for trainees vary from £18,000 in London to around £12,000 elsewhere. On achieving full qualification, you could expect to earn between £30,000 and £37,000 and, if you rise to become a partner in private practice or a senior manager in industry or the public sector, you could easily earn a six-figure salary.

F urther Information

Institute of Chartered Accountants in England and Wales, Central Milton Keynes MK9 2HL Website: www.icaew.co.uk/careers

Institute of Chartered Accountants in Scotland, Edinburgh EH12 5BH Website: www.icas.org.uk

Institute of Chartered Accountants in Ireland, Dublin 4 Website: www.icai.ie

Association of Chartered Certified Accountants, London WC2A 3EE Website: www.accaglobal.com

Chartered Institute of Management Accountants, London W1B 1AB Website: www.cimaglobal.com

Chartered Institute of Public Finance & Accountancy, London SE1 1JA Website: www.ipf.co.uk

Alternative/equivalent entrance requirements can include: ILC, IB, EB, NC/ND and many other similar international systems. For further details see the Equivalent Qualifications section in the Introduction.

What is Involved?

As an accounting technician, you could be working alongside professionally qualified accountants in activities such as keeping financial records, auditing accounts, preparing tax returns or providing information for management reports. You could be running a payroll or credit control system. There are opportunities in virtually every sector of the labour market: you might be based in a specialist accountancy practice, in industry or commerce, in the public or voluntary sectors or you could work from your own home for a variety of clients. Unlike a professional accountant, you would not be legally qualified to conduct a full-scale audit but you could be responsible for much of the groundwork. As a broad rule, you would be more likely to be involved with the detailed, practical applications of day-to-day accounting issues than with the wider areas of financial management dealt with by professionally qualified accountants. As your career develops, you may choose to specialise in a particular area of work, such as taxation or insolvency.

Opportunities for Training

The Association of Accounting Technicians (AAT) and the Association of Chartered Certified Accountants (ACCA) both offer training and qualification routes for accounting technicians. Several major chartered accountancy bodies sponsor the AAT and the qualification would make you eligible for entry to their professional examinations. You would work your way through N/SVQ foundation and intermediate levels 2 and 3 to become a technician at level 4. The completion of these levels, together with a year's relevant experience, achieves the qualification. The training scheme is offered at many different centres, including local colleges, the workplace and training providers. With ACCA, you would work towards their Certified Accounting Technician qualification (CAT). Once you have this, you would be eligible for direct entry to Part 2 of the ACCA professional accountancy examination. Study is flexible and can be full- or part-time at a local college or training provider, by correspondence or online through www.ACCAdemy.com

Requirements

There are no formal academic requirements for training with one of the organisations that award qualifications as an accounting technician, although you must be over 16 years old and should be reasonably numerate with a good command of English.

You may be able to gain exemption from part of the AAT qualification if you have relevant work experience or suitable A level/AVCE/Advanced Higher, Higher or equivalent qualifications.

Kind of Person

As an accounting technician, you would need to feel completely at ease when working with numbers. You would also need to be accurate, with a sharp eye for detail, and you would need good communication skills in order to explain details of accountancy and finance to those less numerate than yourself. You would usually be working as part of a team. Good computer skills are essential. The work would often require you to keep to strict deadlines.

B road Outlook

Opportunities for accounting technicians have grown in recent years, in line with the trend of shifting financial responsibility and decision making away from large central offices towards local, independent control. Qualifying as an accounting technician can be a step on the career ladder leading to full professional status, although many technicians enjoy their work as it is and do not wish to take further exams. With experience, you could move to a senior management position in a company or you could pursue the option of self-employment.

R elated Occupations

You might wish to consider: professional accountant, bookkeeper, insurance clerk, banking executive or financial adviser.

I mpact

Accounting technicians are office based, working traditional office hours five days a week. You may have to move across the private and public sectors – not to mention different parts of the country – in order to gain experience and develop your career. There may be opportunities for working from home and for part-time work.

The work can often be intense and pressurised with a constant need to meet important deadlines.

E arnings Potential

Salaries compare well with those in other sectors. You should see your salary rise from around £11,000 at the foundation stage to £18,000 and beyond once qualified. You can earn considerably more in a senior management post or if you are successful in running your own business.

F urther Information

Association of Accounting Technicians, London EC1R 5AD
Website: www.aat.co.uk

The Institute of Accounting Technicians in Ireland, Belfast BT1 5JE
Website: www.acai.ie

Association of Chartered Certified Accountants, London WC2A 3EE
Website: www.accaglobal.com

Alternative/equivalent entrance requirements can include: ILC, IB, EB, NC/ND and many other similar international systems. For further details see the Equivalent Qualifications section in the Introduction.

What is Involved?

As an actor, you would be a creative interpreter of dramatic works, comedies or musicals, performing in the theatre, in films, on television, video and radio. You should be prepared not merely to act but also to sing, dance and maybe undertake fights and stunt work. Glamour, fame and self-fulfilment might spur you on but can seem far away when you are rehearsing lines or sitting around while scenery and lights are adjusted. The varied working life of an actor might also see you doing voice-overs for advertisements, recording talking books or narrating documentary films.

Opportunities for Training

It is possible to become an actor without any formal training but you would be well advised to consider an accredited training course at a drama school. This would give you a much better chance of gaining employment and acquiring an Equity (the actors' union) Card.

Courses vary a good deal in style, so you should do plenty of research to determine which would be the best for you. Straight from school at the minimum age of 18, you would normally follow a three-year course. There are shorter courses available for graduates and mature candidates. The syllabus should include movement, voice projection, improvisation, singing, dancing, audition techniques and make-up.

You must be careful not to confuse accredited drama school courses with the many drama or performing arts degrees offered by universities and colleges. These tend to be academic, concentrating on the history of drama and the analysis of texts rather than vocational training.

Requirements

Entry to accredited courses is fiercely competitive and you may find that you are one of 20 or so applicants competing for a single place. Admission is usually by audition and interview, with experience of performing regularly in amateur productions or youth theatre a great advantage. You may not need any special academic qualifications, although some drama schools ask for five GCSE/S Grade passes at A-C/1-3 and even two A level/AVCE/Advanced Higher or three Higher or equivalent qualifications.

Kind of Person

Apart from possessing outstanding acting talent – the intelligence, sensitivity and imagination to understand and interpret various roles and the ability to present them to a theatre full of people or to a camera – you must be dedicated, determined and disciplined.

You would need to be strong enough, both physically and mentally, to withstand the long hours of rehearsal, the emotional demands of public performance, the disappointment of rejection at audition and the pain of negative criticism. A good memory is clearly important, together with a mixture of self-confidence and willingness to work in an ensemble. A feeling for music and movement would also be of great benefit.

B road Outlook

You can build a name for yourself by working hard and giving good performances. There is often a degree of luck involved in having the right talents and being available at the right time for a particular project. Many actors, it must be said, spend more time looking for work than they do performing. You need to bring yourself to the notice of casting directors and producers whenever possible and you might find it useful to have an agent to help you get work. Networking and personal contacts are also invaluable tools in the hunt for work. Many actors provide themselves with other qualifications as well, so that they can earn some money in other fields when the going gets tough.

R elated Occupations

You might also consider: drama teacher, dramatherapist or speech and language therapist. If being in the theatre is your main motivation, you might look at: stage manager, musician, dancer, director, production assistant or camera operator.

I mpact

As an actor, you would probably be seen as a member of a glamorous profession. There certainly are great rewards for some in terms of fame and personal fulfilment but you should be aware of the restrictions this could put on your private life. Most performances take place in the evening and at the weekend, and a long run in the theatre could take you out of social circulation for weeks on end. You may find that you would spend a considerable time away from home, staying in a variety of surroundings.

E arnings Potential

When working, you would be entitled to the pay rates negotiated by Equity, with a current minimum wage of just under £300 a week in a London theatre or £240 in the provinces. Lodgings allowances could be available if you are on tour and your agent may be able to negotiate a rate for you above the minimum level. Stardom would entitle you to demand whatever sum you or your agent can command!

F urther Information

National Council for Drama Training, London WC1H 9SS
Website: www.ncdt.co.uk

British Actors' Equity Association, London WC2 9EG
Website: www.equity.org.uk

Conference of Drama Schools, Norwich NR7 0BE
Website: www.drama.ac.uk

Alternative/equivalent entrance requirements can include: ILC, IB, EB, NC/ND and many other similar international systems. For further details see the Equivalent Qualifications section in the Introduction.

What is Involved?

As an actuary, you would use your specialist statistical skills to make financial sense of the future. Using a database of previously accumulated information, statistics, probability theory and compound interest, you would design solutions to questions of financial risk, particularly in the fields of insurance, pensions, risk assessment and investment. For example, you might be asked to consider how much money a company would need to invest in order to pay its employees a reasonable pension when they retire.

You could work for the Government Actuary's Department, reporting to Parliament on such matters as projected population growth or forecasting funding needs for the National Health Service. Alternatively, you might advise an insurance company on the premiums required to make life insurance policies competitive while still offering a reasonable return for customers and shareholders.

Opportunities for Training

There are two professional bodies – the Institute of Actuaries in England and Wales and the Faculty of Actuaries in Scotland – and in order to qualify you would need to become a fellow with one of them. This would mean finding employment with a firm of actuaries and passing a series of professional exams, mainly via correspondence courses and tutorials, taking about 15 to 20 hours a week. The examination system is flexible in that you can take as many exams as you like at one sitting.

In addition to your degree course, it would usually take three to six years to obtain your full professional qualification.

Requirements

For entry to a degree course, you would need at least two or three A level/AVCE/Advanced Higher or three or four Higher or equivalent qualifications, including a good pass in maths, together with five GCSE/S Grade passes at A-C/1-3 or equivalent, including maths and English. While any degree subject is acceptable, you would find it advantageous to obtain a good honours degree in maths, actuarial science or a related subject such as economics or statistics. You would be expected to gain relevant work experience during your university holidays.

Kind of Person

You would need to be the sort of person who finds solving difficult numerical problems very satisfying. Employers would expect you to be highly numerate and analytical, with sufficient people and communication skills to explain your work to non-mathematicians, work with other professionals and manage teams of colleagues. Accuracy and attention to detail would be very important, as would excellent time management, prioritising and IT skills. The training is long and difficult and you would need determination to see it through.

B road Outlook

Employment prospects are excellent. Actuaries can work for the public or private sectors and are involved in all sorts of areas, including corporate finance, asset management, international business and investment. The Financial Services Act and the Pensions Review have both had a big impact and the actuarial market is a growth area.

Very few actuaries are unemployed and hardly anyone feels the need, once qualified, to leave actuarial work. As the UK qualification is highly valued throughout the world, it is possible to spend part or all of your career abroad.

You would be one of only 7,000 qualified actuaries in the UK. About 60% of your colleagues would be working for insurance companies and 30% in consultancy, where they would advise clients mainly on pension provision or insurance requirements.

R elated Occupations

You may wish to consider: accountant, insurance underwriter, investment analyst, stockbroker or financial adviser.

I mpact

You could expect to work long hours whilst training. A good training package from your employer would be very important as you would need their support and study leave for exams. This is a very responsible and demanding work which can be stressful, especially when huge financial risks are involved.

E arnings Potential

This is a very well paid profession. You are paid whilst you are training (usually in excess of £20,000) and on qualification starting salaries range from £40,000 to £50,000 a year. They should rapidly increase afterwards, together with an excellent package of benefits.

F urther Information

The Institute of Actuaries, Oxford OX1 2AW
Website: www.actuaries.org.uk

The Faculty of Actuaries in Scotland, Edinburgh EH1 3PP
Website: www.actuaries.org.uk

Alternative/equivalent entrance requirements can include: ILC, IB, EB, NC/ND and many other similar international systems. For further details see the Equivalent Qualifications section in the Introduction.

What is Involved?

Advertising agencies are employed by their clients to promote almost anything, from products, services and information to health warnings, entitlements to state assistance, job vacancies, sales of houses, flats, holidays, travel and educational opportunities.

• As an **Account Executive**, you would liaise with a client to assess the message the client wishes to promote and then work out and cost, with the help of your colleagues, a suitable campaign. You would report back to your client for final approval. You would then monitor the whole programme and ensure it is completed on time and within budget.

• As an **Advertising Copywriter**, you would write the words for advertisements using suitable slogans, jingles, or scripts for TV commercials – helping to make the advertisements both memorable and persuasive.

• As an **Art Director**, you would plan the visual aspects of a campaign. You would need an artistic training for this career, which could be highly creative, whether in terms of TV commercials, illustration of the script, layout of advertisements, sales literature or the artistic layout of the client's website.

• As a **Media Executive**, you would need knowledge and experience of the media and would know how to place advertisements to influence the maximum number of potential buyers at the most economic cost to your client. You would then buy time on television, cinema or radio, or book space in magazines or newspapers.

• As an **Account Planner** or **Market Researcher**, you would be responsible for ensuring that the advertising campaign is targeted at the right market place or audience. You would carry out market research into the client's field of activity, assess consumer attitudes and look at the techniques used by competitors for similar work.

Opportunities for Training

There are no essential training routes but many new entrants to advertising take an appropriate degree or higher national diploma (HND) course first. Several universities and colleges offer relevant courses, some with modules focusing on either the creative or the business side of advertising. For art director posts, you would probably start your training with a foundation course and a degree in art and design.

Once you are in an agency, you would usually receive in-house training and you may be able to work towards the CAM (Communication Advertising and Marketing) Advanced Certificate or to access courses run by the Institute of Practitioners in Advertising.

Requirements

Courses usually demand at least one or two A level/AVCE/Advanced Higher, three Higher or equivalent qualifications, together with five GCSE/S Grade passes at A-C/1-3. Art and design usually places more importance on a good portfolio of work.

K ind of Person

In all of these fields, you would need a combination of commercial and creative skills. On the creative side, you must have an original imagination with strong visual or writing powers; on the business side, you would need excellent communication skills and a high level of numeracy. Developing campaigns calls for the imagination to see how others would react to your ideas and being flexible enough to change quickly if you get things wrong.

B road Outlook

Advertising is an extremely popular career choice, with many applicants competing for every vacancy. Once you are in employment, promotion tends to be based on experience and proven track record. There is a tendency for creative and commercial functions to merge, so you would improve your prospects if you can combine imaginative flair with sound business sense. Agencies differ in size and speciality and often executives seek promotion by moving between agencies. With sufficient experience, you could start your own business.

R elated Occupations

In the creative field, you might consider: artist/illustrator, graphic designer, photographer, website designer or journalist.

In the more commercial arena, you might consider: marketing or sales manager, public relations officer or market research executive.

I mpact

This job is mainly office based, although you would have to travel to meet clients. To bring in a campaign on time, you might have to work long, irregular hours. Advertising is a young person's world and the great majority of people employed in this field are under 40. A job in advertising tends to be seen as glamorous, but it is recognised as a demanding and difficult world to get in to.

E arnings Potential

Earnings differ greatly from agency to agency. The ones based in London tend to pay the most and as a graduate recruit you could expect to earn between £12,000 and £16,000. With experience you would earn about £40,000, while the most senior posts pay £100,000 plus.

F urther Information

The Institute of Practitioners in Advertising, London SW1X 8QS
Website: www.ipa.co.uk

The Communication, Advertising and Marketing Education Foundation (CAM), Maidenhead SL6 9QH Website: www.camfoundation.com

Alternative/equivalent entrance requirements can include: ILC, IB, EB, NC/ND and many other similar international systems. For further details see the Equivalent Qualifications section in the Introduction.

See also Barrister for England and Wales

What is Involved?

As an advocate, you would work as a member of the Scottish Bar, representing clients in courts of law and giving specialist legal advice. You would work as an expert in a specific area of the law and would be consulted by solicitors or other professionals. You would not work directly for the general public. As well as appearing in court, you might be consulted on a particular point of law or you may appear at a tribunal or enquiry. Advocates can also find employment working for the government or as part of the in-house legal team in a large organisation.

Most advocates work as self-employed independent professionals, based in the Advocates' Library in Edinburgh. A group of advocates who share a clerk are known as a 'stable'. This system offers some support but you would need to build your own reputation in order to get work. It would help to establish a good relationship with the clerk of your stable, who would be, to some extent, responsible for allocating the work that comes in.

Opportunities for Training

You should first complete either an honours degree in Scottish law or an ordinary degree in Scottish law with an honours degree in another subject. (An ordinary degree with distinction in Scottish law is also acceptable.)

You would then have to complete a one-year, full-time post-graduate Diploma in Legal Practice at a Scottish university, before working for a year or longer in an approved solicitor's office. This is intended to give you wide experience of all aspects of the law. You may choose to complete the two-year solicitor's traineeship so that you can practise as a solicitor before going on to become an advocate. This means that you can build up useful contacts, gain experience and start the final stage with fewer debts. Finally, you have to spend a period of time in pupillage, known in Scotland as 'devilling', before being called to the Bar. During the period of devilling, you must get experience of both civil and criminal work with an approved member of the Scottish Bar. You also need to pass an exam set by the Faculty of Advocates, covering court procedure, advocacy, evidence, pleading, practice and professional conduct. At this point, you would have to decide whether or not to practise as an advocate.

Requirements

Degrees in Scottish law are popular and you would need to get good results in your Higher/Advanced Higher subjects in order to be accepted. It would also be helpful if you could show, through work experience, that you have a genuine interest in the law and its processes.

Kind of Person

You would need self-confidence, the intellectual capacity to assimilate large volumes of information in a short time, the ability to work long hours with tight deadlines and high levels of responsibility. The ability to deal with people, to listen to them and then put across a point of view convincingly would be essential. In addition, you would need the motivation and determination to succeed in what can be a daunting profession, particularly in the early years.

B road Outlook

In the early days as an advocate, you may have to work for a reduced fee or work in lower courts in order to get yourself known. It can be hard work for little reward for the first few years, after which it is usually clear whether you are going to be successful.

There are no guarantees of employment, meaning that your job security would depend entirely on your own ability and reputation.

R elated Occupations

You might consider solicitor, civil service administrator, barrister or legal executive (England and Wales).

I mpact

The hours of work can be very long, especially when you are starting out, and can be unsocial as you have to prepare late into the evenings and travel to courts. However, you should be able to do quite a lot of work from home and, if you are successful, to be selective in the sort of work you prefer to do. Payment often comes in some time after the work has been done and this can be a particular problem in the early years.

Advocates who are employed would have the security of receiving a regular wage but may not have the potential for the very high earnings that are possible for advocates in legal practice.

E arnings Potential

Whilst you are working as an intrant in a solicitor's office, you would receive a guaranteed minimum salary. This would be around £9,000 at present for the first year, rising to around £12,000 if you continue for a second year. You would not receive any money during your nine months of devilling. There are scholarships available but you are more likely to be funding yourself. As a practising advocate, you would be self-employed so your earnings would vary enormously, depending on the nature and extent of the instructions you receive and the reputation you develop.

F urther Information

The Faculty of Advocates, Edinburgh EH1 1RF
Website: www.advocates.org.uk

Alternative/equivalent entrance requirements can include: ILC, IB, EB, NC/ND and many other similar international systems. For further details see the Equivalent Qualifications section in the Introduction.

What is Involved?

As an aeronautical engineer, you would be concerned with all aspects of making things fly and keeping them flying. This could range from missiles or one-man microlites right up to the largest passenger planes. You could be involved at all stages of the planning, design and testing of the aircraft. In addition you might be concerned with developing new technology. You would need to consider factors such as aerodynamics, the most appropriate materials to use, electrical systems and the means of propulsion. You could find yourself involved with the design of any aspect of the aircraft, from the wing design to the guidance system used. You might choose to become a specialist in one particular field such as thermodynamics or onboard computer technology. You could find yourself developing ideas for either for civil or military aircraft. This is an industry where you would likely to be working with new, cutting edge technology.

Opportunities for Training

There are 32 UK universities offering degrees in aeronautical or aerospace engineering. Some focus more on production and some on electronics or research, so you should read the prospectuses carefully; there is also a variation in the degree of specialisation as some courses are designed to show the integrated nature of engineering degrees. You should certainly check that your course is accredited with the Royal Aeronautical Society.

In order to become a chartered engineer (CEng), you would need to complete at least four years of academic study on a course leading to an MEng. There are also three-year courses leading to a BEng degree, which could take you to incorporated engineer (IEng) status.

Requirements

In order to study for a degree course in aeronautical engineering or one that incorporates aeronautics options, you are likely to need at least five GCSE/S Grade passes at A-C/1-3 plus three A level/AVCE/Advanced Higher, four Higher or equivalent qualifications, to include maths, physics, and/or another science or technology subject.

Kind of Person

You would need a keen interest in aviation, a very logical and practical approach to problem solving and an ability to understand and to keep up to date with modern technology. You would need to be able to check technical specifications accurately and to follow detailed designs. You might be involved with conducting lengthy equipment tests and would need to show attention to detail. You are likely to be involved with analysing data, so would need to be numerate and able to use computer technology in your work. In addition to your scientific and practical engineering skills, you are likely to be working as a member of a team so you would need to be able to get on well with others. You would be expected to communicate both with fellow professionals and with others who do not have your specialised knowledge.

B road Outlook

This is a relatively small and specialised field but there are good opportunities for well-qualified graduates, particularly if you can demonstrate some work experience. Aeronautical engineers may work for manufacturing companies, airline operators, the armed forces and the Defence Evaluation and Research Agency. There are also opportunities to work abroad. Many employers would be interested in sponsoring you for at least some of your time at university. There has been a low unemployment rate for qualified engineers in recent years but economic factors can cause cutbacks in aircraft production.

R elated Occupations

You might wish to consider: RAF officer, airline pilot, mechanical engineer, electrical/electronic engineer, naval architect, materials scientist or metallurgist.

I mpact

Whilst you may have set conditions of work, there are times when you may need to work long hours in order to meet deadlines or to solve particular problems. You might be based in a laboratory but you could have to work outside or possibly on a wind tunnel project for example. You might be expected to travel to conferences or meetings, which could be in another part of the country or abroad.

E arnings Potential

Salaries for aeronautical engineers are generally quite good and as a recent graduate you could expect to around £20,000. Once you are chartered, your salary is likely to rise considerably and may well exceed £50,000. Average earnings for incorporated engineers are around £37,000.

F urther Information

The Royal Aeronautical Society, London W1V OBQ
Website: www.aerosociety.com

The Society of British Aerospace Companies Website: www.sbac.co.uk

Alternative/equivalent entrance requirements can include: ILC, IB, EB, NC/ND and many other similar international systems. For further details see the Equivalent Qualifications section in the Introduction.

What is Involved?

As an agricultural engineer, you would be working as a specialist in technology related to agriculture or one of the allied land based industries, including forestry, food engineering and technology, renewable energy, horticulture and the environment. These are highly mechanised industries and you would be involved with the design, development and maintenance of the specialised equipment currently in use. You could expect to be involved with: tractors and tillage machines, harvesting equipment, crop processing, animal welfare (handling and transport), irrigation and drainage schemes, earth moving and other construction equipment, pioneer road and bridge construction, forestry machines, horticultural machines and fish farming equipment.

You could also work in areas such as field engineering, land reclamation, drainage and irrigation and the systems used for this or the management of the field-to-table supply chain. You could combine your technical engineering skills with management and economic knowledge and play a valuable role in many aspects of an industry that is undergoing rapid change at the moment.

Opportunities for Training

This is a specialised area and there are few universities or HE colleges that run courses in engineering for the land-based sector. It is possible to take a three-year course that leads to the BEng or a four-year course leading to the MEng degree. There are also sandwich courses available, which allow for time to be spent working in industry as part of the course, and you could combine agricultural engineering with another subject, such as management. In order to become a chartered engineer, you would need to take an accredited course and to complete at least four years of academic study; to become an incorporated engineer, you would need at least a three-year accredited course (see separate article on engineering qualifications).

Requirements

Some universities would require you to have maths at A level/AVCE/Advanced Higher, Higher or equivalent qualification, but even those that do not actually insist on maths would prefer you to have it. Most universities would also prefer you to have physics at A level/Advanced Higher, Higher or equivalent as well.

Kind of Person

You would need to have a strong interest in and understanding of agriculture, horticulture or forestry and the ways that these industries work. You should have a very practical and logical approach to problem solving and a strong mechanical interest. You would need to be able to analyse problems clearly and then to produce workable solutions. In addition to your technical and engineering skills, you would need to be able to communicate your ideas to others. You may well find yourself working as part of a small team, in which case you would be required to tell others what you think and to listen to their points of view. You could find yourself explaining your proposals to others who do not have your expert knowledge, or having to 'sell' your ideas in other cases.

B road Outlook

As with most engineering disciplines, there is a serious shortage of engineering skills in the land based sector. This is particularly evident in the area of servicing. There are good opportunities for well-qualified and knowledgeable engineers who can help to bring solutions to the range of problems facing agriculture, horticulture and forestry today. The industry needs to change and adapt to different demands and conditions both in the UK and abroad. There is a constant need to find more efficient and sustainable ways of using natural resources and more profitable ways of farming, with implications for recycling and environmental concerns. There are opportunities to work abroad, particularly in developing countries.

R elated Occupations

You might be interested in working in another branch of engineering as, for example, a mechanical, automotive, manufacturing or mining engineer. Alternatively, you might like to become involved with farming, commercial horticulture or estate management. You might consider becoming an agricultural adviser, an equipment seller or a food researcher.

I mpact

Whilst you might find yourself working normal office hours, you are also likely to be required to travel out to farms or factories, which could involve longer hours. You may need to be outside in all kinds of weather, which may involve you getting wet, cold and dirty, or hot and dusty in developing countries with primitive facilities. You may have to travel to get to your clients or to the areas where they need your advice. At times you might find yourself working with potentially dangerous equipment and be required to take the necessary safety precautions.

E arnings Potential

You are likely to be paid around £16,000 when you first graduate and this can rise quite rapidly as you gain experience and get nearer to achieving chartered status.

F urther Information

The Institution of Agricultural Engineers, Bedford MK45 4DU
Website: www.iagre.org

Alternative/equivalent entrance requirements can include: ILC, IB, EB, NC/ND and many other similar international systems. For further details see the Equivalent Qualifications section in the Introduction.

What is Involved?

As an air traffic controller, you would be part of a team ensuring the safety of all aircraft taking off, landing and overflying the United Kingdom. You could work at the main control centre at Swanwick, near Southampton or the Scottish centre at Prestwick, near Glasgow, monitoring flights en route to their destinations; alternatively, you may be based at a specific airport, dealing with arriving and departing flights. In all situations, you would be communicating with pilots by radio, providing them with a radar-based picture of all the air traffic in their vicinity and authorising their movements in relation to the flight plans they submit before take-off.

Most air traffic controllers work for National Air Traffic Services (NATS) and this article is concerned primarily with a typical NATS career structure.

Opportunities for Training

Under the NATS training scheme, you would begin your training with an 18-month course at the NATS College of Air Traffic Control, next to Bournemouth International Airport. You would develop teamwork skills, undertake practical training in simulators, do some private flying and visit air traffic control units. In the process, you would work towards ratings for the specific type of work you choose to do: aerodrome approach, approach control, approach radar control or area radar control. You can't do everything and your specialist rating would determine whether you work at a control centre or an airport.

On successful completion of the student phase, you would be posted to an operational unit as a trainee controller and would continue to develop your skills as you work towards your Certificate of Competency as an operational controller.

Requirements

You must be at least 18 and under 30 when you apply, in good overall health, with particular reference to hearing, eyesight and colour vision. Glasses or contact lenses are acceptable within certain limits. You would need at least five GCSE/S Grade passes at A-C/1-3, including English and maths and to have studied through to examination two A level/AVCE/Advanced Higher, three Higher or equivalent qualifications. You must be eligible to work in the UK and you must be security vetted. Following a series of psychometric tests and personality assessments, you would proceed to a second stage of interviews and computer tests.

Kind of Person

Because of the intense nature of the work, much of it sitting at radar screens and computer displays, you would need a high level of concentration and the ability to stay alert for sustained periods. You would need to be able to work both quickly and accurately under pressure and stay calm and focused; to think logically and to react quickly if required. Although the international language of air traffic control is English, you would need to be tolerant when communicating with pilots whose English is not strong, particularly in emergency situations. You must have a clear speaking voice.

You should be a good team player but able to work on your own. You should also have an aptitude to work with complex radar systems and the ability to think in 3D and calculate distances and angles.

B *road Outlook*

With the continuous increase in air travel, despite the downturn in the immediate aftermath of September 11, 2001, the further development of air traffic control is assured. The new 'state of the art' centre at Swanwick is the largest and most hi-tech in the world. All European air traffic control will be integrated at some stage in the future and NATS will have to compete for contracts against other member states of the European Union.

R *elated Occupations*

You might wish to consider: air traffic controller in the armed forces, airline pilot, RAF officer or other posts in civil aviation.

I *mpact*

Although you would work a 40-hour week, you would be expected to complete this in eight-hour shifts, including nights, weekends and public holidays. The work is entirely indoors, mostly wearing headphones and speaking into a microphone. It is extremely tiring and you would normally expect a break of at least 30 minutes after two hours of sitting in front of a radar screen.

You must be prepared to work at any NATS operational unit, anywhere in the UK, depending on vacancies and your specialist qualifications.

E *arnings Potential*

Trainee air traffic controllers earn approximately £17,000 a year, rising to around £25,000 on posting from the College. When fully operational, you would be on a salary scale running from £33,000 to over £60,000.

F *urther Information*

National Air Traffic Services Ltd, London WC2B 4AP
Website: www.nats.co.uk

Alternative/equivalent entrance requirements can include: ILC, IB, EB, NC/ND and many other similar international systems. For further details see the Equivalent Qualifications section in the Introduction.

What is Involved?

As an airline pilot, you would fly aircraft on scheduled and chartered flights, transporting passengers and cargo. You would normally be one of two pilots on the flight deck, starting as first officer or co-pilot and working up to promotion as captain or commander. You would be in overall charge as captain, responsible for the safety of the aircraft and everyone on board.

A typical flight would follow a logical sequence of tasks: before take-off, for example, you would decide on a flight plan, taking into account the weather conditions, the number of passengers and amount of cargo. You would supervise loading and fuelling operations, brief the cabin crew and carry out all the necessary pre-flight checks of operating systems. When ready for take-off, you would liaise with air traffic control for permission to proceed to the runway. During the flight, you would maintain a series of checks on the aircraft's position and technical performance, monitor weather conditions and other air traffic, communicate with air traffic controllers and advise passengers of flight details. Finally, you would land under instruction from air traffic control and would write a report on the flight.

Opportunities for Training

You would need to complete a lengthy and expensive training programme in order to obtain your Airline Transport Pilot's Licence (ATPL), which is essential to work as a captain. Among the different routes, you could start with a Private Pilot's Licence (PPL) and 150 hours of flying experience, working up to the ATPL through part-time attendance (totalling about 26 weeks) at an air training school. If you do not already have a PPL, you can take a longer training course of 47 to 60 weeks at an air training school.

In either case, you should emerge with a 'frozen' ATPL, which you would convert to the full qualification by accumulating 1500 hours of flying experience, about a third of which would be as a co-pilot.

Because of the very high cost of pilot training, you might want to seek full or partial sponsorship by an airline. Schemes vary but you could normally expect to repay up to half of your training costs once you start working.

Requirements

You must hold a medical certificate confirming that you are physically fit, with normal colour vision and good hearing and eyesight. Glasses may be allowed and some airlines specify minimum height requirements.

Most flying schools look for a minimum of five GCSE/S Grade passes at A-C/1-3, including English, maths and a science. Airlines offering sponsorship usually ask for more than this and would normally expect two A level/AVCE/Advanced Higher, three Higher or equivalent qualifications, preferably including maths and physics. There is often an upper age limit of 26 or 28 years.

Kind of Person

Your spatial aptitude must be very high, including the ability to think clearly in three dimensions and to interpret maps quickly and accurately. You would also need a high level of numeracy for making mathematical calculations. Excellent communication skills would be essential for linking with air traffic control, briefing the cabin crew liaising with passengers and producing written reports.

Qualities of leadership, initiative, adaptability and the ability to work well with other people would be required, together with high levels of concentration and attention to detail, the ability to stay calm under pressure and the authority to take charge in an emergency.

B road Outlook

It would normally take you about seven years to reach the required number of flying hours to progress from first officer to captain.

The airline industry is undergoing considerable change and current market conditions favour new, low-cost companies rather than the traditional 'flag carriers.' Job prospects should, however, remain positive as services continue to expand, new airports are constructed and more people choose to fly.

R elated Occupations

You may consider air traffic controller, pilot in the armed services, RAF officer or RAF airman/woman.

I mpact

You would be away from home for extended periods of time, especially on long-haul flights. Your social and family life would have to be fitted around your job. Your hours of work would vary enormously but would usually include nights and weekends.

E arnings Potential

Salaries vary depending on airlines and type of aircraft. As a first officer, you could earn in the region of £22,000 to £36,000; as a captain, £35,000 to £70,000 or more.

F urther Information

British Air Line Pilots Association (BALPA), Crawley RH10 2RD
Website: www.balpa.org.uk

Civil Aviation Authority, Gatwick RH6 0YR Website: www.caa.co.uk

Alternative/equivalent entrance requirements can include: ILC, IB, EB, NC/ND and many other similar international systems. For further details see the Equivalent Qualifications section in the Introduction.

What is Involved?

As an ambulance technician/paramedic, you would respond to 999 and other urgent calls, travelling by ambulance, helicopter, car or motorbike to be at the scene of an emergency as soon as possible. A typical emergency ambulance crew would consist of a technician and a paramedic, both highly trained in all aspects of pre-hospital emergency care from crush injuries to cardiac arrest. Your aim would be to treat and stabilise patients before movement but not to delay hospital admission unnecessarily in order to achieve this.

You would be working primarily in a vehicle designed to provide a clinical workplace with maximum mobility. It would be equipped with a wide range of emergency care equipment, including a heart defibrillator, spinal and traction splints, rescue equipment, intravenous drips, oxygen and a range of drugs for medical and traumatic emergencies. You would carry sophisticated patient monitoring equipment such as a pulse oximeter and cardiac and blood pressure monitors.

Opportunities for Training

Local training routines may vary but the general principles should be broadly similar, with almost all training carried out in-service. Some ambulance services may offer direct entry at trainee ambulance technician level, whilst others recruit new entrants only as ambulance care assistants.

As a trainee ambulance technician, you would attend an intensive training course of up to twelve weeks, learning anatomy and physiology, immediate care and emergency driving skills. You would spend a further period of up to a year gaining operational experience under supervision and taking examinations before qualification.

To become an ambulance paramedic, you would have to be specially selected as an already highly experienced ambulance technician. You would then undertake at least two months additional clinical training in lifesaving procedures. The course would include further training in anatomy and physiology, advanced trauma management and treatment of serious medical emergencies. As a paramedic, you would have to register with the Health Professions Council and would have to re-qualify every three years.

Requirements

Entry requirements vary, with some areas asking for a good level of education while others might specify GCSE/S or A level/AVCE/Advanced Higher, Higher or equivalent subjects; you should be at least 18 to become an ambulance care assistant and probably 21 to become a technician. In order to become a paramedic, you would need to have at least one year's experience of accident and emergency work as a technician. You would need a full clean driving licence and you would have to pass a stringent medical assessment.

Kind of Person

You would have to be highly skilled, quick thinking and decisive, yet able to provide a calm and reassuring environment for the patient and relatives. You would also need to be a good team worker, with excellent communication skills. Physical fitness would be essential to deal with moving and lifting patients and equipment. At the same time, you would need the manual dexterity to carry out treatment in awkward conditions.

B road Outlook

As the ambulance service is run on a local basis, the demand for staff varies across the country, with more vacancies occurring in London and other urban areas. You should contact your local ambulance service for more details. There are some opportunities with ambulance services run by private hospitals or with large industrial companies who run their own on-site ambulance service. There is also some scope to train and work within the armed forces. Promotion to senior management positions can come after successful experience.

R elated Occupations

You might also wish to consider: firefighter, health visitor, nurse, police officer or residential care worker.

I mpact

You would have to work on rotating shifts, going out in all weathers at night, over the weekend and during public holidays. Most of the population respect ambulance personnel for the vital work they do but you should be prepared for the occasional hostile reception, especially when dealing with people under the influence of drink or drugs. As you would be wearing uniform, you would be immediately identifiable. The work can be stressful in that you would rarely know in advance the severity of the emergency to which you were responding; you could be dealing with a train crash or motorway pile-up involving seriously injured casualties.

E arnings Potential

Pay scales vary slightly across the country, with an additional living allowance paid in London. As a general guide, you should earn a basic salary of around £17,500 as a qualified technician and £18,500 as a paramedic. Senior managers can earn considerably more.

F urther Information

Ambulance Service Association, London SE1 8EU Website: www.asa.uk.net

Alternative/equivalent entrance requirements can include: ILC, IB, EB, NC/ND and many other similar international systems. For further details see the Equivalent Qualifications section in the Introduction.

What is Involved?

Archaeology is the study of the past through objects left behind by previous generations. Studying the remains of the past can involve anything from old coins to buried cities. As an archaeologist, you could choose to take up teaching, lecturing, museum work, research or fieldwork.

You would need a broad academic understanding of your subject before specialising in an area such as conservation, heritage management, underwater, computing or environmental archaeology; other specialisms include coins, weapons, ancient languages, chemical analysis and dating of specimens, as well as geographical areas (eg Egyptology) or historical periods (eg the Iron Age).

To show evidence of your commitment and enthusiasm, it would be a very good idea to do as much voluntary work as possible during your university holidays. The Council for British Archaeology (CBA) can help you arrange this, providing information about excavations requiring volunteers.

Opportunities for Training

Nearly all archaeologists are graduates and most have a first degree in archaeology. For some areas of archaeology (eg museum work) a post-graduate qualification is normally required.

There is great variation in the course content but most single honours courses include a basic core of archaeological methods, a broad geographical and chronological view of the subject, science, history and the role of archaeology in today's society.

There is a trend also towards the more scientific aspects of archaeology, with several institutions offering BSc courses in archaeological science. Most courses offer a varying amount of practical fieldwork experience, often on research projects in Britain and abroad.

Requirements

The minimum requirement for a degree course in archaeology is normally three A level/AVCE/Advanced Higher or four Higher or equivalent quali-fications, together with five GCSE/S Grade passes A-C/1-3, including English and maths. Geography, history and a foreign language are all useful subjects. Some science based degree courses ask for physics and chemistry. Archaeology has become a popular subject and high grades are, therefore, required.

Kind of Person

Archaeologists need a dual approach: digs require physical stamina and teamwork, whereas writing up your finds requires attention to detail and patience. You would need to have an academic interest in the past and it is important to realise that the finds made are not always glamorous. You would examine pieces of pottery, coins, human skeletons and bone fragments, which may reveal DNA evidence, together with organic matter which may need dating by processes such as isotopic analysis.

B road Outlook

There are many archaeology graduates but fewer than 5,000 professional archaeologists employed in the UK. The main areas of work for archaeologists are in commercial archaeology units, museums, providing planning and development control advice through local authorities or specialist consultants. Many also work for the national heritage agencies (English Heritage, Historic Scotland and Cadw) or conservation charities, of which the National Trust is probably the biggest employer.

A number of archaeologists continue with academic research after graduation and some of these go on to teach in colleges and university departments. Some archaeologists are self-employed and many of these work as specialist consultants in their particular field, such as pottery or bone analysis. Most archaeology graduates enter the general graduate market, taking up commercial, financial, managerial and teaching careers (eg history, ancient history or classical studies).

R elated Occupations

You may be interested in other careers in this field, such as historical researcher, museum/art curator or archaeological surveyor.

I mpact

Your hours of work would vary according to the type of archaeological activity being undertaken. Museum work usually involves a 36-hour week and some weekends. If you work for a local authority or national agency, you could also expect to work normal office hours. Work on excavations, however, is likely to involve long and sometimes unsocial hours.

E arnings Potential

This varies depending on who you work for and your level of seniority. Generally, the pay tends to be low and you can expect to earn between £11,000 and £14,000 on graduating, rising to between £15,000 and £24,000. If you were working in education, you would be paid on the normal academic scale.

F urther Information

Council for British Archaeology, York YO1 9WA
Website: www.britarch.ac.uk

The Training Online Resource Centre for Archaeology
Website: www.torc.org.uk

Institute of Field Archaeologists, University of Reading RG6 6AU
Website: www.archaeologists.net

Alternative/equivalent entrance requirements can include: ILC, IB, EB, NC/ND and many other similar international systems. For further details see the Equivalent Qualifications section in the Introduction.

What is Involved?

As an architect, you would be involved with designing and constructing new buildings or restoring old ones. You would have the power and the responsibility to shape the environments in which people spend their daily lives. Your designs must be attractive, practical, soundly conceived and not too expensive to turn into reality. You would need to combine both the creativity of using shape, colour, materials and space to meet your client's design requirements and the practicality of understanding planning and building regulations while meeting the physical demands of the construction process.

Opportunities for Training

In order to practise as an architect you would need to complete a seven-year training programme, which involves three stages:

• Firstly, a five-year degree at a recognised school of architecture; this consists of a three year intermediate degree (Part 1) and a two year further degree (Part 2);

• Secondly, two years in professional practice in an architect's office. The first year usually follows Part 1 and the second year follows Part 2;

• Thirdly, the Professional Practice Examination (Part 3).

The title 'architect' is protected in the UK by law. It is only by following this route – or an equivalent route recognised by the Royal Institute of British Architects (RIBA) and the Architects Registration Board (ARB) – that you could be eligible to call yourself an architect.

Requirements

To be accepted for a degree course at a school of architecture, you would need a minimum of two A level/AVCE/Advanced Higher, three Higher or equivalent qualifications, possibly including maths, physics or art.

You could expect an interview by the schools you have applied to and they may want to see your portfolio. They would be looking for evidence of creative skills together with an awareness of architecture. Work experience in an architect's office would be especially valuable here. Your portfolio may include a mixture of photos, sketches of buildings, short notes, collages, still life and life drawings.

Kind of Person

Three-dimensional awareness is important, together with the ability to explain complex structures in the form of drawings. A balance of creative flair and technical skill is essential and you would almost certainly be using computers quite extensively. You should enjoy problem solving and you must have a keen interest in how people react in different types of built environment.

Architects must be able to work as part of a team. They need to be good communicators both with clients and with construction personnel on site.

You would need to be physically fit for the site inspections, which would involve climbing around part-constructed buildings.

B road Outlook

In a recession, building tends to slow down and with it opportunities for architects. When the economy is strong, there is more than enough work for everyone. Training is very long with no guarantee of employment at the end. Most architects work in small private practices with usually fewer than ten staff. To start with, you might be on a short-term contract and then progress with experience to junior and then senior partnerships. Or you could start your own practice. You would be working on a variety of industrial and commercial projects as well as for private individuals. Other architects work in the public sector and are involved with schools, housing, hospitals and so on.

R elated Occupations

You may consider: architectural technologist, civil engineer, interior designer, surveyor and landscape architect.

I mpact

Architecture is regarded as a prestigious profession. Training does, however, take a long time and you can expect to still be a student when your friends are working. Most architects work normal office hours unless there are deadlines to be met. As a self-employed freelance architect, you might experience periods of inactivity and other periods of high workload. You could expect to work some of the time in a light, bright office and some of the time on a potentially hazardous construction site.

E arnings Potential

An architect's average salary is around £30,000 although this varies according to location and size of firms. The public sector tends to pay less. At the top of the profession you could earn considerably more.

F urther Information

Royal Institute of British Architects (RIBA), London, W1N 6AD
Website: www.architecture.com

Architects Registration Board (ARB), London, W1W 5BU
Website: www.arb.org.uk

Royal Incorporation of Architects in Scotland, Edinburgh, EH1 2BE
Website: www.rias.org.uk

Royal Society of Ulster Architects, Belfast BT7 1NZ
ebsite: www.rsua.org.uk

Royal Society of Architects in Wales, Cardiff CF10 3NB
Website: www.architecture-wales.com

Alternative/equivalent entrance requirements can include: ILC, IB, EB, NC/ND and many other similar international systems. For further details see the Equivalent Qualifications section in the Introduction.

What is Involved?

As an architectural technologist, whether designing new buildings or altering existing ones, you would be a member of the architectural team. You would in fact be trained to complete a project from start to finish, in making sure that the building is properly constructed and works as specified in the original design. The design process requires many activities to be undertaken by the architectural team: you would start by deciding exactly what is required, establishing with the client such factors as how the building might be used, how much it would cost, how it would be built and what sort of site might be available, before thinking about its outward appearance.

In addition to the design drawings, detailed specifications and documents would have to be prepared in conjunction with other consultants. You would have to negotiate with the planning and building authorities and work closely with architects and building surveyors. Finally, a 'package' would be prepared to enable the building project to be carried out, often including a management role for your team in supervising work on site.

Opportunities for Training

To apply for associate membership of the British Institute of Architectural Technologists (BIAT), you would need to have one of the following:

• A degree in architectural technology or a related subject

• National/Scottish Vocational Qualification (N/SVQ) level 4 in architectural technology

• Higher National Certificate/Diploma (HNC/D) in architectural design (with additional units)

Degrees last three or four years, full-time or sandwich, while the other routes usually require a similar length of study on a part-time basis. Once accepted as an associate member, you would progress to full membership by completing a further two to three years in practice, maintaining a supervised work diary and passing a professional assessment interview.

Requirements

While there are no specific minimum qualifications, you would be unlikely to be accepted for any training route with less than four GCSE/S Grade passes A-C/1-3. To be accepted for a degree course, you would need at least two A level/AVCE/Advanced Higher, three Higher or equivalent qualifications, together with three GCSE/two S Grade passes (A-C/1-3). English and maths are often required and sometimes a science. The HNC/D route usually requires at least one A level/AVCE/Advanced Higher, two Highers or equivalent qualifications. A driving licence would be useful.

Kind of Person

As a specialist in the science of architecture, building design and construction, you should be able to analyse and solve working problems, both at a computer terminal in the drawing office and on construction sites in all weathers. You would need to be flexible and able to work with others as part of a motivated and effective team.

You would need to be creative as well as technically minded, so you would need an ability to draw in addition to good IT skills. You would need a good memory for facts and figures, including all those building regulations, and you would have to be fit enough to climb around building sites on a fairly regular basis.

B road Outlook

Prospects in architectural technology are linked to the overall health of the construction industry. The current economic climate is encouraging but there can be times when competition for jobs becomes exceptionally intense. Employment can be found in a variety of national and international organisations, from private architectural practices to local authorities and construction companies, and can include new build, conversion, adaptation, restoration or management and maintenance work on many types of commercial, industrial & residential property.

You could eventually set up your own practice or work in partnership or as director with fellow architectural technologists, architects and other professionals within the construction industry.

R elated Occupations

You might also consider: architect, landscape architect, civil engineer, technical surveyor, chartered surveyor or structural engineer.

I mpact

Your working week might vary from one contract to another but you would be mostly office-based and could expect a fairly typical Monday to Friday, nine to five timetable. Particular schedules might demand unsocial hours from time to time to meet deadlines and you might be required to travel to site meetings.

E arnings Potential

There are no set salary scales and how much you earn could depend on your employer and how good you are. As a rough guide, a junior architectural technologist could expect to earn around £13,000, rising to £26,000 + with experience.

F urther Information

British Institute of Architectural Technologists (BIAT), London ECIV INH
Website: www.biat.org.uk

Alternative/equivalent entrance requirements can include: ILC, IB, EB, NC/ND and many other similar international systems. For further details see the Equivalent Qualifications section in the Introduction.

What is Involved?

As an army officer you would be part of the service responsible for the defence of Britain and its allies at home and abroad and playing an increasingly important part in the work of NATO in both humanitarian and peacekeeping operations around the world. You would initially be in charge of a team of up to 50 trained soldiers in any one of the arms of the service, looking after their welfare, discipline and training.

The Army is made up of a number of branches, all of which are specialised and all of which fit into an integrated whole. The Cavalry provide armoured vehicle reconnaissance; the Armoured Corps the heavy battle armour; the Infantry the fighting men; the Air Corps the attack helicopters; the SAS the covert operations force; the Artillery the ground fire and air defence; the Engineers the fighting infrastructure; the Signals the communications; the Intelligence Corps information about the enemy; the Logistics Corps the supply of equipment; and the Electrical and Mechanical Engineers the maintenance of the equipment. The Army also employs lawyers, doctors, nurses, dentists, vets, police, chaplains, physical training instructors and musicians.

Opportunities for Training

At the age of 16, you could apply to attend the Army's residential college at Welbeck to study A level sciences prior to going to university or straight into the Army.

There is an opportunity for gap year students to spend 4–14 months in the Army as officers on Short Service Limited Commission. Most officers, except those entering the army with professional qualifications (doctor, dentist, vet, for example), complete ten months of training at the Royal Military Academy at Sandhurst, learning the basic tactics and weapon training, which all officers need regardless of their specialisation, and acquiring a high level of physical fitness. After leaving Sandhurst, you would join your unit to complete the Young Officers Course for your arm or service. Once qualified, you would continue to be trained by on-the-job experience, working with and observing more experienced colleagues.

Requirements

The minimum entry requirements are five GCSE/S Grade passes A-C/1-3 and two A level/AVCE/Advanced Higher, three Higher or equivalent qualifications. Nearly all new entrants are graduates and you must be of degree calibre even if you choose not to go to university. For the specialist sections of the Army, a degree in a relevant subject, eg in engineering, would be necessary.

You must pass the Regular Commissions Board, where you would be put through a series of selection tests and interviewed at length about your motivation and interests.

Kind of Person

Above all else, the qualities of leadership are important. A high standard of physical fitness is also vital and the programme at Sandhurst ensures that you would leave not only in top physical condition but also able to supervise the fitness training of the soldiers placed under your command. Expeditions involving climbing, sailing, caving, kayaking, diving, trekking and other activities are all encouraged at Sandhurst, with the success or failure of each expedition depending entirely upon your initiative, resourcefulness and courage.

As an officer you must be able to command the respect of those in your care, through your ability to lead in difficult and potentially dangerous situations. You must be able to exercise responsibility, be fit, prepared to work closely with others in combat and mix easily with all sorts of people in whatever context. You must be a team player but able to work alone if required, able to listen but also to make on-the-spot decisions.

B road Outlook

The British Army is very keen to recruit more young men and women in order to build up to full operational strength. You may serve a fixed term as short as three years (Short Service Commission) or a longer term (Regular Commission) until retirement at 55 with good pension provision. Promotion is achieved primarily by examination, experience, training and merit.

R elated Occupations

You might consider RAF officer, Royal Navy officer, police officer.

I mpact

You would be paid to be available 24 hours a day, seven days a week, although when you are not on exercise or operations you are likely to work a fairly normal five-day week.

You could expect to be posted, often at short notice, anywhere around the world, increasingly to work in humanitarian work like peacekeeping or famine relief. You would need to be highly adaptable and broad-minded for you may not always be welcomed by the local community.

All branches of the Army provide exceptional opportunities for personal and professional development and the constant challenge of meeting the unforeseen. Expectations are very high and the pressure of risk considerable.

E arnings Potential

Sixth form sponsorships and undergraduate sponsorship and bursaries are offered to suitable candidates and special rates of pay may be offered to undergraduates whilst studying. Newly appointed Officers earn from £20,000, while a Brigadier is paid over £74,000. Many allowances are provided in terms of accommodation and food.

F urther Information

Available from school and university careers and liaison services, local Armed Forces Careers Offices. Website: www.army.mod.uk

Alternative/equivalent entrance requirements can include: ILC, IB, EB, NC/ND and many other similar international systems. For further details see the Equivalent Qualifications section in the Introduction.

What is Involved?

As an artist, you would probably wish to develop your own creative ideas, perhaps in a specialised area such as sculpture or portraiture. You might receive commissions for some of your work from individuals, private companies or public authorities, although it would be more likely that you would have to persuade galleries or art dealers to exhibit your work for sale, or engage an agent to do this for you. In any case, you would probably have to subsidise your earnings by undertaking some other work such as teaching, illustration or theatre set design.

As an illustrator, you would be employed to carry out a brief or project set by a client. This could include work on magazines, books, greetings cards, technical publications and so on. Most illustrators work as freelances, in their own homes or studios. As either an artist or illustrator, you would spend some time travelling or contacting potential clients to show them examples of the work in your portfolio.

Opportunities for Training

Some successful artists/illustrators are entirely self-taught but a good starting point would normally be to take an art foundation course before going on to a further course of training at an art school or university. Most foundation courses allow you to explore several areas of artistic work before you choose a specialised degree or higher national diploma (HND) course.

Requirements

Entry to foundation courses can be from GCSE/S Grade or A level/AVCE/Advanced Higher/Higher or equivalent qualifications, with great importance placed on a current portfolio of your own artistic work. The courses last for one or two years full-time, and can be found at sixth form colleges, further and higher education colleges, art colleges and some universities.

Entry to an HND course would normally require a minimum of four GCSE/S Grade passes A-C/1-3 and one or two A level/AVCE/Advanced Higher or two or three Higher or equivalent qualifications. The course would last for two or three years, with the possibility of conversion to a degree course. Entry to a degree course would normally require a minimum of five GCSE/S Grade and two or three A level/AVCE/Advanced Higher or three or four Higher or equivalent qualifications. These requirements might be waived if you have foundation course experience and/or an impressive portfolio.

Kind of Person

You would clearly need a high degree of creative artistic talent but there is also a call for other skills. As an illustrator, in particular, you would need to be very well organised, able to stick to deadlines and to interpret the wishes of your clients. IT skills would almost certainly be helpful. As either an artist or an illustrator, you would need to be very determined but able to deal with disappointment if a client or dealer rejected your work. Communication skills, particularly powers of persuasion, would be very important, as you would have to deal with a wide variety of people. Some business sense and an understanding of budgets would also be a great asset.

B *road Outlook*

The traditional image of the starving artist in a lonely garret still has some relevance. It is not easy to make a living purely as an artist but that should not stop you trying if you feel that you have necessary talent and determination. The position is somewhat less bleak for illustrators, although permanent contracts are still something of a luxury.

R *elated Occupations*

You might wish to consider: advertising artist, art teacher/lecturer, art therapist, cartographer, fashion designer, graphic designer, interior designer, photographer, textile designer, theatre set or costume designer.

I *mpact*

Working as an artist or illustrator would put you in a very competitive field, with very little security. You would most likely work on a freelance basis, with extremely variable hours, and you might have to work during the evenings or at weekends if you had a deadline to meet. Also, your earnings might be far from regular and you would have to plan your budget and your domestic and social activities accordingly.

E *arnings Potential*

The price you could ask for your work is governed by many factors and could vary tremendously, possibly requiring you to supplement your income by undertaking some other work. As an illustrator, you would usually receive a fee for each piece of work, the amount being dependent upon the size and scope of the commission. Alternatively, you might charge a daily rate, ranging from, say, £150 upwards. You should also remember that any artists' agent you might employ would charge you a fee.

F *urther Information*

The Association of Illustrators, London EC2A 4QS Website: www.aoi.co.uk

Your Creative Future Website: www.yourcreativefuture.org

Metier, Bradford BD5 0BQ Website: www.metier.org.uk

Alternative/equivalent entrance requirements can include: ILC, IB, EB, NC/ND and many other similar international systems. For further details see the Equivalent Qualifications section in the Introduction.

What is Involved?

As an auctioneer, you would be expected to sell at auction such items as bankrupt stock, commodities, collectables, furniture, household goods, property, land, motor cars, farming equipment or whatever else owners wish to sell in this way. You might work for a firm of surveyors or estate agents who undertake general auctioneering, or for a specialist auction house in the worlds of fine art, furniture, sculpture, antiques, literature, philately, postcards, militaria and celebrity memorabilia, where you would need a very high level of expertise.

In addition to conducting the auction itself, you would assess the value of items for sale, advise clients on setting reserve prices, arrange items into lots, organise a catalogue, insure the goods against loss or damage, arrange the transport of sold and unsold lots and ensure adequate pre-sale publicity.

Opportunities for Training

There are many possible routes to a qualification such as the Royal Institution of Chartered Surveyors (RICS) diploma in valuation or fine arts and chattels valuation. You could, for example, complete a degree or diploma course accredited by the RICS or, if your degree is not accredited, a postgraduate conversion course. You would then undertake two years of practical, on-the-job training leading to the RICS Assessment of Professional Competence. Auction houses, like Christies and Sothebys, run their own courses in fine art, inviting selected participants to join them as trainees in their London or provincial offices. An alternative route would be to progress towards the valuation diploma over a three- to five-year programme offered by Manchester Open Learning.

Requirements

Two to three A level/AVCE/Advanced Higher, three to four Higher or equivalent qualifications, together with supporting GCSE/S Grade A-C/1-3, would normally be required to secure entry to most relevant degree or diploma courses. There are no specific requirements for open learning, although employers may determine their own minimum standards.

Kind of Person

You would need to be capable of inspiring confidence in your clients and of understanding the minds of collectors or purchasers. A sound grasp of the market and its trends and fashions would be essential, as well as a willingness to steep yourself in your specialist field. You would need to have good commercial and business flair. You should be a good public speaker, capable of controlling the auction room and able to explain the special features of items for sale. You should be extremely quick-witted and observant in spotting bids, with excellent hearing and eyesight.

It would be important to know the particular features involved in establishing authenticity, supply and demand, market price and provenance of important or valuable items for sale, especially in the fields of fine art and antique furniture. Writing skills would be needed to produce catalogues, numerical skills to assess bids quickly and IT skills to keep accounts, produce inventories and perhaps maintain a website.

B road Outlook

There are openings from time to time for those with the necessary drive and enthusiasm in this relatively small field of employment. Late starts are feasible in the smaller undertakings but far less easy in the major international auction houses. In many top auction houses it may take up to five or six years to acquire the necessary expert knowledge in a specialised field, such as in 18th century painting or furniture, and even then becoming an auctioneer would not be automatic.

General auctioneering within an estate agency would usually be less demanding. Securing employment in one of the large international auction houses is extremely competitive and you may have to work in a range of practical activities before being accepted into a specialist department where you could learn about and value artistic objects.

R elated Occupations

You might also consider: chartered surveyor, estate agent or museum/art gallery curator.

I mpact

Within a big organisation, travel is likely to be a major consideration. In all auction houses, much pressurised time would be devoted to preparatory activities in itemising and valuing the goods for sale, producing catalogues and displaying and storing the items to avoid awkward delays during sales. Conducting an auction can be very demanding on you mentally and physically.

E arnings Potential

There are huge variations in financial return, depending on the level of business and the profit margins involved. As an auctioneer in a big company, you are likely to be well rewarded, moving on to £30,000+ from a possible starting rate of around £12,000 to £14,000. Where you are running your own business or are an employed director of a firm of auctioneers, hard work and a successful track record would largely determine your financial rewards. The auctioneer normally takes a percentage of the value of each item sold and your own earnings could be directly related to the sale prices you achieve.

F urther Information

Royal Institution of Chartered Surveyors, Coventry CV4 8JE
Website: www.rics.org.uk

College of Estate Management, Reading RG6 2AW
Website: www.cem.ac.uk

Manchester Open Learning Website: www.mancat.ac.uk

Alternative/equivalent entrance requirements can include: ILC, IB, EB, NC/ND and many other similar international systems. For further details see the Equivalent Qualifications section in the Introduction.

What is Involved?

Working as an automotive engineer, you would be involved in a specialised area of mechanical engineering that deals with all aspects of the production of motor vehicles and their components. Your job would be to apply mechanical principles to issues related to the design, development or maintenance of all aspects of motor vehicles. You could be involved with designing new cars or with developing a specific part of a vehicle, such as the transmission system. You would be likely to be working as part of a small team on a particular project, seeing it through from the beginning to the production phase.

Opportunities for Training

There are a number of universities offering degrees in automotive engineering, sometimes combined with mechanical engineering. In order to become a chartered engineer, primarily concerned with research, design and development, you would need to complete at least four years of academic study and would usually achieve this via an MEng degree. If you want to be more involved with the day-to-day management of production processes as an incorporated engineer, you could take a three-year BEng degree.

You don't always have to choose your specific training route from the start, so you should read prospectuses carefully. See also our separate article on engineering qualifications. There are sandwich courses available for both types of degree; these add an extra year but give the opportunity for a period of work experience, which can be very valuable when you are looking for a job. After graduating, you would need to complete a period of industrial training and responsible work experience before you achieve chartered or incorporated engineer status.

Requirements

For degree entry, you are likely to need A level/AVCE/Advanced Higher/ Higher or equivalent qualifications, including maths and/or physics plus one or two other subjects. (An AVCE in engineering could make a valuable contribution for some courses). If maths and physics are not required, they are certainly preferred by universities. In addition, you would need at least five GCSE/S Grade passes at A-C/1-3. You would normally need higher grades for MEng than for BEng admission.

Kind of Person

Your job would involve understanding and solving complex engineering problems. For this you would need a practical and logical mind that might need to show creative approaches to problems. You are likely to find yourself using maths and statistics in your work and you would make extensive use of computers, including specialised and sophisticated software packages.

You are likely to find yourself working as part of a multi-disciplinary team, which means that you would need to be able to communicate with a variety of people. These could be fellow engineers, who would share your technical expertise and understanding, or non-technical specialists in other fields, who would expect you to explain your ideas clearly to them. You could also find yourself managing a team of people working on a project. In addition, you may need to take into account the costs and budget of a project, so you would need some business skills.

B road Outlook

The UK excels in the design and development of motor vehicles, as evidenced by the number of Formula One racing teams based here. Most global manufacturers carry out research, design and development activities in the UK and there are also specialist consultants, such as Lotus Engineering, who employ around 1,000 engineers. There is generally strong demand for qualified automotive and mechanical engineers.

R elated Occupations

You might also consider: manufacturing, mechanical, aeronautical, electrical or electronic engineer. Alternatively, you might want to consider working as an industrial designer, perhaps specialising in motor vehicle design.

I mpact

Whilst you may have set hours of work, you could expect to be under pressure sometimes to meet commercial deadlines and may have to work overtime. You could be based in an office but you are also likely to be working in a more practical, hands-on environment for a large part of your working week. You may occasionally be expected to wear protective clothing of some sort.

E arnings Potential

Average salaries on graduation are currently in the range of £17,000 to £22,000, rising as you achieve chartered or incorporated engineer status. A top engineer in a Formula One racing team, with 10–15 years experience, can earn over £100,000 a year.

F urther Information

The Institution of Mechanical Engineers, London SW1H 9JJ
Website: www.imeche.org.uk

The Engineering and Technology Board, London WC2R 3ER
Website: www.engc.org.uk

The Engineering Careers Information Service
Website: www.enginuity.org.uk

Lotus Engineering Website: www.lotuseng.com

Alternative/equivalent entrance requirements can include: ILC, IB, EB, NC/ND and many other similar international systems. For further details see the Equivalent Qualifications section in the Introduction.

What is Involved?

As a banking executive, you might choose to build your career in an area such as:

• Clearing, retail and private banking – involving the transfer, borrowing and lending of money (sterling and foreign currency) to private customers, sole traders and partnerships

• Corporate and commercial banking – dealing with business clients ranging from small start-up companies to major international corporations

• Investment or merchant banking – involving corporate finance, investment management and dealing in capital markets, usually on a global basis

Opportunities for Training

There is such diversity in the banking sector that there are many possible training routes. All banks/financial institutions recruit school leavers and graduates in varying numbers from year to year. However, each institution has its own specific recruitment and training preferences and you should contact individual banks for current details and an application pack. You can access the websites of all major organisations through the British Bankers Association.

Most management training schemes require a degree as a starting point. The exact subject is not critically important but study in such fields as economics, finance, business or marketing could prove useful. Once in post, you would normally work towards membership of the Chartered Institute of Bankers.

It is sometimes possible to join a management training scheme through internal promotion after gaining experience as a cashier or customer services adviser.

Requirements

For entry to a degree course you would need two to three A level/AVCE/ Advanced Higher, three to four Higher or equivalent qualifications, together with a minimum of five GCSE/S Grade passes A-C/1-3. The degree would usually last three years, although you might like to consider a sandwich course, which would last four years, including a period of paid work experience.

Kind of Person

Since much of your work would be concerned with dealing with a wide variety of people, both colleagues and customers, you would need excellent communication skills, as well as a good head for figures and an understanding of the economic climate. Accuracy and organisational skills would be very important.

As a manager you should be able to inspire confidence and loyalty in your team, and also be capable of selling the bank's services effectively. A high degree of computer literacy would be of benefit, as would proficiency in a foreign language. You would generally be expected to maintain a neat, formal appearance at all times.

B road Outlook

Technology has dramatically changed the face of banking over the past few years, and in such initiatives as telephone and e-banking you would almost certainly face the prospect of continuing change. Opportunities look likely to decline at branch level in retail banking but to increase in specialist areas of head office activity. The vast majority of major UK financial institutions are based within the 'square mile' of the City of London or the Docklands area. Edinburgh is another major location as it has a large concentration of capital market expertise in the form of banks, life assurance companies and unit trust and fund managers. Other banking areas include Glasgow, Leeds, Birmingham, Bristol and Manchester.

R elated Occupations

You might also consider: accountant, actuary, economist, financial adviser, insurance broker, insurance underwriter or stockbroker.

I mpact

In retail banking, you might work normal office hours from Monday to Friday, although increasing competition may mean evening and weekend work. Promotion in this sector of the industry often entails moving to another part of the country. In investment or merchant banking, you would need to be available when colleagues and clients are at work in other parts of the world, which could involve evening and night-time attendance at the office. You may be required to travel extensively.

E arnings Potential

Pay scales would vary widely according to your experience, level of responsibility and the type of banking in which you specialise. As a manager of a small branch, you might earn up to £28,000, while promotion to a larger branch could take you up to £50,000. In addition, you might qualify for profit-related bonuses and other perks such as a subsidised mortgage. Salaries in investment and merchant banking can be considerably higher.

F urther Information

The British Bankers Association Website: www.bba.org.uk

The Chartered Institute of Bankers, Canterbury CT1 2XJ
Website: www.cib.org.uk

The Chartered Institute of Bankers in Scotland, Edinburgh EH3 7SW
Website: www.ciobs.org.uk

Financial Skills Training, London EC2V 7HQ Website: www.fsnto.org.uk

The Bank of England, London EC2R 8AH.
Website: www.bankofengland.co.uk

Alternative/equivalent entrance requirements can include: ILC, IB, EB, NC/ND and many other similar international systems. For further details see the Equivalent Qualifications section in the Introduction.

(See separate entry 'Advocate' for Scotland)

What is Involved?

As a barrister, you would work as an expert in a specific area of law and would be consulted by solicitors or other professionals. As well as appearing in court, you might be consulted on particular points of law or you may appear at a tribunal or enquiry. Your job as a barrister in a higher court would be to present the facts of the case to the judge and jury, using evidence collected by a solicitor. You would cross-examine witnesses and seek to persuade the court to find in favour of your client.

Opportunities for Training

You must either take an approved first degree in law or a degree in another subject, which you then 'convert' by taking a postgraduate qualification known as the Common Professional Examination (CPE)/Postgraduate Diploma in Law (PgDL).

You must join one of the four Inns of Court (Gray's Inn, Inner Temple, Lincoln's Inn, Middle Temple) and attend a number of dinners and education days in order to complete your qualifying units. You must then take the Bar Vocational Course (BVC), a one-year full-time or two-year part-time course of study, which includes practical training in mock trials, drawing up evidence and interviewing clients. It also covers litigation, sentencing and specialist options.

Having completed the BVC you must, if you intend to practise, complete two pupillages of six months each, working under supervision while you gain experience in all aspects of the job. After this you must find a tenancy in a set of chambers, from where you must work for at least three years while you follow a compulsory system of professional development. It is not essential to complete a pupillage if you are going to work in commerce or industry but you would not then be able to appear in court. Most chambers select their junior tenants through the process of pupillage.

Requirements

You would need a minimum of a 2.2 Honours degree but in fact most chambers are looking for at least a 2.1. The entry requirements for a first degree in law are usually quite high and competition for places is strong, with admissions tutors looking for three good A level/Advanced Higher, four Higher or equivalent qualifications.

Kind of Person

Bar Council research shows that the following abilities make an important contribution to success as a barrister: intellectual ability and the ability to cope with large volumes of information to be assimilated in a short time; the ability to withstand the stress of working long hours with tight deadlines and high levels of responsibility; the ability to deal with a wide range of people, to listen to them and then to put across a point of view convincingly. In addition, barristers need the motivation and determination to succeed in what can be a daunting profession, particularly in the early years. You need to be confident both in your work and socially.

B road Outlook

Most barristers work as self-employed independent professionals, often based in chambers, which means they share the offices and costs of support staff. However, you have to build your own reputation in order to get work. It helps to establish a good relationship with the clerk of the chambers who is, to some extent, responsible for allocating work.

Traditionally, barristers start their working life in London but there are opportunities to work in other cities on the legal circuit. It can be very hard work for little reward in your early days as you build up your practice. You may need to work for a reduced fee or in lower courts to build up your reputation. It is usually clear after a few years whether you will make a successful barrister.

R elated Occupations

You might be interested in other legal professions such as solicitor, barristers' clerk or legal executive.

I mpact

The hours of work can be very long, especially when you are starting out, and can be unsocial, as you have to prepare late into the evening and travel to courts. Your life may very well start to revolve around your chambers. However, if you are successful, you can later be selective in the work you choose to do. Payment for work often comes in some time after the work has been completed, which can present problems in the early years.

E arnings Potential

During pupillage, you should receive at least £5,000 for each six-month period but some chambers offer far more than this. As practising barristers are self-employed, your later earnings can vary enormously, from about £20,000 a year to ten or even a hundred times that amount for a real high-flier!

Barristers who are employed have the security of receiving a regular wage but may not have the potential for the very high earnings that are possible for the self-employed.

F urther Information

The General Council of the Bar, London EC4A 1NE
Website: www.legaleducation.org.uk

The Law Careers Advice Network Website: www.lcan.csu.ac.uk

Alternative/equivalent entrance requirements can include: ILC, IB, EB, NC/ND and many other similar international systems. For further details see the Equivalent Qualifications section in the Introduction.

What is Involved?

As a barristers' clerk (*advocates' clerk in Scotland*) you would work for a set of barristers practising in chambers; *the equivalent in Scotland is to work for a stable of advocates based in the Advocates' Library in Edinburgh.* Your job would be to operate as a member of a small team keeping the chamber or stable running efficiently as a business. Each barrister/advocate is self-employed and the senior clerk acts as an agent for them. As such, you would be expected to make and maintain contacts with solicitors to ensure that briefs come to your set or stable. Negotiation of fees and keeping diaries for the barristers would also be your responsibility.

There are 12 stables of advocates in Edinburgh, each with a clerk and at least one deputy. Their remit includes organising members' diaries, scheduling court commitments, arranging consultations, liaising with instructing solicitors, distributing work and negotiating fees.

Opportunities for Training

There is no quick route to becoming a successful clerk to chambers. Training is 'on the job', learning through observation and helping the more senior clerks. When you become a practising Junior Clerk working in London, chambers may agree to send you to the Institute of Barristers' Clerks (IBC) to attend a two-year part-time day release course at Kingsway College in London. This leads to a BTEC National Certificate with special modules in chambers administration.

On becoming an associate member of the IBC and completing five years service in chambers, you could apply for qualified membership. To enable clerks to keep abreast of current legal issues, market changes and administration needs, the Institute organises regular seminars.

In Scotland, there is no formal training or resulting qualification, although there are short courses run by the Faculty Services Ltd and junior clerks are encouraged to attend.

Requirements

While there are no official entry requirements specified in England, the majority of new barristers' clerk entrants start after completing their GCSE, A level or equivalent qualifications. The IBC recommends to chambers a minimum qualification of four GCSE grades A-C in academic subjects, including maths and English.

In Scotland, advocates' clerks need Higher English and must be computer literate and numerate.

Kind of Person

This is still a very small and in some ways old-fashioned profession and in many respects this aspect of the legal profession is still very hierarchical. You would need to be prepared to tackle menial jobs and to respect the established pecking order that exists within the system. Good manners and a smart appearance are important attributes. You would be expected to be loyal to the members of your set or stable.

You must have the confidence to deal with enquiries and problems that arise without having to bother the barristers/advocates. You would have to be tactful, discreet, honest and reliable. At times, you would be expected to think on your feet to solve a problem. To be involved in negotiating the fees, you would have to be reasonably competent at maths. As there is a lot of administration and paperwork, you need to be well organised.

B road Outlook

There are limited opportunities for work as this is a small and close-knit profession but the Institute does run a scheme whereby, for a small fee, you can receive notification of vacancies. Most jobs for barristers' clerks are in London, although there are some openings in chambers in towns on the court circuits. *In Scotland, there are very few advocates' clerks and deputies and turnover is low.*

There is no scope for progressing to professional qualification as a barrister/advocate.

R elated Occupations

You might be interested in other law-related work such as a legal executive or court officer; alternatively, you might consider administrative work in local government or the civil service.

I mpact

The hours worked can be long and can include evenings and weekends. *In Scotland, deputy clerks are paid overtime but this is unlikely to be the case for junior clerks in England and Wales.*

E arnings Potential

Junior barristers' clerks are paid a salary, which usually starts around £9,000 to £10,000 and can rise to over £30,000. Some senior clerks are also paid a salary or a percentage of the fee due to each barrister; alternatively, they may combine a small salary with a percentage of the earnings. This gives senior clerks the potential for very high earnings if they are in a large and successful set of chambers.

Advocates' clerks, all employed by the company responsible for the administration of the advocates' library, earn from £24,000 upwards.

F urther Information

England and Wales: The Institute of Barristers' Clerks, London EC4Y 9AJ
Website: www.barristersclerks.com

Scotland: Faculty Services Ltd., Edinburgh EH1 1RF
Website: www.advocates.org.uk

Alternative/equivalent entrance requirements can include: ILC, IB, EB, NC/ND and many other similar international systems. For further details see the Equivalent Qualifications section in the Introduction.

What is Involved?

Working as a biochemist, you would be a scientist applying the principles of chemistry to the structure and functioning of living things. This is a science at the heart of all areas of biological or life sciences. You might be concerned with organisms from viruses and bacteria to plants and humans; you might find employment in the food, brewing or pharmaceutical industries, where you could help to develop new products or monitor the quality of existing ones; you might work in the agricultural industry, developing high-yielding, disease-free crops; you could be involved in monitoring the environment and advising on pollution or water quality. There are also opportunities for biochemists to work in hospitals. (see clinical biochemist)

Opportunities for Training

Although it is possible to start a career as a biochemist straight from school, a degree is now becoming the more normal requirement. There are degree courses in biochemistry at most universities and it is possible to study for joint honours degrees with a range of other subjects. It is important to read the prospectuses carefully, as the content and emphasis of the degrees can differ enormously. Some universities offer four-year sandwich courses, which give the chance to work in industry or even abroad for a year.

It is also possible to start work as a technician straight from school, taking part-time study leading to a Higher National Diploma and occasionally converting to a shortened two-year degree course.

Requirements

Universities differ widely in their entrance requirements for biochemistry. Most would be looking for an A level/Advanced Higher/Higher or equivalent qualification in chemistry and some would want at least another science at A level or equivalent. Some universities or colleges will accept an AS or Higher in chemistry together with another science or maths and some will specify GCSE/S Grade passes in maths or the sciences at particular levels of achievement. It is best to check directly with the universities to find out what they expect. At some universities, it is possible for candidates without science A level/Advanced Higher, Higher or equivalent qualifications to take a year-long conversion course before they start a degree course. You would need GCSE/S Grade passes at A-C/1-3 in science if you wish to do this. In order to work towards a Higher National Diploma, you are likely to need at least four GCSE/S Grade passes at A-C/1-3, together with one or two A level/AVCE/Advanced Higher, two or three Higher or equivalent qualifications in appropriate subjects. Some colleges specify that the GCSE/S Grade passes must include maths, English and a science.

Kind of Person

You would need to have a strong interest in science and in laboratory techniques. If you do not enjoy your practical science sessions at school, this may not be right choice for you. You will be expected to show a logical and analytical approach to problem solving. At times you may need to show persistence in order to solve particular problems. Some problems may need to be approached with creative thinking and imagination. In addition to your scientific skills, you should be able to communicate well with others. You are likely to be working as part of a team and may have to explain your findings to others, some of whom may not have your scientific background.

B road Outlook

The largest proportion of new graduates move on to further biochemical study or training, mainly registering for MSc and PhD degrees. The majority of these will eventually make a career in scientific research.

Job prospects are generally very good, with a particularly low unemployment rate for biochemistry graduates compared with other life sciences. Although it is very much a laboratory-based science, there are also openings for biochemists in areas such as technical sales or information and management.

R elated Occupations

You might be interested in other careers in a scientific field such as clinical biochemist, pharmacist, microbiologist or forensic scientist.

There are close links with other specialist life sciences, such as cell biology, genetics, microbiology, molecular biology, physiology and pharmacology. In fact, in many cases the distinctions between these disciplines are becoming increasingly blurred.

I mpact

You are likely to be working regular hours without working at weekends or late into the evenings, although there may be occasions when you are required to work late and under pressure in order to meet deadlines. In the laboratory, you may need to wear protective clothing and to take scrupulous care over hygiene; at times you may need to work in sterile conditions. You may need to move around the country in order to find the right job for you.

E arnings Potential

Graduate trainees should earn around £13,000 and this can rise with experience and promotion to £50,000. Salaries in some industries can be even higher than this.

F urther Information

The Biochemical Society, London W1B 1QW
Website: www.biochemistry.org

Alternative/equivalent entrance requirements can include: ILC, IB, EB, NC/ND and many other similar international systems. For further details see the Equivalent Qualifications section in the Introduction.

What is Involved?

Biologists are concerned with all living things including plants, animals or micro-organisms. They, therefore, need the support and practical expertise of technicians in running their experimental work. This means that there would be opportunities for you to work in education, university research, the agricultural industry, pharmaceuticals, food production, brewing, cosmetics and environmental control.

You might find yourself operating testing equipment and recording the results or helping scientists to develop a new drug, fertilizer or weed killer.

Alternatively, you could be setting up equipment in a school, college or university. You would use a variety of practical procedures and techniques in technical and experimental activities, including preparing and analysing samples and maintaining equipment.

Opportunities for Training

There are several possible training routes. You could, for example, take a two-year full-time or three-year sandwich course leading to a Higher National Diploma (HND). The 'sandwich' element would give you periods of practical experience whilst you are studying.

At a lower level, you could consider a course leading to a National Diploma. This could be full- or part-time. Another route would be to work towards NVQ/SVQ at levels 2, 3 and 4. You would normally do this by day release, so that you can work at the same time as studying, and you may be eligible for a Modern Apprenticeship/Skillseeker place to achieve this.

Requirements

The minimum requirements for training would be four GCSE/S Grade passes at A-C/1-3. These must include two sciences, maths and sometimes English. For the HND route, colleges would usually require at least one or two science A level/AVCE/Advanced Higher, three Higher, a national diploma in science or equivalent qualifications.

Kind of Person

You should have a keen interest in science and in particular in biology. You should greatly enjoy practical laboratory work and you should be methodical and accurate with a keen attention to detail. You would at times be involved in routine and repetitive work, so you would need to be patient and persistent.

However, you might equally be working in a fast moving environment that is changing all the time, which means that the results of your work would be much more varied. In addition to your scientific skills, you would need good communication skills, as you would be working as part of a team of scientists. You could find yourself working for more than one person and may be involved with a number of different projects, so flexibility would be necessary.

B road Outlook

There are usually many jobs available for biology technicians and a range of different work environments. You are likely to be working in some sort of laboratory environment, though you may occasionally collect samples outside.

It would sometimes possible to use your scientific knowledge as the basis to branch out into other areas, such as technical marketing or information or some sort of production role in the land-based sector, food manufacturing or medical products.

You may need to move around the country to find a job in the area of work that interests you or to get promotion in another organisation.

R elated Occupations

You might be interested in other science-based careers such as chemistry technician, pharmacy technician or microbiology technician.

I mpact

Most technicians work normal office hours five days a week. In large companies it may be possible to work flexitime provided you work a set number of hours in a week. You may be required to work overtime sometimes when there is pressure to meet a tight deadline.

E arnings Potential

Salaries vary between the private and public sectors. As a qualified technician, you could expect to start earning around £9,000 and this can rise to around £15,000 or above.

F urther Information

The Institute of Biology, London SW7 2DZ Website: www.iob.org

Alternative/equivalent entrance requirements can include: ILC, IB, EB, NC/ND and many other similar international systems. For further details see the Equivalent Qualifications section in the Introduction.

What is Involved?

Working as a biomedical engineer, you would be using your engineering knowledge and skills to help with the treatment and rehabilitation of patients with serious diseases or disabilities. You would work with medical consultants to develop the instruments necessary for diagnosing or monitoring patients. You could be concerned with designing new equipment, such as that used in keyhole surgery, aids for the handicapped, such as replacement joints and limbs, or implants like pacemakers. Your work might be said to harness the techniques of electrical, electronic and mechanical engineering to supplement the mechanics of the human body.

Opportunities for Training

Your first step in training to become a biomedical engineer would probably be to take an accredited degree in mechanical, electrical or electronic engineering. Some degree courses in these subjects include medical engineering options, so it is worth looking carefully at prospectuses when you are researching your university application. There are also postgraduate qualifications in medical engineering, with some training places funded directly by the National Health Service or by a hospital trust.

In order to become a chartered engineer, you would normally need to take a four-year MEng degree and reach a recognised standard on an accredited training programme incorporating suitable periods of practical experience. A three-year BEng degree would normally take you to Incorporated Engineer status, although there is special provision to switch to the chartered route if you wish. (See the separate article on engineering qualifications in the introduction)

Requirements

In order to be accepted on a suitable engineering degree course, you would need at least three A level/AVCE/Advanced Higher, four Higher or equivalent qualifications, normally including maths and physics, together with five GCSE/S Grade passes at A-C/1-3. These should include maths, another science subject and English. Some universities run foundation courses for candidates who do not have the appropriate A level/AVCE/Advanced Higher, Higher or equivalent. A course of this sort would prepare you for the first year of an engineering degree.

Kind of Person

You would need to be interested in discovering practical solutions to the problems experienced by patients. You would therefore need a logical but creative approach to problem solving. In addition to your technical and engineering skills and knowledge, you would have to be able to work as part of a medical health team providing care for your patients. You could find yourself dealing with fellow professionals, patients and their carers as well as with technical and administrative staff. You would need to keep abreast of developments in your field and to share your own specialist knowledge with other professionals at meetings, courses and seminars.

B road Outlook

There are many opportunities for employment within this relatively new and specialised branch of engineering. As a biomedical engineer, you would often work in a hospital department associated with a university and research would usually feature as an important aspect of your activities. In addition to working in hospitals, there are also opportunities to work in the commercial field, for example designing aids for the disabled or diagnostic equipment of all kinds.

R elated Occupations

You might be interested in one of the related engineering professions, such as electronic, electrical, mechanical or telecommunications engineer. Alternatively, you might like to consider another of the professions allied to medicine, such as biotechnologist or medical physicist.

I mpact

You are likely to be able to work regular hours but may need to work overtime if there are tight deadlines to meet. As this is a field that depends extensively on research and new technology, you may find that you have to travel to conferences and meetings in order to exchange ideas with other experts or clients.

E arnings Potential

You could expect to earn in the region of £15,000 when you first graduate and are continuing your training. This can rise to £40,000 and above with age and experience.

F urther Information

Institution of Mechanical Engineers, London SW1 9JJ
Website: www.imeche.org.uk

The Engineering and Technology Board, London WC2R 3ER
Website: www.engc.org.uk

The Engineering Careers Information Service Website www.enginuity.org.uk

Alternative/equivalent entrance requirements can include: ILC, IB, EB, NC/ND and many other similar international systems. For further details see the Equivalent Qualifications section in the Introduction.

What is Involved?

Working as a biotechnologist, you would be involved with using tiny living organisms such as bacteria or yeasts in industrial processes. You might find yourself, for example, working in the food or drinks industry; developing fertilizers or animal foodstuffs; or manufacturing pharmaceuticals. There are also opportunities to work with pollution control and the management of environmental waste. You might become involved with the production of complex molecules, such as hormones or enzymes, which could be particularly useful in the medical field. One area of biotechnology that is expanding at the moment is that of harnessing genetic engineering.

Opportunities for Training

There are approximately 35 courses in biotechnology at undergraduate level, but degrees in biological sciences, molecular biology or biochemistry could also provide a good foundation for postgraduate work in this area. The main recruitment for work in the biotechnological field is from scientists with two to three years' postgraduate experience. To obtain this you would need a first class or upper second class degree, followed by specialist research in the area.

Several universities have postgraduate centres like the Cranfield Biotechnology Centre, where you could undertake your doctoral or post-doctoral research. Career vacancies are advertised in the *New Scientist* and *Nature* magazines. There are opportunities for sixth-formers to attend annual summer schools in national centres for biotechnological education in Aberystwyth and Edinburgh. Many of the institutes such as the Institute of Food Research have summer placement schemes.

Requirements

To gain admission to a degree course, you would need three good A level/AVCE/Advanced Higher, four Higher or equivalent qualifications, including biology and usually chemistry, together with five GCSE/S Grade passes at A-C/1-3 including English and maths. An AVCE or equivalent vocational qualification in engineering or manufacturing could be helpful for some courses, but would not be essential.

Kind of Person

You would need a keen interest in biology and chemistry and in the application of specialised techniques. Attention to detail and a logical approach to problem solving would be essential. If you were involved in research, you would need to be persistent in the face of setbacks because it can take a long time to make headway in solving scientific problems. In return, you could be breaking new ground in an ever-changing world of discovery.

Some of the work would be routine testing and you should enjoy your current laboratory practical work. You would need a facility with statistics as well as good communication skills, as you would be called on to explain your experiments, results and conclusions to others, some of who may not have your technical knowledge. The internet is being used increasingly as a research tool and as a means of communicating by scientists, so you should be happy in using computers. You are also likely to be working as part of a team of scientists and, as you become more senior, would need to direct the work of other members of the team.

B road Outlook

Once qualified, there would be a range of career options available to you. Not only is there choice in the area in which you could work but also in the type of job that you could do. You could, for example, continue with research or move into technical sales and marketing in your particular field. It is often possible to move between industries and so apply your knowledge and expertise in different fields as your career and interests develop. There is normally a shortage of qualified specialised scientists of this nature, although you may need to move to find the job that you really want.

R elated Occupations

You might be interested in working in another area of scientific research by becoming a biochemist, microbiologist, biologist, pharmacist or pharmacologist. You could consider the broad areas of biochemical engineering, process technology or biomedical/clinical sciences.

I mpact

You are likely to be based in a laboratory, although you may also be working in an office attached to a factory, university or hospital. You may need to travel to other laboratories or to meet other scientists or attend conferences or lectures. At times you may have to work late when you have an important deadline to meet or when you are coming close to a breakthrough with a particular experiment.

E arnings Potential

Your salary when you first start working as an assistant scientist is likely to be around £14,000 but this could rise as high as £50,000 or beyond if you were working in industry and had a particular specialism that is in short supply.

F urther Information

Biotechnology and Biological Sciences Research Council, Swindon SN2 1UH
Website: www.bbsrc.ac.uk

The Institute of Biology, London SW7 2DZ Website: www.iob.org

The Biotechnology Group, Glasgow G2 7TP
Website: www.biotech-scotland.org

Cranfield Biotechnology Centre, Silsoe MK45 4DT
Website: www.cranfield.ac.uk/biotech

Alternative/equivalent entrance requirements can include: ILC, IB, EB, NC/ND and many other similar international systems. For further details see the Equivalent Qualifications section in the Introduction.

What is Involved?

As a researcher working in the broadcast media, you would generate new and original ideas for programmes, source information, contacts and contributors and turn ideas into actual broadcasts. As the person responsible for making first contact with potential contributors to programmes, you would have to ensure that they are good speakers and that the stories they provide are accurate and fair. All your sources must be thoroughly corroborated.

On the day of the programme, you would meet the guests you have booked and brief them about what to expect. You may be researching something topical and currently in the news or something more human interest led, and you could spend some time delving into archives, combing newspapers or surfing the internet for background information.

You would have to keep meticulous records of the work you do, notes of interviews with people, copyright details, where permissions to use material have to be obtained and so on. You would also have to work strictly within the constraints of time and budget.

Opportunities for Training

There is no single way to train to become a researcher. It is likely but in no way essential that you would have a degree or bring to the industry transferable skills from another area such as print journalism. Much more important than qualifications would be to prove you have the talent, commitment and knowledge of the industry to make a positive contribution to production research.

Skillset, the Sector Skills Council for broadcast, film, video and interactive media, runs a National Vocational Qualification (NVQ) level 3 in Production Research.

Requirements

You would need two or three A level/AVCE/Advanced Higher, three or four Higher or equivalent qualifications for degree course entry. The subject of your degree is not important, although you could consider a course in journalism or media studies. Three or four years at university would be an opportunity to build experience in student journalism or broadcasting. You should take every opportunity to gain relevant work experience because that is often more highly valued than academic qualifications.

Kind of Person

You must be a team worker, with constant energy, a passion for programming and the ability to generate a variety of ideas for a range of programmes. You must be able to get on with people, particularly contributors, and able to make them feel at ease. You would need a high level of literacy and numeracy skills, together with intellectual rigour. You should be able to work independently and under pressure, to extract relevant details and write detailed notes or reports.

52

Wide general knowledge would be useful, together with good organisation and accuracy, and a high degree of computer literacy. As important as anything would be excellent intellectual and analytical skills. You would have to be very organised and have good communication skills, as you would be dealing with a wide variety of people. You would need mental and physical toughness, to cope with frustration as well as success, and probable long hours. Knowledge of and an ability to analyse different types of programmes would be essential.

B road Outlook

Competition for contracts is intense. Most researchers work on freelance contracts, either directly for broadcasters or for independent production companies. Factual programmes regularly employ researchers, and sometimes drama and light entertainment programmes will too (particularly specialist researchers in, say, music or stills research).

Much of the work is in London and the south east, although major cities such as Cardiff, Edinburgh, Leeds and Manchester are strong regional centres.

R elated Occupations

You might also consider: producer, director, programme editor or presenter, journalist, advertising copywriter or scriptwriter.

I mpact

You should be prepared for short-term contracts, unpredictable hours and tight deadlines. You may have to supplement your income with other work between contracts, especially in the early days as you build up your network of contacts. Your work would probably involve you in a good deal of travel, so a driving licence would be a virtual necessity.

E arnings Potential

If you were in full-time employment with a large TV employer, you could start at about £18,000, with possible progression to about £30,000. The current agreed minimum freelance weekly rate for a researcher is £430.

F urther Information

British Broadcasting Corporation, London W12 8GJ
Website: www.bbc.co.uk

Ft2-Film and Television Freelance Training, London W1B 5LY
Website: www.ft2.org.uk

Skillset Sector Skills Council, London W1V 5RA Website: www.skillset.org

Skills for Media Website: www.skillsformedia.com

Your Creative Future Website: www.yourcreativefuture.org

Alternative/equivalent entrance requirements can include: ILC, IB, EB, NC/ND and many other similar international systems. For further details see the Equivalent Qualifications section in the Introduction.

What is Involved?

As a building services engineer, you could be involved with the design of energy efficient buildings, renewable energy, green architecture, ventilation, lighting, acoustics, electricity and control, many or all of which are necessary in modern buildings. You might also use your skills to meet demands for building energy management systems, fire/smoke control, indoor air quality standards and environmental pollution control. You could design the sophisticated systems that are required and draw up the necessary plans on paper or computer. You would also be expected to supervise the installation of all of these services and ensure they meet the correct specifications and safety regulations. You would often work alongside architects, allowing you to input your creative expertise at the concept stage in the design process.

Opportunities for Training

To qualify as a chartered engineer, responsible for research, development and senior management, the simplest route would be to complete a four-year accredited MEng degree, followed by about four years of structured training with an employer. To qualify as an incorporated engineer, responsible more for the day-to-day management of projects, you could take a three-year accredited BEng degree, followed by a similar period of structured training. There are alternative routes to both chartered and incorporated engineer status and you should consult the Chartered Institution of Building Services Engineers (CIBSE) for more information. Graduates who specialise in IT or acoustics are particularly sought after.

Requirements

Entry requirements vary for different degrees and at different universities. Generally speaking, you would need three A level/AVCE/Advanced Higher, four Higher or equivalent qualifications for the MEng route, including maths and physics, and two A level/AVCE/Advanced Higher, three Higher or equivalent qualifications for the BEng route. In either case, you should also have a broad platform of GCSE/S Grade passes at A-C/1-3. Some universities offer a one-year foundation course for students who do not have the necessary maths or physics passes.

Kind of Person

You would need to be able to display initiative and enterprise in planning and executing a programme for the development of an engineering project and able to work effectively both as an individual and as a member of a team. You should have excellent numeracy and problem solving skills and the ability to communicate ideas verbally, in written reports and by means of presentations to groups.

You would also need good awareness of management methods and of the financial environment in which you would be working. This is a rapidly changing work environment, so you would need to keep up to date with new developments and technology. Computer skills would be essential in your design work – using computer-aided design (CAD) software packages.

You would find yourself analysing and solving practical problems and taking responsibility for your decisions and possibly for large projects. You would need to make site visits during the construction phases, which would require agility and physical fitness.

B road Outlook

Building services engineering is recognised as an important discipline and for many years demand for graduates in this area has outstripped supply. There is, in fact, a nationwide shortage of building services engineers, which means that you would be in an extremely good position to find a job. Organisations that might offer you work include large building contractors, architectural or design practices or equipment manufacturers. Large companies with a buildings portfolio also need building services engineers and there are also jobs in companies that are responsible for the maintenance and servicing of buildings. There are also opportunities to work overseas.

R elated Occupations

You might also consider: quantity surveyor, building surveyor, civil, electrical or mechanical engineer, architect or town planner.

I mpact

If you were office based, you would expect to work regular hours, probably a 36-hour week Monday to Friday. However, you might need to work longer hours when there were important deadlines to meet. If you were working on site, you could expect to work longer and less regular hours than this, including evenings and weekends.

You might need to travel a long distance to reach the site or even to stay away from home whilst you were working. You would also be expected to work all around the site, which could involve climbing ladders or scaffolding. You would need to be prepared to get wet, cold and dirty and probably to wear protective clothing

E arnings Potential

The current shortage of building services engineers means good salaries, secure employment and good promotion prospects. You could expect to start earning around £18,000 when you first graduate and should be able to increase your earnings fairly rapidly, to around £30,000, within a few years. The average annual earnings for experienced chartered engineers are around £45,000 and for incorporated engineers around £37,000.

F urther Information

The Chartered Institution of Building Services Engineers (CIBSE), London SW12 9BS. Website www.cibse.org

Alternative/equivalent entrance requirements can include: ILC, IB, EB, NC/ND and many other similar international systems. For further details see the Equivalent Qualifications section in the Introduction.

What is Involved?

As a building surveying technician, you would carry out a number of tasks that would provide important technical support to a building surveyor. See our separate article on this work. You might find yourself carrying out detailed surveys of buildings, preparing accurate plans and specifications for work, costing work and handling tender documents or dealing with contractors.

You might be required to offer advice to clients on the suitability of buildings for particular purposes, the feasibility of proposed building work or on the soundness of a building. You should be able to advise on relevant legislation and the availability of grants, on the choice of contractors in your area and on maintenance or repair requirements. Another area of work in which you might become involved is that of on-site supervision.

Opportunities for Training

To become a building surveyor technician, you would usually be training whilst working towards qualifying membership of one of three organisations: licentiate of the Architecture and Surveying Institute (ASI), associate of the Association of Building Engineers (ABE) or technical member of the Royal Institution of Chartered Surveyors.

Whichever you choose, you could study full- or part-time for a higher national certificate or diploma (HNC/D) in building surveying or work towards National or Scottish Vocational Qualifications (N/SVQ) at levels three/four. You would normally follow a structured training programme for at least two years and you would need to attain a series of competence levels.

Requirements

For the HNC/D route, you would need at least one A level/AVCE/Advanced Higher, two Higher or equivalent qualifications, together with three GCSE/S Grade passes at A-C/1-3, including English and maths. There are no minimum entry requirements for the N/SVQ route, although individual employers or training providers may set their own standards.

You would almost certainly need a driving licence, as you would be required to visit sites on a regular basis.

Kind of Person

You would be working in a technical field and as such would need to have a methodical and logical approach to solving practical problems. You would have to enjoy working with figures and have some mathematical ability. You may find yourself using quite complicated measuring equipment, so would need some technical skills.

In addition to your practical nature, you would need to be able to communicate with a wide range of people. You might need to read and write reports and convey the information in them to other professionals. You could be talking directly to clients, who may not have your knowledge of buildings. Alternatively, you might be on site dealing with the work force, giving them instructions and organising their work.

B road Outlook

Job prospects for building surveying technicians are generally good, although this does depend somewhat on the state of the housing market. In large companies there is often a recognised career structure and opportunities for promotion are readily available if you are prepared to work hard.

However, promotion can be more difficult in smaller companies and you may need to change jobs and move around to gain experience. It is also possible for experienced technicians to become self-employed or consultants and there are opportunities to work abroad if that appeals to you.

R elated Occupations

You might also consider: building manager, estate agent, technician engineer, town planner or architectural technologist.

I mpact

If you are working in an office-based role then you are likely to work regular hours, mainly Monday to Friday. However, you are also likely to work on sites when you may have to work in wet, cold and dirty conditions. You may need to climb ladders or go up scaffolding and would need to be reasonably fit to cope with the demands of the job. You may need to walk some distance and scramble around sites in order to take accurate measurements. At times you may have to wear protective clothing such as a hard hat.

E arnings Potential

If you start as a school leaver studying part-time, you could earn around £9,000 to £11,000. This is likely to rise to a salary of around £15,000 when you first qualify. Salaries for experienced surveying technicians can vary enormously, depending on demand for staff and also on the particular expertise that you can offer.

F urther Information

The Architecture and Surveying Institute, Chippenham SN15 3WD
Website: www.asi.org.uk

The Royal Institution of Chartered Surveyors, Coventry CV4 8JE
Website: www.rics.org.uk

The Association of Building Engineers, Northampton NN3 8NW
Website: www.abe.org.uk

Alternative/equivalent entrance requirements can include: ILC, IB, EB, NC/ND and many other similar international systems. For further details see the Equivalent Qualifications section in the Introduction.

What is Involved?

As a building surveyor, you would provide detailed advice on the design, construction, maintenance, management or repair of proposed or existing buildings. You would be looking for defects in, or ways to improve, all types in existing buildings. You would also advise on the feasibility and possible costs of repair to the building, of conversion and the suitability of the building for particular purposes.

Your clients would include prospective purchasers, vendors, building societies and property owners. You might find yourself drawing up detailed plans, advising on government or health and safety regulations and on whether a grant might be available for the work. You could also be involved with instructing an architect to prepare detailed plans and with obtaining estimates for carrying out the work.

Opportunities for Training

In order to become a member of the Royal Institution of Chartered Surveyors (RICS), you would need an accredited degree (or equivalent), together with a minimum of two years training whilst you are employed. This on-the-job training must be approved by the RICS before you start. There are full-time degree courses, which take three years to complete. There are also sandwich courses, which include a year of practical work experience that can count towards the required two years training.

If you want to 'earn whilst you learn' there are part-time degree courses available, which you take whilst you are employed. In addition, there are some RICS-accredited distance learning degree or diploma correspondence courses, which can be taken whilst you work, and relevant postgraduate courses.

Requirements

Degree courses in surveying normally ask for a minimum of two A level/ AVCE/Advanced Higher, three Higher or equivalent qualifications, together with least four or five GCSE/S Grade passes at A-C/1-3, often specifying English and maths.

Kind of Person

You would need a practical approach to problem solving. There is likely to be quite a lot of paperwork involved. You would be drawing up and interpreting plans and for this you need to be accurate. You might be involved with reading and evaluating both tender documents and documents relating to the law. You could be involved with making decisions relating to deadlines and budgets for work for which you will need to have a good grasp of maths.

Above all, you would need to bring common sense and logic to your decision making. In addition to this, you are likely to be working with a large number of different people. These can include your employers, who you may need to persuade to your point of view, and the site workers, who you may need to instruct and lead. At times you would be imparting complex technical information to people without your specialist knowledge. You are also likely to be working as part of a team of building professionals, with whom you may need to negotiate the best solution to a problem.

B road Outlook

The demand for the building surveyor's expertise is growing with the increasing refurbishment of urban areas, rural sites and older properties. The largest employer is the private sector, which ranges from very small practices to large companies with overseas operations. Your qualification would be recognised in many countries if you wanted to work abroad. Local authorities also employ a number of building surveyors, as do major companies with a large amount of property, such as major retailers or hotel chains. There are also opportunities to work with large historical buildings for the trusts or charities that manage them and are concerned with their maintenance.

R elated Occupations

You might consider: town and country planner, architect, estate agent, civil engineer, valuer or auctioneer.

I mpact

You are likely to be involved in inspecting buildings very thoroughly; this can involve going into dirty, damp and dark areas such as attics and cellars. You would need to be reasonably fit and agile in order to carry out your surveys effectively. At times you may need to climb ladders or scramble around on scaffolding. Your work could involve you being outside in all kinds of weather and you could need to walk for quite long distances.

A driving licence is likely to be essential to get you to the sites and you may be expected to travel quite long distances within the UK and in some cases to spend time abroad.

E arnings Potential

The salary a building surveyor might expect varies quite considerably and depends on some extent to demand from the market place. If you are a school leaver working and studying part-time, you might expect to earn up to £10,000. Newly qualified building surveyors who are members of the RICS can expect to start earning around £25,000. This can rise to well over £30,000 and in some private practices income is also dependent on the profits made by the business.

F urther Information

The Royal Institution of Chartered Surveyors (RICS), Education and Training Dept, Coventry CV4 8JE Website: www.rics.org.uk

---

Alternative/equivalent entrance requirements can include: ILC, IB, EB, NC/ND and many other similar international systems. For further details see the Equivalent Qualifications section in the Introduction.

What is Involved?

As a building technician, you are likely to find yourself specialising in one or more of the areas of work involved in managing a construction site. For example, you could be working from an architect's or engineer's drawings to estimate the costs of a project or plan the stages of construction. Taking account of the materials and manpower needed, you would calculate the time and costs involved. You might be involved with buying the materials needed and working out how to store the equipment and materials on site. Alternatively, your work could take you on to the site itself where you would check the progress and standard of the work being carried out.

Opportunities for Training

There are several possible training routes. You could, for example, take a part- or full-time higher national certificate/diploma (HNC/D) at a college or training centre; you could take a lower level construction course at a local college or you could train in a craft skill – such as bricklaying or plastering – before taking a National or Scottish Vocational Qualification (NVQ/SVQ) at technician level. Another way of training would be to take a construction apprenticeship, in which you could study part-time up to NVQ/SVQ level 3 while in paid employment. This would probably take three or four years to complete.

Requirements

Practical experience of working on a building site or in a construction environment is usually the most important requirement. For the HNC/D route, you would normally need at least one A level/AVCE/Advanced Higher, two Higher or equivalent qualifications, together with four GCSE/S Grade passes at A-C/1-3, including English, maths and a science. (An AVCE or equivalent in construction/built environment could be helpful). Similar GCSE/S Grade requirements would apply to most apprenticeships and college courses for this type of work. You would often be able to enter a craft level course by passing a selection test.

Kind of Person

You would need to be a practical person with a logical and sensible approach to problem solving. In order to be successful you would need to learn a considerable amount of technical information about the building industry and also gain some knowledge of law and health and safety issues. Your job is likely to involve computers, so you would need to be computer literate. Your job would involve dealing with large variety of people and you would need to have good communication skills. You might, for example, be negotiating with other professionals or supervising workers on a building site.

In either case you would need to make yourself clearly understood. You are also likely to be involved with interpreting plans and with making calculations based on the information you are given. You may need to organise your own work and that of others and should be able to work on your own initiative.

B road Outlook

There are opportunities to work for local and central government, for large building contractors and for large organisations that have property portfolios such as hotel chains or major retailers. The demand for technicians depends to a great extent on the state of the building trade and it may be necessary to move in order to find a first job or promotion. However, there is currently no shortage of opportunities. You may choose to change employers and job roles over time in order to gain the experience necessary to develop your career and perhaps set up your own business.

R elated Occupations

You might consider other construction-related careers, such as: surveying technician, architectural technologist, town planning support worker, building manager, surveyor or estate agent.

I mpact

If you are working in an office-based job, the hours of work are likely to be around 40 hours a week. However, you would also be expected to work overtime in the evenings and at weekend, particularly if you have a contract deadline to meet. The hours of work on building sites can be long, especially in the summer to make maximum use of daylight hours. You could also get dirty, wet and cold at times on a building site and would need to wear protective clothing such as a hard hat, boots and a reflective coat.

E arnings Potential

Salaries for building technicians vary between companies and different parts of the country. Once qualified, you could expect to earn around £11,000 and this would rise as you become more experienced. There are also allowances for working on site and sometimes travel expenses are reimbursed.

F urther Information

Construction Industry Training Board, King's Lynn PE31 6RH
Website: www.citb.org.uk

Alternative/equivalent entrance requirements can include: ILC, IB, EB, NC/ND and many other similar international systems. For further details see the Equivalent Qualifications section in the Introduction.

(Also called Buyer or Purchasing Officer)

What is Involved?

As a buying executive, you would be responsible for obtaining the products and services needed by your organisation to support its key activities. This could include, for example, purchasing the raw materials or components for a manufacturing process, sourcing spare parts for machinery maintenance, ordering the merchandise for a retail outlet or updating the IT facilities in an office environment. You would be expected to negotiate competitive prices at the same time as building relationships with suppliers who understand your needs, can meet your quality specifications and can deliver the right quantity of materials on a reliable basis.

You would have to maintain adequate reserve stock levels to cope with fluctuations in demand and ensure that supplies reach their intended destination on time. You would probably set up automated systems to cope with some of these functions but you would need to discuss contracts with suppliers, monitor deliveries and stock levels, challenge price changes, check sources of new materials and keep pace with technological and design improvements. You could work in almost any sort of manufacturing or service organisation, although you would need special skills to act as a buyer in, say, the retail fashion business or a technical background before you could purchase engineering components.

Opportunities for Training

Most employers would expect you to work towards Chartered Institute of Purchasing and Supply (CIPS) qualifications. These are available on a full- or part-time basis or by distance learning and range from the clerical level Certificate in Purchasing and Supply to the CIPS Graduate Diploma. You could also work towards National or Scottish Vocational Qualifications (N/SVQ) in Procurement or take an accredited degree or higher national diploma (HND). The CIPS qualifications would usually be supported in many companies by an internal training scheme. With appropriate qualifications and experience, you could become a member and then a fellow of CIPS.

Requirements

While there are no specific entry requirements, most employers look for a degree, HND or equivalent qualification. This could be in any subject, although business studies, management science, computing or logistics could be useful. In the engineering/manufacturing industries, a technological qualification would be an advantage, as would chemistry in the chemical industry or computing in IT. (An AVCE/equivalent in retail/distribution service or business could be valuable.) For degree entry, you would normally be expected to have at least two A level/AVCE/Advanced Higher, three Higher or equivalent qualifications, together with four or five GCSE/S Grade passes at A-C/1-3, including English and maths.

Kind of Person

As an essential link in the supply chain, you would be in a very demanding and responsible position. You would need to understand the overall requirements of your own organisation and to be able to assess the relative merits of suppliers' goods or services. A logical and analytical mind would be essential, together with good powers of judgement and the ability to negotiate contracts. You should have strong numerical skills and a grasp of finance and accounting, since you would often be handling large sums of money. In addition to these technical qualities, you would need excellent written and verbal communication skills, a liking for others and a sense of fairness and integrity.

B road Outlook

You might achieve promotion – to senior management or even to board level – within your existing organisation. Alternatively, you could develop your career by moving elsewhere. All kinds of organisation throughout the country need buying executives, so many opportunities to move should be possible. There may be scope to specialise in a particular field calling for special expertise, such as buying art at auction, next season's designs for a fashion store or lorries and vans for a freight company.

R elated Occupations

You might also consider: logistics manager, sales executive, retail manager, freight forwarder or shipbroker.

I mpact

You would work normal office hours but would occasionally need to take work home at night or over weekends, so that you could formulate your strategic plans and analyse your departmental performance, check levels of stock or write a monthly report for directors. You may need to travel fairly extensively, including making trips overseas, in order to check suppliers' procedures, transport systems and quality controls.

E arnings Potential

You could expect to start at around £15,000 as a graduate trainee, with your income rising significantly to, say, £30,000 to £60,000 once you reach middle or senior management levels. If you can demonstrate that your buying skills lead to savings in costs and improvements in efficiency, you could earn significant performance-related bonuses.

F urther Information

Chartered Institute of Purchasing and Supply, Stamford PE9 3NZ
Website: www.cips.org

The Institute of Logistics and Transport, Northants NN17 4XQ
Website: www.iolt.org.uk

Alternative/equivalent entrance requirements can include: ILC, IB, EB, NC/ND and many other similar international systems. For further details see the Equivalent Qualifications section in the Introduction.

What is Involved?

As a careers adviser (or career counsellor), you would help people make decisions about their future. You might work in a careers centre, in schools and colleges, a university or an adult guidance centre, and your clients might need guidance on, for example, their long-term career goals or help with decisions related to their education and training. You would usually work with people individually, although you may occasionally lead groups, using your counselling skills and your knowledge of education, training and employment to help them decide on next steps. You may use psychometric and other interest and ability tests to support the guidance process. After your interview or group work session, you would provide a written report summarising the outcomes of the guidance interview and the implications in terms of career plans. In an educational establishment, your work may involve preparing education programmes related to careers and personal development, taking classes and leading group discussions. You would also be expected to have close, regular contact with employers and other opportunity providers.

In England at present, mainstream careers services are being replaced by the Connexions Service, which provides advice, guidance and information for 13 to 19 year-olds through partnerships with organisations such as youth work, education, health, social welfare and criminal justice agencies. Within this new service a new role of personal adviser has come into being and is still developing. It may replace the current role of the careers adviser but that is not yet entirely clear.

Opportunities for Training

For mainstream work, you should normally obtain the one-year full-time or two-year part-time Qualification in Careers Guidance (QCG), available at 12 approved centres throughout England, Scotland and Wales. You would then, in many cases, undertake the National/Scottish Vocational Qualification (N/SVQ) level 4 in guidance in order to demonstrate your practical competence. Exact details of training arrangements vary from one employer to another, so you should research information carefully. Within the new Connexions Service, you would have to add either the Diploma for Connexions Personal Advisers or the Understanding Connexions training programme. Advisers working in higher education have their own qualification organised by the Association of Graduate Careers Advisory Services.

Requirements

There are no specific entry requirements for the QCG or the N/SVQ, although you would have to demonstrate your ability to cope with the academic aspects of the training. Many new entrants are graduates, with a degree in any subject, but employers also value a broad range of life and work experiences.

Kind of Person

You would need enthusiasm, flexibility and a real interest in helping people to make the most of the opportunities available. Depending on the client

64

group that you were working with, you would also need a wide range of counselling and guidance skills, an understanding of educational systems and knowledge of local, national and international labour markets.

You would need to be able to plan and organise your own time and to be able to work as part of a team. Computer systems are widely used for record keeping, maintaining occupational databases and administering tests, so you would need good IT skills. If your clients are facing difficulties in obtaining employment, you may need advocacy skills as well as the ability to network with relevant agencies.

B road Outlook

At present there is a shortage nationally of both careers and personal advisers. There should continue to be many opportunities as new roles develop within Connexions and new careers organisations in Scotland and Wales. Careers advisers in Northern Ireland are currently part of the civil service but that too is under review. You may find that you need to change employers from time to time, both to broaden your experience and to progress to more senior positions.

R elated Occupations

You might also consider: teacher, social worker, probation officer or youth worker.

I mpact

The work has traditionally been based on normal Monday to Friday hours, with occasional evening and weekend events and some time spent away from home on training courses. This still applies in many cases, although personal advisers may be on call at any time and could find it stressful to work with clients with severe problems.

E arnings Potential

You would probably start on around £15,500, rising to around £21,500. With experience and increased responsibility, your earnings should increase to £25,000 to £40,000.

F urther Information

The Institute of Career Guidance, Stourbridge DY8 1TA
Website: www.icg-uk.org

Connexions Website: www.connexions.gov.uk

The Association of Graduate Careers Advisory Services, Sheffield S3 7QX
Website: www.agcas.org.uk

Alternative/equivalent entrance requirements can include: ILC, IB, EB, NC/ND and many other similar international systems. For further details see the Equivalent Qualifications section in the Introduction.

65

What is Involved?

As a cartographer you would be dealing with the making of maps. You must be careful not to confuse the work of the cartographer with that of the surveyor, nor expect employment to involve strenuous outdoor activity and travel to remote places. With very few exceptions, you would normally be found seated at a desk or graphics workstation, processing original survey data collected and recorded by specialists in the field. The work falls into two areas: the *editorial* side, where the contents of the map are chosen and its appearance is designed, or the *drafting* side, where the map is actually produced.

Cartography has been revolutionised by information technology and traditional methods of map-making continue to change. For example, information is now obtained by photography from satellites. Unlike earlier mapmakers, whose challenge was to obtain the relevant information, today there is so much information available that the problem has become how to select what is required. What we are able to map has also changed and will continue to do so. We can now map the seabed with great accuracy and our increasing exploration of space will bring with it new demands for maps and charts.

Opportunities for Training

Until recently, cartographic education outside the universities was restricted to apprenticeship schemes or programmes created and implemented by the major Government mapping and charting agencies. Today, you can choose between entering a two-, three- or four-year course in cartography, geographical information systems, geography, surveying and cartography, land use (geographical techniques), surveying and mapping science or topographic science. Cartography courses place great emphasis on practical mapmaking and you would gain a lot of 'hands on' experience, either designing on paper or creating maps on a computer screen.

Requirements

To work on the editorial side, you would need a degree in one of the subject areas listed above and possibly a postgraduate qualification. This would require a minimum of two A level/AVCE/Advanced Higher, three Higher or equivalent qualifications, ideally including geography, together with five GCSE/S Grade passes at A-C/1-3, including English and maths. To work on the drafting or production side, you are strongly advised to take geography and/or maths at A level/Advanced Higher, Higher or equivalent followed by a diploma course at college.

Kind of Person

You should have a genuine feeling for maps, combined with the patience and powers of concentration necessary to undertake work which may be both mentally and physically demanding, as the preparation of a single sheet may take several weeks or even months. Artistic flair and a sense of design are valuable assets, as is an ability to work with precision and sometimes against the clock. This is very precise work using complex equipment and techniques. Cartographers have to be experts in communication: in real life roads are not red, nor motorways blue, and there are no dotted lines marking the borders between countries, but we see these things on a map and immediately know what they mean.

In short, you need to love maps, be interested in design, like geography and enjoy designing on a computer screen.

B road Outlook

The IT revolution has meant that far fewer cartographers are needed than before and there is enormous competition for the comparatively few employment openings which occur. Potential employers include government departments and national organisations like the Ordnance Survey, Met Office and Civil Aviation Authority; local, district and regional authorities; and the private sector such as map publishers, the AA or RAC. There are also opportunities to work abroad, for example for oil companies. A growing area of study related to cartography is that of Geographical Information Systems (GIS). This uses digital maps to model the earth in 3D and analyse geographical patterns.

Cartography provides work for around 3,500 skilled personnel in the public sector, although private mapping concerns possibly employ as many as 10,000 more.

R elated Occupations

You might wish to consider: town planner, surveyor, graphic designer or illustrator.

I mpact

This is an office-based job and you could expect to work regular office hours. Many cartographers work freelance on a contract basis and enjoy the freedom of being their own boss. If you have the right qualifications, you can progress from being a map drafter to a map editor and gradually assume responsibility for whole projects.

E arnings Potential

Cartographers themselves will tell you that their rewards are more often aesthetic, or come from knowledge that the end product will be of use to another person, than they are financial. Few, if any, have been known to make their fortune. As a graduate trainee, you could expect a starting salary between £14,000 and £18,000, progressing to about £30,000.

F urther Information

British Cartographic Society, Oxford OX3 OBP Website:
www.cartography.org.uk
(Click on 'publications' to take you to 'careers in cartography')

Alternative/equivalent entrance requirements can include: ILC, IB, EB, NC/ND and many other similar international systems. For further details see the Equivalent Qualifications section in the Introduction.

What is Involved?

As a catering manager, you would most likely work in the rapidly expanding food service management, or contract catering sectors of British industry. This is made up of companies of all sizes, who win contracts to manage the catering needs and related services on behalf a whole range of organisations. It can involve feeding people at work, catering in schools, colleges and universities, hospitals and healthcare or any other companies who prefer to call upon the experts, so that they can get on with taking care of their core business. Food service management companies are now developing their services to include catering for members of the public in such outlets as leisure centres, department stores, airports, railways stations, public events and places of entertainment. Alternatively, you could work in one specific restaurant, hotel or other food outlet, in which case you might be termed a restaurant manager.

In either case, you would be expected to ensure satisfaction with the quality of food and service, manage the whole operation efficiently and profitably and know how to deal with people, both staff and public. The bigger the organisation, the less likely it is that you would be required to cope with front-line welcoming and table organisation; you would concentrate your energies on recruitment, motivation, training, the arrangement and supervision of shifts, quality control, hygiene, health and safety and controlling budgets. Whatever the context, standards would feature high on your priorities.

Opportunities for Training

Opportunities exist at every level, with a range of training routes for school leavers or university graduates. Relevant previous experience or qualifications usually ensure that you are able to join the profession a few rungs higher on the career ladder.

You could go into the business straight from school, perhaps via a Modern Apprenticeship (Skillseeker in Scotland) or a craft course, and develop your career up to a managerial position. Alternatively, you could continue your studies to higher national diploma (HND) or degree level or you could join a company management training scheme.

Requirements

For degree entry, you would need at least two A level/AVCE/Advanced Higher, three Higher or equivalent qualifications, together with a good spread of GCSE/S Grade passes at A-C/1-3. The HND route usually requires one A level/AVCE/Advanced Higher, two Higher or equivalent qualifications. A foreign language would be very useful. You may be able to join a company scheme with A level/AVCE/Advanced Higher, Higher or equivalent, but a degree or HND would be more usual.

Experience in the industry, at however humble a level, would always be proof of your interest and commitment.

K ind of Person

Above all, you should be highly motivated, with a keen interest in food and drink. You would need a smart personal appearance, the ability to communicate effectively with customers and staff and the confidence to operate in a very public setting. You would have to remain calm under pressure and have the flexibility to cope with the occasional crisis in the kitchen. Physical fitness and the stamina to keep going for many hours a day would be important.

B road Outlook

As the catering sector grows, so do the career opportunities available. It is not just about preparing and serving food, although these are vital jobs for the success of the sector. Areas that you could work in include: catering services, corporate events and functions, domestic services, facilities management, food production, human resources, marketing, residential services, sales, service development and support services.

Once you have sufficient experience, you could open your own restaurant or set up a contract catering business.

R elated Occupations

You might also consider: hotel manager, conference and events manager, food service assistant, chef, publican or leisure services manager.

I mpact

In contract catering, your working hours could be reasonably regular; as a restaurant manager, however, you would have to work late into the evening and could expect to be busiest at weekends and during public holidays. You may work on a split shift system and you may find that, rather than having fixed hours, you have to keep working until the last customer leaves.

E arnings Potential

Junior managers usually earn between £9,000 and £15,000, while more experienced managers could expect £20,000 to £23,000. Some senior managers would receive more than £40,000. You may be offered live-in accommodation in some restaurant manager posts. If you can set up and run a successful restaurant or catering business, you should be able to achieve higher financial rewards.

F urther Information

Springboard, London WC2H 8LP Website: www.springboarduk.org.uk

Hotel and Catering International Management Association, London SW17 7HN Website: www.hcima.org.uk

Hospitality Training Foundation, London W5 5DH Website: www.htf.org.uk

Alternative/equivalent entrance requirements can include: ILC, IB, EB, NC/ND and many other similar international systems. For further details see the Equivalent Qualifications section in the Introduction.

What is Involved?

This is not secretarial work in the normally accepted sense. As a chartered secretary, you would play a central role in the administration and management of an organisation. Your work would include advising the directors/trustees of their legal obligations, administering finances, communicating with stakeholders, preparing agendas, taking minutes of meetings and maintaining the statutory records. You would need a wide knowledge of the law, accounting and business organisations.

As a bridge between the management board, stakeholders and other organisations, you would need to be fully aware of every aspect of your organisation, including the nature of the business and its overall direction, the functions of employees and the current finances.

Opportunities for Training

While it is not essential for you to become a member of the Institute of Chartered Secretaries and Administrators (ICSA), you would find this valuable, especially if you were working as a company secretary. You would, for example, be legally qualified to file the annual report with Companies House and you would be able to supply financial information to the Stock Exchange.

The ICSA examination scheme has three stages: foundation, pre-professional and professional. You would be exempt from the first two of these if you have a recognised degree or postgraduate award. Your studies could be full- or part-time, in the evenings or by correspondence course, and would probably take three of four years to complete. You could become an associate member after at least three years (six for a non-graduate) of relevant work experience and a fellow when you are at least 25 and achieve a senior position in your organisation.

Requirements

The ICSA 'open access' policy means that there are no formal academic requirements for the foundation training programme. You would simply need to be at least 17. You would normally, however, require two or three A level/AVCE/Advanced Higher, three or four Higher or equivalent qualifications to gain admission to a recognised degree course. Before you can be accepted as a member of ICSA, you must supply two references confirming that you are a 'fit and proper person' to work as a chartered secretary.

Kind of Person

You would need to be good at administration as this is the core of the work. You would be co-ordinating departments and would therefore need to be good at prioritising and seeing the overall picture. Your management responsibilities would require you to be tactful and discreet. You would also be dealing with financial and legal matters, requiring you to be numerate and also able to work under pressure to comply with legal deadlines.

Minute-taking would require the ability to write clearly and accurately, while explaining technical matters to a non-expert audience would demand excellent speaking skills. This is a very responsible job demanding the highest standards in professional integrity.

B road Outlook

Given that there is a legal requirement for every company in the UK to have a company secretary, there should be plenty of scope to work in this area. Not all company secretaries are chartered – they could have a legal or accountancy qualification instead – but the ICSA qualification is a broad one and can be adapted to a wide variety of administrative work in charities, local government, educational institutions and health organisations. You could go on to become a company director or chief executive.

R elated Occupations

You may wish to consider: accountant, solicitor, barrister/advocate, civil service administrator or human resources officer.

I mpact

This is an office-based job and you could expect to work usual office hours unless there is a deadline to meet, which could mean working unsocial hours. There may be some evening meetings to attend. You would be expected to observe a strict code of personal and professional conduct.

E arnings Potential

Depending on the type and size of the organisation you work for, you might expect a starting figure of around £25,000 as a newly qualified associate member. According to the ICSA, many chartered secretaries go on to earn a salary similar to that of top accountants and lawyers.

F urther Information

The Institute of Chartered Secretaries and Administrators (ICSA), London W1B 1AH Website www.icsa.org.uk

Alternative/equivalent entrance requirements can include: ILC, IB, EB, NC/ND and many other similar international systems. For further details see the Equivalent Qualifications section in the Introduction.

What is Involved?

As a chemical engineer you would apply mainly engineering principles to produce and control the chemical plant and machinery needed to manufacture chemicals, plastics, synthetic fibres, pharmaceuticals, petroleum products, certain food and drink products and medical gases. You would need considerable skill to control reactions which can be highly unstable and where factors such as temperature, pressure, flow rate, heat removal and concentration of reactants must all be taken into account. Your work would often revolve around turning a small-scale laboratory project into a large-scale, economically viable, safe and reliable industrial process.

Apart from this area of new product development, you might work in plant design and construction, in production management or in more general management, technical sales or exports.

Opportunities for Training

Several UK universities offer degrees in chemical engineering. These can last three years for a BEng or four years for an MEng (or a year longer in either case for a sandwich course giving practical experience in industry). In order to become a chartered chemical engineer, you would need to complete at least four years of academic study. The MEng would meet this requirement, whereas you would need to add another year of more specialised study, known as a 'matching section', to top up a BEng qualification.

You would then need, in either case, to follow your degree with a number of years of approved work experience known as the period of Initial Professional Development (IPD). The BEng degree can take you to incorporated engineer status (see our separate article on engineering qualifications).

Requirements

You are likely to need two or three A level/AVCE/Advanced Higher, three or four Higher or equivalent qualifications. These should include chemistry and maths and preferably another science subject, together with at least five GCSE/S Grade passes at A-C/1-3 to include maths, English and a science. Some universities run a foundation course for students who do not have the required science qualifications.

Kind of Person

You would need a strong practical interest in science, with meticulous attention to detail and a logical and methodical approach to problem solving. You would need good communication skills, as you would be required to discuss detailed proposals with other chemists and technologists and to explain technical issues to people who do not have your knowledge and expertise.

You are likely to need good IT skills as computers are used extensively in the design of chemical plants. You would need to work both under your own initiative and as part of a team. You are likely to be working in some sort of industrial, research or business environment and so would need to have relevant management and business skills.

B road Outlook

There are very good job opportunities for chemical engineers and there has been a steady growth in demand across the world. You degree would involve you in a number of disciplines and your employment options would remain open for a long time. There are many areas in which chemical engineers are both highly valued and well paid.

R elated Occupations

You might like to consider another specialism as an engineer, such as mechanical, electrical or civil. Alternatively, you may prefer to work in the scientific field as a pharmacologist, pharmacist, metallurgist or biochemist.

I mpact

Whilst you may have set hours of work, you are likely to be required to work irregular hours, should you be asked for example to manage 24-hour petroleum or chemical production processes or to meet a tight deadline. You may find yourself working under pressure from time to time. If you are working in a laboratory or a chemical plant, you may sometimes need to wear protective clothing. You may need to relocate in order to find the job that you really want and you could be expected to travel, for example to negotiate construction contracts, act as a consultant or attend conferences and meetings.

E arnings Potential

Chemical engineering is generally one of the better paid branches of engineering. You could expect to earn £20,000 or above when you first graduate. This can rise to £50,000 or higher when you become an experienced, chartered chemical engineer.

F urther Information

The Institute of Chemical Engineers, Rugby CV21 3HQ
Website: www.icheme.org

The Engineering and Technology Board, London WC2R 3ER
Website: www.engc.org.uk

The Engineering Careers Information Service
Website: www.enginuity.org.uk

Alternative/equivalent entrance requirements can include: ILC, IB, EB, NC/ND and many other similar international systems. For further details see the Equivalent Qualifications section in the Introduction.

What is Involved?

As a chemistry technician, you might work in industry, where you would be involved with quality control during the production process. Alternatively, you might work with scientists in a research and development department, investigating new products or manufacturing processes. This work could be in any of the industries that are based on chemistry, such as food and drinks, agriculture, pharmaceuticals or oil and chemical manufacture itself. There are also many opportunities to work within the civil service as an assistant scientific officer, in the health service and also in schools and universities.

Your work would tend to focus on the more routine tasks essential to support research and development in chemistry. You might, for example, assemble, maintain and repair laboratory equipment, monitor and record results data, order chemicals to maintain stock levels and constantly look for ways of improving experimental results. You would spend most of your time in a laboratory or workshop, working under the direction of one or more scientists.

Opportunities for Training

There are several possible training routes. You could, for example, work towards a suitable qualification via a Modern Apprenticeship (Skillseeker in Scotland), studying part-time for a National or Scottish Vocational Qualification. Alternatively, you could continue your education with a higher national diploma (HND) or a degree, possibly considering a sandwich course to gain practical work experience whilst studying.

There is often in-service training available within large companies. This may cover more advanced skills, specialised scientific equipment or aspects of management, purchasing and stock control. You could also expect regular updating training in such areas as new techniques and technology, health and safety procedures and computer systems.

Requirements

The minimum requirements for training are usually four GCSE/S Grade passes at A-C/1-3, including English, a science (ideally chemistry) and maths. You would need at least one or two science A level/AVCE/Advanced Higher, two or three Higher or equivalent qualifications for admission to an HND course, while degree entry would require two or three A level/AVCE/Advanced Higher, three or four Higher or equivalent.

Kind of Person

You would need a keen interest in science, particularly in chemistry. You are likely to be working in an environment that is developing and changing all the time, although your work would at times be quite methodical and repetitive, as you would be carrying out routine tests and applications.

You would need to be accurate and to show attention to detail. In addition to your scientific skills, you would have to work as part of a team and provide a fast and efficient service when asked to do so. You may have to explain your work clearly to your colleagues, so you would need reasonably good written and verbal communication.

B road Outlook

There are normally always jobs for chemistry technicians and a wide range of different organisations in which to find employment, although declining opportunities in manufacturing industry may make it necessary for you move to another sector to develop your career. There are jobs within the civil service, industrial research and educational establishments, pharmaceutical companies and hospitals, to name but a few. It should be possible, with appropriate experience, to use your scientific and technical knowledge to branch out into areas such as production or technical sales and marketing.

R elated Occupations

You might be interested in other science-based careers such as a pharmacy technician. You could also move into biochemistry, molecular biology, production supervision, and quality control.

I mpact

Most technicians work normal office hours Monday to Friday, so this work should not disrupt your social or family life. It may be necessary to work overtime sometimes when there are tight deadlines to meet, when research is at a critical point, or if you undertake shift work on a 24-hour production unit. You could find it necessary to move around the country to get promotion and there may be opportunities to work abroad.

E arnings Potential

Salaries vary between the private and public sectors. On average, you could expect to start earning about £9,000 as a technician, rising to around £18,000. In some industries, salaries for experienced, competent technicians can be much higher than this.

F urther Information

The Royal Society of Chemistry, London W1V 0BN Website: www.rsc.org

Alternative/equivalent entrance requirements can include: ILC, IB, EB, NC/ND and many other similar international systems. For further details see the Equivalent Qualifications section in the Introduction.

What is Involved?

As a chiropractor, you would be working in a primary healthcare profession that specialises in the diagnosis, treatment and overall management of conditions related to mechanical dysfunction of the joints, particularly those of the spine, and their effects on the nervous system. Treatment consists of a wide range of manipulative techniques designed to improve the function of the joints, relieving pain and muscle spasm. Your manipulation would have to be highly skilled and very specific, directed at individual joints in order to reduce strains and improve mobility in one area without disturbing another. You would support this treatment with individual counselling and advice about each patient's lifestyle, work and exercise, in order to help in managing the condition and preventing a recurrence of the problem. The work is similar in some ways to that of an osteopath or physiotherapist but with much greater emphasis on manual treatment, including spinal manipulation or adjustment. Your work may involve taking x-rays as part of the diagnostic process.

Opportunities for Training

You must be registered with the General Chiropractic Council (GCC) before you can call yourself a chiropractor. The GCC training standard means that you must graduate from an accredited institution before being accepted onto the register. There are four accredited institutions in the UK – two are independent colleges, whose courses are validated by UK universities, and two are university-based courses.

The four-year BSc in Chiropractic Sciences covers in-depth training in a variety of subjects, including life sciences, biomechanics, clinical medicine and differential diagnosis. You would also undergo practical training in adjustment and supervised clinical training, where you would have hands-on practice in treating patients. After qualifying, you would have to undertake a year's structured training with a qualified practitioner in order to gain the diploma in chiropractic. Finally, you must undertake continuing professional development as a requirement for re-registration on an annual basis.

Requirements

For entry to an accredited course, you would normally need at least two or three A level/AVCE/Advanced Higher, three to four Higher or equivalent qualifications, preferably including biology, human biology, physics or chemistry. Some courses may require GCSE/S Grade passes at A-C/1-3 in English and maths plus science subjects. You must be at least 18 before you can start a course.

Kind of Person

You would need a keen interest in human biology and in chemistry, together with a certain amount of physical endurance, as the manipulative skills required can be hard work at times. Good communication and problem-solving skills would be essential when dealing with a wide range of patients, all expecting a high standard of professional care from you. This would involve you in listening to each patient and then explaining your diagnosis. You would probably be working as a self-employed practitioner, so would need to be approachable and someone in whom patients could have confidence. In addition, you would need to be well organised and to have sufficient commercial skill to run your own business.

B road Outlook

Employment prospects have improved recently as this is an area of medicine that is growing and there should be room for more practitioners to establish themselves. Most chiropractors set up as independent consultants, or possibly as part of a group with other practitioners of complementary medicine. You would have to work for at least a year as an assistant to an established chiropractor before you could set up your own practice. You would not be directly employed in the NHS.

R elated Occupations

You may be interested in investigating other options in complementary medicine, such as osteopath, homoeopath, reflexologist or aromatherapist. Alternatively, you might be interested in other therapy-based professional roles in the medical field, such as physiotherapist, occupational therapist, radiographer or speech and language therapist.

I mpact

Being self-employed means that you would have to work hard to get yourself established and to build a reputation. This may include working long hours in the evenings and at weekends.

E arnings Potential

As most chiropractors are self-employed, incomes vary considerably. Most practitioners charge an hourly rate or per session and this can range from £20 to more than £50 per hour. This income has to cover administrative costs, salaries of assistant staff, plus charges for rent and heating. The British Chiropractic Association quotes a recent survey that suggests that earnings within five years of graduation can be as high as £100,000 per year.

F urther Information

British Chiropractic Association, Reading RG1 1QB
Website: www.chiropractic-uk.co.uk

General Chiropractic Council, London WC1X 8PB Website: www.gcc-uk.org

Alternative/equivalent entrance requirements can include: ILC, IB, EB, NC/ND and many other similar international systems. For further details see the Equivalent Qualifications section in the Introduction.

What is Involved?

As a civil engineer, you would design and manage the construction of bridges, roads, tunnels, pipelines, dams, sewage plants, railways, power stations and major buildings. You would be involved with aspects of the national infrastructure, including transport networks and energy and water supply systems. You would use your knowledge of the properties and behaviour of materials to create imaginative and aesthetically pleasing designs, which meet all relevant safety and durability requirements within specified budgetary constraints.

You would oversee construction projects and this would involve detailed planning and co-ordination with other professionals, including surveyors and architects, together with checking that the actual construction work is being carried out according to specifications. You would liaise in particular with site engineers, who are concerned with the day-to-day activity on site, monitoring such issues as construction methods, delivery of materials, supply pipes and cables and the marking out of the foundations.

Opportunities for Training

In order to become a chartered civil engineer, responsible for research, design and development, you would need to spend at least four years in undergraduate study, followed by postgraduate study and supervised experience. The initial requirement can be achieved by taking a four-year degree course that leads directly to an MEng. Alternatively, you could take a three-year degree course leading to a BEng and follow this with a year of more specialised post-graduate study. To become an incorporated engineer, responsible more for the efficient day-to-day management of projects, you could take the BEng route and follow this with further study and on-the-job training. Another route to incorporated engineer status would be a two- or three-year Higher National Diploma (HND), followed again by further study and relevant experience.

A number of construction companies sponsor undergraduates for some of their time at university, offering work experience and/or sandwich placements.

Requirements

In order to be accepted for an MEng in civil engineering, you are likely to need three A level/AVCE/Advanced Higher, four Higher or equivalent qualifications, including maths and physics, together with at least five GCSE/S Grade passes at A-C/1-3. (An AVCE/equivalent in construction/built environment could be relevant for some courses). Entry requirements for the BEng are usually slightly lower but would still normally include maths and physics at A level/Advanced Higher, Higher or equivalent. HND entry usually requires study of maths and physics to A level/Advanced Higher/Higher, with a pass in at least one of these subjects.

Kind of Person

As a civil engineer, you would need to be creative as well as practical and good at problem solving. You should have a good grasp of both maths and the principles of design. You would need to be a team player. On site, you could find yourself in charge of many people and your leadership skills would be very important. Good communication skills would also be needed, as you would be dealing with a wide variety of people who would need to be very clear about your instructions.

B road Outlook

Civil engineers can take advantage of work opportunities in both the private and public sectors, often changing jobs to gain more professional experience. They tend to specialise in areas such as roads and bridges, oil and gas rigs and pipelines, power stations, docks and harbours or public health and sewerage. There are courses run by the Institution of Civil Engineers for on-going professional development. UK civil engineering qualifications are internationally recognised and there are many opportunities to work on projects abroad. You could eventually become a director or partner in a civil engineering firm. Alternatively, you could join the armed services, become a university lecturer or set up as a consultant.

R elated Occupations

You might also consider: structural engineer, architect, construction manager, surveyor or town planner.

I mpact

When working in the office, you would tend to keep to normal office hours. When working on site or abroad, the hours can be much more unsocial if deadlines need to be met and you could be on 24-hour call in case of problems. Most civil engineers work both in an office and on site. The work on site can be dirty, cold and wet and involve working at heights.

E arnings Potential

As a newly qualified graduate, you could expect to earn about £15,000 to £18,000. This could rise to £30,000 and above as you gain experience, although this would depend on your employer. The average annual earnings for experienced chartered engineers are around £45,000 and for incorporated engineers around £37,000. As a partner, you would have a share in the firm's profits.

F urther Information

The Institution of Civil Engineers, London SW1P 3AA
Website: www.ice.org.uk

The Construction Industry Training Board, King's Lynn PE3 1RH
Website: www.citb.org.uk

Alternative/equivalent entrance requirements can include: ILC, IB, EB, NC/ND and many other similar international systems. For further details see the Equivalent Qualifications section in the Introduction.

What is Involved?

As a civil servant, you would be one of approximately half a million people in a multi-million pound business. You would most likely work in a department or agency – such as Defence, Health or Education and Skills – or in a linked smaller organisation. Whatever your particular role, you would have to work in a non-political capacity for the elected government of the day.

The different parts of the Civil Service have two main functions:

• to advise Government Ministers on the pros and cons of particular decisions.

• to manage and deliver a range of services to the public, such as issuing driving licences, running jobcentres or paying benefits

There is such a wide range of administrative jobs across the departments and agencies that it is impossible to describe the work in detail here. Broadly speaking, you would probably be office-based and would start at one of four possible levels: administrative assistant, administrative officer, junior manager (sometimes called executive officer) or fast-track graduate trainee. One end of the scale starts with routine photocopying and filing, while the other ends with the very highest levels of national administration, researching policy options and advising Cabinet ministers. You should think carefully about your interests and abilities before deciding on an entry point.

Opportunities for Training

There are opportunities for on-the-job training within the departments or agencies and sometimes there are further tests to be passed before promotion is secured. Your training might be linked to the department in which you work, focusing for example on investigating benefit fraud or carrying out immigration checks. The 'Fast Stream Development Programme' can, if you are suitably qualified, speed your progress to top-level appointments. Competition for this programme is exceptionally fierce, with up to 25 applicants per place.

Requirements

Each department and agency sets its own entry requirements, depending on the type and level of work available. In some cases, good communication or decision-making skills can be enough to secure an administrative assistant post but you would need a minimum of two A level/AVCE/Advanced Higher, three Higher or equivalent qualifications for a junior manager position. In practice, around half the junior managers recruited are graduates. The 'Fast Stream' programme normally requires at least a first or second class honours degree.

In addition, you must hold a UK passport or be a citizen of a Commonwealth or European Economic Area country. For the Diplomatic Service, you need to be a UK citizen who has lived in this country for at least five years, with the ability to learn languages easily. Applications for the 'Fast Stream' are normally open only to UK nationals.

Kind of Person

At all levels, you would need to be able to work as part of a team, relate well to others and have a calm, reliable personality. You would also need good organisational skills and the ability to work quickly and accurately under pressure.

You would need to show leadership potential for junior manager or higher appointments, together with the ability to use your initiative, analyse problems and deliver results. The 'Fast Stream' would demand all these qualities and more, especially outstanding intelligence, creative thinking and sound judgement.

B road Outlook

Around 30,000 join the Civil Service each year but this number is falling with more and more jobs being put out to the private sector. With so many different departments and agencies, there are opportunities to work all over the country or even change departments. Most civil servants, however, tend to stay within the fields where they have expertise.

Competition is strong for all parts of the Civil Service, particularly for the 'Fast Stream' programme. Before applying, you are advised to work through the online self-assessment tests on the website.

R elated Occupations

You might also wish to consider: health service manager or local government administrator.

I mpact

Many civil servants work a basic 37-hour week, which may revolve around flexible start and finish times or even shift work. As you become more senior, you may have to work longer hours to complete reports for Ministers if they are needed at short notice.

E arnings Potential

Pay scales are set by individual departments and agencies. As a guideline, 'Fast Stream' salaries in London start from around £19,000, plus a non-contributory pension currently worth a further 13.5%. Many departments offer starting pay above the minimum to reflect relevant experience or qualifications. Increases in pay depend on performance. In London, once you achieve promotion, typically after three to four years, your salary may reach around £31,000 to £33,000, on a range which currently rises to around £48,000. There are considerably higher salaries at the very top.

F urther Information

Civil Service Careers, Bristol BS1 8DG
Website: www.civil-service.gov.uk/jobs/

Fast Stream Development Programme, Basingstoke RG21 7JP
Website: www.faststream.gov.uk

Alternative/equivalent entrance requirements can include: ILC, IB, EB, NC/ND and many other similar international systems. For further details see the Equivalent Qualifications section in the Introduction.

What is Involved?

As a clinical biochemist (or chemical pathologist), you would be largely concerned with the use of biochemical investigations to diagnose diseases in which the body's chemistry goes wrong: diabetes, for example, or kidney failure. A major part of your work would be to provide scientific leadership in the pathology laboratory, through the direction of scientific services and the interpretation of test results for the doctor in the clinic or at the bedside. You could attain equivalent status to a medical consultant and become head of a laboratory. Although your expertise would contribute to the management of patients, you would not be medically trained and so could not take clinical responsibility for patients. In other words, you would not be able to treat them.

You might specialise in a particular area, such as toxicology or endocrinology, using sophisticated equipment to carry out tests on body tissues. Like the majority of clinical biochemists, you would most likely work within the National Health Service, the National Blood Service (blood transfusion) or the Public Health Laboratory Service.

Opportunities for Training

Clinical biochemists are graduates, usually with a first or upper second honours degree in a subject like biochemistry or chemistry, and often with a PhD. They usually undertake a three-year programme of basic training, followed by four to five years of specialist training regulated by the Health Professions Council.

Virtually every university in the country offers a degree course in biochemistry or one in which biochemistry is a major component. It is important to read the prospectuses carefully to find out what each course involves. The emphasis can be quite different, depending on factors such as the other degree programmes available. Many universities offer sandwich courses, which give the opportunity to spend a year working in industry. Because biochemistry is a research-based discipline, many graduates continue into postgraduate training.

Requirements

To gain entry to a degree course in this field, you would need A level/AVCE/Advanced Higher/Higher or equivalent passes in biology and chemistry, together sometimes with maths or physics. At some universities it is possible for applicants without such science qualifications to take a 'conversion course' before starting their degree. You would also need a broad platform of GCSE/S Grade passes at A-C/1-3, including English and science subjects.

Kind of Person

You would need to have a strong interest in science and in laboratory procedures. If you do not enjoy your practical science lessons at school, this is probably not the career for you. Patients' lives could depend on your accuracy and efficiency in carrying out tests and interpreting results. You would need to have a logical and methodical approach to your work.

Although you would be primarily based in a laboratory, you would be working as part of a team of professionals. You would need to make clear explanations of your findings and opinions, which would demand good communication skills.

B road Outlook

There are good prospects for employment in this field, particularly in some specialised fields. Opportunities vary across the country, so you may need to move to gain promotion. It is possible to advance your career by taking on more responsibility and by gaining wider or more detailed experience. Senior clinical biochemists often have managerial responsibilities by taking charge of a department or section or by moving to production, sales or marketing departments in the pharmaceutical industry. These opportunities can arise quite early in your career.

R elated Occupations

You might be interested working in other science-based fields particularly those involving biology or chemistry. Such careers as research chemist or biologist, doctor, pharmacologist, pharmacist, chemical analyst or forensic scientist could be of interest. In researching this career, you need to be clear about the distinction between a clinical biochemist, a medically qualified doctor and a biomedical scientist. Each has a different and essential role and requires different qualifications and training.

I mpact

You are likely to be working regular hours and a 37-hour week, which should not normally include weekend or evening work. However, you may be expected to be on call at times in cases of emergency.

E arnings Potential

In the NHS assistant clinical biochemists with a degree can expect to earn anything from £13,000 and this can rise to around £50,000 for senior posts. Higher salaries can be sometimes earned if you are prepared to take on responsibility for management, overtime work or teaching commitments. Salaries may be higher at times if you choose to work in the private sector.

F urther Information

The Association of Clinical Biochemists, London SE1 2TU
Website: www.acb.org.uk

The Biochemical Society, London W1N 3AJ Website: www.biochemistry.org

The Royal College of Pathologists, London SW1Y 5AF
Website: www.rcpath.org

The Health Professions Council, London SE11 4BU
Website: www.hpcuk.org

Alternative/equivalent entrance requirements can include: ILC, IB, EB, NC/ND and many other similar international systems. For further details see the Equivalent Qualifications section in the Introduction.

What is Involved?

As a construction manager, you would be responsible for running a construction site or a section of a large project. You might also be known as a site manager, site agent or building manager. Your work would include developing a strategy for the construction of the project, planning ahead to anticipate problems and solve them before they happen, making sure all processes are carried out safely, reporting on the progress of the project and motivating the workforce to get the best out of them. You would be responsible for liaising with the architects and planners, for carefully assessing the specifications and site plans. You would consult engineers, surveyors, quantity surveyors and estimators, checking costs of labour, supervision and materials before producing time schedules, agreeing labour force requirements and placing orders. You would be in control of the site throughout the construction process.

Opportunities for Training

There are several possible training routes. You could, for example, take a three- or four-year degree in a relevant subject such as construction, building, construction or building management, building studies or technology; you could take a full- or part-time higher national certificate or diploma (HNC/D) in a similar subject; or you could start as a technician with a national certificate or diploma. Sandwich courses are available, which give the opportunity for practical paid experience during your degree. There are also opportunities for sponsorship during your degree course, usually with the larger construction companies. Following your academic training, you could work towards professional qualifications awarded by the Chartered Institute of Building or the Association of Building Engineers.

Requirements

The degree route would normally require two or three A level/AVCE/Advanced Higher, four Higher or equivalent qualifications often including passes in maths and/or physics, together with at least five GCSE/S Grade passes A-C/1-3, including English, maths and a science subject. For the HNC/D, one or two A level/AVCE/Advanced Higher, three Higher or equivalent qualifications, or a national certificate/diploma would be necessary.

Kind of Person

You would need to apply all your knowledge of construction techniques to ensure that each project is completed to time, on budget and safely. You would have to be able to motivate people and would need excellent communication skills. You would also have to be able to stay calm when things don't go quite as planned. Other people would expect to rely on your judgement. Your decisions would need to be based on your knowledge of technical, legal and health and safety factors but above all on practical common sense and experience. You may find yourself working under pressure when, for example, schedules are slipping or materials fail to arrive.

B road Outlook

There are approximately 133,600 construction managers within the industry. Most work for a construction company or a specialist sub-contractor. There are jobs throughout the country and opportunities to work abroad as well. The building industry is affected by the national economic situation and as such the job opportunities may vary. At the moment there is good demand for construction managers.

R elated Occupations

You might also consider: civil engineer, architect, building services engineer, quantity surveyor, town planner or estate agent.

I mpact

Whilst your basic hours of work are likely to be around 40 hours a week, you could expect to be working longer hours than this when you are on site. The hours of work on building sites tend to be particularly long during the summer, when there are a lot of daylight hours, but much shorter in the winter. At times, you may be expected to work in the evenings and at weekends. In addition you can expect to be working outside in all kinds of weather, and would need to wear protective clothing such as a hard hat when on site. Most of your working day would be spent on site or even travelling from site to site. Some managers move from one location to another as projects are completed and new ones start. Some are able to reach the site by travelling every day; others live away from home during the week and return home at weekends.

E arnings Potential

You would expect to start on a salary of about £13,000 to £15,000, depending to some extent on where in the country you are working. This can be raised by allowances for being on site or for travelling. Experienced construction managers can expect to earn between £26,000 and £37,000. Salaries are higher in London.

F urther Information

Construction Industry Training Board, Norfolk PE31 6RH
Website: www.citb.org.uk

The Chartered Institute of Building, Ascot SL5 7TB
Website: www.ciob.org.uk

The Association of Building Engineers, Northampton NN3 8NW
Website: www.abe.org.uk

Alternative/equivalent entrance requirements can include: ILC, IB, EB, NC/ND and many other similar international systems. For further details see the Equivalent Qualifications section in the Introduction.

What is Involved?

As a countryside conservation officer, you would be an environmental specialist responsible for advising on issues concerned with protecting and conserving the countryside. You would ensure that conservation laws are being observed and would take steps to enforce them if necessary; you could be responsible for managing a site of special scientific interest or for designating a new one; or you may assess the environmental impact of proposed major construction developments. While you might spend some time outside on site surveys, you would be largely office-based, reading and writing reports, consulting maps and charts, preparing talks or checking details of legislation.

Opportunities for Training

Although there is no set training route, you would be unlikely to secure a post without a relevant degree and even a postgraduate qualification. Possible degree subjects would include ecology, environmental science, geology, geography, conservation and countryside management, biology or estate management. There is fierce competition for jobs, so part-time and voluntary experience is very important. You should take every opportunity to show your commitment by undertaking voluntary projects and you should check degree courses for the amount of fieldwork and other practical experience they offer. A postgraduate qualification at MSc or PhD level in conservation, ecology or land management would also be advisable.

Requirements

Degree entry requirements would vary depending on your choice of both subject and university. However, you would normally need a minimum of two A level/AVCE/Advanced Higher, three Higher or equivalent qualifications and five GCSE/S Grade passes at A-C/1-3. In order to be accepted for postgraduate study, you are likely to need first class or upper second honours in your first degree.

A full driving licence would almost always be essential.

Kind of Person

You may find yourself having to negotiate with people who are opposed to your ideas, so you would need to show diplomacy and tact in your approach to them. At the same time, you would have to have confidence in your point of view and powers of persuasion to make your case clear. This may involve communicating complex scientific or technical information to non-specialists. You could be required to write reports and to speak at public meetings. You would need to be prepared for criticism of your work from people who do not understand your point of view or your recommendations. You would find yourself working as part of a team but you would need to be able to work unsupervised and to manage your own time. A real commitment to, and knowledge of, preserving the environment would be essential.

Broad Outlook

There are jobs for countryside conservation officers with government agencies such as English Nature or Scottish National Heritage, with local government and with organisations such as The National Trust. However, there is very strong competition for jobs and each advertised post often has a large number of applicants. You may well need to move around the country and to apply for a large number of jobs in order to secure a suitable post. Some positions are on short-term contracts or are purely seasonal, and you may have to gain experience with one or more of these before finding a full-time position. There would be opportunities to progress to managing a team of conservation officers or to pursue a specific interest, which could lead you into research, lecturing or specialist consultancy work.

R elated Occupations

You might also consider: countryside ranger, forest manager, town planner, landscape architect, rural practice surveyor, research biologist, cartographer, geologist, microbiologist or zoologist.

I mpact

You would nominally work a normal week of around 40 hours, Monday to Friday. You may, however, have to attend evening and weekend meetings and you would have to work whatever hours it takes to write up a report in the required time.

E arnings Potential

As a countryside conservation officer working for a government agency, you would be likely to have a starting salary of around £17,000, rising to around £26,000. Senior positions may command salaries of around £34,000. Local government salaries are likely to be similar but charitable organisations often start at lower levels, perhaps around £13,000.

F urther Information

British Trust for Conservation Volunteers, Wallingford OX10 0EU
Website: www.btcv.org

The Countryside Agency, Cheltenham GL50 3RA
Website: www.countryside.gov.uk

English Nature, Peterborough PE1 1UA
Website: www.english-nature.org.uk

The Countryside Council for Wales, Bangor LL57 2LQ
Website: www.ccw.gov.uk

Scottish Natural Heritage, Edinburgh EH9 2AS Website: www.snh.org.uk

The Environment and Heritage Service, Belfast BT1 1FY
Website: www.ehsni.gov.uk

The National Trust, London SW1H 9AS Website: www.nationaltrust.org.uk

Alternative/equivalent entrance requirements can include: ILC, IB, EB, NC/ND and many other similar international systems. For further details see the Equivalent Qualifications section in the Introduction.

What is Involved?

As a countryside ranger or warden, your job would be to protect, manage and develop a particular area of countryside. This might be something like a wildlife habitat or a site of special scientific interest. Your role would also involve helping the public to enjoy that particular area of countryside. You are likely to be working somewhere like a national park, an area of outstanding beauty or a nature reserve.

Your job might include patrolling the area to look for repairs that need doing or developments that could be achieved to enhance the site. You may carry out the necessary work yourself or organise teams of people. You could become a specialist in a particular area relevant to your area of work. In addition to the outdoor activities, you might also work in an information centre or an office, producing information booklets or planning exhibitions and site visits to explain the flora and fauna and geographical features of your site.

Opportunities for Training

Countryside management is a high-qualification, training-conscious industry, with nearly two-thirds of employed workers having degrees, Higher National Certificates/Diplomas or equivalent professional qualifications. While opportunities are available for non-graduates through routes such as Modern Apprenticeships (Skillseekers in Scotland) and National Diplomas, there is a tendency for graduates to apply for jobs at all levels, including the most basic.

Requirements

While there are no specific entry requirements for many of the training schemes, competition for places is strong and you should have a good standard of education. You would probably need at least four GCSE/S Grade passes at A-C/1-3 or equivalent, including English, maths, a science subject and another academic subject.

Many applicants, as noted above, have a degree or HND in a relevant subject such as ecology, biology, environmental science, land management, agriculture, leisure and recreation, geography or geology. You would need to show evidence of part-time or voluntary work in a countryside or conservation field and you would probably need to be able to drive.

Kind of Person

You would need to be physically fit and prepared for hard practical work. Your employers would be looking for evidence of a genuine interest in the countryside. You would probably be dealing with the public, who may need you to explain aspects of the site or the work. For this you would need a pleasant and tactful manner.

You may be expected to speak in public, giving presentations to publicise your area of work. Depending on where you work, you may need to have knowledge of the law relating to countryside rights and to health and safety issues. Your personal, practical skills and willingness to learn are likely to be as important as your academic achievements.

B road Outlook

The environmental conservation industry is expected to continue expanding in the future but it is estimated that there are 200,000 volunteers and a mere 49,000 paid staff. Included in this number are some 5,000 countryside rangers or wardens. Competition for full-time jobs is intense and there is almost always an expectation of considerable voluntary or part-time experience before you apply. There are limited opportunities for promotion, although it is possible – depending on your qualifications and experience – to move into some of the related occupations listed below. You may need to be prepared to move around the country in order to find a suitable vacancy.

R elated Occupations

You might like a job in a related field such as conservation officer, land agent, forest manager, amenity horticulturalist, agricultural adviser, microbiologist or marine biologist.

I mpact

Your job as a countryside ranger is likely to involve working in the evenings and at weekends. You might be working in a fairly remote countryside area, which could be quite isolated. You may find the work tiring, as it can include walking many miles or handling heavy equipment. You will be exposed to the elements at all times of the year.

E arnings Potential

Countryside rangers are usually paid between £11,500 and £20,000, with senior rangers or site managers earning up to £25,000. A vehicle is usually provided for use at work but you would also need your own transport.

F urther Information

Lantra, Coventry CV8 2LG Website: www.lantra.co.uk

The Growing Careers Partnership Website: www.growing-careers.com

The British Trust for Conservation Volunteers, Wallingford OX10 OEU
Website: www.btcv.org.uk

The Countryside Agency, Cheltenham GL50 3RA
Website: www.countryside.gov.uk

The National Trust, London SW1H 9AS Website: www.nationaltrust.org.uk

Alternative/equivalent entrance requirements can include: ILC, IB, EB, NC/ND and many other similar international systems. For further details see the Equivalent Qualifications section in the Introduction.

What is Involved?

As a dental technician, you would be involved in the design and construction of appliances prescribed for their patients by dental surgeons. These would include dentures, crowns and bridges and orthodontic appliances such as braces designed to correct misalignment of the teeth. You would most likely work in a commercial dental laboratory, using a wide range of materials – metal alloys, gold or porcelain for crown and bridge work, acrylic or metal for braces, plastic or chrome cobalt for dentures – to meet the specific requirements of each prescription. The work requires great precision and technical skill but only rarely involves actually meeting the patient for whom you are ultimately working.

You might carry out work for a number of local dentists or even offer a postal service for dentists from a wider area. Alternatively, you might work in a hospital, supporting oral and maxillofacial surgeons in restructuring patients' faces and mouths.

Opportunities for Training

There are three main training routes leading to the National Diploma in Dental Technology: you can obtain a training place within a commercial laboratory and attend college on a part-time basis for four or five years; you can take a three-year full-time course incorporating periods of practical experience; you can seek a place on a hospital or health authority training scheme, usually following a four-year NHS sandwich course where part of the time is spent at college and part in the laboratory. Once qualified, you may be expected to continue your professional development by taking evening classes in specific aspects of your work.

Successful completion of this route would entitle you to apply for inclusion in the United Kingdom voluntary National Register of Dental Technicians, maintained by the Education and Training Advisory Board. There are also Higher National Diploma/Certificate courses, together with three university degrees (at Manchester Metropolitan, Sheffield and the University of Wales Institute, Cardiff) in Dental Technology.

Requirements

For the national certificate or diploma courses you should have at least four GCSE/S Grade passes at A-C/1-3, including English, maths and a science. Entry to higher-level courses can be a natural progression from your initial national qualification; alternatively, you could seek direct entry with A level/AVCE/ Advanced Higher, Higher or equivalent qualifications to a HND or degree course.

Kind of Person

The work you would be involved in is highly skilled and you would need to be practical, with a high level of manual dexterity and some artistic flair. You would need a keen eye for detail; the ability to concentrate on what is often very precise work and sufficient scientific understanding to follow detailed technical instructions. You may work alone or as part of a team. Good eyesight with or without glasses and good colour vision are important.

B road Outlook

According to the Education, Training and Advisory Board, there is a shortage of skilled dental technicians, which should mean that finding a job is relatively straightforward. Most of the 8,000 dental technicians in the UK work in commercial laboratories but there is also scope in the NHS, in individual dental practices or in the armed services. There may be opportunities to work abroad or to set up your own laboratory once you have the required experience.

R elated Occupations

You might also consider: medical technical officer, orthotist/prosthetist, goldsmith/silversmith.

I mpact

You would probably have a normal working week of 37 to 39 hours in the NHS, slightly longer in a commercial laboratory. If you specialise in maxillofacial work, you may expect to be called out at any time in cases of emergency.

You may have to be reasonably flexible about where you work, for many laboratories are concentrated in the larger population areas.

E arnings Potential

You could expect to receive £6,000 to £10,000 a year while on a training scheme, rising to £13,000 on qualification. Subsequent salary increases would depend to a certain extent on whether you were in a commercial laboratory, a private dental practice or part of the NHS but could take you well above the qualified level.

F urther Information

Dental Education Resources on the Web Website: www.derweb.co.uk

The Dental Technician's Education, Training and Advisory Board, Northants NN13 7XY Website: www.dtetab.co.uk

Alternative/equivalent entrance requirements can include: ILC, IB, EB, NC/ND and many other similar international systems. For further details see the Equivalent Qualifications section in the Introduction.

What is Involved?

As a dentist, you would be responsible for the dental health of a group of clients, examining, diagnosing and treating patients in line with your professional judgement. Your work would include fillings, removing teeth and fitting bridges or crowns. When necessary, you may refer patients for specialist treatment such as orthodontics. You would usually have a dental nurse to assist you and, with the increasing emphasis on dental health and hygiene and the prevention of decay, you might employ a dental hygienist.

Alternatively, you might choose to work in a hospital and specialise in a particular area such as oral surgery – which could include repairing damage to the jaw caused by accident or disease and also corrective surgery to repair birth defects. This could also include carrying out more complicated bridgework or surgery to gums that cannot be performed by a general dentist. Another area is orthodontics, which is concerned with straightening teeth. In hospital there is a hierarchy of dentists that works up to a consultant level as with doctors. The majority of dentists work in general practice, on their own or as part of a group. You could also work in the armed forces, as a company dentist in a large organisation or as a community dentist in a clinic.

Opportunities for Training

You would have to take the Bachelor of Dental Surgery (BDS) degree before you could register with the General Dental Council and start to work as a dentist. This is a five-year course, which combines theoretical subjects such as anatomy, physiology and dental materials science with the practical and clinical skills needed to treat patients. In addition, you would need to learn about anaesthesia and radiology, how to design and fit dental aids as well as relevant aspects of dental law and ethics. Most dental students start practical work on patients in the second or third year of study, although some courses offer integrated courses with clinical work in the first year. If you want to work for the NHS, you would have to undergo a year of supervised practice before you could become independent.

Requirements

Competition for places at dental schools is very fierce and you would have to offer three very good A level/Advanced Higher, five Higher or equivalent qualifications to get in. While some schools require three A level/Advanced Higher, Higher or equivalent qualifications to be in science subjects, the minimum is usually chemistry plus another science subject or maths. A few dental schools allow students without the right subjects to take a pre-dental year, although this would severely limit your choice of school. In addition to academic success, you should have a strong interest in the subject and should arrange some work experience with a dentist before you apply.

Kind of Person

Dentists need to have good interpersonal skills, to be interested in people and able to communicate with all types of people. Patients may be worried about the visit and it is important that the dentist is friendly and can help them to relax. All dentists need to be able to work as part of a team with a number of different people – dental nurses, receptionists, hygienists or other medical staff in hospital. Dentistry requires an interest in science, good eyesight and manual dexterity. Working in general practice also involves some business and marketing skills.

B road Outlook

With greater awareness of oral hygiene, the need to maintain dental health and the increased use of fluoride, there is less corrective work for dentists and fewer dentists are being trained. There are still good job prospects for dentists, although you may have to be prepared to move for a suitable job, particularly if you are seeking a career in hospital work.

R elated Occupations

You might consider: doctor, medical laboratory scientific officer, pharmacist or pharmacologist. Look at dental hygienist or dental nurse if you want to specialise in oral care.

I mpact

In general practice, you could be quite flexible about the hours you work, although NHS dentists often have to offer emergency cover on a rota basis. Dentists in hospital may have to work anti-social hours and be prepared to be on call.

The work can be physically very tiring as it involves a lot of standing and bending of the spine.

E arnings Potential

There is a scale of fees for NHS work in general practice. This means that your salary would be dependent on how much and what type of work you take on. You may also carry out private work, for which you could set your own fees. Average earnings for general dental practitioners are over £50,000 per annum but there are usually business expenses to meet. Hospital dentists start as a house officer on about £17,000, whilst consultants can earn in excess of £60,000.

F urther Information

The British Dental Association, London, W1M 8AL
Website: www.bda-dentistry.org.uk

Alternative/equivalent entrance requirements can include: ILC, IB, EB, NC/ND and many other similar international systems. For further details see the Equivalent Qualifications section in the Introduction.

What is Involved?

As a dietitian, you would need a fascination with food and health, together with the ability to translate medical advice and scientific findings about food into practical diets that people can understand. You may work as part of a healthcare team in a hospital or in the community, offering advice on a well-balanced diet to ensure healthy living. In a hospital or GP's clinic, you may be helping patients with problems such as difficulty in swallowing or checking that the meals provided are nutritionally balanced and appropriate for each individual. You may run clinics in outpatients departments for people who are overweight, people with eating disorders or those who have to live with diabetes, food allergies or other conditions. You might also be involved in health promotion activities or talking to groups such as pregnant women or those with young children.

In the food industry, you might provide specialist advice to manufacturers or trade associations. You would analyse food products and check information leaflets to ensure that the content is correct and nutritionally sound.

Opportunities for Training

To become a state registered dietitian, you must take an approved degree or post-graduate diploma. Degree courses are generally full-time and take four years. However, some part-time courses are being introduced. All courses include practical training in a hospital or community setting. In addition to nutrition and dietetics, you would study physiology and biochemistry, medicine and pharmacology, psychology and social science, some microbiology and food science, with statistics and research methods to help with your final Honours project.

There are also a few postgraduate courses for students with relevant first degrees in science subjects.

Requirements

You would need a sound base in science to gain entry to an honours degree course. You would need chemistry and another science A level/AVCE/Advanced Higher, Higher or equivalent qualification, as well as five GCSE/S Grade passes at A-C/1-3 including English and maths. Some universities run foundation courses, which can give access to the degree if you do not have the required A level/AVCE/Advanced Higher, Higher or equivalent qualifications.

Kind of Person

Your role as a dietitian would require tact and perseverance to convince people who are ill that, by changing their diet, they can reduce their symptoms and put themselves more in control of their illness. You would need to be able to interpret scientific and medical information so that your patient can understand it.

In order to give advice, you must be aware of how a person's personal circumstances can affect their lives and how your dietary recommendations might need to be adjusted to make them workable. You would have to accept your patients' lifestyles and religious or cultural beliefs without passing judgement.

B road Outlook

With increased interest in healthy living and growing awareness of the importance of well balanced diets, the prospects for dietitians look extremely promising. There are lots of jobs at the moment in the NHS but, if you want to do research, you'll need to look around and be prepared to move. Other opportunities include work in the food industry, in retail chains such as supermarkets, acting as a nutrition adviser, or in product development and marketing for food companies producing specialist dietary products.

R elated Occupations

If your main interest is in food and nutrition, you might also consider: food scientist or technologist or hotel and catering manager. If you want to work with people on health-related issues, you might prefer to explore alternative careers such as nurse, pharmacist, radiographer, speech therapist or occupational therapist.

I mpact

An NHS dietitian works a 36.5-hour week, which can include some weekend work or hours on call.

Your job may require you to work with vulnerable groups of people and, as a result, you would need to declare any criminal record. You would also need to complete a health declaration. Problems in either of these areas may not stop you from completing a university course but they may not allow you to become State Registered, which means that you would not be able to practise at the end of your course.

E arnings Potential

Newly qualified NHS dietitians earn around £15,000 per year; senior dietitians earn from £19,000 per year, rising to around £33,000. Salaries are likely to be higher than this in the private sector.

F urther Information

The British Dietetic Association, Birmingham, B3 3HT
Website: www.bda.uk.com

Alternative/equivalent entrance requirements can include: ILC, IB, EB, NC/ND and many other similar international systems. For further details see the Equivalent Qualifications section in the Introduction.

What is Involved?

As a member of the diplomatic service, you would be working for one of the major departments of the civil service. You would be primarily involved with representing British interests abroad and advising government ministers on aspects of foreign policy. The service is based in London, with high commissions in Commonwealth countries and embassies in other countries around the world, together with missions to international organisations such as the European Commission and United Nations. During the course of your career, you might work in several different areas of the service, including commercial, information, consular, immigration, political assessment and liaison and general administrative or managerial duties. You would normally spend much of your career working abroad, with tours of duty of two to four years.

Opportunities for Training

The first two years of your career in the service would be spent in the UK, initially learning the broad outline of diplomatic work and then acquiring the knowledge and skills for the specialisation in which you are going to work. For some postings, full-time language training would be provided as part of a continuous programme of preparation for working in a particular country. All staff would have the opportunity to learn the local language before taking up an appointment.

As a graduate with at least a second class honours degree, you could compete for selection to the Fast Stream Development Programme.

Requirements

You would have to be a UK citizen with a minimum of five years residence in the UK before you can apply. Competition for places is intense and the majority of successful applicants are graduates with good honours degrees. In the past, arts graduates have predominated but science, business, economics and technological degrees are increasingly welcome.

You could apply for clerical entry with five GCSE/S Grade passes at A-C/1-3 including English and a maths-based subject and five years' work experience or two A level/Advanced Higher, three Higher or equivalent qualifications and three years' work experience. Linguistic ability would be useful but is not essential.

Kind of Person

Because of the nature of the work, you would be expected to have a keen interest in international issues and recognise Britain's unique role in world affairs. You should be a natural team player; confident, friendly, calm and reliable in your dealings with others, particularly with those you do not know. You should be keen to travel and prepared to visit and live in some of the less developed parts of the world. Much of your work would require a good organisational approach and the ability to work to precise and demanding standards as well as to think on your feet.

B road Outlook

The traditional view of the civil service offering a job for life with good promotion prospects is less true today than it might once have been. The diplomatic service could be said to have been less vulnerable to this change, with prospects remaining very bright for those with the right qualities and attitudes. There may be opportunities to work in related government departments, such as the Department for International Development.

Regular appraisal of your work and detailed assessment of your performance would give you a clear picture of your progress and of the prospects for your future career development.

R elated Occupations

If you have the qualities demanded by the diplomatic service, with high levels of integrity and excellent communication and organisational skills, you could aspire to high level positions elsewhere in the civil service, in industry or in export/import organisations. You might also find a role in the media.

I mpact

The majority of your service would be in overseas locations and you would need to uproot your family, adjust to new climates and cultural systems, make new friends and leave others behind. You would need to be adaptable, to see changes as exciting challenges and to build up your contacts within and outside the service. If you have children, you would need to help them cope with an interrupted family life and adjust their education to your travels.

E arnings Potential

When stationed abroad, you would be entitled to a range of payments on top of your basic salary to cover the local cost of living, in addition to rent-free accommodation, educational allowances for your children and various fare paid allowances for travel to and from the UK. Your salary would compare very favourably with the main professions and would rise with promotion and the relative importance of your work.

F urther Information

Civil Service Careers, Bristol BS11 8DG
Website: www.civil-service.gov.uk/jobs

Fast Stream Development Programme: Capita RAS, Basingstoke RG21 7JP
Website: www.faststream.gov.uk

The Foreign and Commonwealth Office Website: www.fco.gov.uk

Alternative/equivalent entrance requirements can include: ILC, IB, EB, NC/ND and many other similar international systems. For further details see the Equivalent Qualifications section in the Introduction.

What is Involved?

As a dispensing optician, you would supply and fit glasses and other optical aids but you would not be trained to carry out eye tests or treat disorders of the eyes. You would be qualified to interpret the prescriptions you are given by an optometrist or ophthalmic surgeon and then make an order for the glasses to be made up by a prescription house. You could also fit contact lenses after additional training.

You would most likely work in private practice in a high street retail outlet, ensuring that clients get the correct glasses or lenses for their needs and lifestyle. You would need to spend time with each patient, taking precise facial measurements and discussing with them the optimal balance between the prescription requirements and their own feelings about appearance, comfort and the conditions in which the glasses or contact lenses are to be used. You would also ensure that the final choice fits securely and matches the prescription.

Opportunities for Training

You must pass the exams of the Association of British Dispensing Opticians (ABDO) and register with the General Optical Council. You can do this in several different ways: by taking a full-time degree or diploma in ophthalmic dispensing; by taking a part-time diploma; or by completing the ABDO distance learning course while working with a qualified optometrist. In this very specialised field, you would choose to study for your degree or diploma at one of the following institutions: Anglia Polytechnic University, Bradford and Ilkley Community College, the City and Islington College or Glasgow Caledonian University. If none of these locations is convenient or if you prefer to study and work at the same time, distance learning is the remaining option.

Whichever route you choose, you would have to follow your course with a pre-registration year of paid work supervised by a registered optometrist. The ABDO final examination then has to be passed.

Requirements

You would need at least five GCSE/S Grade passes at A-C/1-3, to include English, maths or physics and another science based subject. The degree courses offered at universities or colleges require two A level/AVCE/Advanced Higher, three or four Higher or equivalent qualifications and some specify science subjects such as biology, physics, chemistry and/or maths. It is essential to check prospectuses before you apply. Some diploma courses call for one or two A level/AVCE/Advanced Higher, three to four Higher or equivalent qualifications but others may specify GSCE/S Grade passes, in maths and science subjects.

Kind of Person

You must like people and you must be able to deal with them tactfully and confidently. In addition, you would be required to understand the information contained in prescriptions and to operate a number of scientific instruments. You would be to some extent selling frames and accessories, so you would need to know which styles are in fashion and which colours are available. A smart appearance, patience and a sense of humour would all be helpful.

B road Outlook

Most dispensing opticians work in general practice either for an independent optometrist or for one of the big chains. There are also some openings in hospital clinics and in prescription houses (lens manufacturers), together with opportunities to be self-employed or to work in partnership. The job market is becoming more competitive but there are still lots of opportunities for work, especially if you are prepared to move and are confident enough to take on management responsibilities. There are opportunities for job sharing and part-time employment.

R elated Occupations

You might be interested in other professions concerned with visual problems or disorders, such as optometrist or orthoptist. You might also consider therapeutic professions in the medical field, such as occupational therapist, speech and language therapist or dietitian.

I mpact

Most dispensing opticians work a five-day week, but in a high street shop you would certainly find yourself working on Saturdays and possibly one or two evenings a week.

E arnings Potential

Trainees working full-time can earn about £9,000. On registration, dispensing opticians earn from £15,000 and this can rise according to experience and responsibility to as high as £35,000 for a manager. You could earn even more if you establish your own business.

F urther Information

The General Optical Council, London W1N 2DJ Website: www.optical.org

The Federation of Ophthalmic and Dispensing Opticians, London W2 6LQ Website: www.fodo.com

The Association of British Dispensing Opticians, London SW6 3DU Website: www.abdo.org.uk

Alternative/equivalent entrance requirements can include: ILC, IB, EB, NC/ND and many other similar international systems. For further details see the Equivalent Qualifications section in the Introduction.

What is Involved?

As a doctor you would be responsible for promoting good health to try to prevent illness or working to restore patients' well being after an illness or an accident. You would work either as a General Practitioner (GP), dealing with a wide range of patients with many different problems, or as a hospital doctor specialising in a particular field of medicine.

Opportunities for Training

Learning to be a doctor involves a long and expensive course of study. You would generally spend at least five years as an undergraduate at medical school before becoming a pre-registration house officer for a further year. After this, you can apply to the General Medical Council to become a fully registered doctor but you would need at least three more years of further education to become a GP or seven to become a hospital consultant.

Traditionally, medicine courses began with two years of 'preclinical' work, involving study of the basic medical sciences, followed by the 'clinical' course, of approximately three years, which involved work in hospital wards under the supervision of consultants. Throughout these three years, students also attended lectures on all aspects of medical practice. In the last ten years, however, there has been a marked shift towards new medical curricula, with more integration of the preclinical and clinical courses, less emphasis on learning vast quantities of factual information and more time devoted to communication skills, problem-based learning, practical clinical tasks and in-depth study of modules chosen by the students. Most schools have now introduced integrated courses but each course is different and uses different methods of teaching, so you are advised to think carefully about the kind of course that would suit you.

Requirements

Most medical courses require a good set of GCSE/S Grade results in most subjects, followed by three good A level/Advanced Higher, five good Higher or equivalent qualifications. Most courses require chemistry at least to A level/Advanced Higher, Higher and another science subject and/or maths. Biology is particularly useful for understanding anatomy and physiology. Competition for places to read medicine is very intense. You would need to show that you have a genuine interest in the subject and if possible demonstrate relevant paid or voluntary work experience, such as work as a hospital auxiliary, in nursing or residential care. You can also find more about what it is like to be a doctor by having a formal period of work observation.

An inadequate science background would involve taking a one-year pre-medical course (sometimes called a 'first MB'), which is not offered at all medical schools.

Kind of Person

You would need to be dedicated and prepared for an enormous amount of hard work, absorbing vast amounts of technical information while developing highly tuned listening and communication skills. Practical ability and manual dexterity are also important.

You would need to deal with a wide range of people, to be tolerant of their weaknesses, pain and fear and to help them when they are at their most vulnerable. At times you would need to show emotional resilience as you may be faced with making rational and objective decisions in difficult and distressing circumstances. Other people would need to be able to trust you and to depend on you to keep calm in a crisis.

B road Outlook

Employment prospects are good for both GPs and hospital doctors, although it would take a number of years of hard work, further study and examinations before you could become a senior hospital doctor. There is enormous scope for specialisation in one of the many branches of medical work. Doctors are also needed in the armed services, in the police and forensic services, in public health and pharmacology, in industry and academic research.

R elated Occupations

You may be interested in other medical based professions such as physiotherapist, radiographer, pharmacist, pharmacologist, osteopath or nurse.

I mpact

The hours can be very long and anti-social, particularly in the early years. The training takes a long time, which means that you would be working hard for little financial reward for much longer than in many other careers. You need to be prepared for shift work and to have the determination to continue even when you are tired and over worked.

On the positive side, doctors are generally among the most valued, highly regarded and trusted members of any community.

E arnings Potential

Salaries for hospital doctors in the NHS start at around £18,000 for a pre-registration House Officer and rise to £69,000 for a consultant. Earnings in the private sector are likely to be higher than this. GPs have a higher income earlier in their career though the potential to earn more with experience is ultimately not so great.

F urther Information

British Medical Association (BMA), London WC1H 9JP
Website: www.bma.org.uk

General Medical Council, London W1N 6JE Website: www.gmc-uk.org

Alternative/equivalent entrance requirements can include: ILC, IB, EB, NC/ND and many other similar international systems. For further details see the Equivalent Qualifications section in the Introduction.

What is Involved?

As a dramatherapist, you would use improvisation, mime and other dramatic techniques to support people who are experiencing physical, psychological, psychiatric or social problems. You could be working with people of any age, including those with autistic tendencies, those with mental health problems, those living with HIV or AIDS, those in prison or children who have been abused.

You would be applying your knowledge and experience of drama to promote healing, open up new experiences and improve the quality of life for each individual.

Opportunities for Training

You could become a dramatherapist either through a part-time course undertaken while working in the health or community services or through a full-time postgraduate course run by the Central School of Speech and Drama in conjunction with the Sesame Institute. This is a charity which also organises and runs short courses for those who are interested in dramatherapy and wish to find out more before committing themselves to a longer course.

The full-time course lasts for one-year and combines a strong practical element with theoretical and academic study. You would go out on clinical placements in addition to studying core subject areas such as drama and improvisation, myth, analytical psychology, human development, movement with touch and sound and group therapy in training.

Requirements

In order to qualify for entry to the postgraduate course, you would need to be at least 23 years of age, probably already having achieved an arts or psychology degree. Experience in one or more of the following fields would also be valuable: teaching, drama, social work or nursing. Selection is by interview and audition, with applicants coming from all over the world.

To apply for one of the shorter or part-time courses, you should normally be working in the fields already mentioned.

Kind of Person

As a drama and movement therapist you would be working with a wide range of clients, some of whom could have very difficult and deep-seated problems. Respect for each individual would be vital.

You would have to be strong – mentally, emotionally and physically – since you could be working in a variety of demanding environments. You would need to be totally committed to your work, able to enthuse your clients and talented enough to demonstrate dramatic techniques. Resilience would be another valuable quality, together with the ability to cope with both success and apparent failure.

B road Outlook

You could work as a dramatherapist in hospitals, schools, connexions or careers companies, prisons, community centres and in private practice. You could work full-time or part-time. You might decide to specialise in one particular area of work or go on to train as a course leader. You may work on a freelance basis, building up your reputation through effective practice over a period of several years.

R elated Occupations

Other occupations which might interest you would include: actor, occupational therapist, psychiatric nurse, psychotherapist, social worker, speech and language therapist or teacher.

I mpact

Given the very demanding nature of dramatherapy, you would have to be totally committed to your work. You would almost certainly be expected to work within a wide variety of work environments. You should be prepared to give up time in the evenings and at weekends for some sessions.

E arnings Potential

Payment would vary widely, according to the type of work and whether the sessions were with individuals or with groups. As a freelance dramatherapist, you might charge £30 to £35 per hour. Detailed advice on a suitable fee structure can be obtained from the British Association for Dramatherapists.

F urther Information

British Association for Dramatherapists, London SW6 3DP

Central School of Speech and Drama, London NW3 3HY
Website: www.cssd.ac.uk

Roundabout (a charity which organises dramatherapy sessions for disadvantaged people in Greater London) Website:
www.roundabout.nildram.co.uk

Sesame Institute UK, London SE1 8NY
Website: www.btinternet.com/~sesameuk

Alternative/equivalent entrance requirements can include: ILC, IB, EB, NC/ND and many other similar international systems. For further details see the Equivalent Qualifications section in the Introduction.

What is Involved?

As a professional economist, you would be one of a small group of advisers working for the government, a financial institution or a very large organisation. Alternatively, you might be part of a specialist consultancy. Your work would involve analysing information about what is happening in world financial and employment markets in order to identify significant trends or other points that might influence future policy or strategy. You might study, for example, the ways in which labour markets determine wages and unemployment, why some countries take a bigger share of the world market than others or the role of government in providing goods and services.

Your work might vary considerably according to the sector in which you are working but certain tasks would be similar in any employing organisation:

• You would research data from every relevant source and analyse it using mathematical, statistical and logical tools, particularly computer-based simulations

• You may focus on macro-economic – concerned with large economic units such as nation states – or micro-economic issues – concerned with the financial characteristics of firms, industries or individual households, and the way individual elements in an economy (such as consumers or commodities) behave. A typical macro-economic task might be to forecast the GDP (gross domestic product) of the USA in the coming year, whilst at the micro-economic level you could be concerned with predicting the demand for furniture in South East England over the next quarter

• You would produce a report based on your research and analysis.

Opportunities for Training

To work as a professional economist, you would need a good (first or upper second class) honours degree, usually in economics although a joint degree may be acceptable as long as economics forms the major part. You may find it useful or even essential to continue your studies with a postgraduate award before seeking employment. Similarly, you should consider joining a professional organisation such as the Society of Business Economists or the Royal Economic Society in order to receive their journals and attend their programme of events. The Government Economic Service (GES), the largest single employer of economists in the UK with 600 economists in 30 departments and agencies, runs a 'fast track' programme for selected graduates and also a European scheme for which a foreign language would be essential.

Requirements

To take an honours degree in economics you would need two or three A level/Advanced Higher, four Higher or equivalent qualifications, usually including maths. You would also need a minimum of five GCSE/S Grade passes at A-C/1-3, including maths and English. A good honours degree would be essential for admission to a relevant postgraduate course.

Kind of Person

You would need to enjoy analysing data, to be comfortable with figures and able to communicate your findings to non-specialists. Logic and accuracy are also very important, as are advanced computing skills. You would need to work as part of a team, to meet deadlines for producing reports and to be quick thinking during meetings. As your role would usually be that of an adviser, you must be prepared to accept that your recommendations might not always be acted upon.

B road Outlook

Economics is a relatively small profession and competition for jobs can be fierce. It is estimated that fewer than 10% of economics graduates go on to work as professional economists and you would have to be both exceptionally able and determined to succeed. You could join the GES as an assistant economist, rising to economic adviser usually within four or five years. The Bank of England is another major employer, followed by other banks and financial institutions, large companies, consultancies and other organisations.

R elated Occupations

You might also consider: accountant, actuary, chartered secretary, civil service administrator, financial adviser, investment analyst or statistician.

I mpact

Economists are office based and tend to work regular office hours, although deadlines can mean evening and weekend work from time to time. You may be involved in travel abroad depending on your employer.

E arnings Potential

The GES current starting salary in London for an economist with a first degree is £20,000 and £22,000 for an MSc. Successful senior economists can expect to earn around £50,000, although a few earn considerably more.

F urther Information

The Society of Business Economists, Watford WD17 4RX
Website: www.sbe.co.uk

Government Economic Service, London SW1P 3AG
Website: www.ges.gov.uk

The Royal Statistical Society Website: www.rss.org.uk

The Bank of England Website: www.bankofengland.co.uk

The Civil Service Fast Stream Development Programme
Website: www.faststream.gov.uk

The Royal Economic Society, London NW1 4SA Website: www.london.edu

Alternative/equivalent entrance requirements can include: ILC, IB, EB, NC/ND and many other similar international systems. For further details see the Equivalent Qualifications section in the Introduction.

What is Involved?

As an electrical engineer, you would be largely concerned with generating and supplying electrical power, although you might branch into the closely related field of electronic engineering, where you would be more involved with designing and making machines that use electricity. Electrical engineers work mainly with large power applications, generating and harnessing electrical power. You could be researching more efficient power generation systems, developing alternative energy sources or planning the future development of the electricity supply network.

In the move away from burning fossil fuels to generate electricity, your work might involve designing an improved wind turbine, re-examining the advantages and disadvantages of nuclear reactors or exploring ways of harnessing the power of the oceans.

Opportunities for Training

There are a number of universities offering degrees in electrical engineering either as a single subject or in combination with electronic or manufacturing engineering, management, languages or other subjects. It is important to read prospectuses carefully and to ensure that your final choice is accredited by the Institution of Electrical Engineers. In order to become a chartered engineer, focusing on research, design, development and management, you would need to complete four years of academic study. Your degree should be an accredited four-year Master of Engineering (MEng) or three-year Bachelor of Engineering (BEng) qualification. You would have to follow the BEng with an extra year of specialised study, known as a matching section, in order to progress to chartered status. In either case, you could take a sandwich course, which would include a year working on an industrial placement. After graduating, you would need to complete a period of approved work experience in order to achieve chartered status. If you want to be more involved with the day-to-day management of production processes as an incorporated engineer, you could take the BEng route and follow it with a period of formal training.

Requirements

For degree entry, you would need at least two A level/AVCE/Advanced Higher, three Higher or equivalent qualifications, usually including maths and physics, together with a broad platform of GCSE/S Grade passes at A-C/1-3. There are foundation courses available at some universities for students who do not have the required passes in maths and physics.

Kind of Person

Electrical engineers work in a rapidly developing environment and you would need to be creative, imaginative and prepared to keep up to date with changes in your field. You should have a logical and practical approach to solving complex scientific problems. A useful indicator at this stage could be how much you enjoy maths, design and technology and science (especially experiments with wires and batteries) at school. In addition to your scientific

106

skills, you are likely to need good communication skills. You would probably be working as a member of a team and may need to communicate with a wide range of people, not all of whom would have your technical knowledge and skills. You may be involved in some form of cost management, so some awareness of financial or business management would be helpful.

B road Outlook

There are good opportunities for employment for electrical engineers and, with our increasing reliance on technology and the need for cleaner energy supply systems, this situation is likely to continue. Chartered engineer status is recognised throughout Europe and there are other chances to work all over the world.

R elated Occupations

You might also consider: civil, mechanical, manufacturing, chemical or aeronautical engineer, materials scientist, metallurgist, physicist, medical physicist, biotechnologist, geophysicist or computer scientist.

I mpact

You may be working set hours and a five-day week. However, you are also likely to work overtime and under some pressure when you have a tight deadline to meet. There might be occasions when you are rushing to solve a problem or finish a product ahead of a competitor. You may need to wear protective clothing in some environments. You could be required to travel for your job, both in the UK and overseas.

E arnings Potential

There is a shortage of qualified electrical engineers, so you are likely to be quite well paid and could expect to earn around £20,000 straight after you graduate. Once you are chartered, your salary is likely to rise considerably and should exceed £50,000. Average earnings for incorporated engineers are around £37,000.

F urther Information

The Institution of Electrical Engineers (IEE), London, WC2R OBL
Website: www.iee.org.uk

The Engineering and Training Board, London WC2R 3ER
Website: www.egc.org.uk

The Engineering Careers Information Service.
Website: www.enginuity.org.uk

Alternative/equivalent entrance requirements can include: ILC, IB, EB, NC/ND and many other similar international systems. For further details see the Equivalent Qualifications section in the Introduction.

What is Involved?

As an electronic engineer, you would be concerned with designing or making equipment that uses low power electric current. Your work would be likely to have a large impact on the way that people live their lives in the modern world, and could range from communications satellites through to the smallest calculator or digital camera. As society demands ever more sophisticated technological development, you could be among the team of people exploring new possibilities in robotics, artificial intelligence and the information superhighway. There is considerable overlap with electrical engineering (see our separate article on this subject) or you might specialise in areas such as communications, computing, software, control, informatics or manufacturing.

Opportunities for Training

There are a number of universities offering degrees in electronic engineering either as a single subject or in combination with electrical or manufacturing engineering, management, languages or other subjects. It is important to read prospectuses carefully and to ensure that your final choice is accredited by the Institution of Electrical Engineers (IEE). In order to become a chartered engineer, focusing on research, design, development and management, you would need to complete four years of academic study. Your degree should be an accredited four-year Master of Engineering (MEng) or three-year Bachelor of Engineering (BEng) qualification. You would have to follow the BEng with an extra year of specialised study, known as a matching section, in order to progress to chartered status. In either case, you could take a sandwich course, which would include a year working on an industrial placement. After graduating, you would need to complete a period of approved work experience in order to achieve chartered status. If you want to be more involved with the day-to-day management of production processes as an incorporated engineer, you could take the BEng route and follow it with a period of formal training.

Requirements

For degree entry, you would need at least two A level/AVCE/Advanced Higher, three Higher or equivalent qualifications, usually including maths and physics, together with a broad platform of GCSE/S Grade passes at A-C/1-3. There are foundation courses available at some universities for students who do not have the required passes in maths and physics. The MEng route usually requires higher grades (or more UCAS points) than the BEng.

Kind of Person

You would be working in an area of rapid change and advance and would need to keep up to date with the latest developments, and indeed to be one step ahead of the opposition. You are likely to be continually learning and solving problems in new and creative ways. You would need to have good analytic and logical skills to apply to problems. You should enjoy maths, physics and design and technology lessons at school, as these point towards the types of problems that you would be working on. In addition to your technological skills, you would also need to be able to work on a project as a member of a team. You would need good communication skills as you may be required to make presentations to people who do not share your technical knowledge. You could require a sound business sense, as you might be involved with feasibility studies to assess whether a project is worth starting or completing.

B road Outlook

This is an area of work that is expanding at the moment with the rapid developments in technology and there are excellent job opportunities in a wide range of fields. There are chances to work both in the UK and abroad. The IEE is the largest group of professional engineers in Europe. It has 130,000 members, including 30,000 based outside the UK, and they are to be found in industry, consultancy, education and the public sector.

R elated Occupations

You might also consider: civil, mechanical, manufacturing, chemical or aeronautical engineer, materials scientist, metallurgist, physicist, medical physicist, biotechnologist, geophysicist or computer scientist.

I mpact

Although you may have specified hours, you are likely to have occasions when you are working under considerable pressure to meet a tight deadline or to keep ahead of the opposition and this may require you to work overtime. In addition, you are likely to need to read a lot and to keep up to date with developments in this field. You may be required to travel to conferences or meetings in order to liaise with other specialists or to advise or solve the problems of clients.

E arnings Potential

As there is a demand for electronic engineers, you are likely to be well paid with the potential to advance quickly. You could expect to earn around £20,000 straight after you graduate. Once you are chartered, your salary is likely to rise considerably and should exceed £50,000. Average earnings for experienced incorporated engineers are around £37,000.

F urther Information

The Institution of Electrical Engineers (IEE), London WC2R OBL
Website: www.iee.org.uk

The Engineering and Technology Board, London WC2R 3ER
Website: www.engc.org.uk

The Engineering Careers Information Service
Website: www.enginuity.org.uk

Alternative/equivalent entrance requirements can include: ILC, IB, EB, NC/ND and many other similar international systems. For further details see the Equivalent Qualifications section in the Introduction.

What is Involved?

As an environmental health officer, your job would be to protect people from environmental hazards, which could include pollution by chemicals, fire risks and health problems arising from rundown housing or tainted food. You might specialise in, for example, atmospheric pollution. You would be empowered to make unannounced visits to such places as shops, factories and offices, leisure facilities, abattoirs, restaurants and hospitals; you could issue warnings, give advice on how to correct matters or even serve notices of closure if you were to find a situation which contravened the law.

Opportunities for Training

You would need to complete a first degree or postgraduate course accredited by the Chartered Institute of Environmental Health (CIEH). Several of these courses include the statutory 48 weeks' practical work experience necessary for qualification, but it would be possible for you to do your work experience after graduation. Alternatively, you could study for a degree part-time, while working as an environmental health technician or technical officer. You would need to register with the Environmental Health Officers Registration Board (EHORB) before undertaking your work experience. After graduating, you would take the professional exams set by the CIEH and, if you complete these satisfactorily, you would be entitled to the award of the Certificate of Registration of the EHORB. The training is similar in Scotland but you would register with the Royal Environmental Health Institute of Scotland and study for the Diploma in Environmental Health.

Requirements

The minimum entry requirements for an undergraduate degree course in environmental health or science (BSc) would be two to three A level/AVCE/Advanced Higher, three to four Higher or equivalent qualifications, of which at least one should be in a science, together with five GCSE/S Grade passes at A-C/1-3 (including English, maths and a science). The course would last three or four years. Alternatively, you could qualify for entry to a two-year postgraduate course in environmental health (MSc) after completing a first degree in a relevant science subject.

Kind of Person

A concern for the environment and for the welfare of your fellow citizens would be very important. You would need excellent communication skills, balancing sympathetic understanding with the need to explain your findings and decisions clearly and firmly, since you would be talking to people of widely differing backgrounds, sometimes in difficult situations. You would also have to be able to express yourself very clearly in your written reports. You might not always be welcome (or at least your findings might not be), so you would need to be resilient, scrupulously fair, and willing to back your judgment. You should be able to assimilate and understand a large amount of scientific, technical and legal detail and, while you would be working on your own quite a lot, you should also be a willing member of a team.

110

B road Outlook

Local authorities employ approximately 95% of environmental health officers, and our increasingly complicated lifestyles will continue to demand their services. There is a clearly defined promotional ladder, with the possibility of attaining management status. You may find it possible to work part-time. Some officers decide to specialise in particular areas of work, perhaps entering industry in posts concerning hygiene or health and safety, becoming housing managers or environmental consultants or setting up their own advisory consultancies when they have gained sufficient experience. Some organisations, such as hotels, food manufacturers and stores, also employ their own environmental health advisers.

R elated Occupations

You might also consider: food technologist, forensic scientist, health and safety inspector and trading standards officer.

I mpact

You would normally work a standard five-day week, but you should be prepared to put in extra hours in the evening or at weekends in an emergency. The work would involve a good deal of travelling and you might well have to move to another area of the country for promotion. Some of the places you would have to visit might be unpleasant, such as abattoirs, and you might encounter some hostility, so you would have to be mentally and physically tough. It is not a job for those of a squeamish disposition.

E arnings Potential

Newly qualified environmental health officers working for a local authority can earn between £20,000 and £23,500. With experience and promotion, you could earn up to £40,000. Pay scales in the private sector would be generally higher, particularly if you reached managerial status, and could rise to well above £45,000 in the oil, gas and chemical industries.

F urther Information

The Chartered Institute of Environmental Health (CIEH), London SE1 8DJ
Website: www.cieh.org

The Royal Environmental Health Institute of Scotland, Edinburgh EH3 7DH
Website: www.rehis.org

Alternative/equivalent entrance requirements can include: ILC, IB, EB, NC/ND and many other similar international systems. For further details see the Equivalent Qualifications section in the Introduction.

What is Involved?

As an estate agent, you would specialise in the buying and selling of property, including house, commercial, industrial and land sales. You would normally act for the seller *(vendor)*, taking a percentage of the selling price as commission when you have completed a successful sale. You might also deal with the letting and management of properties. As an agent involved with buying and selling houses, you would be known as a *negotiator*. In this capacity, you would visit the client's house, advise on a suitable selling price and then try to find a suitable buyer by marketing the property and contacting your database of potential buyers. If a buyer is not willing to pay the full purchase price, you would negotiate with both sides to reach an acceptable agreement. Often more than one prospective buyer could become involved and you would have to negotiate on your client's behalf.

Opportunities for Training

You might start by doing general office work in an estate agency and gradually training to become a negotiator. The National Association of Estate Agents offers National Vocational Qualifications (NVQs) in Residential Estate Agency and the examination-based Certificate of Practice in Estate Agency, both of which are open to practising estate agents and those just starting in the business. You may find that you have access to funded training on a Modern Apprenticeship (Skillseeker in Scotland).

When looking for a position within an estate agency, you should ensure that you clarify their policy on training and developing staff and insist that they provide you with the opportunity to gain a qualification, attend relevant training courses and/or undertake a relevant, structured in-house training programme.

Some estate agents are qualified chartered surveyors. In order to qualify, you would need to complete a degree or diploma accredited by the Royal Institute of Chartered Surveyors. It is also possible to do a degree course in a relevant subject, such as estate management or building and land surveying and valuation.

Requirements

There are no specific qualification requirements to become an estate agent, although you would have the opportunity to qualify with the National Association of Estate Agents after three years experience (minimum age 21).

Whilst academic qualifications are always helpful and applicable, personal qualities and abilities are the most important aspect. Increasing legislation means that estate agents require a good knowledge of relevant law and it can help to be able to show clients or potential employers that you are a professional with a good knowledge of the business.

Kind of Person

You would have to like meeting all sorts of people and be good at negotiating and communicating. Buying or selling a house is often the single most important financial transaction that people make. The housing market is complicated, often involving 'chains' of buyers and sellers, deals often fall through and as a consequence feelings can run high. You would need to be a tactful and sympathetic person to cope with this. You would also need to be a good salesperson.

B road Outlook

At this moment, the housing market is buoyant, as a result of low interest rates and a strong economy. However, this is a field that fluctuates and your pay may well rise or fall according to how much commission you earn. You would probably start as a salaried employee and could then rise to partner or start your own agency. You would have a greater variety of opportunities if you were a qualified chartered surveyor.

R elated Occupations

You might also consider: surveyor, solicitor, legal executive, auctioneer/valuer or estate manager.

I mpact

You would probably be expected to work during some evenings and on Saturdays at weekends. You would be out of the office a great deal, going to see clients and showing them around houses, other property or land. The workload tends, however, to be seasonal and to fluctuate.

E arnings Potential

This can be up to you. Starting pay is usually about £15,000 but you would often receive commission, so the more houses you sell the more you would make. Working hard, networking and getting your name and face known would all be important here. You would be dealing closely with solicitors, banks and other lending organisations and it would be to your advantage to build up personal contacts. If you progress to become a partner, you could earn significantly more depending on the success of the agency and the state of the economy at the time.

F urther Information

National Association of Estate Agents, Warwick CV34 4EH
Website: www.naea.co.uk

Royal Institution of Chartered Surveyors, Coventry CV4 8JE
Website: www.rics.org.uk

Alternative/equivalent entrance requirements can include: ILC, IB, EB, NC/ND and many other similar international systems. For further details see the Equivalent Qualifications section in the Introduction.

What is Involved?

In the ever more competitive world of business and commerce, events, conferences and corporate hospitality days are being used to promote and increase awareness of products, stimulate customer loyalty and reward staff. As an events or conference manager, you would be in charge of the overall organisation of an event, including the venue, the catering, the staffing and the reception arrangements. You might be employed by a large organisation or company, or by a particular venue, or by a specialist company brought in to do the job. Your work could involve a good deal of travel and would certainly mean that you had contact with a wide variety of people, both clients and your own staff. You would discuss and agree what the organisation wanted and what size budget would be at your disposal.

You would need to be aware of all the facilities required to ensure that delegates gain the maximum benefit from each event under your control.

Opportunities for Training

There is no single route into events or conference management but many entrants would have experience of working in hotels or restaurants, or perhaps in a managerial position in such areas as personnel (human resources), leisure, marketing or tourism. You could also work your way up through the ranks. Training would usually be carried out on-the-job. The Association for Conferences and Events runs short courses and can provide lists of companies and venues, together with other useful information.

Requirements

While there are no particular educational qualifications required, increasing numbers of graduates are being employed. Almost any subject would be acceptable, although you might give particular consideration to courses in hospitality management or leisure and tourism, or to others including elements of business studies or marketing.

For entry to a degree course, you would normally need a minimum of two A level/AVCE/Advanced Higher, three Higher or equivalent qualifications, together with five GCSE/S Grade passes at A-C/1-3, or equivalent. Courses usually last three or four years and many would be described as 'sandwich courses', which means that they incorporate periods of industrial experience. There are also Higher National Diploma (HND) courses, which are usually a year shorter than corresponding degrees. For HND entry, you would need one or two A level/AVCE/Advanced Higher, two or three Higher or equivalent qualifications, together with five GCSE/S Grade passes at A-C/1-3.

Kind of Person

You would need excellent communication skills to deal with a wide variety of people. The ability to persuade others to your point of view would be particularly valuable. A good head for business and an understanding of how particular companies work would stand you in good stead. You would need to be tough, both mentally and physically, as the work would probably involve you in long hours, weekend and evening work. You would need to be a good organiser, concerned with getting all the details right while juggling several priorities at any time. You would be on show, so a smart appearance would be important.

B road Outlook

Events and conference management is being seen more and more within the hospitality industry as an important tool for commercial and business success. It is, however, very much at the mercy of the national economic climate. Competition for the top jobs is intense but the rewards can be substantial. As a successful manager, you could progress to setting up your own company or go on to a senior managerial position.

R elated Occupations

You might also consider: advertising executive, hotel/catering manager, leisure services manager, marketing manager or public relations officer.

I mpact

You would have to be prepared to work long hours, at the weekends and in the evenings, sometimes in order to meet deadlines and sometimes to conduct actual events or conferences. There would almost certainly be quite a lot of travel involved.

E arnings Potential

There is a considerable range in earnings, since the type of work involved varies so widely. You might be expected to start on a relatively low salary but your earnings should increase substantially once you gain experience and can demonstrate success.

F urther Information

The Association for Conferences and Events, Huntingdon PE18 6SG
Website: www.martex.co.uk/ace

Hospitality Training Foundation, London W5 5DB Website: www.htf.org.uk

Springboard, London WC2H 8LP Website: www.springboarduk.org.uk

Alternative/equivalent entrance requirements can include: ILC, IB, EB, NC/ND and many other similar international systems. For further details see the Equivalent Qualifications section in the Introduction.

What is Involved?

As a farm manager, you would oversee the running of a farm as an efficient and profitable business. You might work for the owner of a large estate or for a big commercial organisation and the exact nature of your work would depend on the size of the business and the type of farming involved. Broadly speaking, you would be likely to work in one of three areas:

• An arable enterprise would see you producing crops such as wheat, potatoes, sugar beet, linseed, flax, lavender or turf. You might choose to specialise in the rapidly expanding business of organic production, avoiding the use of artificial fertilisers and pesticides on your land.

• The livestock sector would involve you in the production of pigs, beef, dairy cattle, sheep and poultry or, more rarely, deer and ostrich. Here you would have the opportunity to work with animals both outdoors and indoors and to plan breeding programmes.

• A mixed farm would offer you a combination of both arable and livestock elements.

While your work may involve you being outside in all weathers, you would spend at least some of your time in an office, planning ahead, dealing with staffing issues, keeping records and managing the accounts. You would be responsible for the financial success of the farm, making sure that whatever you produce arrives at the right market at the right time and sells for the best possible price.

Opportunities for Training

You would normally have a degree or a (Scottish) Higher National Diploma in agriculture or agricultural business management from university or agricultural college, as well as considerable relevant experience. Courses last three or four years and may include work placements or opportunities for work or study abroad.

Course content varies enormously and is often specifically geared to arable or livestock farming as outlined above. Other relevant courses could range from wildlife conservation to soil science.

Requirements

At least two A level/AVCE/Advanced Higher, three Higher or equivalent qualifications are required for entry to degree courses. Chemistry is often specified; biology and geography are regularly mentioned. For diploma courses, you should have at least one A level/AVCE/Advanced Higher, two Higher or equivalent qualifications, together with three or four GCSE/S Grade passes at A-C/1-3 including English, maths and a science subject. You would need considerable work experience and you would find it difficult to survive without a driving licence.

Kind of Person

In the rapidly changing world of modern agriculture, you may find that business management and IT skills are even more important than a thorough grounding in farmyard skills and a love of the countryside. Farming can be highly unpredictable as weather conditions change, crops lose their market value or animals become sick. As a manager, you would need to be adaptable, unflappable and able to rearrange plans at very short notice. Good communication skills would be essential for working with staff, advisers, suppliers and customers.

B road Outlook

Farming is going through difficult times at present and this could affect the number of managerial jobs available. As they diversify into less traditional activities to 'add value' and increase profitability, farm businesses will be looking to use traditional resources, such as land, labour, buildings and equipment, for uses over and above livestock, milk and crop production. You could improve your overall prospects by trying to apply innovative thinking to the process of moving away from intensive production towards such areas as leisure pursuits, organic farming and conservation.

R elated Occupations

You may wish to consider: horticultural manager, conservation officer, landscape architect, estate manager, forest manager, countryside ranger or fish farmer. You could move into other commercial aspects of agriculture, such as technical sales or contracting. With the increase of tourism in the countryside, you could specialise in the management of tourist facilities.

I mpact

Many people view agriculture as an industry that offers long hours for poor reward. You should find in reality that, while there are rarely any set hours and you are expected to vary your workload according to the changing demands of the seasons, farming is becoming increasingly 'market aware', calling for flexible, innovative and enthusiastic people who are well rewarded for their commitment. Running a farm tends to become a way of life and early mornings, late evenings and weekend commitments can often be part of the lifestyle.

E arnings Potential

There is no official salary scale for farm managers. Your annual earnings could range from £12,000 to £35,000 or more depending on the size of the farm and your level of responsibility. You could have a car and a house on the farm as part of your employment package and you may even be able to participate in a profit-sharing scheme.

F urther Information

Lantra, sector skills council for the environmental and land-based sector, Kenilworth CV8 2LG Website: www.lantra.co.uk

Growing Careers Website: www.growing-careers.com

Alternative/equivalent entrance requirements can include: ILC, IB, EB, NC/ND and many other similar international systems. For further details see the Equivalent Qualifications section in the Introduction.

What is Involved?

As a fashion designer, you would work with others in designing and making clothes and accessories. There are three areas of fashion design: 'haute couture', 'designer ready-to-wear' and 'high street fashions'. Haute couture is the top end of the market, where individually designed clothes are made for exclusive clients. The fashion houses involved – Armani, Dior, Calvin Klein, Chloe, for example – all display their latest collections at glitzy shows and it is often these designs that influence what the rest of us wear over the next season. Designer ready-to-wear clothes are produced by the haute couture fashion houses and are emblazoned with their all-important designer label or logo. These are usually limited runs of the design, sold in specialist boutiques. Most fashion garments are sold in high street stores, including French Connection, Marks and Spencer, Debenhams and TopShop. Fashion is one of the largest industries in the UK, employing more than 165,000 people and contributing significantly to British exports.

You could work in the dominant womenswear market or you could choose to focus on the growing menswear and childrenswear segments. Other possible areas include accessory design, millinery, shoe and sportswear design or you could even specialise in costume design for film, TV and theatre work.

Opportunities for Training

With over 250 fashion degrees and higher national diplomas (HNDs) currently available in the UK, you would need to research training courses carefully before making a final choice. A good starting point could be a one- or two-year foundation course in art and design, allowing you time after school to explore a range of options in creative design and to develop a suitable portfolio of your work. Courses should take you through all the stages from an initial design idea to a prototype garment.

You may find an on-the-job training place with a design studio but you would need to be sure that you would focus on design rather than on manufacturing garments.

Requirements

Most institutions offering degree and HND courses require five GCSE/S Grade passes at A-C/1-3 or equivalent, preferably with maths and English, together with relevant AS/A level/AVCE/Advanced Higher/Higher or equivalent qualifications including an art related subject, and/or the completion of an art foundation course. You must be able to present a portfolio of work, with evidence of good drawing skills and a lively interest in fashion. Work experience is important and it would be helpful to demonstrate that you have made up a garment, taken photographs or assembled your own fashion scrapbook.

Kind of Person

You would need a real passion for fashion, with a love of clothes, textiles, colour, texture and pattern. Good drawing skills would be essential, together with the ability to communicate your ideas to buyers or manufacturers and the practical ability to make up sample garments. You would need to work as part of a team, to be able to use fashion-specific IT packages and to have some knowledge of the business constraints of budgeting and costing. For haute couture, in particular, you would need to be exceptionally creative and determined to succeed.

B road Outlook

Competition in fashion design is intense and success can be as dependent on getting a lucky break as on having talent, drive and irrepressible determination. You may want to gain experience by working in the UK or abroad, possibly for low pay in a very junior position, in the fashion centres of London, Paris, Milan and New York. The majority of actual jobs in the UK are at the high street end of the market and may be somewhat removed from the glamour associated with stars such as Galliano, Westwood and McQueen. You should ask about career destinations of previous students before selecting a degree or HND course.

R elated Occupations

You may wish to consider other designer areas such as: textile, interior, industrial product, jewellery or graphic. Alternatively, you might wish to consider other fashion options such as: photographer, buyer, illustrator or journalist.

I mpact

Fashion design could well become dominant in your life as you work through the night to meet deadlines for fashion shows and rearrange holidays to fit work schedules. Inspiration can come at any time and you would need to capture ideas before they disappear again.

E arnings Potential

You could expect to start on about £13,000 to £16,000 a year, usually more in London. Depending on your talent and opportunities, you could be earning in the region of £30,000 to £40,000 after a few years and, if you become a top design director, you might earn £100,000 or more.

You may choose to work on a freelance basis, in which case your earnings would depend totally on how hard you work and how successful you are in selling your designs.

F urther Information

CAPITB Trust, Leeds LS28 6BN Website: www.careers-in-clothing.co.uk

Your Creative Future Website: www.yourcreativefuture.org

Alternative/equivalent entrance requirements can include: ILC, IB, EB, NC/ND and many other similar international systems. For further details see the Equivalent Qualifications section in the Introduction.

What is Involved?

As a financial adviser, you could work in one of two major areas:

• You may be tied to an individual bank, building society or insurance company, advising solely on the financial products of your organisation;

• You may have a broader role as an independent adviser, recommending suitable investments, mortgages, pensions and insurance policies on an impartial basis.

In either case, you would need a detailed knowledge of investment opportunities, insurance policies, pension plans, mortgages and savings schemes. You would analyse each client's financial position and draw up plans to help meet his or her future requirements and commitments. For example, in addition to house purchase and retirement planning, a client might wish to educate their children privately and you would advise how they could best achieve this through structuring their savings and investments. You could work as a completely independent financial adviser, charging clients by the hour in the same way as an accountant, or you could offer your advice free of charge, earning commission on the financial products you promote and sell.

Opportunities for Training

You are most likely to receive your training on the job, observing and learning from experienced colleagues as well as attending short courses on market trends, product knowledge and sales techniques. During your first year of training, you would have to work towards the three-stage Financial Planning Certificate (FPC) or an equivalent qualification and you may then find it useful to progress to the Advanced FPC.

You must keep up with changes in financial and taxation legislation, together with government incentives to promote individual investment and financial planning, ensuring that the advice you offer is completely up to date.

Requirements

While there are no formal academic entry requirements, the most prestigious employers would require a degree or at least A level/AVCE/Advanced Higher, Higher or equivalent qualifications, together with evidence of numeracy. Many people starting as financial advisers are graduates in business studies, accountancy or similar subjects, although this is not an essential requirement. Some people become financial advisers after gaining experience in clerical positions, although this could take some time because of the level of maturity expected by clients.

Kind of Person

This is a job for a 'people' person. You would have to be good at communicating – both listening carefully to your client's requirements and being able to explain your proposed solutions to their financial needs. You would meet all sorts of people and you would need to inspire confidence in them. You would need to be numerate and have an understanding of financial products and the legal or taxation implications of making certain investment decisions.

Good IT skills are essential. If working on commission for a company, you would have to be good at selling. Honesty is vital here, both in terms of explaining the extent of your independence and of treating personal information confidentially. You would normally be expected to dress smartly and conventionally for this type of work.

B road Outlook

Financial advice is an area undergoing rapid change and considerable growth. As more and more people change jobs throughout their working lives, they need financial planning advice. The financial services sector has had some bad publicity in recent years but its image is changing with tighter regulation and the introduction of the compulsory FPC for financial advisers.

You could progress into management or training or you could start your own business.

R elated Occupations

You may consider: accountant, banker, insurance broker or investment analyst.

I mpact

Generally financial advisers are office based, working normal office hours. However, you might be expected to visit clients in their homes and this could involve having to see them in the evening or at weekends.

E arnings Potential

This can vary considerably. Your method of payment could range from a full salary to a salary with bonuses for achieved targets, to commission only or fees only. So, to a certain extent, what you earn would be up to you. As a graduate, you could expect to earn up to £20,000 in your first year and considerably more later if you exceed your targets. You could achieve very high earnings as an experienced and successful independent adviser.

F urther Information

The Financial Services Authority, London E14 5HS Website: www.fsa.gov.uk

The Society of Financial Advisers, London EC2V 7HY
Website: www.sofa.org

The Association of Independent Financial Advisers, London EC2N 2HD
Website: www.aifa.net

The Institute of Financial Planning, Bristol BS1 2NT
Website: www.financialplanning.org.uk

Financial Services National Training Organisation, London EC2V 7HQ
Website: www.fsnto.org

Alternative/equivalent entrance requirements can include: ILC, IB, EB, NC/ND and many other similar international systems. For further details see the Equivalent Qualifications section in the Introduction.

What is Involved?

As a fire officer or firefighter, you would be working as part of a team to reduce deaths and losses from fire. While you would certainly be involved in the often dangerous and stressful process of actually fighting fires, you would also be responsible for making the general public aware of fire hazards, visiting public and commercial premises to advise on fire regulations and safety standards and responding to other emergency calls. These may range from floods to road, rail and air crashes or working with other emergency services at sites of major disasters. You would be trained in first aid so that you could administer immediate help before the arrival of the emergency medical services.

As a more senior officer, you might organise the response of your service to call-outs and you might attend major incidents to co-ordinate the work. At other times, you could be reviewing the operating policies of your brigade or organising the training of the firefighters under your command.

Opportunities for Training

As a new recruit, you would train for approximately four months at a local training centre or fire station. Initial training is tough, with an emphasis on strict discipline and high standards of physical fitness. You would cover both the theory and practice of all aspects of the firefighter's role, including the use of ladders and hoses, wearing protective clothing and breathing apparatus and learning about fire regulations. You would then be on probation at a fire station for up to two years, during which time you would learn from experienced colleagues and you would be continuously assessed to determine your ultimate suitability for this demanding job. You would be encouraged to work towards National or Scottish Vocational Qualifications in Emergency Fire Services and you would be expected to continue to train throughout your career.

Requirements

There are no formal entry requirements, although some brigades may require specific GCSE/S Grade passes, and you would have to pass a series of initiative and fitness tests. There is no separate entry scheme for candidates with higher level qualifications but you should be able to pass training and promotion exams relatively more quickly.

You must be at least 18 before you can join the Fire Service, fully fit and able to meet national fitness standards in lung capacity and upper body strength. Good vision in both eyes is essential and you should have normal colour vision.

Kind of Person

You must be able to work as part of a highly disciplined team but with the capacity to respond to challenges by showing initiative when required. You would be required to accept the brigade dress code and restrictions on your personal appearance.

Handling specialist equipment calls for a variety of practical skills and you must be able to react calmly but quickly in dangerous situations. Good communication and interpersonal skills are vital. You would need to be physically strong to carry your equipment and mentally resilient in view of the sometimes harrowing situations you would encounter.

B road Outlook

There is fierce competition for Fire Service positions and there are always many more applicants than vacancies, although there is scope in rural areas to work as a part-time 'retained' firefighter.

All new entrants start on the same grade and promotion is strictly on merit. You could rise to the rank of station commander through internal promotion but would need to move to different areas to obtain more senior appointments.

R elated Occupations

You might also consider: armed forces serviceman/woman, army, RAF, Royal Navy, merchant navy, police or security officer or ambulance technician/paramedic.

I mpact

Firefighters work a shift system, which means both day and night time working and work at weekends. Occasionally, you may be expected to work overtime but can expect on average to have two days off each week. Because of the nature of the job you may be called out on emergency work at short notice and would have to see the job through however long it takes for you to be relieved.

E arnings Potential

From a starting salary of approximately £16,000, you could expect to earn over £20,000 within five years. Station Officers are paid around £27,000 and senior Divisional Officers up to £40,000.

F urther Information

Contact the recruitment department of your local fire service.

You can also obtain useful background information by visiting the Fire Service Inspectorate website at: www.safety.dtlr.gov.uk/fire/fepd/hmfsi.htm

Alternative/equivalent entrance requirements can include: ILC, IB, EB, NC/ND and many other similar international systems. For further details see the Equivalent Qualifications section in the Introduction.

What is Involved?

As a food scientist, you would examine the chemistry and biology of manufactured foods from the raw materials through to the final product. As a food technologist, you would use food science and other technological expertise to turn raw materials into finished products for the consumer, often with the aid of sophisticated equipment. You might work for a food processing company, for a large supermarket chain, for the civil service or for the environmental health service, ensuring that food products are safe to eat and economical to produce, that they taste good and look inviting. You could be testing products in a laboratory to monitor chemical and microbiological changes during cooking and storage; you could be developing new products to meet changing consumer demands; you may be creating low-fat, ready-to-eat meals for airlines; you may be experimenting with new ways of preventing fruit from rotting. While there is considerable overlap between the two types of work, you would be more likely to work in a laboratory as a food scientist and in a food production establishment as a food technologist.

Opportunities for Training

There are over 30 institutions in the UK offering Food Science, Food Technology or closely related subjects at degree or higher national diploma (HND) level or N/SVQ level 4. Some of the courses are sandwich-based, giving you a chance to combine your academic study with practical experience in the industry. It is also possible to train on the job, without a higher education qualification, possibly starting on a Modern Apprenticeship (Skillseekers in Scotland). There may be opportunities to specialise in areas such as meat and poultry processing, baking technology or brewing.

If you are interested in working abroad, some degrees and HNDs offer study in Europe as part of the course. You would be expected to continue to study throughout your working life in order to keep up to date with new developments in the food market.

Requirements

You should be thinking of studying chemistry plus at least one subject from food science, maths, biology or physics as a grounding for a degree or HND. Most universities require three good A level/AVCE/Advanced Higher, four Higher or equivalent qualifications for degree entry, including chemistry. The HND route would normally require one A level/AVCE, two Higher or equivalent qualifications.

It is possible to work as a technician in food and drink production if you have four GCSE/S Grade passes A-C/1-3 in English, maths, biology and chemistry or an equivalent qualification.

Kind of Person

You would need a genuine interest in food and drink, coupled with a meticulous approach to detail and hygiene when you are conducting trials or laboratory tests on food. You would also need good communication skills and the ability to work as part of a team. Knowledge of food safety law is required, to ensure that you work within relevant health and safety regulations.

B road Outlook

Food and drink is a large, expanding and changing industry, with new jobs being created all the time. There is wide range of possible employers, from food or drink manufacturers, large retailers or supermarket chains to Government research establishments, local authorities or universities.

To gain promotion in a large organisation, you would need to develop specialised skills relevant to the company and to demonstrate the broad qualities sought for management responsibility. You may find it necessary to change employers a few times in order to develop your career.

R elated Occupations

You may be interested in working in the food industry as a dietitian, nutritionist, biochemist, biotechnologist, microbiologist, environmental health officer or chef.

I mpact

You would most likely work a typical 35- to 40-hour week. Some manufacturing companies may have a 24-hour production programme, in which case you would work shifts in order to supervise and test the quality of the food during production. This may include some weekend work.

Meticulous hygiene requirements would mean that you would at times have to wear special clothing, including a hat or hairnet, gloves and even a mask.

E arnings Potential

As a graduate food scientist or technologist, you should earn in the region of £18,000 to £30,000. This could rise to £50,000 or more for a senior managerial position, depending on the size of the organisation, your responsibilities and your qualifications.

F urther Information

Food and Drink NTO, London WC2B 5JJ
Website: www.foodanddrinknto.org.uk

Institute of Food Science and Technology, London W6 7NL
Website: www.ifst.org

Alternative/equivalent entrance requirements can include: ILC, IB, EB, NC/ND and many other similar international systems. For further details see the Equivalent Qualifications section in the Introduction.

What is Involved?

As a forensic scientist, you would be working at the meeting point between science and the law, examining and analysing minute traces of materials in the search for physical traces which might be useful for establishing or excluding an association between someone suspected of committing a crime and the scene of the crime or victim. Such traces commonly include blood and other body fluids, hairs, textile fibres from clothing, materials used in buildings such as paint and glass, footwear, tool and tyre marks, flammable substances used to start fires and so on. Much of your work would be carried out in close co-operation with the police and would make a very valuable, at times critical, contribution to the process of the law. You are likely to be involved with cases of arson, burglary and fire and murder investigations. You might also be concerned with car accidents or cases involving drugs. You would work in a laboratory, possibly analysing samples of DNA, and occasionally visiting the scenes of crimes.

Opportunities for Training

Most of the training for the Forensic Science Service in England and Wales or the police laboratories in Scotland would be carried out once you have started working. While you can become an assistant forensic scientist with at least one A level/Advanced Higher or two Highers, you would need a good honours degree in a relevant subject in order to become a forensic scientist and progress to senior level. There are some universities offering degrees in Forensic Science either as single or joint honours but it is possible to start training with a good degree in a subject such as chemistry, biochemistry, pharmaceutical chemistry, biology or metallurgy, followed by a one- or two-year post-graduate course in forensic science. This is the route currently recommended by the Forensic Science Society. However, there is no route that will guarantee you a job in this oversubscribed field.

Requirements

For entry to a relevant science degree, you would need A level/AVCE/ Advanced Higher, Higher or equivalent qualifications in chemistry and another science subject, with some universities specifying maths or biology. If the university does not specify maths as an A level/Advanced Higher, Higher or equivalent subject, you are likely to need at least a B/2 in maths at GCSE/S Grade. There are just a handful of Forensic Science degree courses available and admission offers can be higher than for other chemistry- or biology-based courses.

Kind of Person

You would need a strong interest in science and a methodical and analytic approach to problem solving. At times you would be required to make very detailed examinations of the scene of an incident. The tests that you carry out would call for accuracy and a sound understanding of maths. In addition to your scientific and analytical skills you would need to express yourself clearly both verbally and in written reports. You may be required to stand up in court and give evidence, in which case you may have to face cross-examination. You are likely to become an expert in one particular area of forensic science and would, therefore, work fairly independently but always as a team member. Finally, you would have to cope with crime scenes, which can be very unpleasant.

B road Outlook

This is a fiercely competitive area of work, with many well-qualified candidates chasing every vacancy. You may have to move around the country in order to secure a post.

The majority of forensic scientists in the United Kingdom are employed by the Forensic Science Service (in England and Wales), by specific police forces (in Scotland) and by regional government (in Northern Ireland). There are also private companies, which specialise in providing primary forensic science services to the police, together with organisations which focus on specific areas of forensic science such as fire investigation.

R elated Occupations

You might be interested in other careers with a scientific base such as research chemist, pharmacologist, chemical engineer, metallurgist, biochemist or pathologist.

I mpact

You may be called out to a crime scene at night or at weekends, and this could clearly have an impact on your social life. Apart from being available on an on-call rota of this sort, you could expect your normal working week to be around 40 hours spread over five days. Some of the scenes of crime you attend may be distressing, so this is not a career for the faint-hearted!

E arnings Potential

As an assistant forensic scientist with the Forensic Science Service, you could expect to earn between £12,000 and £24,000; this could rise to 30,000 as a forensic scientist and £50,000 as a senior forensic scientist. Pay rates vary in Scotland from around £12,000 for a technician to £45,000 for a principal scientist.

F urther Information

The Forensic Science Society, Harrogate HG1 1BX
Website: www.forensic-science-society.org.uk

Alternative/equivalent entrance requirements can include: ILC, IB, EB, NC/ND and many other similar international systems. For further details see the Equivalent Qualifications section in the Introduction.

What is Involved?

Forestry is defined as the science and practice of managing forests and woodlands but modern multi-purpose forestry is about far more than just growing trees for timber. Your work as a forest manager could embrace everything from planting and managing large coniferous forests to creating and tending small broadleaved woodlands; from raising young trees in nurseries to felling and delivering timber to wood-using industries. Timber production still underpins the work but your remit would be much broader, including managing woods and forests to offer multiple benefits for people, wildlife and the environment in general. Forests can provide havens for wildlife, can screen and enhance the landscape, filter the air and cater for many types of recreation.

You would usually commence your career as a technical manager or supervisor, known in the industry as a forester. You would plan and control forest operations and ensure that the forest environment is protected and enhanced. You might also manage public recreation and access. There are chances to specialise in wildlife conservation, recreation, training, research, harvesting, marketing and processing. You would probably spend about three days a week out in the forest and the rest of the time in an office.

Opportunities for Training

There are several possible training routes. You would normally need a degree, postgraduate qualification or a higher or national diploma in forestry (ND/HND). A Modern Apprenticeship (Skillseeker in Scotland) could also enable you to progress to a similar level. A degree would take three or four years to complete and ND/HND two or three years. You should obtain relevant work experience before starting any of these courses. You may find it useful to work towards full membership of the Institute of Chartered Foresters, which carries with it recognition of your experience and success in passing their examinations.

Requirements

For entry to a forestry degree, you should have at least two A level/ AVCE/Advanced Higher, three Higher or equivalent qualifications in science subjects and five GCSE/S Grade passes A-C/1-3. The HND would require at least one A level/AVCE/Advanced Higher, two Higher or equivalent qualifications and GCSE/S Grade passes A-C/1-3 in maths, English and a science subject; for the ND you would need similar GCSE/S Grade passes. A full driving licence would be essential.

Kind of Person

You would need to be interested in the successful development and economic viability of forests, in their conservation and their environmental roles. You would have to be fit and to enjoy working outdoors. You would need good team skills, the ability to organise the schedules of those working for you and to communicate effectively with colleagues and members of the public.

B road Outlook

The UK is one of the few places in the world where the tree cover is actually expanding as more and more trees are planted with the advent of community forests and the National Forest. Recent government initiatives in the expansion of leisure facilities in both private and public forests, coupled with grants to encourage the use of more land for forestry, have increased employment possibilities.

Nevertheless, competition is keen and gaining work experience is vitally important. The Forestry Commission employs about 20% of people in forestry, private estates and the wood-processing industry account for about 60%, with the balance working for forest management and timber harvesting companies.

Openings exist with national and local government agencies, forest management companies, private estates, land agency firms, timber companies and independent consultants. There are forestry opportunities in New Zealand, Canada and the USA. Volunteer forestry workers can also be employed by charities working in underdeveloped countries. There are opportunities for postgraduate work and research in forestry with universities and the Forestry Commission.

R elated Occupations

You might also consider: countryside ranger/warden, conservationist, horticultural manager, landscape architect, chartered surveyor or land agent.

I mpact

You may have to work long hours, especially in commercial forests to meet contract deadlines. The Forestry Commission has an official 42-hour week, although that may include evening and weekend work. You are likely to be based in a very rural and possibly quite remote environment.

E arnings Potential

As a graduate you could expect to start earning between £14,000 and £23,000, depending on your experience and qualifications. As a senior manager you could earn in the region of £35,000. The commercial forests tend to pay rather less than the Forestry Commission but there may be additional benefits.

F urther Information

Forestry Commission, Edinburgh EH12 7AT Website: www.forestry.gov.uk

Institute of Chartered Foresters, Edinburgh EH3 6AA
Website: www.charteredforesters.org

Royal Forestry Society, Hertfordshire HP23 4AF Website: www.rfs.org.uk

Alternative/equivalent entrance requirements can include: ILC, IB, EB, NC/ND and many other similar international systems. For further details see the Equivalent Qualifications section in the Introduction.

What is Involved?

In today's global economy, we buy our everyday needs from all around the world: mobile phones from Finland, furniture from Sweden, televisions from Japan and computers from the USA. We also sell our own goods all over the world. As a freight forwarder, you would be part of the international industry that uses ships, planes, trucks and railways to transport these goods to their markets around the globe.

You might work as a freight forwarding agent, assisting exporters or importers by collecting and delivering between them and the shipping line or airline, buying space on sailings or flights, handling documentation and dealing with HM Customs. Alternatively, you might work for an airline, a shipping company, a road transport operator or a courier, dealing in high volumes of small and urgent packages. See also our separate article on 'Logistics Manager.'

You would need a clear knowledge of the advantages and disadvantages of all types of transport and of the handling techniques at ports, railway stations, road transport terminals and airports worldwide.

Opportunities for Training

While there is no single recommended training route, there are many relevant higher national diploma (HND) and degree courses in international trade, business and logistics management. These can lead to a fast-track development programme within some of the larger freight organisations. You could also follow a part-time or correspondence course organised by a body such as the British International Freight Association or the Institute of Logistics and Transport.

Requirements

For degree course entry, you would normally need two or three A level/ AVCE/Advanced Higher, three or four Highers or equivalent qualifications, together with a good platform of GCSE/S Grade passes A-C/1-3. HND entry would normally require one A level/AVCE/Advanced Higher, two Higher or equivalent qualifications. There are no specific subject requirements but subjects such as economics, foreign languages and geography could be useful. You should try to spend some time on a relevant work experience placement before making an application.

Kind of Person

The main qualities required would include an analytical mind with a practical side to it, as you could be constantly called upon to unravel problems such as goods going astray, suffering damage or failing to connect with a container ship or cargo plane. You would need to examine the fine detail without losing sight of the wider picture. You must be willing to assume independent responsibility, to communicate clearly and decisively, to insist on getting the facts, to negotiate and be adaptable and to cope with all these stresses and frequent changes. Excellent communication skills, both

130

verbal and written, would be vital to carrying out your tasks, in which efficiency of operation, speed of turn-around time and the availability of return freights would be essential.

B road Outlook

Freight forwarding offers a good degree of job security because, even during periods of economic downturn, there is still huge demand for the movement of goods around the world. Many people come into the freight industry by accident but then stay for a life-long career. There are several thousand freight-forwarding offices in the UK, from large companies (with 30 or more branches) down to single-outlet operators. All the pointers suggest that this is an industry facing significant change but one in which there is considerable room for expansion in line with greater world trade.

R elated Occupations

You might also consider: logistics manager, shipbroker, marketing manager, insurance broker, insurance underwriter or tour operator.

I mpact

The freight industry operates 24 hours a day, seven days a week. It could make major demands on your time, especially if you are in regular contact with people living on the other side of the world. Your hours of work could be long and irregular and you may be expected to travel extensively.

E arnings Potential

The average starting salary for a graduate management trainee is around £15,000, although this can vary according to company size, location and so on. Other salaries are difficult to gauge but a recent survey by the Institute of Logistics and Transport shows that many senior managers receive a salary in the £50,000 to £75,000 range.

F urther Information

The Institute of Logistics & Transport, Corby NN17 4XQ
Website: www.iolt.org.uk

Institute of Chartered Shipbrokers, London EC3V 0AT
Website: www.ics.org.uk

British International Freight Association, Middlesex TW13 7EP
Website: www.bifa.org

Alternative/equivalent entrance requirements can include: ILC, IB, EB, NC/ND and many other similar international systems. For further details see the Equivalent Qualifications section in the Introduction.

What is Involved?

As a geologist or geoscientist, you would study the structure, evolution and dynamics of the planet Earth and its natural mineral and energy resources. You would investigate the processes that have shaped the Earth through its 4600 million year history in order to unravel that history and reveal its direct relevance to modern society. By mapping the distribution of rocks exposed at the Earth's surface, looking at how they are folded, fractured and altered by geological processes and determining their ages and field relations, you could produce the geological maps and databases which are the basic tools underpinning the use of all geological resources. You might analyse how energy resources such as oil and gas, coal and uranium are formed and where they may be found, or you might be involved in the search for sources of geothermal energy. You may be employed in exploration and surveying on land and sea, using aerial or satellite photography and electro-magnetic measurements (remote sensing). If you were to specialise in engineering, you might advise on the best locations for the construction of mines, roads, buildings and bridges.

Opportunities for Training

To pursue a professional career, you would need a BSc degree in geology or geoscience. Most students follow a broadly based course, although you could concentrate on a particular aspect such as environmental geology or geophysics. It is also possible to combine geology with other subjects in joint or modular degree programmes. Fieldwork plays a vital part in most courses and you should be prepared to spend time out of doors to undertake group expeditions lasting from a few days to one or two weeks. Increasingly, students wishing to become geoscientists go on to take a postgraduate qualification, such as a one-year taught MSc course concentrating on a particular area of interest to employers (eg petroleum geology, geophysics or hydrogeology). The Geological Society runs an accreditation scheme for geoscience degrees and successful completion of an accredited course can be the first stage of becoming a chartered geologist (CGeol).

Requirements

For degree entry, you would normally need two or three A level/ AVCE/Advanced Higher, three or four Higher or equivalent qualifications. Science and technological subjects, especially chemistry, physics, biology, mathematics and engineering, are preferred and a foreign language can be useful. As geology is not available in the majority of UK schools, it is not a university entrance requirement.

Kind of Person

You would need good spatial awareness and practical skills to use sophisticated instruments and you would have to possess good IT skills. You would sometimes work alone and sometimes as part of a team; you would need to be fit and healthy, since you may be working in physically challenging environments anywhere in the world. Any colour blindness could be a serious problem. Good communication skills would be essential for writing reports, making presentations and participating in discussion with professional colleagues.

B road Outlook

There is a wide range of career opportunities open to geology graduates, including the hydrocarbons, mining and quarrying and civil engineering industries, government and government-supported scientific establishments, geological surveys, specialist geological consultants and research companies and teaching. These industries are susceptible to economic fluctuations and employment opportunities can be variable. The British Geological Survey is the largest single employer of geoscientists in the UK.

Currently only a third of graduates in the geosciences are taking up a career in the profession and short-term contracts are now being offered by many employers.

R elated Occupations

You might also consider: geochemist, surveyor, petroleum, civil, structural or mining engineer, hydrographic surveyor or cartographer.

I mpact

Most professional geologists spend at least part of their working career doing fieldwork, sometimes in remote areas in difficult conditions. You could be land-based, in mining operations or take part in underwater drilling operations. Temperatures can be extremely high in desert areas in the day and very low at night. In locations like Alaska you would experience sub-zero conditions and very short daylight hours. You would need a wide range of safety equipment and protective clothing to cope with each situation.

E arnings Potential

Newly qualified entrants to the profession may earn from £16,000 to £21,000 depending on the company they work for, and those with five years experience up to £30,000. Additional allowances may be paid for working offshore and abroad. Senior geologists may earn as much as £80,000 or more.

F urther Information

The British Geological Survey, Nottingham NG12 5GG
Website: www.bgs.ac.uk/

The Geological Society, London WIJ 0BG Website: www.geolsoc.org.uk/

Alternative/equivalent entrance requirements can include: ILC, IB, EB, NC/ND and many other similar international systems. For further details see the Equivalent Qualifications section in the Introduction.

What is Involved?

As a golf course designer, you would be commissioned by a client or golf club to work on a new project or to make alterations to an existing course. Your work is likely to fall under four headings: *conceptual design*, covering the ideas and development of the concept of the project; *detailed design*, focusing on the engineering detail and associated documentation of the architecture to greens, tees, bunkers, drainage, irrigation and so on; *design management*, involving inspections and supervisory visits during the construction and irrigation phases; *establishment management*, in which final visits and inspections would be made.

Opportunities for Training

There is no direct career path within what is a relatively small profession, though it has now been given a European dimension by the creation of the European Institute of Golf Course Architects (EIGCA). In conjunction with Heriot-Watt University in Edinburgh, Elmwood College in Cupar, Fife, and Merrist Wood College in Surrey, the EIGCA runs two courses: 1) a master's degree in golf course architecture, full-time for 12 months; 2) a part-time postgraduate diploma in golf course architecture, comprising part-time attendance and distance learning opportunities.

As a result of your training, you would be expected to have a grasp of the following disciplines:

> The principles and form of architecture, landscape architecture, agronomy, civil/mechanical/hydraulic engineering, soil science, botany, plant physiology, plant chemistry, bacteriology, mycology (fungi), turf culture, quantity surveying and computer technology amongst technical matters.

Requirements

For the master's degree you would require a good first degree, preferably with first or upper second class honours, or an equivalent qualification. Similar standards would apply to the postgraduate diploma but account would also be taken of any relevant vocational training and prior practical experience.

Kind of Person

You must possess and be able to display a feeling for shape and form in design terms, coupled particularly with an appreciation of nature. Although you may well be based in an office, your essential work would be out on site. With the worldwide expansion of golf, opportunities for travel and for meeting clients from different countries with differing customs and cultures are numerous. The ability to enjoy and cope with this aspect of the job would, therefore, be vitally important.

You would need good communication and presentation skills to convince golf club officials and members that your plans meet all of their specifications, and you would need to be aware of legislation relevant to protecting and preserving the environment. In the context of developing existing course, you would need the ability to analyse, identify and select the strengths and weaknesses of any course and then recommend ways to improve it. You would probably arrive at this specialism as a result of a keen interest in playing golf.

B road Outlook

You would find that this is a small and very specialised profession, with approximately 100 practising architects in Europe. However, golf is an expanding game, which has undergone amazing growth in the last 50 years. There are still countries with no golf courses at all, so there is considerable potential in areas like central Eastern Europe, Mid-Asia and the Middle East. The EIGCA is currently structuring a positive education programme and career path, even though many golf course design practices are owned and run by individuals.

It remains, however, a difficult career to enter, unless you can secure employment, internship or a studentship with one of the larger, more dynamic practices. Some 150 golf course architects run practices in the USA and are members of the American Society of Golf Course Architects, but you would have to obtain a green card if you wish to find employment in America as an intern.

R elated Occupations

You might also consider: architect, landscape architect, chartered surveyor, rural practice surveyor, countryside conservation officer or golf professional.

I mpact

This is not a job with regular office hours from Monday to Friday. With the frequent travel necessitated, it would be common for golf course designers to put in many additional hours per week, which may be unsociable but could also be enjoyable. Projects may well not be close to hand, so some disruption of your social and domestic life would be inevitable.

E arnings Potential

As a student or intern, you could expect a relatively low salary, whereas you would certainly earn in excess of £20,000 once qualified. Those who run their own practices would earn considerably more, dependent on the value of projects in hand at any time.

F urther Information

The European Institute of Golf Course Architects (EIGCA), Guildford GU3 3PE. Website: www.eigca.org

Alternative/equivalent entrance requirements can include: ILC, IB, EB, NC/ND and many other similar international systems. For further details see the Equivalent Qualifications section in the Introduction.

What is Involved?

As a graphic designer, you would add a dimension of visual flair to the words and pictures making up magazine and newspaper layouts and covers, advertisements, posters, book jackets, sales brochures, catalogues, websites and product packaging. Graphic design is about drawing and presentation skills and about the ability to handle colours, lettering and patterns. Increasingly too, because of the development of design software, it is about a high degree of computer literacy. You might work on a wide range of projects or you could become a specialist in, for example, typography (print), illustration, packaging, corporate identity or magazine design.

You would often be expected to suggest a number of designs and colour combinations for consideration, possibly modifying layouts, typestyles and overall emphasis according to the wishes of your client or art director. Branding and house style, costing/budgeting, delivery dates and media to be used would all need to be agreed before your design work is finalised and handed over for printing or publication.

Opportunities for Training

There are no required qualifications but a good starting point would normally be to take an art foundation course before going on to a further course of training at an art school or university. A foundation course would give you a broad introduction to working in different areas of design and would provide the opportunity to build up a portfolio of your best work before you choose a specialised degree or higher national diploma (HND) course. In Scotland, the foundation would be the first year of a four-year course.

Requirements

Entry to foundation courses can be from GCSE/S or A level/AVCE/Advanced Higher, Higher or equivalent qualifications, with great importance placed on a current portfolio of your own artistic work. The courses last one or two years full-time and can be found at sixth form colleges, further and higher education colleges, art colleges and some universities.

Entry to an HND course would normally require a minimum of four GCSE/S grade passes and one or two A level/AVCE/Advanced Higher, Higher or equivalent qualifications. The course would usually last two years, with the possibility of conversion to a degree course. Entry to a degree course would normally require a minimum of five GCSE/S Grade passes and two or three A level/AVCE/Advanced Higher, Higher or equivalent qualifications. These requirements might be waived if you have foundation course experience and/or an impressive portfolio.

Kind of Person

You would need to be artistically creative and imaginative. You would also need to have good technical and drawing skills and the ability to visualise a design concept. You would need to be able to understand the technical aspects of printing and, if applicable, multimedia systems. Computer skills would be essential, as graphic design is almost always based on specialist design software. You would need to communicate well with your clients, to listen carefully to their ideas and suggestions and be able to explain your own design concepts. In addition, you would need some understanding of budgeting and costing when preparing your plans.

B road Outlook

Britain has the largest number of higher education courses in graphic design in Europe, which means that entry to the profession is competitive. However, there are more openings in graphic design than in any other area of design – in advertising agencies, design studios, in-house company departments and consultancies as well as in the freelance sector. Most agencies and studios are based in the larger cities, with a particular concentration in the London area. There is growing demand for designers specialising in television and video graphics and in website design.

R elated Occupations

You might also consider: advertising art director, photographer, artist/ illustrator, exhibition designer or webmaster.

I mpact

You may have a contract that states your hours will be nine to five, Monday to Friday. At times, however, you would be expected to be flexible and work longer than this if there is a tight deadline to meet. You may find yourself travelling to visit clients and having to meet them at times that are convenient to the client rather than to you. As a junior designer, you are likely to find yourself working in an open plan environment with other designers.

E arnings Potential

There is a wide range of starting salaries depending on your age and experience, but you can expect to earn around £12,000 when you first start. This can rise to around £40,000 for a senior designer. There are good opportunities for experienced designers to work freelance, in which case your salary would depend on your skills, your ability to market yourself and the hours you are prepared to work.

F urther Information

The Chartered Society of Designers (CSD), London EC1N 8FH
Website: www.csd.org.uk

Your Creative Future Website: www.yourcreativefuture.org

Alternative/equivalent entrance requirements can include: ILC, IB, EB, NC/ND and many other similar international systems. For further details see the Equivalent Qualifications section in the Introduction.

What is Involved?

As a health and safety inspector, you would visit a wide variety of workplaces and other sites, including building sites, farms, factories, fairgrounds, schools and hospitals, to ensure that all aspects of relevant health and safety law are being upheld. You would be a civil servant, working for the Field Operations Directorate of the Health and Safety Executive (HSE). In seeking to protect the welfare of the workforce and the general public, you would have the power to arrive at premises, unannounced, to examine equipment and machinery, manufacturing processes and working methods, and write up a full report.

If you find evidence of unsafe practice, you would make recommendations for change to the employer and you would have the sanction, in extreme cases, of issuing a prohibition order – closing the premises until the required improvements are made – or even taking the employer to court. You would work alone for much of the time, although you would be part of a small team of six to eight inspectors, and you would have a fair degree of freedom to organise your own work within the overall limits set by your principal inspector.

Opportunities for Training

You would have to complete a two-year training course, the first year of which would be probationary. HSE training is carried out mainly on the job, accompanying experienced inspectors. During the second year, you would study part-time at the University of Aston for the Diploma in Occupational Health and Safety and would have to complete the National or Scottish Vocational Qualification level 4 as a regulatory specialist. Once qualified, you would be expected to keep up to date with changes in the law and with developments in workplace technology.

Requirements

Although it is not actually laid down as an educational requirement, you would in practice be expected to come into the profession with a degree or equivalent qualification. You would have to pass a civil service test of observation, flexible thinking and reasoning and you should have completed a year or two of work experience.

The subject of your degree would not be crucial, although agricultural inspectors might be expected to have studied a related subject and other specialist inspectors might enter via industrial experience and professional qualification in an area such as engineering. Entry to a degree course would normally require two or three A level/AVCE/Advanced Higher, three or four Higher or equivalent qualifications. A full driving licence would be essential.

Kind of Person

An interest in people's welfare would be important. This is a very responsible job and you would need to be confident and tough enough to back your own judgment in potentially awkward situations. Good communication skills would be vital (particularly in the realms of tact and diplomacy), as you would be dealing with a wide variety of people at all levels of employment, and you would need to write clear and detailed reports.

You might have to present your findings in a court of law. You would need to be able to assimilate large amounts of knowledge (some of it quite technical) and apply this in practical situations. You would need good powers of observation and would have to pay great attention to detail.

B road Outlook

There is always a demand for health and safety inspectors, although the overall number employed by the Health and Safety Executive is not very large. You might like to specialise in one particular area or branch out into the field of policy making.

Inspectors are also employed by large organisations to advise on health and safety matters, while some experienced inspectors start up their own advisory consultancies or work on a freelance basis. Promotion can be gained into management positions.

R elated Occupations

You might also consider: environmental health officer, operational research/work study officer, human resources (personnel) manager or trading standards officer.

I mpact

You would normally work a standard five-day week, but you should be prepared to put in extra hours in the evening or at the weekend in cases of emergency. As well as being involved in a fair amount of travel, you might have to move around the country in order to gain further experience and/or promotion. You would also have to be prepared to visit some rather unsavoury places – possibly cold, wet, dangerous or noisy – and sometimes wear protective clothing.

E arnings Potential

You would be paid on the HSE national salary scale, starting at around £17,500 (just over £20,000 in London). Promotional increments could take your salary to over £32,000. Your earnings as a consultant in the private or freelance sectors would depend entirely on your reputation, experience and ability to negotiate suitable contracts.

F urther Information

Health and Safety Executive, Bootle L20 3QY Website: www.hse.gov.uk

Alternative/equivalent entrance requirements can include: ILC, IB, EB, NC/ND and many other similar international systems. For further details see the Equivalent Qualifications section in the Introduction.

What is Involved?

As a health service manager, you could work in the private or public sector, although you would be more likely to operate within the public National Health Service (NHS). Depending on your qualifications and experience, your post may be operational or based around policy-setting, planning or strategic development. Health service management is such a large and varied sector that your role could be that of an administrator running a doctor's surgery or that of a chief executive controlling a large hospital with a budget of many millions of pounds.

Opportunities for Training

It is possible to enter healthcare management at all the major stages: post-16, post-18 and post-college/university. Alternatively, you could enter after gaining experience in the voluntary or social care sectors. However, most managers are experienced healthcare professionals who move into managerial positions after achieving state registration in their specialised area. All staff in the NHS can work towards management qualifications through the MESOL programme (Management Education Scheme by Open Learning). As a new graduate in England, you could join the NHS Management Training Scheme. Split into general and financial management, the scheme includes a three-month induction and orientation to the NHS, two nine-month work placements and the opportunity to spend three months working outside the NHS either in the UK or abroad. On successful completion of the scheme, you would gain a postgraduate Diploma in Health Care Management from the University of Birmingham and a National Vocational Qualification (NVQ) level 4 in management. Scotland, Wales and Northern Ireland administer their own management training schemes.

Requirements

You could join the NHS at a clerical level without any formal qualifications and work your way up through the MESOL and/or NVQ routes (or the Scottish equivalent). For the NHS general management training scheme, you would need a degree in any subject or an equivalent professional qualification in a health or management-related discipline. For the financial management specialism, you must have a degree and evidence of ability in maths and English. A good way of checking that you meet the requirements is to try the NHS on-line self-assessment questionnaire, which takes around 15 minutes to complete.

Kind of Person

You would need excellent communication skills, the ability to lead through example and to influence others through persuasion and negotiation. Other qualities listed by the NHS include: *conceptual skills* – seeing the implications of actions and decisions; *analytical skills* – using and interpreting data and facts; *impact and influence* – making informed decisions, justifying your position and persuading others; *taking action* – planning your work, setting priorities and dealing with problems in a flexible and proactive way; *numerical skills* – understanding and applying figures.

B road Outlook

Entry to the NHS management training scheme is very competitive but successful completion should mark you out as a high flyer with considerable potential. The skills you gain could take you to a senior position in the NHS or on to other executive roles in the public and private sectors.

R elated Occupations

You might also consider: civil service administrator, local government administrator, accountant or human resources/personnel manager. Alternatively, you could begin by qualifying as a nurse, radiographer, physiotherapist, speech and language therapist or other healthcare professional.

I mpact

Advances in medical technology, tough expenditure targets, a high political profile and rising public expectations mean that, at the higher levels, this can be a very demanding job. You may need to move around the country to broaden your experience and seek promotion.

E arnings Potential

As a management trainee, you should start on around £17,500 (excluding London allowance), with the prospect of future earnings of £60,000–£80,000 as a director in a large health organisation or £100,000+ as a chief executive. If you are already working as a healthcare professional, you may be able to retain your existing salary while working through the management training programme.

F urther Information

Institute of Healthcare Management, London SW1W 0EB
Website: www.ihm.org.uk

NHS Management Training, London W2 3QR Website: www.mts.nhs.uk

Scottish Executive Health Department, Edinburgh EH1 3DG
Website: www.scotland.gov.uk

Centre for Health Leadership Wales, Pontyclun CF72 8YS
Website: www.chl.wales.nhs.uk

Northern Ireland Dept of Health, Belfast BT4 3SJ
Website: www.dhsspsni.gov.uk

Alternative/equivalent entrance requirements can include: ILC, IB, EB, NC/ND and many other similar international systems. For further details see the Equivalent Qualifications section in the Introduction.

What is Involved?

As a homoeopath, you would be working in a branch of complementary medicine based on the 'like cures like' concept, in which minute doses of a medicine that could produce similar symptoms in a healthy person are used to stimulate the body's own natural healing powers. You would examine a patient's whole physical, emotional and social state and look closely at those aspects of their lifestyle, including diet, posture, exercise and relationships, which could be contributing to their symptoms. The idea is that you would develop a clear picture of your patients and would match your remedy to each individual, encouraging them to take a major role in helping themselves. You could choose to specialise in homoeopathic treatment of animals.

Opportunities for Training

There are several bodies offering different training routes for homoeopaths. The Society of Homoeopaths, for example, lists 15 training centres in the UK offering courses lasting three years full-time and four years part-time. The courses are structured in four main ways:

• Part-time courses – four years, usually meeting for 10–15 weekends each year or for a similar number of two-day blocks mid-week

• Part-time courses with initial correspondence course – four years, with the first one or two years available through a correspondence course. The clinical education aspect would make your physical presence essential in the later stages

• Full-time courses – three years, with attendance typically for three days each week, during three terms each year

• Degree courses – similar to diploma courses but with additional academic components, often in the wider field of health studies

All routes would take you to the same status as a licensed homoeopath. You could become a registered member by completing a course successfully, practising for at least a year and presenting cases for inspection by the society. The Faculty of Homoeopathy, on the other hand, promotes training at five centres but only if you are already a qualified healthcare professional, such as a doctor, dentist, vet, pharmacist, podiatrist or nurse.

Requirements

You would normally need five GCSE/S Grade passes at A-C/1-3 and three A level/AVCE/Advanced Higher, four Higher or equivalent qualifications, preferably including biology or human biology, chemistry and physics, for entry to a course accredited by the Society. (Vocational subjects which could be helpful: health and social care, science, care/health.)

Late entry is common, especially if you have already met the registration requirements of a conventional healthcare profession and wish to join the faculty as outlined above.

Kind of Person

You would need excellent interpersonal skills, particularly when it comes to

142

listening and explaining. You should have a genuine desire to help people (or animals), be confident and emotionally stable yourself and able to treat your patients with objectivity. You would need to assess conditions, offer clear advice and be able to recognise when a patient needs referral to a conventional practitioner. As you are likely to be self-employed, you would need sufficient commercial awareness to run your own business.

B road Outlook

Complementary medicine has expanded rapidly in the last twenty years and homoeopathy has steadily acquired respect and recognition by the NHS. You may work in private hospitals or clinics or in the NHS with patients recommended to you by their GPs.

Demand continues to increase, with opportunities throughout the UK.

R elated Occupations

You may choose to qualify first as a conventional healthcare professional such as doctor, dentist, vet, pharmacist, podiatrist, nurse or health visitor. Alternatively, you may wish to consider other specialisms in complementary medicine such as aromatherapist, osteopath, chiropractor, herbalist or naturopath.

I mpact

As most homoeopaths are self-employed, you could enjoy considerable flexibility both in the hours you choose to work and the places you work in. On the other hand, there are few promotion prospects, fluctuations in demand for treatment and the costs to consider of maintaining a therapy room and associated expenses.

You may find that patients are most keen to see you when they are not themselves at work, keeping you busy in the evening and at weekends.

E arnings Potential

Your income would depend on how many people you see and how much you charge. Earnings vary considerably, usually based on charges of between £25 and £60 per hour.

F urther Information

The Faculty of Homoeopathy, London EC1R OAA
Website: www.trusthomeopathy.org/faculty

The Society of Homoeopaths, Northampton, NN1 4HU
Website: www.homeopathy-soh.org

The Homoeopathic Medical Association, Kent, DA12 5DZ
Website: http://www.the-hma.org

Alternative/equivalent entrance requirements can include: ILC, IB, EB, NC/ND and many other similar international systems. For further details see the Equivalent Qualifications section in the Introduction.

143

What is Involved?

There are two main branches of horticulture: commercial and amenity, sometimes referred to as production and non-production horticulture respectively.

As a **commercial horticultural manager,** you would be involved in the production for sale of fruit, vegetables, glasshouse crops, mushrooms, herbs, pot plants, shrubs, trees, bulbs and flowers. As a manager you would decide what to grow, bearing in mind local growing conditions and your knowledge of the market. You would have to recruit the right staff, buy the seeds, plants and other materials needed for the next crop cycle, keep detailed planting and cropping records, control your finances and deliver consistent product quality to your customers at competitive prices.

As an **amenity horticultural manager**, you would be responsible for planning and maintaining large public parks, sports grounds, private estates and green spaces in towns and cities. Your role as a manager might include determining how to make your park or garden attractive and accessible, supervising the work of gardening staff, controlling the budget for park maintenance, publicising your amenity and keeping abreast of plants that are currently in vogue. You would also normally want to be actively involved with the practicalities of digging, sowing, lopping, grass-cutting and so on.

Opportunities for Training

There are many possible training routes, ranging from degree and postgraduate courses through specialist qualifications offered by the Royal Horticultural Society or the Royal Botanic Gardens to part-time National/ Scottish Vocational Qualifications. Degree courses in horticulture normally take three years full-time or four years if they include a 'sandwich' of industrial experience. They may specialise in commercial or amenity horticulture, so it is important to read prospectuses carefully before you apply. All courses would normally include the underlying science of horticulture, crop characteristics, growing techniques and marketing and finance. Higher national diploma (HND) courses cover similar ground at a more practical level.

Requirements

For a degree course, you would normally need two or three A level/ AVCE/Advanced Higher, four Higher or equivalent qualifications in one or two sciences, especially chemistry and biology; for the HND route, one or two A level/AVCE/Advanced Higher, two to three Higher or equivalent, would be required. For either route, your application should ideally be supported by periods of work experience in horticultural or agricultural organisations. There are no entry requirements for some of the specialist qualifications.

Kind of Person

You would need to be physically robust, very interested in the cultivation of plants, good at teamwork and willing put up with irregular hours depending on the seasons of the year and the weather. You would need a strong sense of priorities in meeting essential deadlines and a firm grasp of production costing, aided by good numeracy and book-keeping/accounting skills and a reasonable level of computer literacy. Communication skills would be essential in dealing with clients and suppliers and in clearly explaining your requirements to staff.

B road Outlook

Opportunities are forecast to increase in commercial horticulture. Ever-growing technological demands are creating an ongoing requirement for higher-level skills in information and production technologies as well as the ability to understand and operate complex production systems. There is also a demand for business management and marketing abilities. The amenity side is slightly less positive, with local authorities in particular cutting back staffing levels. Specialised skills associated with historic gardens, restoration and environmental conservation are, however, in increasing demand.

R elated Occupations

You might also consider: landscape architect, forest manager, countryside conservation officer or countryside ranger/warden.

I mpact

You would normally work a theoretical 39-hour week but you might at times have to tailor your hours to fit the demands of particular growing seasons. Many people in horticulture like to start work early in the morning to make the most of daylight hours. Sports grounds and public gardens are often busiest at the weekend. In setting up your own nursery or garden centre, enormous efforts and sacrifices would be essential, with often a seven-day week, in order to meet strong weekend demand.

E arnings Potential

As a junior manager, you would start at between £11,000 and £15,000, rising to £16,000 to £30,000 as a senior manager within a well-established company. The rewards for owner managers can be considerably greater.

F urther Information

Lantra, Warwickshire CV8 2LG Website: www.lantra.co.uk

The Royal Botanic Garden, Kew, Richmond TW9 3AB
Website: www.rbgkew.org.uk

The Royal Botanic Garden, Edinburgh EH3 5LR Website: www.rbge.org.uk

Institute of Horticulture, London SW1X 8PS
Website: www.horticulture.org.uk

The Royal Horticultural Society, Wisley GU23 6QB
Website: www.rhs.org.uk

Alternative/equivalent entrance requirements can include: ILC, IB, EB, NC/ND and many other similar international systems. For further details see the Equivalent Qualifications section in the Introduction.

What is Involved?

Hotels vary enormously in size and scope but your job as a hotel manager would include ensuring that the day-to-day running of the establishment is well organised and efficient and that guests enjoy using your services.

You might have responsibility for accommodation, food and drink, conferences, special events and leisure facilities. You could be in overall control of every department, with a number of assistants, or you might have to manage several of these responsibilities yourself, especially in a smaller hotel.

Opportunities for Training

There is no single training route for hotel management and you do not always need academic qualifications. You may decide, for example, to gain experience at a lower level and work your way up, or you may enter the industry from an allied occupation such as human resources, accountancy or restaurant management. If, however, you want to obtain direct entry to a hotel management trainee scheme, you would do well to consider a relevant higher national diploma (HND) or degree course.

The HND in Hospitality Management would take two or three years, while a similar degree would take three or four years to complete. Alternatively, you could consider the two-year professional certificate offered by the Hotel and Catering International Management Association (HCIMA).

Requirements

To enter a hospitality/hotel management degree course, you would need two or three A level/AVCE/Advanced Higher, three or four Higher or equivalent qualifications, together with a minimum of five GCSE/S Grade passes A-C/1-3.

Entry to an HND course would require a minimum one A level/AVCE/Advanced Higher, two Higher or equivalent qualification, together with four GCSE/S Grade passes A-C/1-3. It is vital to check each institution's entry requirements and it would help to obtain work experience before applying. (A relevant AVCE/Higher: hospitality/catering.)

Kind of Person

You should be able to communicate effectively with other people, both staff and guests, and take a keen interest in their welfare and comfort. You would need to be tough, both physically and mentally, to cope with long hours and the need to be constantly available for decision making and problem solving.

You should also be well versed in IT, with acute business awareness, good organisational skills and the ability to deal with financial matters. A smart appearance would be essential and knowledge of foreign languages would certainly be an asset.

B road Outlook

Although competition for hotel manager positions is intense, the hospitality industry usually has no shortage of opportunities on offer. Much importance is placed on experience and proven performance. Managers of small hotels can be promoted to jobs in larger or more prestigious establishments, or to responsible jobs in the administration of chains of hotels.

Working for a hotel chain could lead to travel or work abroad. You may need to move several times to develop your career, while there is always the prospect of using your experience to set up your own guest house or hotel.

R elated Occupations

You might also consider: events and conferences organiser, leisure services manager, marketing executive, personnel (human resources) manager, public relations officer, restaurant manager or travel and tourism consultant.

I mpact

As a hotel manager you would be expected to work long hours, including regular evening and weekend commitments. If you worked in a small hotel or owned your own establishment, you would probably have to accept that the work could sometimes even spread over 24 hours, with considerable implications for your family and social life. Accommodation is often provided as part of the job but that can make it difficult for you ever to be completely off duty.

E arnings Potential

There is a wide range of salaries, according to the size and type of hotel you would be working in and the level of management responsibility you achieve. Some managers can receive profits or performance bonuses, and there could be financial advantages to living in (although there could be obvious disadvantages as well).

You might start as a trainee manager on about £10,000. This could rise to around £15,000 as a deputy manager and £30,000 or more for an experienced general manager.

F urther Information

Hospitality Training Foundation, London, W5 5DB Website: www.htf.org.uk

Hotel and Catering International Management Association, London SW17 7HN Website: www.hcima.org.uk

Springboard, London WC2H 8LP Website: www.springboarduk.org.uk

Alternative/equivalent entrance requirements can include: ILC, IB, EB, NC/ND and many other similar international systems. For further details see the Equivalent Qualifications section in the Introduction.

What is Involved?

Your job as a human resources (HR) or personnel manager would focus on getting the best from the people who work in your organisation, from selecting the right people in the first place to managing them effectively when they are in post. The exact nature of your work would depend on what your organisation does, whether it is in the private or public sector, how large it is and whether it has strong union representation.

However, common issues would include understanding what your organisation needs in terms of workforce skills and experience, planning future recruitment and training and devising policies for health and safety, equal opportunities, communication, training and development, pay and conditions of employment. You might also design procedures to measure performance, handle complaints, maintain discipline and keep employee records.

You could operate as a generalist across all of these areas or you could choose to specialise in a topic such as health and safety, employee relations or recruitment and selection.

Opportunities for Training

There is no single route into HR management but a degree or higher national diploma (HND) would be a good starting point. Any subject would be acceptable but business studies, law or psychology could be particularly relevant and may give some exemption from the professional qualifications awarded by the Chartered Institute of Personnel and Development (CIPD). Your goal, whether achieved by exemption or by full- or part-time study, would be graduate membership of the CIPD. Many large organisations also offer their own in-house training schemes.

Requirements

You would normally need two or three A level/AVCE/Advanced Higher, three or four Higher or equivalent qualifications, together with five GCSE/S Grade passes A-C/1-3, for degree course entry. HND entry would require at least one A level/AVCE/Advanced Higher, two Higher or equivalent qualifications, together with similar GCSE/S Grade passes.

Relevant experience is always regarded as important.

Kind of Person

You should be genuinely interested in the way people work and behave. In order to succeed, you would have to be able to deal with many different situations in a fair and even-handed way, balancing the needs of each individual employee against the overall interests of the organisation. Tackling issues such as discipline or redundancy can be extremely stressful.

Excellent communication skills, both oral and written, would be necessary, together with willingness to work in a team, both as a leader and member. Tact, discretion and an understanding of the need for complete confidentiality when dealing with people's personal details would be essential.

B road Outlook

Competition for the available vacancies, especially for inexperienced graduates, continues to be very keen. Indeed, some employers indicate that they have a higher percentage of applications for HR work than any other function.

All kinds of organisations employ HR professionals, including banks, local government, health services, airlines, hotels, retail organisations and manufacturing industries. Two relatively new areas are further and higher education institutions and the health service. Many of these organisations are now self-governing, employ their own staff and are responsible for their own budgets.

You might start out as a trainee manager and work your way up the ladder in one organisation or move to a larger one with more scope. With sufficient experience, you might set up your own business, offering specialist recruitment, training or other services. You could have the opportunity to travel, if you work for a multi-national organisation.

R elated Occupations

You might also consider: personal or careers adviser, occupational psychologist, office manager, recruitment consultant or training consultant.

I mpact

You would normally work the usual office hours from Monday to Friday, though you might have to work overtime at certain times, for interviewing or attending meetings. Weekend work would be unusual.

E arnings Potential

Starting salaries paid to graduates entering HR traineeships immediately after a first degree are very similar to those entering other trainee posts. Salaries paid by local authorities and the smaller retailers show a tendency to be lower than those paid by large manufacturing firms and public corporations. Graduates with relevant postgraduate qualifications or experience may be able to command slightly higher starting salaries.

A survey carried out in 1999/2000 showed the following average earnings: Assistant HR Officer £16,700; HR Officer £21,000; Senior HR Officer £25,959; HR Manager £32,500; HR Director £55,000.

F urther Information

The Chartered Institute of Personnel and Development, London SW19 4UX
Website: www.cipd.co.uk

Alternative/equivalent entrance requirements can include: ILC, IB, EB, NC/ND and many other similar international systems. For further details see the Equivalent Qualifications section in the Introduction.

What is Involved?

Working as a hydrographic or marine surveyor, you would be concerned with mapping the vast expanse of the earth's surface that is underwater. You might measure and chart the seabed or survey underwater for mineral resources, gas and oil deposits. You could get involved with land reclamation schemes, with dredging or with defining international boundaries. You might also survey ports, oceans, channels and inland waterways.

Another area in which you could become involved is the search for hazards to shipping, such as rocks or wrecks, strong currents and tides. You would be likely to use advanced technological equipment, including sonar scanning, to obtain information about the seabed and aerial or satellite photography for mapping and charting. In common with all measurement at sea, precise positioning is essential and you would use a range of systems, from lasers for short-range, very high accuracy work to global satellite navigation systems for positioning throughout the world's oceans.

Most of the processing and presentation of the data collected at sea is undertaken using computers. In many cases survey data can be processed on board ship, providing immediate access to the end product charts and maps. Certain types of survey data processing would require access to large computing resources and very elaborate processing software.

Opportunities for Training

Hydrographic surveying is part of the geomatics faculty of the Royal Institution of Chartered Surveyors (RICS). There are various routes to full RICS membership but the most likely in this case would to take an accredited degree or postgraduate course in hydrographic surveying or a similar subject with a hydrographic option. On completion of your accredited course, you would be eligible to move to the two-year RICS structured training stage, concluding with an RICS professional assessment interview known as the Assessment of Professional Competence (APC).

Requirements

You would normally need three A level/AVCE/Advanced Higher, four Higher or equivalent qualifications to enter an accredited degree in a surveying discipline, together with five GCSE/S Grade passes A-C/1-3, including English and maths.

You would find it helpful to have a driving licence and RYA powerboat qualifications.

Kind of Person

You would need to be quite technically minded in order to operate and understand all the sophisticated equipment involved. The use of computers is also an important aspect of this work. You would need to be physically robust and able to cope with being at sea in all kinds of weather. You may be out on a boat for extended periods of time.

Whilst some of your time would be spent out on location, you would also

150

need to be prepared to work in an office, usually with a computer, analysing data and writing up and explaining the results of your surveys. You are likely to be part of a team and at times this could be an international team of professionals. As you may be working in confined conditions on a boat for several days at a time, you would need to be tolerant of others.

B road Outlook

Career opportunities are good in both the private and public sector. Many of the opportunities in the private sector are associated with the offshore oil and gas industry, which is exploring ever-deeper waters for hydrocarbon reserves, and there are a number of specialist marine survey companies. Many of the companies and organisations concerned with marine survey operate on a worldwide basis and hence offer careers with considerable opportunity for overseas travel.

The Royal Navy also employs quite a number of hydrographic surveyors as naval officers.

R elated Occupations

You might be interested in another specialist career in surveying, such as mineral or land surveyor, or in another career involving the sea, such as oceanographer or marine biologist. Alternatively, you might consider a career as a cartographer or meteorologist.

I mpact

You would need to be prepared to work at sea in hostile environments when the weather is rough, or even when it is extremely hot. You are likely to have to spend extended periods of time away from home, which could sometimes make family and social life difficult.

E arnings Potential

As a new graduate, you could expect to earn in the region of £19,000. This can rise to above £60,000 with experience or as a partner or senior executive. You may be paid extra when you are spending extended time away from home on ship. If you choose to join the Royal Navy as a hydrographic surveyor, your salary would be set by the normal officer pay scales.

F urther Information

The Royal Institution of Chartered Surveyors (RICS), Coventry CV4 8JE
Website www.rics.org.uk

The Society for Underwater Technology, London EC3 7JN
Website www.sut.org.uk

The Hydrographic Society, Dagenham RM8 2AS
Website www.hydrographicsociety.org

Alternative/equivalent entrance requirements can include: ILC, IB, EB, NC/ND and many other similar international systems. For further details see the Equivalent Qualifications section in the Introduction.

151

What is Involved?

As a newly qualified chemistry graduate, you could decide to work in such industries as chemicals and pharmaceuticals, food and drinks, oil refining or agricultural chemicals and polymers. Alternatively, you could become an analyst in the water industry, join one of the environmental protection agencies or enter the general graduate employment market.

You could go into *research and development* in industry. Research is normally carried out in teams with other scientists, seeking to discover new chemical entities such as a new drug, enzyme or plastic. Development is more about turning research knowledge into commercially valuable products to meet customers' needs. This requires skills beyond chemical knowledge, such as marketing, economics, safety and management.

You could go into *production management*, ensuring that the manufacturing process is run efficiently and cost effectively, that chemical plant operatives are given adequate supervision and that production schedules are maintained.

Alternatively, you could opt for UK or export *sales* or you could provide *techno-commercial support* for a range of your company's products. In most of these cases, your insight and understanding of chemistry would be of great advantage.

Opportunities for Training

Many universities have degree courses in chemistry, biochemistry, pharmacology and similar subjects and these usually take between three and four years of full-time study. It is also possible to read chemistry as a joint honours degree with a range of different subjects. For example, it might be useful to read chemistry and a foreign language, which could be beneficial for working on chemical exports, or perhaps chemistry and law for organising legal agreements to make sure new discoveries are protected by patent and are economically viable.

Requirements

A levels/AVCE/Advanced Higher or Higher qualifications in chemistry and ideally in maths or another science are likely to be required for entry to a chemistry degree. However, if you choose to combine chemistry with a very popular subject, such as law, you may need to obtain higher grades than are required for chemistry alone. It is possible for students without these qualifications to take a foundation course before starting their degree, either at a university or a college of further education.

Kind of Person

In order to be successful as a chemist, you would need to have a technically enquiring mind. You would want to know why chemical reactions occur and what the effects of these changes might be. Chemistry is an investigative science, so you would need to have an analytical approach to problem solving. You would be required to be extremely accurate in measuring and recording your results.

152

In addition to your scientific and intellectual abilities, you would need to communicate with a wide range of other people. You are likely to be working as part of a team and may find yourself supervising production workers, technicians or sales staff. You would need to communicate in technical or sales discussions and requests for further information and samples in regular written reports to your colleagues.

B road Outlook

There are good prospects of employment for chemists in all areas. Should you decide that you want to continue with postgraduate study, it is sometimes possible to get your research funded by your company once you start. Depending on the type of career you choose to pursue, you could find yourself working in a chemical production plant, a laboratory or an office.

Chemistry graduates also work in completely unrelated fields such as chartered accountancy, merchant banking, investment banking, stock market analysis, financial exchange and law, where their powers of numerical analysis can prove valuable.

R elated Occupations

You might consider other careers in the field of chemistry, such as chemical analyst, dietitian, pharmacologist, forensic scientist, biochemist, microbiologist or pathologist.

I mpact

Although you are likely to work office hours mainly during the week, you may at times need to work late and in production management to cover shift work. You may have tight deadlines to meet, a report may be needed to brief a senior director or a piece of research may require you to work extra hours to complete it. In addition, you would be expected to keep up to date with the numerous developments in your subject, which would involve reading scientific and technical literature in your own time.

E arnings Potential

As a scientist who has recently graduated, you might expect to earn £14,000 to £16,000 initially. This could rise to £50,000 and beyond in some industries when you start to take on managerial responsibilities.

F urther Information

The Royal Society of Chemistry, London W1V 0BN Website: www.rsc.org

Alternative/equivalent entrance requirements can include: ILC, IB, EB, NC/ND and many other similar international systems. For further details see the Equivalent Qualifications section in the Introduction.

What is Involved?

As an industrial or product designer, you could design almost any sort of product from toys, toasters, television sets or washing machines to bicycles, cars and even spacecraft. You would be given a design brief and would have to consider not only the aesthetic appeal of the product but also its viability in terms of cost, materials used, ease of manufacture, safety and marketability. You would quite often be working in a team of designers but, even if you were working alone, you would be in constant consultation with other professionals, such as engineers, manufacturers, computer experts and marketing managers, as well as with your client.

You would prepare plans (often computer-generated) with models for inspection and discussion, and would have to be prepared to modify them as necessary. You would normally be based in a design studio or workshop. Some industrial or product designers have extensive knowledge of engineering and manufacturing techniques, and many tend to concentrate on particular technical areas of design work.

You may also be involved in packaging design, specialising in finding ways of making products look attractive while you protect them until they are safely in the hands of the consumer.

Opportunities for Training

While it is not essential, the best-established training route is a degree or higher national diploma (HND) in a design-based subject. The usual way into this is via a foundation course in art and design (general year in Scotland). Universities and art colleges offer many relevant courses, with varying titles but usually classified under a heading such as 'three-dimensional design'.

Requirements

For entry to a one-year art foundation course in England or Wales, you would need a good portfolio of work, relevant A level/AVCE/Advanced Higher, Higher or equivalent qualifications, together with five GCSE/S Grade passes A-C/1-3. You could then progress to your chosen HND or degree course. In Scotland, the first year of a four-year degree is broadly similar to the foundation course.

Again, you would need a good portfolio of work, together with two A level/ AVCE/Advanced Higher, three Higher or equivalent qualifications. Some universities and colleges place a greater emphasis on the technological aspects of industrial/product design and may require passes in maths or physics, so you must check prospectuses very carefully. Equally, some admissions staff for art and design courses could accept you purely on the strength of an exceptionally good portfolio of work.

Kind of Person

You would need a high degree of artistic, creative talent but this would have to be matched with an appreciation of the various constraints, particularly those of attractive appearance and good function versus cost of production and materials. You should be able to persuade others of your point of view, but you should also be able to take criticism and suggestions for improvement, and be happy working as part of a team.

You should have a good grounding in maths and an understanding of basic engineering principles and properties of engineering materials. A high level of computer proficiency would be essential to take advantage of the design software tailor-made for this field. Poor colour vision would limit your potential in industrial/product design but would not necessarily be a complete barrier.

B road Outlook

As manufacturers have become more conscious of the marketability of good design, so the demand for industrial and product designers has increased, particularly for those with specialised knowledge of technology. Some large companies have their own design departments, while others employ design consultancies. Experienced designers also work on a freelance basis, having set up their own businesses.

R elated Occupations

You might also consider: architect, mechanical engineer, graphic designer, interior designer, theatre, television and film set designer.

I mpact

Designers employed by a company usually work normal office hours, but you would need to be prepared to work in the evenings and at the weekend if there were deadlines to be met. If you work as a freelance you would have to face the possibility of financial insecurity until you become established.

E arnings Potential

Earnings vary a great deal, depending on the nature of the work, location and type of employer. Trainees working in-house could start at around £15,000, with those in consultancies getting more. Senior designers and freelancers can earn around £60,000 or more.

F urther Information

Your Creative Future Website: www.yourcreativefuture.com

The Institute of Engineering Designers, Westbury BA13 3TA
Website: www.ied.org.uk

The Design Council, London WC2E 7DL
Website: www.designcouncil.org.uk

The Chartered Society of Designers, London SE1 3YY
Website: www.csd.org.uk

Alternative/equivalent entrance requirements can include: ILC, IB, EB, NC/ND and many other similar international systems. For further details see the Equivalent Qualifications section in the Introduction.

What is Involved?

As an insurance broker, you would be an independent expert helping clients decide what sort of insurance cover they need, where to look for it and how much they should pay for it. You would use your knowledge and experience to assess risks thoroughly and accurately, and to find the appropriate policy or policies. You must put the interests of your client first, even though it is the insurance companies who pay you commission for the business you put in their direction. The range of insurance products is expanding all the time and it is possible to insure virtually anything, from cars, ships and aeroplanes to pets, pianists' hands and even the risks associated with a country's politics. You would have to know who to contact among over 700 insurance companies. This could include Lloyd's, a London market consisting of individuals or syndicates offering insurance cover, but not all brokers are authorised to do this.

You would normally be able to deal instantly with straightforward cases, such as motor insurance, but more complex risks would involve you in compiling a detailed report to present to the underwriters. You would use the report to negotiate cover with the insurers and obtain a quotation for your client. For very large risks, such as ships and aircraft, the risk is spread among a number of insurers, with each underwriter accepting only a small percentage of the risk. You would then have to contact many different insurers to obtain full cover for your client.

Opportunities for Training

Training for insurance brokers is generally provided in-house, under the supervision of experienced staff. In order to gain promotion, you would find it useful to take examinations set by the British Insurance Brokers Association (BIBA) or the Chartered Insurance Institute (CII). These can take up to three years to complete and some employers would allow you time off for study. If you work for a Lloyd's brokers, you would have to sit the Lloyd's Introductory Test within 15 months of starting.

Requirements

Whilst there are no specific educational requirements, many organisations prefer graduates or A level/AVCE/Advanced Higher, Higher or equivalent students for their trainee broker positions. However, a great deal of emphasis is placed on personal characteristics, making it possible to join a broking firm as a 16 year-old school leaver and progress to a post with quite considerable responsibility. For entry to a degree course, you would need two or three A level/AVCE/Advanced Higher, three or four Higher or equivalent qualifications.

Kind of Person

You would need good communication skills, both oral and written, since you would be dealing with a wide variety of people and often explaining complex matters. The information in a report must be presented to the underwriter logically and clearly, with great attention to detail. When approaching underwriters, you would require confidence and good negotiating skills. Numeracy would also be important. Another essential quality would be honesty, together with discretion, since you could be dealing with confidential and sensitive issues. You would benefit from an outgoing personality and business flair. In particular, you would need an analytical mind and the ability to assimilate large amounts of information. Much of your work would be on computer, so good IT skills would be essential.

B *road Outlook*

Opportunities for brokers are increasing in line with the overall growth of the insurance market. You could develop your career by taking on greater responsibility as your experience increases, or you might choose to specialise in particular insurance fields, such as marine and aviation or life and pension. You could eventually set up your own business or act as a consultant.

R *elated Occupations*

You might also consider: insurance underwriter, accountant, actuary, loss adjuster, stockbroker, banking executive or financial adviser.

I *mpact*

Broking can be very demanding and at times frustrating when things go wrong and, despite hard work, a deal is lost. You would have to be persistent and calm even when underwriters are being uncooperative or clients impatient. You would usually work normal office hours during a five-day week, but you would need to be prepared to work in the evenings or at the weekend to meet particular clients.

E *arnings Potential*

You could expect to earn around £18,000 (more in London) as a graduate trainee. Earnings of experienced brokers vary widely, according to the scope and responsibility of their work and their performance. At the top end, a top broker in the City of London could earn well over £60,000.

F *urther Information*

The Chartered Insurance Institute, London EC2V 7HY
Website: www.cii.co.uk

British Insurance Brokers Association, London EC3A 7NT
Website: www.biba.org.uk

Financial Services Authority, London E14 5HS Website: www.fsa.gov.uk

Alternative/equivalent entrance requirements can include: ILC, IB, EB, NC/ND and many other similar international systems. For further details see the Equivalent Qualifications section in the Introduction.

What is Involved?

As an insurance underwriter, you would work for one of the major insurance companies or Lloyd's of London, assessing the extent of any given risk and deciding whether your organisation should accept it and on what terms. You would have to determine the appropriate premium for the risk, setting an amount high enough to reflect the potential loss that could result but low enough to attract the business away from any competitors.

In order to carry out these tasks, you would have to build up a thorough understanding of the risks you handle. In the early stages of your career, the risks you underwrite would be those for which there are well-established statistical data and for which rating guides are available. However, with more complex or more unusual risks, you would rely on your skill and the experience to assess and rate risks appropriately.

You could specialise in, for example, large-scale risks in marine or aviation insurance or you could focus on smaller-scale but hugely valuable sectors such as motor car, life or property insurance. Lloyd's itself is an insurance marketplace, where underwriters and brokers meet to agree terms on what might be very straightforward or highly unusual or complicated risks.

Opportunities for Training

Training for insurance underwriters is usually in-house, under the supervision of experienced underwriters, or by moving from department to department to learn how premiums are charged, and claims checked and paid out. You can study by day release, evening classes or distance learning for the Associate examination of the Chartered Insurance Institute (CII), which is not essential but could be valuable when seeking promotion. To work for a Lloyd's company, you would have to pass the Lloyd's Introductory Test within 15 months of starting there.

Requirements

Most underwriting trainees are school and college leavers with two A level/AVCE/Advanced Higher, three Higher or equivalent qualifications, but increasing numbers of graduates are joining the insurance industry. As there is no school or degree subject which would fully equip you for an underwriting career, employers are unlikely to specify any particular course of study. However, subjects such as business studies, economics, law, science and engineering can be helpful, as can some interest in biology, physiology or medical matters for life underwriting. Some universities offer degrees in insurance, business studies or financial services with modules giving partial exemption from the CII Associate examinations. You could, on the other hand, enter a clerical post in an underwriting department with GCSE/S Grade passes at A-C/1-3, including English and mathematics, and work your way up, with experience, training and study for further academic or vocational examinations, to an underwriting position.

Kind of Person

You would need to be decisive and capable of justifying your decisions with

158

logical and sound argument. Given that you would often be dealing with extremely confidential information about an individual or organisation seeking insurance protection, you must be able to handle these details with the utmost discretion. For the more unusual risks, the ability to think and solve problems creatively could be extremely valuable. You would need a logical, analytical and retentive mind and the ability to take into account many different factors before making decisions. You would need to feel confident when dealing with numerical and statistical data, and would need to communicate clearly with actuaries, insurance technicians and other members of your team. It would be vital to be able to write up contracts covering the terms and conditions of your underwriting agreements.

B road Outlook

The insurance industry is changing and many companies now have call centres and websites to deal with straightforward risks, cutting out some of the traditional work of the underwriting department. There are still, however, good career opportunities in over 700 insurance companies, including household name groups, small specialist insurers and Lloyd's of London.

R elated Occupations

You might also consider: insurance broker, actuary, accountant, banking executive, loss adjuster, stockbroker, surveyor or financial adviser.

I mpact

Underwriting can be a very intense way of life, with a huge responsibility to get your quotations right and avoid unacceptable levels of loss. This calls for courage and confidence and the ability to accept worry and stress when large claims are made. Otherwise normal office hours should apply with very little disruption of your family and social life, although you may have to work unsocial hours if you need to be available to answer the more unusual call centre enquiries.

E arnings Potential

You could expect to earn up to £16,000 (more in London) as a graduate trainee. Your salary should increase rapidly with experience, increased responsibility and successful performance. At the top end, as a senior Lloyd's underwriter on a performance-linked salary, you might expect to earn in excess of £250,000 a year.

F urther Information

The Chartered Insurance Institute, London EC2V 7HY
Website: www.cii.co.uk

Alternative/equivalent entrance requirements can include: ILC, IB, EB, NC/ND and many other similar international systems. For further details see the Equivalent Qualifications section in the Introduction.

What is Involved?

Interiors are big business. As an interior designer, you could be hired to create a desirable ambiance in a pub, club or restaurant to attract big-spending customers. You could be working with a chain of DIY stores to market a new range of wallcoverings, paint effects or soft furnishings. You could be adding a touch of designer style to private homes. In work that is often more technical than is suggested by TV programmes such as 'Changing Rooms', you would liaise with your clients (or their architects) about design schemes to take account of the purpose of the space involved, the needs of the people using it, their budgets and timescales. Your brief may include curtains, carpets, furniture, lighting, fixtures and fittings.

This would involve design sketches, mock-ups, samples of fabrics and colour schemes and sourcing items such as light fittings. You would then oversee your projects, which would involve liaising with contractors. Closely associated specialist design work is also available in film, television and theatre set design; exhibition and display design; and any other interior space, from an aeroplane to a department store. You could work freelance, for an interior design consultancy, within an architectural practice or for a large hotel or store group or furniture manufacturer.

Opportunities for Training

Most entrants have a formal qualification in art and design. There are numerous degree courses in interior design, which are available either as specialist courses or as an element in other art and design courses. There are also Higher National Certificates/Diplomas and postgraduate courses.

Requirements

To obtain entry to an art and design course, you would usually have completed a foundation course in art and design (general year in Scotland). The foundation courses in England and Wales take two years for students aged 16 with five GCSE/S Grade passes A-C/1-3, or one year for students aged 17, who might also have an A level/AVCE/Advanced Higher, Higher or equivalent qualification in a relevant subject. In most cases, a good portfolio of your best artistic work is more important than exam passes. Progression to a degree course would then be via interview, at which your portfolio would be carefully examined by the staff and questions asked.

Kind of Person

As a designer you would not have as much of a free hand as you would as an artist. You would have to meet your clients' needs and wishes, which can sometimes be difficult for creative people, and you would need to be tactful and persuasive but be prepared to compromise when it is wise to do so. You would need good drawing skills and must be able to communicate your ideas to the client. Team working skills would also be important, together with a willingness to meet deadlines.

You would need to be practical as well as creative, have a technical understanding of the materials you are working with and the sensitivity to assess their suitability for use. You would need a keen interest in fashion and an eye for colour, texture and pattern.

B road Outlook

Interior design is seen as a glamorous profession and demand for jobs outstrips supply, although there is always a place for good creative talent. Most entrants start as an assistant in order to learn the practical aspects of the work, which can be for the company sector or for private clients. Self-employment is an option for experienced and established designers.

R elated Occupations

You might also consider: architect, artist/illustrator, fashion designer, graphic designer or industrial product designer.

I mpact

As an interior designer, you would be working both in a studio and on site as well as visiting clients in their homes. Designs have to be prepared, discussed and changed; furniture, fittings, fabrics and colour schemes have to be agreed…which is all very time consuming and calls for much patience, charm and diplomacy.

Although the work tends to be done in regular office hours, there are always deadlines to meet and contractors to engage and supervise, which could involve working evenings and weekends. Then there is the problem of finding time to assess work, produce written quotations, compete for prestigious contracts with hotels, restaurants, new housing estates, time-shares, property, land developments, holiday chalets and furnished flats, without which business would grind to a halt.

E arnings Potential

Earnings would vary widely, depending on your talent, your location and who you are working for. As an assistant designer, you could expect to earn between £17,000 and £20,000. You could earn considerably more if you manage to make a name for yourself.

F urther Information

Interior Decorators and Designers Association, London SW10 0XE
Website: www.idda.co.uk

Your creative future Website: www.yourcreativefuture.org.uk

Alternative/equivalent entrance requirements can include: ILC, IB, EB, NC/ND and many other similar international systems. For further details see the Equivalent Qualifications section in the Introduction.

What is Involved?

As an interpreter, you would be a highly skilled linguist specialising in the spoken word. You could be involved in simultaneous or consecutive interpreting, usually translating into your mother tongue from one or several other languages. Simultaneous interpreters generally work from a soundproof booth at multi-language conferences, listening to speeches through headphones and relaying an instant translation into a microphone; at smaller meetings, for one or two people and certain court proceedings, direct whispering may replace the technology. Consecutive interpreting occurs when the speaker pauses at intervals to allow you to translate what has been said into the target language. You might need to take notes in order not to forget anything that the speaker has said.

You would be expected to have a broad understanding of the cultural, technical, professional or practical issues under discussion, with the requisite vocabulary in the target language to convey what is necessary. Linguistic skills alone would not be enough.

Opportunities for Training

You would normally need a degree in interpreting or in languages followed by a postgraduate course. Your training should give you language laboratory practice in interpreting techniques, experience of technical vocabulary, note-taking and memorising exercises and practical work experience. You may be expected to work towards the National/Scottish Vocational Qualifications (N/SVQ) in interpreting and you would usually need to join and pass the examinations of professional organisations such as the International Association of Conference Interpreters (AIIC), the Institute of Linguists (IOL) and/or the Institute of Translation and Interpreting (ITI).

Requirements

You would need two or three A level/Advanced Higher or three or four Higher passes (or equivalent) for degree entry, including one or more foreign languages. At least a year of your course should be spent in another country. The N/SVQ route does not require any formal academic qualifications and could prove attractive if you have advanced linguistic skills, cultural awareness or technical knowledge but do not want to go to university. You would have to provide evidence of your ability in the form of recordings and simulated performance.

Kind of Person

Interpreting would require you to be alert, confident, capable of spontaneous reactions and articulate enough to communicate ideas rather than exact translations. You must have total mastery of your mother tongue and of one but preferably more foreign languages, together with a thorough knowledge of the institutions, culture, attitudes and practices in the countries where your languages are spoken, normally acquired through residence there. You would also need, for much of the work, a flair for technical subjects and a readiness to keep up to date with new developments. A good memory, the ability to concentrate for extended periods and a clear speaking voice would all be essential.

B road Outlook

Starting up as an interpreter is not easy. The competition is intense and only the really skilled succeed. Few organisations employ full-time interpreters and, if they do, it is normally on short contracts. It is much more common for interpreters to be freelance. This would give you a great deal of freedom but it could take several years to establish your reputation and build up a network of contacts.

You could operate in international organisations such as the European Union, the United Nations and its agencies, NATO or aid agencies; you could work in law courts and conferences as well as in multinational corporations and companies. Public services employ interpreters for liaising with ethnic communities, or in legal work in court when a person does not understand the English language adequately.

R elated Occupations

You might also consider: translator, teacher, secretary linguist, tour operator, journalist, solicitor or diplomat.

I mpact

The implications for your domestic life are considerable, since you would be expected to travel extensively, sometimes at short notice. Conferences often take place in the evenings or at weekends and the work can be extremely tiring. Given the unpredictable nature of the work, you may need to supplement your income with other activities, such as teaching or translating.

E arnings Potential

The European Commission salary range starts at around £32,000, rising to around £70,000 for a very experienced interpreter. Freelance rates vary enormously but average around £300 per day plus expenses. The public service rate is about £200.

F urther Information

Institute of Translation and Interpreting (ITI), London EC1V 1ND
Website: www.iti.org.uk

Languages National Training Organisation (LNTO), London WC2N 4LB
Website: www.languagesnto.org.uk

Institute of Linguists (IOL), London SE1 1UN Website: www.iol.org.uk

International Association of Conference Interpreters (AIIC),
CH-1202 Geneva, Switzerland Website: www.aiic.net

European Commission Recruitment Unit, B-1000 Brussels, Belgium
Website: www.europa.eu.int/en/

Alternative/equivalent entrance requirements can include: ILC, IB, EB, NC/ND and many other similar international systems. For further details see the Equivalent Qualifications section in the Introduction.

What is Involved?

As an investment analyst, you would study the performance of companies on the stock markets of the world in order to advise your clients or employers on good new investment opportunities, or to warn them of any growing weaknesses in performance, which could undermine their existing investments. You would initially work in a team under the supervision of a qualified senior analyst. Typically, you would study company accounts, relevant newspaper articles or announcements, information on the Internet and statistical data on past performance. You would also visit companies to discuss their profit forecasts and the development of their trading activities.

This information would then be collated and written up in report format for your clients or managers, with your recommendations to buy, hold or sell the stocks concerned. You could advise investment banks or fund managers of pension funds or you could deal directly with companies needing advice on investment, including stockbrokers who wish to help their own clients. The roles of investment analyst and fund manager are quite similar but the fund manager would make buying decisions after considering the research/advice of the investment analyst.

Opportunities for Training

Almost all entrants are graduates, often with a professional qualification in a related field and with experience of a specialist market sector. You would normally train on the job and would be expected – after at least six months' experience – to obtain the Investment Management Certificate (IMC), which is assessed by the UK Society of Investment Professionals (UKSIP). The syllabus would cover financial regulations, investment in equities, commodities, currencies, accountancy, portfolio management, economics and taxation (including capital gains tax).

Requirements

You would need a degree or professional qualification for which typically two or three A level/AVCE/Advanced Higher, three or four Higher or equivalent qualifications would be required in the first place. For non-graduates, the minimum requirements of UKSIP for the IMC would be five GCSE/S Grade passes at A-C/1-3 or equivalent – usually including English and maths.

Kind of Person

You would need to be strongly interested in the stock market and financial news and prepared to keep up to date with trends and developments. Numerical and statistical skills would be vital to deal with the huge amount of financial data you would have to analyse, summarise and assess for future trends. You would need reasonable IT skills, as you would be using computers for much of your work. Sound judgement would be essential, with the ability to see behind the headlines and not to be swept into recommending excessively speculative investments.

A grasp of international politics and geography would be necessary to recognise the possible impact of war, conflict or other economic and financial problems on levels of world trade. It would also be helpful to earn the trust and respect of managers whose company results you are analysing, given that your recommendations could have a huge impact on their future trading. You would be expected to dress smartly and conventionally.

B road Outlook

This is a highly competitive profession, with only 5,000 qualified analysts spread over the principal UK cities. Most analysts are based in London but there are also opportunities in Manchester, Liverpool, Birmingham and Edinburgh. You might have to move to achieve promotion or simply to find a job. If you are successful, the prospects can be extremely good, although unpredictable global economic factors can cause serious disruptions to share prices, which could in turn upset your best-laid plans.

R elated Occupations

You might also consider: insurance underwriter, actuary, accountant, statistician, merchant banker, stockbroker or financial adviser.

I mpact

Although this is an office-based career, stock markets are global and financial news arrives on a 24-hour basis. This can mean working irregular hours at times and keeping in touch with clients and colleagues around the world by telephone, fax and email every day.

Your performance would be continuously assessed, so you would need to be alert to significant news and to move fast in channelling this to clients. You would need to travel abroad to assess the soundness of some overseas companies and to hold meetings with overseas clients. Considerable disruption of your social and family life could occur at times in keeping pace in this highly demanding career field.

E arnings Potential

Starting salaries range from £16,000 to as high as £30,000 in London. Your salary could then rise rapidly to well above £250,000, with well-established analysts earning significantly in excess of this when taking into account frequently large annual bonuses to reward successful performance.

F urther Information

The UK Society for Investment Professionals (UKSIP), London EC2V 8EY
Website: www.uksip.org

The London Stock Exchange, London, EC2N 1HP
Website: www.londonstockexchange.com

The Securities Institute, London EC3R 8AJ
Website: www.securities-institute.org.uk

The London Investment Banking Association, London EC2R 8BT
Website: www.liba.org.uk

Alternative/equivalent entrance requirements can include: ILC, IB, EB, NC/ND and many other similar international systems. For further details see the Equivalent Qualifications section in the Introduction.

What is Involved?

As a **newspaper journalist** working for a local or national newspaper you would gather information about relevant people, places, events, politics, sport or crime. If you are reporting a football match, for example, you would describe the match, interview the coaches and goal scorers to find their reactions to the game and do any research necessary before writing your 'copy'.

As a **magazine journalist** working for the ever-increasing number of magazines from the world of business, computing, sport, fashion, art and leisure, you would find many similarities with your newspaper journalist colleagues. You would, however, be less likely to spend your time chasing news stories and more likely to write specialised feature articles. The process of recording interviews, researching information, writing up copy and sub-editing is largely the same, although deadlines can be measured in weeks rather than minutes!

As a **broadcast journalist** working for national and local radio and television companies, you may benefit from earlier experience as a magazine or newspaper journalist. You would be involved in researching, writing and presenting programmes and you may also have to operate studio equipment.

As an **agency journalist** you would supply news, stories and photographs to magazines, newspapers and television stations.

Opportunities for Training

There is no standard entry route into journalism. The National Council for the Training of Journalists (NCTJ) regulates training for newspaper work, offering possibilities linked to 'direct entry' or 'pre-entry.' Direct entrants usually follow a two-year training contract, working as journalists while studying part-time; pre-entry means following an accredited full-time course before finding a job. If you are sure that you want to make a career in journalism, you can take an NCTJ-approved post-A level/Advanced Higher, Higher, degree or postgraduate course. You could also consider Modern Apprenticeship skillseeker training in newspaper journalism.

While the NCTJ is also involved with training for magazine journalism, you should be aware of courses accredited by the Periodicals Training Council. Training for broadcast journalism focuses rather more on ad hoc provision organised by individual companies, although there are courses accredited by the Broadcast Journalism Training Council.

Requirements

The majority of journalists enter as graduates but not necessarily with a degree in journalism. You need to have a strong command of English, good communication skills and to be interested in people and news. Previous experience can often prove to be as valuable as academic achievement. Being on the editorial staff of your school/college magazine or undergraduate newspaper can show this, as can working as a volunteer on your local hospital or campus radio station or work-shadowing a journalist. It is important to build up a portfolio of your writing and any published articles to give evidence of your work.

Kind of person

You would need to be familiar with computers and modern methods of communication and to meet deadlines. If you struggle to hand in your homework on time, consider whether you're really likely to succeed in the heat of the newsroom! You would need to be self-confident and persistent, to relate well to others and to be willing to work hard, often at unsocial hours. Any interests you have such as sport, fashion or a hobby may also be useful.

B road Outlook

Despite the number and range of newspapers and magazines, competition for jobs and promotion is fierce and success is achieved solely on merit. There are always more candidates than places available and a constant stream of fresh young graduates serves to remind even experienced journalists that they are only as good as their last story.

Some freelance journalists become well established before embarking on their own and selling articles to newspapers and magazines. Others only write the occasional article and are not dependent on journalism for their income.

R elated Occupations

You may be interested in other jobs in this field such as press and information officer, advertising copywriter, public relations officer, media researcher.

I mpact

You may work irregular hours, often at weekends and evenings, and when a story breaks you have to be there. It is a job many people would like to do, and those in it have to be dedicated. Magazine journalists are more likely to work regular hours, although deadlines can still require staying on the job until your material is ready to print.

E arnings Potential

For trainee journalists, the rate for local newspapers is in the range of £9,000 to £13,000 but the pay varies considerably according to experience. An experienced journalist can earn £45,000 or more.

F urther Information

National Council for the Training of Journalists, Harlow CM18 7BL
(Send a stamped addressed envelope) Website: www.nctj.com

Periodicals Training Council, London WC2A 3LJ Website: www.ppa.co.uk

Broadcast Journalism Training Council, London W2 5NR
Website: www.bjtc.org.uk

Alternative/equivalent entrance requirements can include: ILC, IB, EB, NC/ND and many other similar international systems. For further details see the Equivalent Qualifications section in the Introduction.

What is Involved?

As a land surveyor, you would be primarily concerned with the accurate measurement of the natural and built environment, the description and classification of features, the analysis and collation of relevant data and the presentation of data in forms required by users such as architects, civil engineers, property developers, planners, solicitors, environmentalists, geologists, archaeologists, geographers and map makers. Your work would be an essential preliminary to virtually all planning, property development and construction, major engineering and other projects relating to the natural environment and urban infrastructure.

You would learn about the traditional survey methods of triangulation and traversing, and would use them when appropriate, but you would come to rely more and more on satellite geodesy and computerised mapping and Geographic and Land Information Systems. Your detailed surveys would often be based on plotting from aerial photography and the use of sophisticated computer driven plotting equipment.

Opportunities for Training

Land surveying is part of the geomatics faculty of the Royal Institution of Chartered Surveyors (RICS). There are various routes to full RICS membership but the most likely in this case would to take an accredited degree or postgraduate course in land surveying or a similar subject with a land or geomatics option. Your course should introduce you to the major methods of measuring and recording data, from levels, theodolites and simple maps to techniques involving the modern technology outlined above.

An introduction to positioning and navigation using the Global Positioning System (GPS) would also be given and a residential field course would ensure that you could apply your knowledge to real-world tasks. On completion of your accredited course, you would be eligible to move to the two-year RICS structured training stage with an employer, concluding with an interview known as the Assessment of Professional Competence (APC). Alternatively, you could seek corporate membership of the Architecture and Surveying Institute (ASI), usually following a similar route of accredited degree and two years of approved practical experience.

Requirements

You would normally need three A level/AVCE/Advanced Higher, four Higher or equivalent qualifications to enter an accredited degree in a surveying discipline, together with five GCSE/S Grade passes at A-C/1-3, including English and maths.

Kind of Person

Your job would involve the interpretation and analysis of data, requiring you to be observant and comfortable with numerical work. There would be extensive use of computers, so you would need to be confident in using the relevant software packages. You would need to be well organised and ordered in your approach to work as you would be collecting data from a number of different sources, often at enormous expense. You would usually work as a member of a team, particularly on larger projects. This might involve you in managing and coordinating the work of members of your team. In addition to liaising with fellow professionals, you might have to explain quite complicated and technical information to clients with little previous knowledge. You would need to be physically fit, as you are likely to spend a lot of time out on site or in open countryside.

B road Outlook

The opportunities for employment are somewhat dependent on developments in construction and civil engineering but in recent years there have been a reasonable number of vacancies. There are opportunities to work abroad, or to branch out into areas such as archaeological surveying. Land surveyors are employed in certain government departments, large construction and civil engineering companies and by local authorities. There are also increasing opportunities to work in private practice or as an independent consultant.

R elated Occupations

You might also consider: hydrographic, quantity, rural practice or building surveyor, town planner, architect, cartographer or civil engineer.

I mpact

This is unlikely to be a nine to five job. Whilst there would be times when you are based in an office with regular hours, you would also be expected to go out to sites. When on location, you could be in a remote area, which might take a long time to reach.

E arnings Potential

The average graduate salary is £19,000, which would increase with experience and can rise to well over £50,000 a year. Salaries in the commercial fields tend to be greater than those in the public sector and surveyors working in cities earn more than their rural counterparts.

F urther Information

The Royal Institution of Chartered Surveyors, Coventry CV4 8JE
Website: www.rics.org.uk

The Architecture and Surveying Institute, Chippenham SN15 3WD
Website: www.asi.org.uk

Alternative/equivalent entrance requirements can include: ILC, IB, EB, NC/ND and many other similar international systems. For further details see the Equivalent Qualifications section in the Introduction.

What is Involved?

As a landscape architect, you would work to preserve the natural scenery and ecology of an area while creating attractive settings for construction projects such as housing developments, roads, parks, play areas, offices or industrial buildings.

You might also work on preserving parts of the coastline, rescuing derelict factory sites or restoring disused pits and quarries. You could specialise in countryside issues or you could focus on urban projects. Whatever the particular project, you would hold discussions with your clients to find out what the job is about, make visits to the site to carry out surveys and then draw up plans and projected costs.

Once these have been agreed, you would visit the site from time to time to check that the landscaping work is progressing smoothly. In order to produce workable design solutions, you would need an understanding of topics such as civil engineering, surveying, geology, horticulture and earth-moving techniques. Indeed, you would usually be part of a team including architects, civil engineers, town planners and construction technicians.

Opportunities for Training

There are two possible routes to qualification: a degree in landscape architecture or postgraduate study after taking a degree in a related subject, such as architecture, horticulture or botany. The higher degree can be taken straight away or, on a full- or part-time basis, after you have spent some time in related work.

Being a Member of the Landscape Institute (MLI) is the recognised professional qualification in landscape architecture. To achieve this status, you must first attain associate membership by completing your first degree or postgraduate course and then gain at least two years of approved practical experience before taking the Institute's professional practice examination.

Requirements

The minimum requirements for degree entry would normally be two A level/AVCE/Advanced Higher, three Higher or equivalent qualifications, plus supporting GCSE/S Grade passes at A-C/1-3, which should include English and either maths or a science. The Landscape Institute regards subjects such as art, biology, botany and geography as particularly relevant, although you should check with university prospectuses to be sure of exact entry requirements. You would also be expected to show a portfolio of artwork, including landscape designs, to provide evidence of your creative potential. For entry to a postgraduate course, you would need a good first degree.

Kind of Person

You would need a genuine concern for the environment, an understanding of conservation issues, creative vision, good drawing ability and excellent communication skills. You would almost certainly use a computer for your design work and would need a reasonable standard of IT literacy. Good organisational and negotiating skills would be very important for working as part of a team. Inspecting construction sites can be demanding physically, so you would need to be reasonably fit.

B road Outlook

This is a small profession but one that is growing quite rapidly, offering good job prospects if you are properly qualified. There are opportunities to work all over the country and overseas. About half of all landscape architects work in private practice for small firms or consultancies, with the rest employed by large organisations such as major building companies, the forestry commission or local government.

There is a formal career structure in the public sector, with corresponding security, but many landscape architects prefer to move to private practice when they have some experience, in order to develop their ideas more freely.

R elated Occupations

You might also consider: chartered surveyor, forest manager, horticultural manager, town planner, civil engineer or architect.

I mpact

You would need to be prepared to go on site in all weathers but you would usually spend less than a quarter of your time outdoors. Far more of your time would be taken up with deskwork and meetings. Landscape architects working in private practice are likely to spend quite a lot of time travelling, undertaking commissions around the country.

In the public sector, you would normally work a basic 37-hour week, whereas private practice is more likely to include long and irregular hours, often involving evening and weekend meetings with clients.

E arnings Potential

Your salary once you have graduated and are gaining professional experience is likely to be around £12,000 to £18,000. When you are fully qualified, this can rise to around £25,000 in the public sector and more in private practice, depending on the amount of work you can attract and the number of hours you are prepared to put in.

F urther Information

The Landscape Institute, London SW11 1QU Website www.l-i.org.uk

The British Association of Landscape Industries, Keighley BD21 3DR Website www.bali.co.uk

Alternative/equivalent entrance requirements can include: ILC, IB, EB, NC/ND and many other similar international systems. For further details see the Equivalent Qualifications section in the Introduction.

What is Involved?

As a legal executive in England and Wales (there is no direct equivalent in Scotland), you would report to a solicitor or senior legal executive and would be involved in a specialist area of the law. For example you could choose to specialise in family law, probate, criminal or civil cases or conveyancing.

You may well find yourself as the main point of contact for clients concerned about their legal affairs and may have an administrative or managerial role within a legal practice. Your day-to-day work would be similar to that of many solicitors and you could continue to train, should you wish to do so, until you qualify as a solicitor.

Opportunities for Training

Most trainee legal executives work in a solicitor's office and study part-time to gain qualification as a Fellow of the Institute of Legal Executives (ILEX). The examinations are in two stages:

• Part I, set at A level standard, can either be studied 'academically'- in which case you sit four papers on aspects of law and the legal system – or 'vocationally', where you compile case studies and a portfolio before taking a test on elements of the legal system.

• Part II, set at degree standard, involves four specialist exams, three of which are in specialist areas of law and one in related legal procedure.

Having passed both levels, which usually takes three to four years, you are eligible to apply for Membership of ILEX. To achieve the Fellowship, you must be 25 years old and have had at least five years' experience of working in a legal office. At least two of these years must be after becoming a member of ILEX.

Some law degrees incorporate ILEX Membership on graduation.

Requirements

You would need at least four GCSE/S Grade passes at A-C/1-3 or equivalent. These must include English and at least another two academic subjects. However, there is strong competition for places in legal practices, so you may need more that these minimum stated requirements. You can make valuable contacts by doing holiday work in a solicitor's office or in a local court. This should show that you have a genuine interest in and knowledge of this sort of legal career.

Kind of Person

You would meet a wide range of people in your job, so you would need the ability to communicate effectively at all levels. You would be required to express yourself fluently and persuasively, both verbally and in writing, with a clear understanding of technical legal terms.

At times you would have to work under pressure and you would have to analyse and solve problems as and when they arise. It would be important that you have good attention to detail. You would be working in an office, possibly dealing with several different cases at the same time, and would need to have good organisational and administrative abilities.

B road Outlook

Although it can be difficult to find a place in a legal practice, becoming a legal executive offers the chance to earn money at the same time as studying for a professional qualification. It also provides an alternative route to becoming a solicitor and you will already be an experienced lawyer by the time you qualify.

Once qualified as a Fellow, you could act as a Commissioner for Oaths and administer oaths, declarations and affidavits. You would also have extended rights of audience in the County Court and Magistrates Court and could become a fully qualified Legal Executive Advocate, allowing you to manage clients' cases from start to finish.

R elated Occupations

You may be interested in other careers in the legal field such as barristers' clerk, solicitor or shorthand writer.

I mpact

Although you would be working in an office, your hours may at times be long when you have a deadline to meet or when there is a large volume of work to complete. In addition, you would need to be prepared to use your free time in the early years to study for your exams.

E arnings Potential

There is no recommended minimum salary for trainee legal executives but, if you start working in a legal office straight from school, you could expect to earn £12,000 to £15,000 a year, depending on the size and location of the practice. Your salary is likely to rise to £20,000 to £24,000 once you are qualified. Experienced Fellows of ILEX can earn over £40,000.

Many employers help out with course or examination fees while you are working for them.

F urther Information

The Institute of Legal Executives, Bedford MK42 7AB
Website: www.ilex.org.uk

Alternative/equivalent entrance requirements can include: ILC, IB, EB, NC/ND and many other similar international systems. For further details see the Equivalent Qualifications section in the Introduction.

What is Involved?

As a leisure services manager, you would be responsible for the efficient operation of a leisure and sports complex or centre. You would ensure that the whole organisation runs smoothly on a day-to-day basis, that there are sufficient suitably-trained staff on the premises, that safety procedures are in place and that the customers are enjoying themselves. You would be in charge of the sports coaches and instructors, together with office, catering and maintenance staff, and you would be dealing with every aspect of running the centre, including financial control and book-keeping, the recruitment of staff and the organisation of timetables and special activities (such as school holiday courses and tournaments).

You might have some face-to-face involvement with customers, dealing with complaints and possibly doing some sports coaching yourself, if you are suitably qualified. Leisure and sports centres vary widely in size and scope, with the largest quite possibly encompassing indoor and outdoor facilities, such as swimming pools, gymnasia and fitness centres, badminton, squash, tennis and basketball courts, football and cricket pitches. They may also include dance floors, saunas, and children's activity centres, and there will almost always be cafés, usually with bars too. Some centres specialise in outdoor and adventure pursuits, such as rock-climbing and canoeing.

Opportunities for Training

While there are several possible routes to a responsible position of this kind, employers are increasingly looking to appoint graduates with professional qualifications and relevant experience. A good starting point would therefore be a degree in sports and leisure studies or sports science or a degree in another subject followed by a postgraduate course.

You could then work towards professional qualifications awarded by the Institute of Leisure and Amenity Management or the Institute of Sport and Recreation Management. An alternative would be to start at a lower level and study part-time for degree and professional qualifications.

Requirements

Degree course entry would normally require two or three A level/ AVCE/Advanced Higher, three or four Higher or equivalent qualifications, together with five GCSEs/S Grade passes at A-C/1-3. You should check course details carefully because they vary a great deal and may not contain the right elements for you. A talent for sport, and proven success, would be an advantage and the ability to drive could be useful. Lifeguard qualifications and first aid training might also be looked for.

Kind of Person

You should be well-motivated, organised and efficient, in order to make sure that the centre functions smoothly at all times. If there is a problem, you should be able to deal with it or delegate someone else to do so. You should have a good sense of business, in order to promote the centre and attract new customers, and you should be able to cope with financial matters where necessary.

Good communication skills, both verbal and written, would be extremely important and you should enjoy being both a leader and member of a team, so that your staff will respect you and enjoy working with you. You should also be enthusiastic and knowledgeable about sport, enjoying the contact with the customers, and helping them to enjoy what the centre has to offer.

B road Outlook

Leisure and sports centres have proliferated over the past few years, all over the country, and are usually very popular. Opportunities to progress to senior management positions have generally kept pace with the growth in leisure provision. There is scope for managers to be promoted to bigger centres, or to take up administrative and managerial posts with local authorities in their sports and recreation departments.

R elated Occupations

You might also consider: marketing manager, PE teacher, public relations officer, retail manager or sports coach.

I mpact

By the very nature of the industry, you would have to expect to work some weekends and in the evenings, as well as normal office hours. Usually a rota would be worked, in order to share out the unsocial hours. You should also be prepared to work additional hours whenever necessary. You may have to move around the country to find a new post as you develop your career.

E arnings Potential

Salaries vary widely, according to the size and location of the centre (with higher pay in London), and between the public and private sector. There are national pay scales for those employed by local authorities. In general, an assistant manager could earn around £15,000, with promotion to around £23,000 as a manager. Heads of leisure departments could earn up to £40,000.

F urther Information

Institute of Sport and Recreation Management, Melton Mowbray LE13 1XJ
Website: www.isrm.co.uk

Institute of Leisure and Amenity Management, Reading RG8 9NE
Website: www.ilam.co.uk

Central Council for Physical Recreation, London, SW1P 1DE
Website: www.ccpr.org.uk

Alternative/equivalent entrance requirements can include: ILC, IB, EB, NC/ND and many other similar international systems. For further details see the Equivalent Qualifications section in the Introduction.

What is Involved?

As a librarian, you might just as likely be known as an information manager or scientist, since the management, storage, retrieval and presentation of information would be at the core of your job, and the amount and variety of information, both in content and form, would be absolutely huge. Gone are the days of the stereotypical librarian, surrounded by mounds of dusty or dog-eared volumes, fussily telling readers to "shush"! Books, periodicals and printed catalogues are still of vital importance but information now comes via a great many other media, including the internet, CD-ROM, video and DVD, making your work as a librarian increasingly diverse.

You might be based in a public library, with plenty of contact with readers and responsibility for a wide variety of topics; you might specialise in a particular field (possibly medical or legal) and work for a learned or professional organisation; you might like the idea of working in an academic library in a university or other institution of higher education.

Whatever type of library you chose, the basic principles of your work would be the same: to make sure that your acquisitions are up to date and meet the needs of your clients; to organise the material in the most accessible way; to help users find the information they require, if necessary researching and acquiring new material for them. You might also, in a public library, organise events to promote the library and encourage new readers.

Opportunities for Training

While you could become a library assistant by learning on-the-job, to become a chartered librarian or information professional you would need to follow one of two routes: (1) complete an undergraduate degree accredited by the Chartered Institute of Library and Information Professionals (CILIP); (2) take a degree in another subject, followed by an accredited postgraduate course.

You may be expected to participate in a graduate traineeship before starting a postgraduate course. Look for schemes meeting the SCONUL (Standing Conference of National and University Libraries) Code of Practice. This means that you would gain systematically planned and supervised experience of library work prior to starting your course.

Finally, you would undertake a period of professional training with an employer in order to gain chartered status.

Requirements

The minimum entry requirement for undergraduate degree courses is two A level/Advanced Higher, three Higher or equivalent qualifications, together with five GCSE/S Grade passes A-C/1-3, though in practice many courses will be looking for more than this. The courses usually take three or four years full-time or four or five years part-time. Postgraduate courses take one year full-time or two or three years part-time. It is sometimes essential and always useful to undertake some relevant work experience before starting a course.

Kind of Person

You should have excellent communication skills, since you would be dealing with a wide variety of people and would need to understand what they want and how to direct them to the information they require. In any library, a high level of computer literacy would be important, together with a methodical approach and excellent record keeping. Wide-ranging general knowledge and active intellectual curiosity would be clear assets in this type of work, together with specialised knowledge if you are working in an academic library.

Broad Outlook

As a librarian/information professional, you would be at the heart of the information revolution. This does not necessarily indicate a huge shortage of suitably qualified people but it does acknowledge that library work is changing rapidly. Indeed, your career development may depend on how willing you are to embrace new methods of storing and accessing information and to move between different employment sectors in order to broaden your experience.

Related Occupations

If you like the sound of librarianship/information management, you might also be interested in: archivist, museum curator, academic researcher or teacher.

Impact

Your working hours as a librarian would depend very much on where you are based. You might well have to work on a shift basis, including evenings and weekends, particularly in the public library service or in university libraries. On the other hand, you might have a term-time only contract in a school library. There is considerable potential for part-time working or job-sharing. You may have to move around the country to develop your career.

Earnings Potential

Earnings vary massively from job to job and you are advised to consult the CILIP website for detailed salary guides. You should be able to earn around £18,000 to £22,000 once qualified, with the prospect of applying for posts in the £40,000 to £50,000 range when you have sufficient experience.

Further Information

The Chartered Institute of Library and Information Professionals, London WC1E 7AE Website: www.cilip.org.uk

Alternative/equivalent entrance requirements can include: ILC, IB, EB, NC/ND and many other similar international systems. For further details see the Equivalent Qualifications section in the Introduction.

What is Involved?

As a licensed conveyancer, you would be a specialist property lawyer, trained and qualified in all aspects of the law dealing with property transfer in England and Wales. You could act for buyers, sellers and lenders in the process of transferring the ownership of a house, flat, commercial property or piece of land from one person to another, otherwise known as conveyancing.

Your work would be office-based and would involve conducting searches into the ownership of properties, their leasehold or freehold status, likely planning changes, rights of way, checking the new owner's liability for unsound building structures and repairs, planned changes to roads and highways and local factory and property developments. You might work for a licensed conveyancer, solicitor, local authority, bank or building society, provided that an appropriately qualified conveyancer or solicitor is head of the legal department.

Opportunities for Training

In order to qualify, you would need to work for at least two years in a legal environment, gaining practical experience of conveyancing. At the same time, you would have to pass the foundation and final examinations of the Council for Licensed Conveyancers (CLC). You could study for these by part-time attendance at a college or university or through distance learning. The topics covered would include all aspects of conveyancing law and practice, law of contract, land law, landlord and tenant agreements and accounts.

Having successfully completed the examinations and practical training, you would be eligible to apply for a limited licence, allowing you to offer conveyancing services through your employer. After a minimum period of three years at this level, you could apply for a full licence and become a partner in a firm or even set up your own business as a sole practitioner.

Requirements

You would need to have at least four GCSE/S Grade passes A-C/1-3 or equivalent which must include English and three other approved subjects. However, many applicants have A level/AVCE/Advanced Higher, Higher or equivalent qualifications as well. A degree in law would give you exemption from many of the qualifying examinations.

Kind of Person

You would need to be well organised in order to deal efficiently with the large amount of paperwork involved. Attention to detail would be important to avoid potentially costly errors in the documents you are preparing. At times these documents could be quite complex, so you would need to have the patience and perseverance necessary to work your way through them. In addition, you would need good communication skills to explain legal matters to your clients. If you establish yourself as an independent practitioner, you would need the relevant commercial skills to run your own business. The CLC will not approve your licence until it is satisfied that you are a 'fit and proper person' to practise as a licensed conveyancer.

B road Outlook

This is a very new profession, which started in 1987 after the law was changed to end the effective conveyancing monopoly held by solicitors. The number of practising conveyancers is now growing and the qualification is becoming increasingly sought after, both by people wishing to practise on their own account and by employers responsible for providing legal services.

In recent years, low mortgage interest rates have created a very buoyant property market in the UK, with people buying and selling houses regularly. Traditionally, however, the housing market is very volatile and there could in future be times of greater or lesser demand for conveyancing services.

R elated Occupations

You might also consider: legal executive, solicitor, civil service administrator, accountant or insurance underwriter or broker.

I mpact

You would be working office hours but may well need to work into the evenings and at weekends to meet deadlines. This would be particularly true if you were trying to establish a business and develop your own customer base. You might need to offer a faster, cheaper, more efficient service in order to entice clients away from traditional providers of conveyancing services. The initial training can be expensive and you may wish to seek financial support from your employer to help you through this phase of your professional development.

E arnings Potential

There are no guidelines given either for licensed conveyancers who are employed and still training, or for the fees that those holding a full licence can charge. However, there is currently plenty of work available in this area. If you choose to become self-employed, your earnings potential would be dependent on how much work you could attract and complete.

F urther Information

Council for Licensed Conveyancers, Chelmsford CM1 1QG
Website: www.conveyancers.gov.uk

Alternative/equivalent entrance requirements can include: ILC, IB, EB, NC/ND and many other similar international systems. For further details see the Equivalent Qualifications section in the Introduction.

What is Involved?

As a local government administrator, you would be part of a huge workforce of some two and a half million people employed by a network of unitary authorities, county and district councils and London boroughs. Your work would address the needs, conflicts and concerns of the local population in a variety of services ranging from education, leisure and environmental protection to trading standards, social services and waste collection. You could be engaged in a range of management challenges relating to any one of these services, working alongside specialist professionals such as architects, surveyors, social workers, teachers and environmental health officers.

Local authorities are led by elected councillors and you would have to implement their policies. You might advise on the initial decision-making process and you would certainly be involved in setting up procedures to carry out decisions, manage systems efficiently and ensure that public money is being spent wisely. You would be expected to report back to councillors on a regular basis. You might work from a large public building such as a county hall or from a smaller office in the area covered by your authority.

Opportunities for Training

There are several different training routes. You could, for example, join as a clerical or administrative assistant and work your way up to administrator level by achieving a relevant National or Scottish Vocational Qualification (N/SVQ). Alternatively, you could take a degree in any subject and apply for the National Graduate Development Programme (NGDP), which is specifically designed to create a new generation of managers with the ability to take on senior roles.

Though recruited at a national level, you would join a local authority and would spend two years there, taking on strategic project work, obtaining a postgraduate management qualification and participating in short-term placements with other public and private sector partners. As you progress through the programme, you would gain the capabilities and experience to make an impact on the direction local government might take in the future.

Requirements

The NGDP aims to attract high calibre graduates with a wide range of abilities and knowledge. You would therefore need at least an upper second class honours degree in any subject. There are no formal requirements for the N/SVQ route, although most employers would stipulate A level/AVCE/ Advanced Higher, Higher or equivalent qualifications.

Kind of Person

According to the NGDP, you would need to demonstrate the following range of skills and personal characteristics: *teamwork* – using your skills to complement others and sharing your talents to achieve a common goal; *leadership* – inspiring, directing and influencing staff at every level with enthusiasm, energy and assertiveness; *analysis* – identifying, analysing and interpreting relevant information from a range of sources to develop well-informed solutions; *communication* – talking, writing and presenting your ideas clearly and logically; *organisation* – managing your time and priorities to deliver to deadline-driven objectives; *IT awareness* – understanding the benefits and pitfalls of computer applications within local government; *motivation* – personal and career drive to achieve success through continued learning, perseverance and proactivity.

B road Outlook

You might be expected to move around the country to broaden your experience as you seek to develop your career. Administrators are needed in every department of every local authority and you should be able to progress to middle or senior management if you have the necessary talent, ambition and commitment. Many traditional local government services have been privatised or contracted out in recent years, leading to increased opportunities for switching between the public and private sectors. Once you have gained sufficient experience, you could set up your own consultancy specialising in areas such as drawing up service specifications, negotiating contracts and monitoring contractor performance.

R elated Occupations

You might also consider: civil service administrator, health service manager, human resources/personnel manager or chartered secretary.

I mpact

You would normally work a fairly standard 37-hour week, Monday to Friday, although you may be expected to attend some evening meetings. Local government employers often make provision for very flexible working patterns, including flexitime, job sharing and term-time only contracts.

E arnings Potential

As a graduate recruit to the NGDP, you would receive a starting salary of between £18,500 and £22,000 (depending on location). If you start as an administrative assistant, you would be paid on a scale ranging from around £9,000 to £17,000. Your entry point would depend on such factors as the grade of the job and your level of responsibility.

F urther Information

Local Government Opportunities (LGO), Sidcup DA15 7BJ
Website: www.lgcareers.com

National Graduate Development Programme, Newbury RG14 1AF
Website:www.ngdp.co.uk

Convention of Scottish Local Authorities (COSLA), Edinburgh EH12 5XZ
Website: www.cosla.gov.uk

Alternative/equivalent entrance requirements can include: ILC, IB, EB, NC/ND and many other similar international systems. For further details see the Equivalent Qualifications section in the Introduction.

What is Involved?

As a logistics manager, you would specialise in organising and improving the supply chain, the complex sequence of events and decisions which connects sourcing raw materials with manufacturing and the end consumer. You may work for a large organisation, such as a manufacturer or retail company, aiming to get the right quantity of a product to the right place, at the right time, in the right condition and at an acceptable cost.

You might be responsible for the smooth operation of a manufacturing process or for managing a distribution centre. Equally, you may plan a new supply strategy or be involved in production scheduling or vehicle routing. Getting the supply chain exactly right is vital, as late deliveries, over-ordering of stock or miscalculating delivery times could cost your company their competitive edge. You would aim to make things happen 'just-in-time', which means being involved with buying, manufacturing, movement of goods by say road or rail, warehousing and general distribution. All of these areas are inter-dependent and you would have to co-ordinate them efficiently, making considerable use of IT to process data.

Opportunities for Training

Entry into the industry is usually via a graduate training scheme. There are industrial placements available both for sandwich course students and also summer internships for undergraduates. Once in employment, you would receive in-house training and have the opportunity to study for a professional qualification in logistics.

The Institute of Logistics and Transport offers professional qualifications at junior, middle and senior management levels, with courses covering the development of general management skills, key personal abilities, professional standards, road freight regulations, operations and administration, transport economics, inventory management, movement of people, government transport policy and resource management. Companies may offer full-or part-time training or distance learning, including postgraduate study to MSc level.

Requirements

The minimum requirements for degree course entry would be two or more A level/AVCE/Advanced Higher, three Higher or equivalent qualifications, together with five GCSE/S Grade passes A-C/1-3 including English and maths. There are some degree courses in logistics management but many employers would accept a good quality degree in other subjects.

Kind of Person

To manage, co-ordinate and improve the total supply chain demands high-level managerial skills and the capacity to play a key part in meeting your company's longer-term strategic objectives. You would need to be numerate and able to solve problems, think on your feet and manage people. The ability to use IT packages and electronic communication methods would be vital, not least because, with the growing use of Internet shopping, the supply chain is at the heart of developments in telecommunications and e-commerce. Foreign language skills would be a great advantage, since you could be in contact with suppliers or buyers all over the world.

B road Outlook

Career opportunities in logistics continue to grow. Even during downturns in the business cycle, when companies are cutting costs, the demand for able and experienced supply chain managers tends to remain high. You could expect to achieve managerial level after about five years and could go on to be a director. There should be many opportunities to move to other companies wishing to develop their logistics expertise or you could consider setting up your own consultancy business.

Environmental concerns are creating new areas of opportunity. For example, the supply chain no longer ends with the consumer but includes consideration of how goods can be recycled; you might be involved in ensuring that a distribution centre is energy efficient or in minimising the pollution impact of a large fleet of lorries.

R elated Occupations

You might also consider: marketing manager, shipbroker or freight forwarder.

I mpact

As this job is all about deadlines, you would be expected to work extra hours when the occasion demands, especially during emergencies such as transport delays. Logistics management often operates 24 hours a day, seven days a week. It could make major demands on your time, especially if you are in regular contact with people living on the other side of the world. Your hours of work could be long and irregular and you may be expected to travel extensively.

E arnings Potential

On entry you could expect to earn between £15,000 and £18,000 a year. A manager would earn about £35,000 and a director considerably more. The Institute of Logistics and Transport website quotes examples of recent vacancies advertised to include a logistics controller at £60,000 plus car, plus relocation package, and a distribution manager at £30,000.

F urther Information

The Institute of Logistics and Transport, Northants NN17 4XQ
Website: www.iolt.org.uk

Alternative/equivalent entrance requirements can include: ILC, IB, EB, NC/ND and many other similar international systems. For further details see the Equivalent Qualifications section in the Introduction.

What is Involved?

As a management consultant, your job would be to help companies and organisations improve their success rate by investigating their current structure and work practices, searching out any weaknesses and suggesting or implementing appropriate remedies. This would involve in-depth research, including the consideration of staffing, marketing strategies, growth potential, financial controls and the strength of the competition where appropriate.

In a time of technological change, as now, you might also be called upon to advise on and often oversee the implementation of new methods of working, bearing in mind the implications this would have on existing staffing and traditional work patterns.

Opportunities for Training

There is no single route of training to become a management consultant. Many practitioners come into the work after successful management experience in industry or commerce and, quite often, with a postgraduate qualification such as the MBA (Master of Business Administration).

However, some very large management consultancies do recruit recent graduates and give them intensive in-house training. You can become a member of the Institute of Management Consultants, the professional body which regulates standards of qualifications and competence.

Requirements

Although there is no educational requirement actually laid down for entry into the profession, it is virtually all graduate. The subject of your first degree could be drawn from a wide variety, followed by management training. There are, however, plenty of degrees in management and related fields or a combination of, say, a modern language and management/business, financial or engineering studies, which could provide a good introduction.

If you like the idea of studying for a degree in management, you should look very carefully at the subjects required at A level/AVCE/Advanced Higher, Higher or equivalent for entry. Some courses might specify maths beyond GCSE/S Grade levels.

Kind of Person

You would need excellent communication skills, both spoken and written, as you would be dealing with a wide variety of people, at all levels of seniority, and would have to write clear, cogent reports on your findings and recommendations. Some of these would not necessarily be very popular, and you would need tact, resilience and understanding to deal with this. You would almost certainly be working as a member of a team, but should also have considerable independence of mind and the confidence to make decisions based on your own judgment.

You should enjoy problem solving and analysing situations and you should have plenty of stamina, both physical and emotional, as you might be working long hours in order to meet deadlines and you would be making far-reaching decisions. You should be able to work comfortably with a variety of IT systems.

B road Outlook

Given the ever-increasing pace of change, management consultants often find it necessary or desirable to specialise in different aspects of the work, such as finance, marketing or IT, or in particular types of organisation, such as manufacturing, commercial sales/exporting, retailing or even charities. Competition for places in the best-known management consultancies is very great but, if you make the grade, the potential for promotion is good, particularly with the growth of multi-national companies, and increasing competition and mergers. Some experienced consultants set up their own agencies.

R elated Occupations

If you think you have the skills and qualities to be a management consultant, you might also like to consider: accountant; economist; information technology specialist; operational research/work study specialist; human resources (personnel) manager; recruitment consultant.

I mpact

Management consultants are generally called in to do a particular job, and are given a budget and a timescale. This means that you would have to be prepared to work long hours, possibly at the weekend, in order to fulfil your contract. You could also be expected to travel anywhere in the world.

If you were employed by a firm of consultants, your income would be steady but, if you were on a fixed-term contract, you might have to face a certain amount of insecurity from job to job. You would also have to be sure that you could handle the knowledge that your recommendations, based on your professional judgment, could result in people facing unemployment.

E arnings Potential

Earnings vary a great deal but are generally well above average for graduates, depending upon the size and nature of the contract. For senior management consultants the rewards can be very high. As with many competitive professions, it is getting the first job that can be the hardest.

F urther Information

Institute of Management Consultancy Website: www.imc.co.uk

Institute of Business Administration Website: www.ibauk.org

Alternative/equivalent entrance requirements can include: ILC, IB, EB, NC/ND and many other similar international systems. For further details see the Equivalent Qualifications section in the Introduction.

What is Involved?

As a manufacturing engineer (sometimes known as a production engineer), you would be concerned with all stages of the conversion of raw materials into usable products either for the general public or for other industries. In some instances, your job would be very similar to that of a mechanical engineer but you would be more concerned with broad manufacturing technology. You could be involved with overseeing the production processes and systems involved in making any sort of manufactured goods. As a result, your job is likely to include designing or maintaining complex machinery. You could be using robotics or involved with other computer driven equipment. Your main concern could be with designing, testing and maintaining the equipment itself or you could be involved with the design and layout of the plant in a factory. In order to present your product(s) to the marketplace at the time, price and quality that the customer expects, you would need a wide range of knowledge and skills, from product design, marketing and accounting to management, economics and finance. You would also need to appreciate the blend of people, machines and materials necessary to impart quality to the manufacturing process.

Opportunities for Training

There are a number of universities offering degrees in manufacturing engineering, sometimes combined with product design or with mechanical engineering. In order to become a chartered engineer, primarily concerned with research, design and development, you would need to complete at least four years of academic study and would usually achieve this via an MEng degree. If you want to be more involved with the day-to-day management of production processes as an incorporated engineer, you could take a three-year BEng degree. You don't always have to choose your specific training route from the start, so you should read prospectuses carefully. See also our separate article on engineering qualifications. There are sandwich courses available for both types of degree; these add an extra year but give the opportunity for a period of work experience, which can be very valuable when you are looking for a job. After graduating, you would need to complete a period of industrial training and responsible work experience before you achieve chartered or incorporated engineer status.

Requirements

For degree entry, you are likely to need maths at A level/AVCE/Advanced Higher, Higher or equivalent and usually physics plus another one or two subjects one of which could be an AVCE equivalent in engineering. If maths and physics are not required, they are certainly preferred by universities. In addition, you would need at least five GCSE/S Grade passes at A-C/1-3. You would normally need higher grades for MEng than for BEng admission.

Kind of Person

You would need the ability to learn and develop the multidisciplinary knowledge, competencies and skills relevant to manufacturing so that, on graduation, you would be able to undertake the diverse range of management functions found in industry. You would be involved with the application of computer technologies to integrate management and processes, requiring advanced IT skills, and you would find foreign language skills useful.

You might find yourself giving or taking orders, liaising with others and co-ordinating the work of fellow team members. In addition, you may need to give presentations to senior staff, to explain your ideas and discuss plans with people who do not always have your expertise.

B road Outlook

High quality manufacturing engineers are in great demand, and you would be entering a profession where your skills, knowledge and competencies would be sought by manufacturing companies in the UK and abroad.

R elated Occupations

You might consider: mechanical, automotive, electrical/electronic, telecommunications, civil, chemical, mining, petroleum or marine engineer. Alternatively, you might be interested in robotics or cybernetics.

I mpact

Whilst you may have specific hours of work you are also likely to be asked to work overtime on occasion, when there is a deadline to meet or a problem with production. Some production lines run continuously, so you may be required to be on call when problems arise.

Depending on the area of production with which you are involved, you may need to spend at least some time working in a factory or manufacturing area. Occasionally this could be dirty or noisy and you may be required to wear protective clothing.

E arnings Potential

You are likely to earn around £15,000 to £18,000 when you first start work after graduating but this has the potential to rise sharply as you gain experience. Once you are chartered, your salary is likely to rise considerably and may well exceed £50,000. Average earnings for incorporated engineers are around £37,000.

F urther Information

The Institution of Mechanical Engineers, London SW1H 9JJ
Website: www.imeche.org.uk

The Engineering and Technology Board, London WC2R 3ER
Website: www.engc.org.uk

The Engineering Careers Information Service
Website: www.enginuity.org.uk

Alternative/equivalent entrance requirements can include: ILC, IB, EB, NC/ND and many other similar international systems. For further details see the Equivalent Qualifications section in the Introduction.

What is Involved?

Working as a marine biologist, you would be concerned with the astonishing diversity of plant and animal life in the world's oceans. Your area of study could include anything from microscopic bacteria to the largest whales. You could concentrate on a specific group of marine organisms or you could look more broadly at marine ecology and the interaction between groups of organisms. You might work in an area such as monitoring fish stocks and developing sustainable methods of harvesting food from the sea; you might be searching for new chemicals for the pharmaceutical industry; you might be measuring the effects of dumping waste in the oceans.

Opportunities for Training

There are about 25 universities offering degrees in marine biology, mostly organising their courses on a modular basis. This structure should give you experience of a range of biological disciplines, such as genetics, ecology, zoology, biochemistry, botany and microbiology. Other modules would be designed to give you a necessary background in marine chemistry, physics and geology and an understanding of how these disciplines interact to explain what is found in the ocean and why. You could also undertake more specialised postgraduate study in marine biology and you may find this essential before you enter the labour market.

You would find that most courses have a large fieldwork component, giving you plenty of opportunity to get your hands wet as you go to sea in a research vessel or collect samples on the shoreline. You may also have the opportunity to gain a diving qualification, which could prove highly useful.

Requirements

To gain admission to a degree course in marine biology, you would normally need three A level/AVCE/Advanced Higher, four or five Higher or equivalent qualifications, together with at least five GCSE/S Grade passes A-C/1-3 or equivalent, including English and maths. Some universities specify A level/ Advanced Higher, Higher or equivalent in biology and another science subject.

Kind of Person

You should have a keen interest in science generally, with a particular passion for the sea. You would probably be involved in research work and much of this would involve careful attention to accuracy and detail. You would be expected to communicate your results to others, some of whom may not have the same scientific background as you. You should therefore have good written and verbal communication skills. You would almost certainly make extensive use of computers for obtaining, processing and storing data and would therefore need excellent IT skills. Your work would involve you in being out of doors in all sorts of weather, sometimes at sea. For this you would need to be quite fit and robust.

B road Outlook

Job prospects in this area are not good in the UK, where there are many more marine biology graduates than there are vacancies. There is only a limited amount of research being undertaken and this is often commissioned on short-term contracts.

There is some work in the commercial sector but marine departments tend to be small, with limited promotion prospects. You may find that a specialised postgraduate qualification is essential before you can get started in the labour market.

R elated Occupations

You might wish to consider: biologist, biochemist, oceanographer, geologist, conservation officer or environmental scientist.

I mpact

If you are working in a land-based, laboratory environment you are likely to be working normal office hours. However, you might at times have to go to sea, which would involve working longer hours, in harder conditions and could take you away from home for several weeks. Wherever you work as a marine biologist, you should be prepared to get wet at times.

It can be difficult to plan your career progression if you are restricted to a succession of short-term contracts.

E arnings Potential

The salaries for marine biologists usually start at around £15,000, although there can be some variation in this, rising to around £30,000 for an experienced senior scientist. Some marine biologists become specialists in a particular area, boosting their income with consultancy or lecturing fees.

F urther Information

Natural Environment Research Council, Swindon SN2 1EU
Website: www.nerc.ac.uk

Centre for Environment, Fisheries and Aquaculture Science (CEFAS), Lowestoft NR33 OHT Website: www.cefas.co.uk

Marine Conservation Society, Ross on Wye HR9 5BU
Website: www.mcsuk.mcmail.com

Department for Environment Food & Rural Affairs, London SW1P 3JR
Website: www.defra.gov.uk

> *Alternative/equivalent entrance requirements can include: ILC, IB, EB, NC/ND and many other similar international systems. For further details see the Equivalent Qualifications section in the Introduction.*

What is Involved?

As a marine engineer, you could be involved in the design, management and maintenance of many different sorts of systems and equipment used in a maritime environment, including:

• Ocean engineering, involving all aspects of the exploration and production of oil, gas and minerals found under the seabed. The range of activities includes oil and gas extraction, mining the seabed for minerals, and development of renewable energy resources.

• Offshore engineering, involving the design, construction, commissioning and operation of fixed and mobile offshore platforms and their associated systems. Designers and operators have to find ways of overcoming the problems presented by winds, waves, currents and the nature of the seabed, while dealing with high pressure, high temperature and corrosive fluids and gases.

• Seagoing engineering, involving the safe and efficient operation of a vessel's main propulsion machinery, associated equipment and systems. The traditional career path here would be to train with the Merchant or Royal Navy, gaining qualifications and experience at sea. See our separate articles for Royal Navy and Merchant Navy Officer.

Opportunities for Training

Both BEng (Bachelor of Engineering) and MEng (Master of Engineering) courses are available. BEng courses usually last three years (four years in Scotland); MEng courses are a year longer. The MEng provides a broader engineering education than the BEng. On the other hand, the BEng would allow you to complete your academic studies more rapidly, and to enter industry a year earlier to continue your education in the workplace. Both routes provide a pathway to chartered engineer status but additional study would be required to supplement the BEng. See our separate article on engineering qualifications.

Your academic education would normally be followed by a period of structured training and experience known as Initial Professional Development.

Requirements

For degree entry, you would normally need at least two A level/AVCE/Advanced Higher, three Higher or equivalent qualifications, including maths and usually physics or a subject which includes physics. In addition, an AVCE in engineering could be helpful for some courses. You would also be expected to have supporting GCSE/S Grade passes A-C/1-3 or equivalent, usually including English. Other useful subjects would include technology and foreign languages. At many universities, students without the necessary background in science and mathematics can take a one-year foundation course.

Kind of Person

Maritime engineering is a practical subject, attracting people who are interested in science and technology and finding out how things work and who have an affinity with the sea. You should have an open and enquiring mind, with a creative approach to problem solving. Teamwork skills are important because co-operation is essential in maritime engineering, particularly for engineers who serve at sea. You would need to be good at numerical reasoning and at using computers for your work. You would also have to be able to explain your thoughts and ideas clearly to other members of the engineering team.

B road Outlook

Research into the exploration and recovery of minerals from under the seabed is progressing rapidly and enormous engineering expertise will be required to carry out deep-sea operations in a sustainable and environmentally friendly way. Although the size of the UK shipbuilding industry has reduced dramatically over the past 20 years, market forces are beginning to work in favour of the remaining shipyards. The emphasis now is on building specialist vessels, particularly for the offshore industry and the Royal Navy, and there is a continuing demand for engineers in this area.

R elated Occupations

You might also consider: naval architect, offshore, aeronautical, automotive, mechanical, civil or electrical engineer, oceanographer or hydrographic surveyor.

I mpact

Traditionally, the engine room at sea is run on a continuous watchkeeping system, which involves working four hours on, eight hours off, round the clock. On more modern automated ships, the majority of engine room staff work during the day, with a single engineer on duty at night, although passenger vessels maintain continuous watchkeeping systems. Leave time is generous, to compensate for time spent on board and away from home. For example, after a voyage of around four months, you could get as much as two months or so off at home. Most ships have excellent facilities for those living and working on them and some provide facilities for officers to be accompanied by their husband or wife.

E arnings Potential

You are likely to start earning around £18,000 when you first graduate and this will rise quite rapidly as you gain experience and take on more responsibility. The average salary of a chartered marine engineer is over £40,000.

F urther Information

The Institute of Marine Engineering, Science and Technology, London EC3R 7JN Website: www.imarest.org

Alternative/equivalent entrance requirements can include: ILC, IB, EB, NC/ND and many other similar international systems. For further details see the Equivalent Qualifications section in the Introduction.

What is Involved?

As a market researcher, you might be employed by manufacturing companies or other organisations to find out what people think and what they want. Manufacturers, politicians, pressure groups and others need to know the public response to various products, advertising campaigns and initiatives. You might work as a freelance, for an independent agency or as a member of the research department of a large company.

It would be your job to target an appropriate sample of people, to ensure that the right questions are asked, to collate the results efficiently and to present them in the best possible way. Depending on your circumstances and seniority, you might be involved in interviewing and making presentations of your findings. Market research is increasingly being conducted on an international basis, and there might well be scope for travel.

Opportunities for Training

The Market Research Society (MRS) is the official awarding body in the UK for vocational qualifications in this field. As well as running short courses, the MRS offers the Advanced Certificate in Market and Social Research Practice and the Diploma of the Market Research Society. Many companies offer new graduates the opportunity to take part in the MRS graduate development scheme.

Several business-related degree and higher national diploma (HND) courses offer options in market research and allied subjects, and there are some postgraduate courses available. Work experience or work shadowing would be an advantage when applying for courses or employment opportunities.

Requirements

While there are no particular educational requirements laid down for entry into market research, graduates are becoming increasingly in demand. The actual subject of your degree or HND would not be of critical importance, but business studies, economics or other subjects including evidence of numeracy would show that you have the aptitude for coping with numbers and statistics. Psychology or sociology could also be useful, and languages might give you an advantage in certain situations.

The minimum entry requirements for university degree courses are two A level/AVCE/Advanced Higher, three Higher or equivalent qualifications, together with five GCSE/S Grade passes A-C/1-3. In practice, you should aim to offer more than the minimum. Courses last three or four years. For HND courses, you would need one or two A levels/AVCE/Advanced Higher, two or three Higher or equivalent qualifications. The courses last for two or three years.

Kind of Person

In order to succeed in market research, you would need excellent communication skills, both spoken and written, as you would be in contact with a wide variety of people. Persuasive skills would also be an asset, and the ability to deal with disappointment in a highly competitive world.

A keen sense of business would be an advantage. You should be able to absorb and analyse data quickly and accurately, and you should have a high level of computer literacy. You should be able to work independently and also as part of a team, and be capable of working under pressure in order to meet deadlines. It would help if you were inquisitive and interested in how people think and behave.

B road Outlook

In an increasingly competitive business world, the work of the market researcher is becoming extremely important, and agencies concerned with consumer research have proliferated over the past few years. Another growth area has been social research, with increased use of researchers by local and national government.

Competition to enter the profession is fierce but the rewards can be high, with good promotion prospects if you can demonstrate the right levels of drive and determination. Later on, you could set up your own agency or head a large department for a major employer.

R elated Occupations

You might also consider: advertising executive, economist, marketing manager, personnel (human resources) manager, public relations officer, retail manager or statistician.

I mpact

Since many market research campaigns are linked to deadlines, you should be prepared for some long hours, together with working weekends and in the evenings. There would quite likely be travelling involved, maybe abroad. You would need to be tough and be prepared to fight your corner.

E arnings Potential

Salaries vary according to employment circumstances, since many market researchers are freelance. As a graduate, you could expect to start at around £15,000, while a senior executive might earn around £45,000 or more, depending on their track record and degree of managerial responsibility.

F urther Information

The Market Research Society, London EC1V 0JR Website: www.mrs.org.uk

Alternative/equivalent entrance requirements can include: ILC, IB, EB, NC/ND and many other similar international systems. For further details see the Equivalent Qualifications section in the Introduction.

What is Involved?

Your role as a marketing executive would be to secure the best possible match between the goods or services produced by your organisation and the perceived needs of your actual or potential clients. This could mean conducting market research to find out what customers want and what they understand about the market. You might then use the results of your research to identify your own and your competitors' shortcomings, decide on improvements needed, locate the main target markets in the UK and abroad and then put forward your proposals for the next steps. Typical approaches could include producing new promotional material, revamping your image, repositioning your products and upgrading your packaging. You might propose an advertising campaign, employ a public relations (PR) agency or department to enhance your public image, or introduce more effective distribution facilities. Your work might involve industrial products, consumer goods or services or the public sector.

Opportunities for Training

Although it is possible to start as a marketing assistant and progress through promotion, the majority of entrants join by direct entry on graduate trainee schemes. You could take a degree in marketing or a related subject but you would find that any degree subject is acceptable. You could also take a higher national diploma (HND) in business studies with a marketing specialism. Another method of entering this very competitive field is to start by gaining experience in a related area, such as customer service or market research, and then moving across. In most companies, you would train in-house by working alongside an experienced marketing executive. There are formal qualifications run by the Chartered Institute of Marketing (CIM) and the Communication Advertising and Marketing Education Foundation (CAM).

Requirements

For degree entry, you would need two or three A level/AVCE/Advanced Higher, three or four Higher or equivalent qualifications, together with a supporting platform of GCSE/S Grade passes A-C/1-3. HND requirements are usually slightly less demanding. A similar level of achievement would be required for direct entry as a marketing assistant. In all cases, evidence of skills in English and maths would be important.

Kind of Person

Above all, you would need commercial flair to recognise and exploit market opportunities. You should have an analytical mind, capable of assessing the essentials of each situation, with a clear understanding of your organisation and the position of its products and services within an ever changing market place. Good communication skills, both written and verbal, would be essential, together with the ability to relay your enthusiasm to others and motivate them to meet your marketing targets.

You would frequently face deadlines and would have to produce marketing briefs for senior management or prepare for negotiations with important clients. Numeracy would play a key role in assessing and analysing costs and estimating the effects of changes in pricing policy. You would need writing skills to produce reports or promotional literature and good IT skills. The ability to speak one or more foreign languages would be valuable.

B road Outlook

Opportunities for promotion would usually exist within your own organisation if you can prove you are effective and produce good results, although competition for senior posts is likely to be fierce. Marketing is considered to be a good basis for moving into general management and promotion could eventually lead a post such as managing director or chief executive. Additional qualifications in marketing would enhance your chances. Marketing is recognised as one of the most important activities in manufacturing and service industries, and vacancies are widely available throughout the country. Marketing is closely linked with advertising and public relations and a great deal in interchange between these sectors is possible.

R elated Occupations

You might also consider: advertising executive, public relations officer, retail manager, market researcher or logistics manager.

I mpact

This is a high pressure careers field, with a constant need to keep in touch with other people and to achieve deadlines and objectives. You would be expected to produce information in reports, analyse new data or travel to clients, at home and abroad, often at short notice, especially when you reach more senior levels of management.

E arnings Potential

As a school leaver trainee, you would start at around £11,000. As a graduate, you could expect around £16,000 to £17,000. Executives could soon rise to above £30,000, depending on their success, and directors to much higher salaries.

F urther Information

The Chartered Institute of Marketing, Maidenhead SL6 9QH
Website: www.cim.co.uk

The Communication Advertising and Marketing Education Foundation, Maidenhead SL6 9QH Website: www.camfoundation.com

Alternative/equivalent entrance requirements can include: ILC, IB, EB, NC/ND and many other similar international systems. For further details see the Equivalent Qualifications section in the Introduction.

What is Involved?

As a materials scientist, you would specialise in the physical and chemical properties of the materials used to manufacture products. You would be looking for the highest possible standards of performance and long-term reliability. You might, for example, work in the aerospace industry, developing stronger and lighter alloys for airframes or high temperature alloys for engines. Pressure for reductions in pollution and noise and increases in durability would drive your work forward. Other examples could include selecting the best combination of materials (plastics and metals) for a mobile phone, a replacement hip joint or the parts used in a domestic dishwasher. You would need to know the limitations and advantages of a variety of metal, plastic, ceramic, glass and carbon fibre resources and you would be expected to know how best to mould, extrude, shape and manufacture them. Thousands of different materials are available to deal with such problems as corrosion and rusting, high or low temperatures, vibration, bending, stretching, elasticity, resistance to chemical attack and simple daily wear and tear. The right combination of materials, allied to good design, can greatly enhance the performance, appearance, sales and profitability of a product.

Opportunities for Training

You would normally need a degree in materials science, metallurgy, materials engineering or similar. You should look carefully at the content of each course to find the right one for you, as they can vary widely. There is often the opportunity to include the study of a language and spend some time abroad, or to incorporate a management module; you might also consider a sandwich course, which would take a year longer but would offer a period of paid work placement. Some materials engineering courses are accredited for registration with the Engineering Council and could be the first step towards qualifying as a professional engineer. There is also the option of following a postgraduate materials science course, sometimes with sponsorship from an employer.

Requirements

For degree entry, you would need two or three A levels/AVCE/Advanced Higher, three or four Higher or equivalent qualifications selected from physics, chemistry, maths or design and technology, together with at least five GCSE/S Grade passes A-C/1-3. Materials and metallurgy courses are often under-subscribed and at some universities it is possible for students without the right A levels/AVCE/Advanced Higher, Higher or equivalent qualifications to take a foundation course before starting their degree. To be accepted for a postgraduate course, you would need a good honours degree in a relevant scientific or engineering subject.

Kind of Person

You should be interested and have reasonable ability in mathematics, physics and chemistry, but there is more to being a good materials scientist than that. You should enjoy applying scientific theory to practice, and be able to work accurately at all times. Good communication skills, both spoken and written, would be important, as you would be working as part of a team and would be expected to write up regular reports of your work. A logical approach would be required, although the ability to think laterally could be an asset in problem solving. You should also have a high level of computer skills. You may need good eyesight and colour vision for some aspects of the work.

B road Outlook

The pace of scientific and technological change seems ever increasing, and you should have no difficulty in finding work in many areas of materials science. Opportunities arise with private employers, at home or abroad, in research and development, quality control, and management. You could also work for universities or government organisations such as the National Physical Laboratory. Promotion could be within an organisation to a senior position, while some experienced materials scientists establish their own private consultancies or diversify into technical writing, teaching or sales and marketing.

R elated Occupations

You might also consider: biomedical scientist, aeronautical, chemical, civil, electrical, manufacturing or mechanical engineer, management consultant, research scientist, industrial chemist or product designer.

I mpact

In most parts of industry, you would work a fairly typical nine to five week from Monday to Friday. In production or quality control, however, you may need to work on a rota basis as the production line is likely to be in 24-hour operation. You would need to wear protective clothing when dealing with some dangerous substances and at other times you might be required to wear anti-contamination clothing in a scrupulously clean environment.

E arnings Potential

Pay scales vary widely between companies but generally you might start at around £16,000, with progression as you became more experienced and undertake more responsibility to around £35,000. Some materials scientists can earn appreciably more than this, particularly if they go into management.

F urther Information

Institute of Materials Mining and Metallurgy, London SW1Y 5DB (moving to Stoke on Trent, June 2002) Website: www.instmat.co.uk

Polymer Training Ltd, Telford TF7 4NA Website: www.bpta.co.uk

Alternative/equivalent entrance requirements can include: ILC, IB, EB, NC/ND and many other similar international systems. For further details see the Equivalent Qualifications section in the Introduction.

What is Involved?

As a mechanical engineer, you would be concerned with applying engineering principles and rules to all sorts of machines and their components. This means that you could be dealing with anything from the largest manufacturing equipment down to the nuts and bolts used in production. Depending on your interests and your level of qualification, you could become involved in design, manufacture, research, development, management or marketing or a combination of these.

Broadly speaking, you would focus more on research, design and development if you pursue your education, training and experience through to chartered status; you would be more involved with production processes as an incorporated engineer. See our separate article on engineering qualifications for a more detailed analysis of these issues.

Opportunities for Training

Training as a mechanical engineer would lead you into one of the broadest areas of engineering. There are many universities offering degrees in mechanical engineering and there is a wide variation in the types of courses and specialisms offered within these degrees, so it is a good idea to check the prospectuses carefully before applying. It is important to ensure that your degree is an accredited course recognised by the Institution of Mechanical Engineers. There are four-year courses, usually leading to an MEng qualification, which can take you to chartered engineer status.

Alternatively, there are three-year courses, usually leading to a BEng qualification, which can take you to incorporated engineer status. It is possible to add a further year of specialised study, known as a matching section, to enable you to progress to the chartered route. There are also sandwich courses, which include a year spent in industry gaining practical work experience, and you should find many opportunities for sponsorship.

Requirements

Most universities would either prefer or require you to have A level/AVCE/ Advanced Higher, Higher or equivalent in maths and physics, together with five GCSE/S Grade passes A-C/1-3, including maths and English. An AVCE or equivalent in engineering or manufacturing could be helpful.

Kind of Person

Your job would probably involve understanding and solving complex engineering problems. For this you would need a practical and logical mind that might need to show creative approaches to problems. You are likely to find yourself using maths and statistics in your work and you would make extensive use of computers, including specialised and sophisticated software packages.

You are likely to find yourself working as part of a multi-disciplinary team, which means that you would need to be able to communicate with a variety of people. These could be fellow engineers, who would share your technical expertise and understanding, or non-technical specialists in other fields, who would expect you to explain your ideas clearly to them. You could also find yourself managing a team of people working on a project. In addition, you may need to take into account the costs and budget of a project, so you would need some business skills.

B road Outlook

There are excellent job prospects for mechanical engineers and currently about 70% of graduates go into full-time careers associated with engineering. Mechanical engineering can provide a good starting point for a career in management because it is a wide-ranging subject area that requires and develops a number of different technical, people management and business skills. There are opportunities for mechanical engineers in just about all areas of industry and in many other fields of employment.

R elated Occupations

You might be interested in working in another branch of engineering or in specialising to become an expert in a particular field such as CAD (computer-aided design) or marine systems. Alternatively, you might consider science-based options such as: medical physicist, metallurgist, geophysicist, oceanographer or biotechnologist.

I mpact

You might be working set office hours or you might be expected to work long hours or on a rota system if you are involved with industrial production. You are likely to have to work extra hours from time to time in order to meet deadlines, when you could find that you are working under some pressure. Working towards chartered status can involve several years of further study after you have completed your degree course.

E arnings Potential

You could expect to start earning around £15,000 when you first graduate. Given the shortage of engineers in general, you should expect to be able to increase your earnings fairly rapidly and you should see your salary rise to around £30,000 within a few years. The average annual earnings for experienced chartered engineers are around £45,000 and for incorporated engineers around £37,000.

F urther Information

The Institution of Mechanical Engineers, London SW1H 9JJ
Website: www.imeche.org.uk

The Engineering and Technology Board, London WC2R 3ER
Website: www.engc.org.uk

The Engineering Careers Information Service Website: www.enginuity.org.uk

Alternative/equivalent entrance requirements can include: ILC, IB, EB, NC/ND and many other similar international systems. For further details see the Equivalent Qualifications section in the Introduction.

What is Involved?

As a medical physicist, you would be a specialist within a hospital clinical science group, applying science and technology for the benefit of the sick. Although your education and training would be different from that of a doctor, you could still be intimately involved in assessing and treating illness and disability. Close collaboration between a medical physicist and a doctor can achieve much more than either in isolation. You would work in many different medical fields, with a mixture of research, development and routine services to patients.

The main areas are nuclear medicine, radiotherapy, radiology and various aspects of physiological monitoring and investigation, but other specialities range from anaesthetics to urology. You could, for example, be responsible for establishing correct doses of radiation for treating malignant tumours, without causing unnecessary damage to other body tissues, and for ensuring that therapeutic and diagnostic radiographers use radiation equipment safely. You might also devise and erect special monitoring equipment, which can record patients' progress during or after surgery.

Opportunities for Training

With a good honours degree in physics or a closely related subject such as electronic engineering, you could join the two-year NHS training programme in an accredited department. Successful completion of the training programme, incorporating an accredited Master of Science (MSc) award, would result in the Diploma of the Institute of Physics and Engineering in Medicine (IPEM).

You would be given time off and support for your studies during this training period. It would be possible to complete your MSc before starting the training period, although this is a less popular route. Having completed this stage, you would have the option of taking a further course of advanced training, which could lead to a doctorate (PhD). You cannot become state registered without completing the MSc course and without gaining at least four years of practical experience.

Requirements

Entry to most relevant degree courses would require two to three A level/AVCE/Advanced Higher, three to five Higher qualifications or equivalent, together with a good platform of GCSE/S Grade passes A-C/1-3. Since there is a shortage of applicants, grade requirements in some universities are not high but all departments would be looking for good grades in physics and maths. For postgraduate study, you would usually need a first degree passed with first or upper second class honours.

Kind of Person

You would be working in a field that is developing fast, so you would need to keep up to date with new discoveries and advances in technology and a very strong interest in physics, maths and technology. Getting your calculations and measurements right could be critical to the patient. You would need to have an interest in and be at ease with patients. You would be expected to work as part of a team of clinical science professionals, so you would need to communicate clearly and to explain your diagnoses or recommendations.

B road Outlook

This is a small and very specialised field of medical science, but it is also one that is expanding rapidly. Within the NHS, you would follow a formal career structure, entering as a trainee at grade A. Once in possession of the IPEM diploma, you could compete for posts at grade B, the main professional grade, covering a wide range of responsibilities.

The highest level in the profession is Grade C, where you might be in charge of a scientific department or a major departmental sub-division. The most senior medical physicists have equivalent status to medical consultants. You could also seek employment in the healthcare industry, where your career would be less structured than in the NHS.

R elated Occupations

You might also consider: doctor, physicist, radiographer, electrical or electronic engineer, clinical biochemist, pharmacologist, optometrist or biomedical engineer.

I mpact

You would normally expect to work a 37-hour week in the NHS but might be expected to work extra hours to cover emergencies. You might need to attend lectures or conferences in order to complete your studies, which could be outside your normal working hours, as would keeping up to date on new developments in medical physics.

E arnings Potential

The NHS has a set pay scale and you are likely to average around £16,000 whilst you are completing your training. Once qualified, your salary could rise from around £20,000 to £40,000, with senior clinical scientists reaching £55,000 and beyond.

F urther Information

The Institute of Physics and Engineering in Medicine, York YO24 1ES Website: www.ipem.org.uk

The Institute of Physics, London W1B 1NT Website: www.iop.org

Alternative/equivalent entrance requirements can include: ILC, IB, EB, NC/ND and many other similar international systems. For further details see the Equivalent Qualifications section in the Introduction.

What is Involved?

As an officer in the merchant navy, you would work for a fleet which operates all over the world, consisting largely of ferries, container ships, passenger ships, survey ships and oil tankers. Additionally, some ships operate as auxiliary vessels for civilian and Royal Navy operations such as updating charts of shipping lanes. The person in charge of a ship is known as the master or captain. This post carries full responsibility for the ship, the crew, the cargo, passengers, the safety of the ship and everyone on board, and for navigating the ship to where it needs to go. The person in charge of a ship's engineering and technical systems is the chief engineer. This post carries full responsibility for the operation and maintenance of complex electrical and mechanical plant and associated control systems. As a ship's officer, you would have responsibility for a range of tasks in either the deck or the engine department. There are also some dual officer roles, covering both departments. You may also control the work of ratings, who perform a wide range of technical and non-technical jobs and have a lower level of responsibility.

Opportunities for Training

You can start your training at 16, 18 or 21, with a range of entry routes, and you can choose from deck or engineering options. Whether you join as a cadet, undergraduate or graduate, you would follow a programme of learning and experience, with alternating periods at college and at sea, obtaining the relevant qualifications and professional maritime certificates. Each route provides progression opportunities to the next stage, through the ranks to master/captain or chief engineer, depending on your chosen option, ability and ambition. You would be sponsored during your training. The sponsorship package would vary according to the training programme and the company concerned but your tuition fees would be paid and the total cost of practical training and experience at sea met by the company. In some cases, sponsorship can include a salary or training allowance to cover residential costs at college.

Requirements

You must be in good health and you would have to pass a statutory medical examination before being employed at sea. A good standard of eyesight is also required for prospective deck (navigation) personnel. You should generally be aged between 16 and 21, although older candidates are sometimes considered. For officer cadet training, you can enter with at least four good GCSE/S Grade passes A-C/1-3 including English, maths and physics or combined science; or with A level/AVCE/Advanced Higher, Higher or equivalent, preferably including maths and/or physics. For graduate entry, you would need to have a science-based degree.

Kind of Person

You must be prepared to accept responsibility not only for making important decisions yourself but also for inspiring confidence in the crew. You would need the knowledge, leadership, communication and team-working skills to keep complex systems running in extremes of temperature and weather, to demanding schedules and within safety and efficiency requirements. You would need to be able to cope with living, possibly for several months at a time, in a confined space far from friends and family.

B road Outlook

The merchant navy has in recent years had more vacancies (approximately 1000 per year) than it has applicants to fill them, so prospects are currently good. This is despite the fact that fewer crew will be required for the larger and more technically advanced ships of the future.

There are good opportunities for both men and women to obtain promotion but further training and examinations are involved, whilst length of service and personal characteristics also play an important part. After retirement from the service, there are civilian employers who look favourably on those with a successful merchant navy career behind them.

R elated Occupations

You might also wish to consider: Royal Navy officer or the other uniformed services.

I mpact

Life on board a ship is a 24-hour a day operation, seven days a week, 52 weeks a year. The work is divided into shifts called watches, which are typically four hours on watch, followed by eight hours off watch. At busy times this may increase to six hours on watch and six hours off watch.

Leave time is generous, to compensate for time spent on board and away from home. For example, after a voyage of around four months, you could get as much as two months or so off at home. Most ships have excellent facilities for those living and working on them and some provide facilities for officers to be accompanied by their husband or wife.

E arnings Potential

Pay rates and other conditions of service vary from company to company but cadets can expect to earn up to £7,500 and newly qualified officers approximately £21,000. In addition, food and accommodation are provided on board and travelling expenses are paid when joining and leaving ship.

F urther Information

Merchant Navy Training Board, London EClM 6EZ
Website: http://www.mntb.org.uk/

Alternative/equivalent entrance requirements can include: ILC, IB, EB, NC/ND and many other similar international systems. For further details see the Equivalent Qualifications section in the Introduction.

What is Involved?

As a metallurgist, you would be a specialist in the science and engineering of metals, concerned with examining how they behave during use, what we can make them do and how we can use them to our best advantage. There are literally thousands of different metal products with widely different physical and chemical properties. You could work in research to overcome problems of metal failure or corrosion in aeroplanes or motorcars, or on the formulation and quality control of new steels/alloys.

There is considerable overlap between the work of a metallurgist and that of a materials scientist, as more and more manufactured products use combinations of metals, plastics, ceramics and carbon fibre, which need to fit together and survive impacts, dampness and high or low temperatures whilst meeting the need for attractive product design and commercial viability.

You might specialise in the manufacturing processes of converting metals and alloys into products, or you might concentrate on the extraction of metals from ores or recovery from scrap.

Opportunities for Training

You would normally need a relevant degree and there are several universities offering suitable courses in metallurgy or materials science. Some courses cover a wide range of metals, plastics and ceramics, while others might concentrate on just one material, so it is important to examine prospectuses carefully to make sure that courses cover the areas you expect. Metallurgy can also be studied as a joint honours subject with languages, business, management or economics, for example. You could choose to continue your studies in metallurgy with a postgraduate course at MSc or PhD level.

Requirements

For degree entry, you would need two or three A level/AVCE/Advanced Higher, three or four Higher or equivalent qualifications selected from physics, chemistry, maths or design and technology, together with at least five GCSE/S Grade passes A-C/1-3. Metallurgy courses are often under-subscribed and at some universities it is possible for students without the right A level/AVCE/Advanced Higher, Higher or equivalent qualifications to take foundation courses before starting their degree. To be accepted for a postgraduate course, you would need a good honours degree in metallurgy or a related subject such as mechanical engineering.

Kind of Person

You would need to have a strong interest and proven ability in maths, physics and chemistry. You should enjoy the practical aspects of science, such as your practical laboratory work at school. You would need to have a methodical approach to your work and meticulous attention to precise detail.

You may need deep reserves of patience as you carry out repeated tests on particular metals before discovering an acceptable alloy. You are likely to use computers in analysing data from test equipment. You would also need to communicate well and to be prepared to seek advice from other experts when necessary. You may need to instruct technicians who are helping in your research, and to communicate clearly with others who do not have your scientific background. The ability to write clear, unambiguous reports would be essential if you work in scientific research.

B road Outlook

There are excellent job opportunities for metallurgists at the moment. You might be employed by a steel producer or by an automotive, aeroplane, armaments, shipbuilding or railway engine manufacturer. There are opportunities to work in metallurgical research laboratories and for government science research centres, as well as in university research departments. Many other industries employ metallurgists at all stages of their production processes, including electricity and power companies and the oil and chemical industries. There are good opportunities to work abroad and also to work as an independent consultant.

R elated Occupations

You might also consider: mechanical, aeronautical, civil, structural, mining or chemical engineer, physicist or geologist.

I mpact

In most parts of industry, you would work a fairly typical nine to five week from Monday to Friday. In production or quality control, however, you may need to work on a rota basis, as the production line is likely to be in 24-hour operation. You would need to wear protective clothing when dealing with some dangerous substances and at other times you might be required to wear anti-contamination clothing in a scrupulously clean environment.

E arnings Potential

As a newly qualified graduate, you are likely to start earning in the region of £15,000. This can rise to £40,000 and above with experience.

F urther Information

The Institute of Materials, Mining and Metallurgy, London SW1Y 5DB (moving to Stoke on Trent, June 2002) Website: www.instmat.co.uk

Alternative/equivalent entrance requirements can include: ILC, IB, EB, NC/ND and many other similar international systems. For further details see the Equivalent Qualifications section in the Introduction.

What is Involved?

As a meteorologist, you would be a specialist in the science and study of the earth's atmosphere and the interaction of the atmosphere with the earth itself. Meteorology seeks to understand and to predict the behaviour of weather, the climate and the atmosphere in general, from the surfaces of land and sea to the edge of space.

The Royal Meteorological Society, the professional body for meteorologists, lists 27 separate areas where meteorologists work. They range from weather forecasting to climatology and from horticulture to the planning and operation of great engineering undertakings. They include the development of complex mathematical representations of the way the atmosphere works and can be predicted, the manipulation of vast data resources, the design, development and testing of new instruments, and the use of modern communications and data- management systems. There are also close links with sister sciences such as hydrology and physical oceanography.

The Met (Meteorological) Office, currently in Berkshire but moving to Exeter in 2003, is the largest employer of meteorologists. It is a government institution involved in research, applied and operational meteorology.

Opportunities for Training

A university degree would be essential. This could be in meteorology but an alternative approach would be to enter meteorology at postgraduate level following a first degree in physics or maths or an associated subject such as computing, environmental studies, physical geography or electronics.

The Met Office has its own college in Reading providing training courses for new entrants and for continuing professional development. With a high level of knowledge and experience, you could become a chartered meteorologist. This professional qualification corresponds to others such as chartered accountant or chartered engineer. While it is not essential, accreditation can satisfy clients and employers that you have reached and continue to maintain a specified level of knowledge and experience and that you are conversant with current best practice.

Requirements

For a meteorology degree, you would need maths and physics at A level/Advanced Higher, Higher or equivalent level. You should research the exact entry requirements of individual universities. There are some Met Office opportunities for non-graduates, where you would need A level/AVCE/ Advanced Higher, Higher or equivalent passes including maths and/or physics.

Kind of Person

You would need a genuine and enthusiastic interest in the weather and climate phenomena, with a good working knowledge of maths and physics. You would also need to be observant, have good communication skills, enjoy problem solving and have a logical approach to collating data. You must be highly numerate and able to cope with sophisticated computer systems and software.

B road Outlook

The Met Office is the main employer and has a promotion structure which operates on merit. There are jobs with the Natural Environment Research Council and Agricultural and Fisheries Institutes but as they only employ a small number of meteorologists there is less chance of internal promotion. There are some opportunities for working abroad with the Met Office, with British companies or with the United Nations.

There are opportunities for pure research, applied research, operational work, scientific and commercial management, entrepreneurial ventures, teaching and consultancy.

R elated Occupations

You may be interested in training as a physicist, oceanographer or hydrographic surveyor.

I mpact

You may be expected to move your work base from time to time in order to broaden your experience. Indeed, it is a condition of Met Office employment that you agree to work wherever required. Some weather stations are located in remote spots, carefully chosen for their extreme weather conditions! As the earth interacts with the atmosphere around the clock, you may have to work shifts, weekends and sometimes long hours.

Although a few meteorologists appear on television as weather forecasters, most of this work is carried out by professional broadcasters after a short course at the Met Office college.

E arnings Potential

As a graduate you could begin by earning in the region of £16,000. Experienced research meteorologists earn in the region of £30,000 to £35,000 depending on their experience and qualifications. Senior meteorologists may earn in the region of £40,000 to £45,000.

F urther Information

Royal Meteorological Society, Reading, RG1 7LL
Website: www.royal-met-soc.org.uk

The Meteorological Office, Bracknell, RG12 2SZ
Website: www.meto.gov.uk

Alternative/equivalent entrance requirements can include: ILC, IB, EB, NC/ND and many other similar international systems. For further details see the Equivalent Qualifications section in the Introduction.

What is Involved?

As a microbiologist, you would study micro-organisms such as fungi, bacteria, viruses or algae, investigating their growth conditions and sources. You would also consider the impact of microbes on the environment and the relationship between microbes and other living organisms. If you choose to specialise in the hospital service, you could work as a *medical laboratory scientific officer* (MLSO), dealing with samples from patients and isolating and identifying the microbes that cause illness (pathogens). Alternatively, you could practise as a *clinical microbiologist*, working alongside hospital doctors, general practitioners and environmental health officers in the diagnosis and prevention of disease. In this role, you would be responsible for more complex and specialised techniques than an MLSO. You may, on the other hand, choose to develop new products in the food industry or work in a public health laboratory, testing food, milk and water supplies for microbiological contamination. There are other openings in areas such as the pharmaceuticals, cosmetics and oil industries, where micro-organisms can be used to produce chemicals, hormones, antibiotics and enzymes, all of which can be of great benefit to society.

Opportunities for Training

Most microbiologists are graduates and you would need a good honours degree or higher national diploma (HND), preferably in microbiology or in another life science such as biology, biochemistry or biomedical science. To qualify as an NHS clinical microbiologist, you would then undergo three years of training that would include an MSc course, practical work and a research project. You would have to register with the Health Professions Council and complete a one- or two-year postgraduate training course if you want to work as an MLSO in the National Health Service. In other areas of microbiology, employers offer work based training. There are also a limited number of training placements for school leavers.

Requirements

For degree entry, you would need A levels/Advanced Highers, Highers or equivalent passes in biology and one other science subject, together with five GCSE/S Grade passes at A-C/1-3 including maths, English and two sciences. Some universities may specify chemistry A or AS level/Higher, Advanced Higher or equivalent qualifications but offers are likely to vary considerably between institutions. If you decide to take an HND, you are likely to need a science subject at A level/AVCE/Advanced Higher or Higher, together with four GCSE/S Grade passes at A-C/1-3 including maths, English and a science subject.

Kind of Person

You would need a strong interest in science, particularly biology, although an interest in chemistry is also useful. You should enjoy the practical side of your science lessons at school and be able to work accurately and in a well organised way in the laboratory. Some types of work include following set procedures with rigorous attention to detail and this needs patience and persistence. You would have to show a responsible approach in carrying out your tests and analyses. Communication skills are very important since you would probably be working in a multi-disciplinary team and would need to explain your work to people who do not share your scientific background.

B road Outlook

Microbiology is an essential component of medical diagnosis, a tool in tracking down serious infections and epidemics, which can threaten human and animal health. National Health Service and other medical laboratory work is therefore likely to be in demand. Microbes can be beneficially harnessed in food production, in the manufacture of all alcoholic beverages, cheeses, and yoghurt, and in the disposal of sewage or of harmful industrial waste, so careers are likely to expand in these fields too.

R elated Occupations

You might be interested in other scientific careers such as biochemist, pharmacist, biological researcher, food scientist or forensic scientist.

I mpact

Shift or night work is sometimes necessary in manufacturing plants and on-call work is expected when providing a round the clock service, such as in the NHS. Occasionally you may have to work extra hours to meet deadlines. It is usual to wear protective clothing, which varies according to the work and includes laboratory coats, gloves and eye protection.

E arnings Potential

Starting salaries for graduate trainee biomedical scientists and microbiology technicians are about £13,000 (rising to more than £27,000). Clinical microbiology trainees and graduate research assistants earn about £16,000, which rises with experience and expertise. You may earn more by taking on management responsibilities or perhaps teaching commitments. Starting salaries in industry are usually around £18,000 upwards.

F urther Information

The Society for General Microbiology, Reading RG7 1AG
Website: www.biocareers.org.uk

The Institute of Biomedical Science, London EC1R 5HL
Website: www.ibms.org

The Health Professions Council, London SE11 4BU
Website: www.hpcuk.org

The Institute of Biology, London SW7 2DZ Website: www.iob.org

Alternative/equivalent entrance requirements can include: ILC, IB, EB, NC/ND and many other similar international systems. For further details see the Equivalent Qualifications section in the Introduction.

What is Involved?

As a midwife, you would work in the community or in healthcare settings such as hospital maternity units, providing care and support for expectant mothers both during pregnancy and throughout labour and the postnatal period. Apart from delivering babies, you would carry out clinical examinations, provide health education, help mothers and their partners prepare for their parental role and give them advice on feeding their baby. You would also work in partnership with other health and social care professionals to meet the particular needs of people such as teenage mothers, socially excluded mothers, disabled mothers and mothers from diverse ethnic backgrounds. Your priority would be to provide a 'woman-centred' integrated care service, offering choice and continuity of support to mother and child.

Although you would be working as a healthcare professional, you would have a client group who are on the whole very healthy and in need of help and advice only because they are expecting a baby. The birth itself may be at the heart of the process, but midwives provide support to women, their babies, their partners and families, from conception to the first phase of postnatal care.

Opportunities for Training

You could enter the profession directly by undertaking a specialised three- or four-year course leading to a midwifery qualification. These course are provided at both diploma and degree level by a number of universities. You could also take a shortened (18 months) midwifery course after first qualifying as a nurse. Courses combine theory and practice, with periods of university-based study interspersed with supervised work in local hospitals, clinics and the community. The diploma route offers free tuition and non means-tested bursaries, while the degree route generally includes free tuition and some means-tested bursaries.

Before you can practise, you must be registered with the Nursing and Midwifery Council and you must maintain a portfolio of evidence of your continuous professional development. This would mean updating your skills and knowledge on a regular basis.

Requirements

For entry to a diploma course you would need at least five GCSE/S Grade passes A-C/1-3 or equivalent, usually including English and maths or a science. Many alternative qualifications are acceptable, especially for mature candidates. Entry to a degree course would require a minimum of two A level/AVCE/Advanced Higher, three Higher passes or equivalent qualifications, plus supporting GCSE/S Grade passes. A pass in a science subject may be required.

You must be over 17 before you start training and you must pass a medical test.

Kind of Person

You would be providing professional support and reassurance to a huge

210

diversity of women, during some of the most emotionally intense periods in their lives. You must be kind and caring, flexible and adaptable, prepared to look after all women regardless of their class, creed, economic status, race or age. You would need to be able to stay calm and alert in times of stress and enable women to feel confident and in control. On the rare occasions where something goes wrong, you would have to be ready to react quickly and effectively. Good organisation and record keeping are essential.

B road Outlook

There should be no difficulty in getting work once you qualify. Your first job would probably be within the National Health Service but there are openings within the private sector and some midwives practise independently. There are also opportunities for work abroad, although some countries specify that midwives must have full nurse training. Promotion can come as, for example, head of midwifery services or you might like to take further qualifications and become a midwifery teacher.

R elated Occupations

You might also wish to consider: nurse, nursery nurse, dietitian, doctor, health visitor, occupational therapist, physiotherapist, social worker or teacher.

I mpact

You must be prepared to work shifts, including nights, weekends and holiday periods. You would also have to respond to emergency calls and you would need your own transport in order to travel between the hospital or clinic and people's homes. You would wear a uniform all the time you are on duty.

E arnings Potential

Midwives working in the NHS usually start on a salary of around £16,500 a year. After that, allowances are paid for additional skills, overtime, shift working, responsibilities and experience. Senior midwives can earn more than £30,000 and an additional allowance is paid to those working in London.

F urther Information

Royal College of Midwives, London W1G 9NH Website: www.rcm.org.uk

NHS Careers, Bristol BS99 3EY Website: www.nhscareers.nhs.uk/

Nursing and Midwifery Council, London W1B 1PZ
Website: www.nmc-uk.org

NHS Education for Scotland Website: www.nes.scot.nhs.uk

Alternative/equivalent entrance requirements can include: ILC, IB, EB, NC/ND and many other similar international systems. For further details see the Equivalent Qualifications section in the Introduction.

Mining Engineer

What is Involved?

The scale of industrial operations in mining can be immense, requiring teams of trained professional engineers. As a mining or quarrying engineer, you would design and manage systems used in the extraction of ores; as an environmental engineer, you would provide essential planning and monitoring services; as a minerals engineer, you would design and manage plants for processing the minerals into metals and saleable concentrates or for recycling metals and related minerals. You would be expected to apply environmental best practice in all of these activities and you may find increasing opportunities to work solely in cleaning up the environment and in conservation. This is a very technologically driven industry and one that tries to balance ever-increasing demands for raw material resources with environmental issues.

Opportunities for Training

You would need a degree in mining engineering from one of the small group of universities specialising in this area. In order to become a chartered engineer, primarily concerned with research, design and development, you would need to complete at least four years of academic study and would usually achieve this via an MEng degree. If you want to be more involved with the day-to-day management of production processes as an incorporated engineer, you could take a three-year BEng degree. You don't always have to choose your specific training route from the start, so you should read prospectuses carefully. See also our separate article on engineering qualifications. There are sandwich courses available for both types of degree; these add an extra year but give the opportunity for a period of work experience, which can be very valuable when you are looking for a job. After graduating, you would need to complete a period of industrial training and responsible work experience before you achieve chartered or incorporated engineer status.

Requirements

For a degree course, you are likely to need A level/AVCE/Advanced Higher, Higher or equivalent passes in two or three subjects selected from maths, physics and chemistry. If the latter subjects are not actually required, they will be strongly preferred by universities. (An AVCE or equivalent in engineering could be acceptable for some courses). In addition, you would need five GCSE/S Grade passes (A-C/1-3), including English, maths and at least one science subject. You would also be expected to have visited some mines and to have an understanding of the key issues in the industry.

Kind of Person

You should be interested in technology and in keeping up to date with developments in your field. You would need a strong interest in maths and science and it might be helpful to have an interest in geology or physical geography. You would probably be expected to find practical solutions in your work, so you should have a logical and creative approach to problem solving. You are likely to be analysing complex information, and may be required to use computers so you would need IT skills. Some of your work is also likely to require you to show meticulous attention to detail. In addition to your technical skills you will need to communicate well with others. You are likely to be working as a member of a small team. In addition to talking to other engineers, you may be expected to direct the work of others and also to explain your ideas to people who may not have your technical expertise.

B road Outlook

There are good employment prospects for mining engineers both in this country and abroad. Employers range from large multinational organisations, such as the major oil and gas producers, to small companies offering specialised services. With long-term reductions in commodity pricing, mining cannot afford to be inefficient and outdated. It is very capital intensive and is becoming increasingly technologically driven in order to realise lower costs. Owing to the diversity and geographical spread of the industry, it is not possible to describe an average career in mining and minerals engineering. You could focus exclusively on coal or salt, for example, or you could travel extensively – anywhere from Antarctica to Zambia with spells in the UK – gaining experience of mining for, say, copper, zinc, lead or gold.

R elated Occupations

You might also consider: petroleum, chemical, civil, mechanical, energy or nuclear engineer, materials scientist/metallurgist or geologist.

I mpact

If you want to stay involved in mining operations, you have to go where the mines are. Given that many mines are in remote locations, you can't always live where you would ideally like. You may sometimes work normal office hours in a relatively clean environment but you may equally work highly irregular hours, outdoors or deep underground, in conditions that could be difficult, dirty and at times dangerous.

E arnings Potential

Starting salaries for graduates can range from £18,000 to £25,000 and, ten years after graduation, they can rise to £60,000.

F urther Information

The Institute of Materials, Mining and Metallurgy, Doncaster DN1 2DY
Website: www.imm.org.uk & www.uk-rocks.net

The Engineering and Technology Board, London WC2R 3ER
Website: www.engc.org.uk

The Engineering Careers Information Service
Website: www.enginuity.org.uk

Alternative/equivalent entrance requirements can include: ILC, IB, EB, NC/ND and many other similar international systems. For further details see the Equivalent Qualifications section in the Introduction.

What is Involved?

As a curator or keeper, you would usually manage a section of a large museum or art gallery (exhibiting, for example, paintings/sculpture, archaeological objects, historically important documents and artefacts or furniture), and would be responsible for the acquisition, identification, display and care of the exhibits. This would include seeing that they are kept in appropriate lighting and atmospheric conditions and arranging for any necessary restoration or conservation. You may also find yourself involved in the design of exhibitions and in administrative tasks: including cataloguing, preparing exhibition catalogues, articles and poster displays; giving talks and looking after members of the public.

In a large gallery or museum, jobs can be highly departmentalised and you might specialise in, say, 16th Century Italian art, 19th Century sculpture, Egyptian artefacts, Greek vases or the paintings of JMW Turner. In a small museum or art gallery, you could be responsible for everything from developing an acquisition policy, working with school groups, preparing a touring exhibition and managing volunteers to raising sponsorship and writing press releases.

Opportunities for Training

There is no formal training route in this very small, competitive and highly academic field. You should have a good degree in a relevant subject area – which could mean anything from history, anthropology or history of art to ceramics, textile design or a science or technology subject – followed by a postgraduate course in museum or heritage studies. The Courtauld Institute, University of London or University of East Anglia are among universities offering relevant postgraduate provision. Many other opportunities are available and could even include a doctorate at an overseas university such as Harvard, Stamford or Rome.

You would need to show your commitment by undertaking voluntary work experience in a museum or gallery and you would find that some employers run formal schemes leading to National/Scottish Vocational Qualifications in cultural heritage management. You might find it useful to work over a period of several years towards Associateship and then Fellowship of the Museums Association.

Requirements

You would normally need two or three A level/AVCE/Advanced Higher, three or four Higher or equivalent qualifications for degree entry, together with a broad platform of GCSE/S Grade passes at A-C/1-3. For a postgraduate course, you should have a relevant first degree and evidence of your commitment (usually in the form of voluntary experience).

Kind of Person

You would need to have a genuine interest in art and historical artefacts, good organisational skills and the ability to explain and arrange exhibits in an imaginative way for visitors to enjoy. You might well be expected to have very detailed knowledge of a particular subject area. Good communication skills would be essential both for giving talks on your specialism and for writing associated articles and catalogues or even books.

B road Outlook

This is not an easy career route to follow: there is increasingly intense competition for jobs, the pay would generally be described as poor and the level of qualifications and experience demanded is extremely high. In addition, career progression can be difficult – you would have to be willing to move anywhere in the country to widen your experience and gain promotion – and short-term contracts are often seen as the norm.

The Museums Association website contains details of current opportunities. Potential employers include independent museums and galleries, universities, local authority museums and galleries and national museums and galleries. There is also some scope for overseas work, especially in Commonwealth countries.

R elated Occupations

You may also wish to consider: archaeologist, archivist, art auctioneer, conservator, art restorer, or fine arts/antiques dealer.

I mpact

While you would generally work around 36 hours per week, you should expect some weekend commitment in line with the opening hours of the museum or gallery. You may find yourself working late into the evening when a new exhibition is being launched, usually with an opening reception for friends of the museum or gallery or for local counsellors and sponsors. As noted above, you would almost certainly have to move home from time to time to pursue opportunities for promotion.

E arnings Potential

You might start as an assistant curator on around £15,000 a year, depending on the size and location of the museum or gallery. Progression to senior curator could take your salary to £30,000 or more.

F urther Information

Cultural Heritage National Training Organisation, Bradford, BD5 0UP
Website: www.chnto.co.uk

Museums Association, London, EC1 0PA
Website: www.museumsassociation.org

Alternative/equivalent entrance requirements can include: ILC, IB, EB, NC/ND and many other similar international systems. For further details see the Equivalent Qualifications section in the Introduction.

What is Involved?

As a professional musician, in classical or popular music, you would play one or more instruments and/or sing. You could be a performer or composer, a teacher working from home or in a school, college or university, an administrator, publisher, record company executive, instrument manufacturer, librarian, broadcaster or journalist. Many musicians combine some of these activities, especially those who both perform and teach. As an orchestral player, you may spend many years with one orchestra or work freelance, taking session work for concerts, recordings, backings and jingles. You could also join the armed forces or the police for service with a regimental or police band. In popular music, you might combine singing with playing an instrument either as a soloist or in a small group. Your main contact with the public would be through performing, perhaps supported with recordings and videos.

Opportunities for Training

Whatever area of music you choose, there is no standard training programme and no fixed career path. Any performing career would demand very high standards, simply because the competition is so intense. For classical musicians, the specialist music colleges and conservatoires offer three- or four-year degree courses with the emphasis on performance. Alternatively, you could study music to degree level at university, where courses may have more academic content, before taking a postgraduate course to concentrate on technique and performance. Music therapy training is also at postgraduate level. The armed services train musicians (including string players) for military bands. Recruits are brought in from the age of 16 and are given two-and-a-half years of professional training. There is limited formal training for popular music, although there are some courses. You should gain as much performing experience as possible, while trying to get noticed by a recording company.

Requirements

For degree course entry, you would need at least two A level/AVCE/Advanced Higher, three Higher or equivalent passes plus supporting GCSE/S Grade passes (A-C/1-3), and you would need to have reached an advanced level of instrumental or vocal performance (at least grade 8). To teach in a maintained school, you would need a recognised professional qualification for teaching as distinct from training in music. See our separate article for 'Teacher'.

Kind of Person

Qualities such as artistry, determination and dedication must be combined with general musicianship and technical mastery of your instrument or voice. As a performer, you must be confident in your ability and enjoy being in front of an audience. As a private teacher, you should like working with people and would need good communication skills, patience, perseverance and the ability to run your own business. To work in a school, you must like and understand young people and want to teach them, no matter what their ability.

B road Outlook

Competition is fierce and the pay is generally below that of other jobs requiring similar levels of skill, training and expertise. To succeed, you must have more than talent alone; you must also have absolute dedication and determination. To get work, you have to be known and this means taking every opportunity – concerts, auditions, awards, bursaries and competitions – to show that you are worth engaging. Even after becoming established, you would find that earning a living as a performer – out of recordings, broadcasts and concerts – is hard work. Many performers combine a performing career with teaching or other work in the community, perhaps as a music therapist.

Job prospects for classroom teachers are good, since the demand for music teachers exceeds the supply. Pop musicians often start informally as a group of students at school or college, usually with a manager who organises gigs and recording contracts. Some become rich and famous. Others work more or less full-time in pubs, clubs and concert halls.

R elated Occupations

You might also consider: teacher, music therapist, recording engineer or radio/TV producer.

I mpact

Working hours can be long and irregular, with evening and weekend performances and rehearsals during the day, often linked with extensive travel to concerts or gigs. As a music teacher, you would work more regular hours but would usually be expected to organise evening and weekend events.

E arnings Potential

Top performers command extremely high fees but, for the majority, earnings are moderate. The Incorporated Society of Musicians publishes on its website recommended rates for most types of musical activity. Music teachers, permanent members of major orchestras and musicians in the armed forces are among the few to enjoy the luxury of a regular income, although many musicians make a reasonable living.

F urther Information

Incorporated Society of Musicians, London, W1C 1AA
Website: www.ism.org

Musicians' Union, London SW9 0JJ Website: www.musiciansunion.org.uk

Association of British Orchestras, London SE1 9PQ
Website: www.abo.org.uk

Alternative/equivalent entrance requirements can include: ILC, IB, EB, NC/ND and many other similar international systems. For further details see the Equivalent Qualifications section in the Introduction.

What is Involved?

As a naval architect, you would be a professional engineer responsible for the design, construction and repair of ships, boats and other marine vessels and offshore structures. You could be involved with merchant ships, passenger ferries, naval warships, offshore drilling platforms or yachts, powerboats and other recreational craft. Given the size and complexity of many of these vessels, you would work as a member of a team containing many specialist engineers. Part of your role as a naval architect would be to integrate their activities and take overall control of a project. You would also have a specialist role in ensuring that the final product is safe, efficient and seaworthy.

Apart from the architectural aspects of ship form and layout, you must be able to use complex mathematical and physical models to ensure that your design is satisfactory technically and that it meets the relevant safety rules and standards. Alternatively, you may specialise in construction, usually taking responsibility for the management of a yard or for sections of it such as planning, production or fitting out. There is a continuous striving to make savings on existing techniques and equipment through the adoption of new processes and practices and by better training for the work force. You would also organise the supply of materials and components, inspection and testing as well as the vital resources of manpower.

Opportunities for Training

You would normally undertake a degree course in Naval Architecture, Marine Technology, Offshore Engineering or Ship Science. The course should be accredited by the Royal Institution of Naval Architects (RINA) and lead to registration with the UK Engineering Council as a Chartered Engineer (CEng) or Incorporated Engineer (IEng). There is also scope to qualify below degree level as an Engineering Technician (EngTech). You must have an aggregate of seven years of education, approved training and responsible experience in industry after reaching the age of 18 years before you can achieve full RINA membership and CEng status.

Requirements

You should take a broad range of subjects at GCSE/S Grade, covering both the arts and sciences and including maths, physics and English. You should then add three A level/AVCE/Advanced Higher, five Higher or equivalent qualifications, including good pass grades in maths and/or physics. These studies should lead to qualifications satisfying the entry requirements for either an accredited masters degree (MEng) course if you want to become a chartered engineer, or a degree (BEng) course if you are intending to become an incorporated engineer. (See the separate article on engineering qualification in the introduction).

Kind of Person

You would need a creative, practical, enquiring and logical mind, excellent communication skills in speech and writing, mature judgement and evidence of leadership ability. A keen interest in sailing, windsurfing or other maritime pursuits can be extremely helpful. You must have a broad understanding of many different branches of engineering together with advanced skills in computer-aided design.

B road Outlook

Naval architecture is a truly global profession and you should find that your qualifications and experience would open up career opportunities all over the world. You may become a specialist in one particular aspect of ship design or construction or you may use your professional skills in project management to develop a broader management career, possibly outside the maritime field.

Potential employers include ship and boat builders and repairers, offshore constructors, design consultants and, for the ships and submarines of the Royal Navy, the Ministry of Defence. Major equipment manufacturers also employ teams of engineers, including naval architects, on the design of such products as propulsion systems, auxiliary systems, sub sea production systems and control systems.

R elated Occupations

You may wish to consider: mechanical engineer, electrical/electronic engineer, civil engineer, offshore engineer, officer in the Royal or Merchant Navy, architect or systems analyst.

I mpact

Achieving CEng status can mean considerable extra work in the years immediately following your degree but this should be a good long-term investment. You may have to travel extensively as you seek to develop your career.

E arnings Potential

While you would probably start on around £16,000, the most recent Engineering Council survey (2000) shows average earnings for experienced CEng graduates of around £45,000 and for experienced IEng graduates of around £36,500.

F urther Information

The Royal Institution of Naval Architects, London SW1X 8BQ
Website: www.rina.org.uk

Alternative/equivalent entrance requirements can include: ILC, IB, EB, NC/ND and many other similar international systems. For further details see the Equivalent Qualifications section in the Introduction.

What is Involved?

As a registered nurse, you would be working as part of a multi-disciplinary team providing health care in hospitals, specialist clinics and the community. You would specialise in one of four main branches:

In the **adult branch**, your main focus would be patients from the age of 16 upwards.

As a **children's nurse**, you might be looking after a very sick baby on a life support machine, a 10 year-old needing urgent surgery to repair a broken leg and a 14 year-old with a damaged liver.

As a **mental health** or **psychiatric nurse**, you would be working with patients suffering from problems such as depression, anxiety, alcohol dependency and severe eating disorders.

As a **learning disability nurse**, you would be least likely to work in a hospital and could spend most of your time with patients in their own homes or in residential care centres.

Opportunities for Training

You would have to undertake a university-based diploma or degree programme, leading to registration with the Nursing and Midwifery Council (NMC). Training usually lasts three years (some degrees take four years) and includes equal amounts of theory and practice. You would gain experience in a variety of care settings, including hospitals, nursing homes and the community.

The three-year course is divided into two distinct parts:

• the first year, the "Common Foundation Programme" or CFP, is undertaken by all students, regardless of branch choice. It includes core issues and topics, together with experience of a wide variety of care environments

• the second part, the branch programme, concentrates on specific branch subjects and practice placements

You should investigate the area of nursing which you would like to study and ultimately work in, as the choice of branch for the second part usually has to be made upon application. However, some universities enable you to make a more informed choice after you have started.

Requirements

The baseline entry requirements are set by the NMC as five GCSE/S Grade passes A-C/1-3, or equivalent. However, universities also set their own entry criteria, which may be higher. You should therefore contact the university of your choice to check on the exact requirements. For a degree course in nursing, you would normally need at least two A level/AVCE/Advanced Higher, three Higher or equivalent qualifications, together with supporting GCSE/S Grade passes. The more scientific courses may specify science subjects at AS or A level, Advanced Higher or Higher, with biology being the most popular. Admissions officers are usually looking for commitment, motivation and experience as well as academic qualifications, so it is a good idea to get some relevant work experience. You have to be at least 17 years old to start training as a nurse.

*K*ind of Person

You would need to be very resilient, both physically and mentally, to face the many challenges involved in caring for people who are ill or disabled. You would be constantly interacting with other people, so would need to be good at both talking and listening. You would need to be able to inspire trust and confidence, displaying tact, sensitivity and maturity. At times, you would have to put people at ease in stressful situations. You would also have to work closely with others as part of the healthcare team.

*B*road Outlook

Employment prospects depend on where you want to work but there is no problem at present accessing employment as a registered nurse in the UK. There is a shortage of registered nurses in all disciplines and, even if permanent employment is not available, most hospitals and a number of nursing homes run 'nurse banks,' which may be a useful way of testing the environment whilst also earning!

*R*elated Occupations

You may wish to consider physiotherapist, occupational therapist, radiographer, dietitian or speech and language therapist. Alternatively, you might develop your career as a midwife or health visitor.

I mpact

Depending on your chosen branch, you might have to work on a shift basis, including nights, weekends and public holidays, although not usually more than 37.5 hours per week in total. There is currently such a shortage of nurses that many employers would be prepared to discuss all types of flexible working arrangements.

*E*arnings Potential

The starting salary for a newly qualified nurse is just over £16,000 per annum within the NHS, more in London. You could earn substantially more with overtime and experience. Salaries in the private sector are likely to be higher.

*F*urther Information

NHS Careers, Bristol BS99 3EY Website: www.nhscareers.nhs.uk/

Nursing and Midwifery Council, London W1B 1PZ
Website: www.nmc-uk.org

Alternative/equivalent entrance requirements can include: ILC, IB, EB, NC/ND and many other similar international systems. For further details see the Equivalent Qualifications section in the Introduction.

What is Involved?

As an occupational therapist, you are most likely to work as part of a multi-disciplinary team. Your job would be to assess and treat people of all ages with physical and mental health problems, to help them regain, develop or maintain an independent lifestyle. You may be involved with helping someone who has had a stroke or a person with an eating disorder return to a normal lifestyle.

Alternatively, you could find yourself helping burns victims recover from their injuries, work which may include applying make-up to camouflage any scarring. This rehabilitation can start before the patient leaves hospital and continues once they have been discharged, either in the patient's own home or in the occupational therapy department at the hospital. You might also work with long-stay patients in hospital, helping them maintain contact with 'normal' life, and you may become involved with supporting patients' families.

Opportunities for Training

You would need to be state registered with the Health Professions Council, which means in most cases that you must take a validated three-or four-year degree course in Occupational Therapy. All training courses are about two thirds academic, covering such areas as anatomy, physiology, psychiatry and orthopaedics, together with the particular skills and techniques used by occupational therapists, the organisation and management of occupational therapy departments and how to provide suitable aids and equipment for patients. The remaining third of the course is clinical and is spent in departments and hospital clinics learning about practical day-to-day occupational therapy. During this time, you would learn to assess and treat patients under the guidance of a registered therapist and then build up to treating your own small caseload under supervision.

An alternative route to qualification is the four-year, in-service, day-release course for people already working as assistants in occupational therapy departments. Accelerated postgraduate courses are also available, enabling graduates of other disciplines to obtain a licence to practise in two years.

Requirements

You would need a minimum of two A level/AVCE/Advanced Higher, three Higher or equivalent qualifications, together with at least five GCSE/S Grade passes A-C/1-3. Normally, this requirement includes at least one science subject at GCSE/S Grade, while some courses look for A level/Advanced Higher or Higher biology. Demand for courses can be quite high, which means that applicants often need more than the minimum requirements. It is best to check with admissions tutors to be sure of meeting the entry requirements for particular courses.

Kind of Person

Since the job is very varied and you would have to meet and deal with a large number of people with different problems and needs, you would need to be creative and flexible. Each patient will require their own particular programme to work on and will make progress at their own rate. You will need to be able to gain the confidence of your patients both to find out what their needs are likely to be and to be able to encourage them to keep trying. At times progress can be frustratingly slow and hard work. As well as being able to establish supportive relationships with patients, you would have to be able to explain the treatment clearly and adjust the programme as necessary. You would have to keep good records on each patient and you would need to liaise with other healthcare professionals, sometimes taking part in case conferences.

B road Outlook

Employment prospects are good as there is currently a shortage and there is an increasing demand for the services of occupational therapists. There are opportunities for specialisation in areas such as burns and plastics, neuroscience or working with handicapped children. There are also increasingly openings for occupational therapists to promote safe procedures at work and in the home, in order to reduce the risk of injury.

Most occupational therapists work for the NHS, in social services or in education departments but there are also opportunities to become self-employed or to work freelance or in private practice.

R elated Occupations

You might consider social worker or other therapy-based professions in the medical field, such as radiographer, physiotherapist, speech and language therapist or nurse.

I mpact

The work can be demanding, stressful and, at times, frustrating so you need to have commitment and a real desire to help others to achieve their potential. You would have to keep up to date with what equipment or exercises are available to help your patients. Occupational therapists usually work a 36-hour week, although you might sometimes be required to work extra hours.

E arnings Potential

In the NHS, a typical starting salary would be around £14,000 rising to £34,000 for a district superintendent. Prospects for promotion are excellent and there are growing numbers of research posts available and opportunities to work abroad.

F urther Information

College of Occupational Therapists, Education and Practice Group, Southwark, London SE1 1LB Website: www.cot.org.uk

Alternative/equivalent entrance requirements can include: ILC, IB, EB, NC/ND and many other similar international systems. For further details see the Equivalent Qualifications section in the Introduction.

What is Involved?

As an oceanographer, you would be a scientist concerned with the chemistry, biology, physics or geology of the marine world. This could include studying coastlines, waves and tidal flow, the structure of the seabed, estuaries and coastal waters or organisms that live in the sea. You work could relate to the pollution of the seas or issues of climate change.

If your main interest is biology, you might study sustainable methods of seafood production; as a marine chemist, you might focus on how pesticides or nuclear waste enter and move through the oceans; if you are interested in physics, you might prefer to study the interaction between the wind and ocean currents; as a geologist, you could study the deposition of sediments in the oceans.

Whatever your principal science, the additional dimension of oceanography would give you a broad range of skills and knowledge relevant to understanding and managing the marine environment.

Opportunities for Training

An ocean science degree would give you a broad overview of all the disciplines of oceanography, so that you can understand how they combine to explain the ways in which the oceans interact with the earth and the atmosphere. Most courses are modular, giving you a chance to specialise if you wish to as your awareness grows. There are also universities offering degrees focusing on a particular area of oceanography, such as marine biology or marine chemistry. For postgraduate study, it is more common to specialise in one of these specific areas of oceanography.

Requirements

For entry to a degree course, you would need at least two A level/AVCE/ Advanced Higher, three Higher or equivalent qualifications, usually including passes in sciences related to your main interest. Some universities specify more than the minimum, so you should research admission requirements carefully. Employers of oceanographers often require postgraduate qualifications.

Kind of Person

You would need a strong interest in science and the sea, with an enquiring mind and a keen attention to detail and accuracy. You would probably need to spend extended periods of time on a boat gathering data. You may need to go down to the seabed in a submarine vehicle or by diving. You would need IT skills to carry out detailed calculations.

Some of your work is likely to be carried out on your own but you would also need to work as part of a team. You may need to write up reports and explain to people what you have found out or what you are aiming to explore. These may be other scientists but could also be people who do not share your technical knowledge, so you would need to be able to communicate clearly.

B road Outlook

While competition for posts is fierce, there are opportunities for oceanographers to work as researchers and the Natural Environment Research Council is a major employer. There are also opportunities to work in a commercial environment or for an organisation like the National Rivers Authority, a harbour authority or the Royal Navy. As environmental concerns become more important there is an increasing number of consultancies being set up, creating opportunities to work in private practice.

R elated Occupations

You might also consider: hydrographic surveyor, geologist, meteorologist, biologist, chemist, physicist, microbiologist or biochemist.

I mpact

You are likely find yourself working away from home, sometimes abroad or living on ships. When you are working out in the field you would out in all sorts of weathers, sometimes cold and wet, sometimes basking in bright sunshine! You would generally work normal office hours but when you are at sea you may be expected to work long hours on a rota to finish your project in the time available.

E arnings Potential

You are likely to start on a salary of around £15,000, although you may get allowances for time spent working away from home. This can rise to over £30,000 for a senior scientist. Some oceanographers boost their income by undertaking lecturing duties at a university. Salaries in the commercial sector or for consultants may well be higher but are often based on short-term contracts.

F urther Information

National Environment Research Council, Swindon SN2 1EU
Website www.nerc.ac.uk

Southampton Oceanography Centre, Southampton SO14 3ZH
Website www.soc.soton.ac.uk

The Society for Underwater Technology, London EC3 7JN
Website www.sut.org.uk

Alternative/equivalent entrance requirements can include: ILC, IB, EB, NC/ND and many other similar international systems. For further details see the Equivalent Qualifications section in the Introduction.

What is Involved?

All companies and organisations rely on well-run offices to maintain their profitability or success. As an office manager, you would be responsible for making sure that every aspect of the organisation's administration were carried out in the most efficient and satisfactory way. You could be dealing with the outgoing and incoming information and communication and its accurate storage and retrieval, in both paper and electronic form. You would probably have a team of clerical and administrative assistants to deal with the day-to-day office duties, such as answering queries (in person or on the telephone), typing letters or emails, taking and passing on messages, providing help at meetings and filing information. You should set the tone of the office.

Opportunities for Training

There is no single route into office management, but many managers gain promotion from other administrative positions and are employed because of their experience and proven success in other fields. Training is often carried out on-the-job. Another route would be to take a degree or higher national diploma (HND). There are a good number of university courses in subjects such as business studies or management and allied options; postgraduate courses are also available.

More specific training courses could include the OCR (Oxford, Cambridge and Royal Society of Arts) Diploma and Higher Diploma in Administrative and Secretarial Procedures or the London Chamber of Commerce Executive Secretary Diploma. There are also National/Scottish Vocational Qualifications in administration.

Requirements

While there are no particular educational requirements laid down for office managers, graduates are increasingly being employed. Most subjects are acceptable but it would be useful to be able to show that you are numerate and have some idea of what business organisation entails. You might consider a course in business studies (though they vary widely and you should look carefully at their content before making your choice) or another subject containing an option in some aspect of business. Just as important as the actual subject of the course, however, would be your personality, general interest and understanding of the business world. A sandwich course, which includes an industrial or business placement, could be useful.

For entry to a degree course, you would need two or three A level/AVCE/ Advanced Highers, three or four Higher or equivalent qualifications, together with five GCSE/S Grade passes A-C/1-3. The courses last three or four years. For the HND route, you would need one or two A level/AVCE/Advanced Higher, two or three Higher or equivalent qualifications. The courses last two or three years.

Kind of Person

You should be organised, efficient and confident; you should also be willing to take responsibility and to make decisions quickly and fairly. As a manager, you should be happy working both as leader and member of a team, delegating sensibly and making sure that everything is working smoothly. Excellent communication skills would be important, as you would probably be in contact with a wide variety of people, both in the organisation and outside it. Computer literacy and a good standard of written language would be valuable.

B road Outlook

While the numbers of clerical and administrative staff may have fallen with the arrival of computers, there is still a need throughout the country for skilled office managers. Increasingly, business is becoming internationally based, making office managers with some ability in foreign languages particularly in demand. Non-commercial areas, such as national and local government and higher education, also need efficient office managers.

R elated Occupations

You might also consider: accountant, accounting technician, banking executive, chartered secretary, hospitality manager, leisure services manager, local government administrator, management consultant; personnel (human resources) manager; retail manager or civil service administrator.

I mpact

As an office manager you would normally work regular office hours but you might have to work overtime at certain times of the year. Weekend work would be unusual but, as the one in charge, you would be expected to take the lead if extra time should be needed.

E arnings Potential

There is considerable variety in salary scales, according to the size of the organisation and the amount of responsibility involved. In a large company or organisation, a skilful and ambitious manager could gain high rewards, with possible share in company bonuses. Salaries of between £20,000 and £30,000 should be possible, with more in London.

F urther Information

The Institute of Customer Services, Essex CO1 1EW
Website: www.ics-nto.com

The Association of Medical Secretaries, Practice Managers, Administrators and Receptionists, London WC1H 9LN Website: www.amspar.co.uk

OCR, Cambridge CB2 1GG Website: www.ocr.org.uk

London Chamber of Commerce, Sidcup DA15 7BJ
Website: www.lccieb.com

Alternative/equivalent entrance requirements can include: ILC, IB, EB, NC/ND and many other similar international systems. For further details see the Equivalent Qualifications section in the Introduction.

What is Involved?

As an operational researcher, you would specialise in applying mathematical, statistical, computing and other analytical techniques to help organisations evaluate their operational procedures, improve their efficiency and devise strategies for future development. Operational research (OR) work can be very varied, giving you the opportunity to move around and experience many different business environments, ranging from central government, health, defence or transport to manufacturing industry, retailing, financial services or power, water and telecommunications supply companies. Within these, you might consider areas such as information storage, handling and access, management decision making, manufacturing processes, sales administration, accounting systems, logistics, forecasting or scheduling. In a rapidly developing economy, OR techniques are in great demand to keep organisations efficient, economically viable and competitive.

Your work would often involve visiting the workplace to talk to operational personnel and management in order to establish what changes need to be looked at, what kinds of problems arise regularly to disrupt efficient operation and where information bottlenecks are causing delays in, for example, the delivery of goods or in reordering raw materials. You would then apply appropriate OR techniques, such as mathematical modelling and computer simulations, to analyse the problems and come up with pragmatic solutions for the management team or company board to consider. Finally, you could be directly involved in the installation and testing out of new systems.

Opportunities for Training

Most people employed in OR are graduates and many would have followed courses with a significant mathematical, statistical or computing content. However, opportunities can exist for people from other disciplines and those who move into OR from other professions. Many undergraduate courses in mathematics, statistics, business studies and management include some OR, although it is not always necessary for entrants to the profession to have studied OR. Many employers would look firstly for quantitative, logical and communication skills and then provide any further appropriate training. In fact, graduates are recruited from many disciplines – and most OR groups have members contributing a variety of skills. After graduating, you could either seek employment straight away or follow a postgraduate course. Many significant employing organisations prefer candidates with an MSc in OR and a list of suitable courses can be found on the Operational Research Society website.

Requirements

For entry to an appropriate degree course, you would normally need to have at least two A level/AVCE/Advanced Higher, three Higher passes or equivalent, in most cases including mathematics. After successfully completing your degree and demonstrating that you have the required analytical and business interest skills, you could progress to employment or postgraduate study.

228

K ind of Person

A solid grounding in maths, statistics and computing would be an important asset for a career in OR. However, before launching into data analysis, you would have to assemble and understand the information relating to the problem area. This would often involve in-depth discussions with people at all levels. Good communication skills and business awareness would, therefore, be crucial in winning co-operation, whilst literacy, numeracy and computer literacy would be vital in the execution of your work. You would need an excellent grasp of business operations, with an insight into management controls, communications, production and administration systems. You would have to pay careful attention to detail and you might need strong powers of persuasion to convince managers and directors that your proposals would solve their problems.

B road Outlook

Opportunities for promotion often occur within a high demand field of this sort, both in your existing organisation and by moving to another. Some 250 companies, government departments, financial institutions, retailing, transport, health, management consultancy groups and university departments offer openings for OR staff. This is a field in which you can gain a remarkable overall grasp of organisational structures and is likely to open up many opportunities for rapid promotion to senior general management levels and even to board level, where your training would give you a considerable technical advantage.

R elated Occupations

You might also consider: organisation and methods/work study officer, management consultant, software engineer, statistician or actuary.

I mpact

Your work could involve a great deal of travel in the UK and abroad, with often lengthy periods spent away from home and therefore with some disruption of social and family life. Disentangling complex systems and coming up with better ones would often be accompanied by the pressure of meeting deadlines, writing reports and proposals and making presentations to managers or senior executives.

E arnings Potential

Qualified operational researchers can earn around £35,000 and senior managers from £50,000 to £85,000 or more for department heads or directors.

F urther Information

Operational Research Society, Birmingham B1 2RX
Website: www.orsoc.org.uk

Alternative/equivalent entrance requirements can include: ILC, IB, EB, NC/ND and many other similar international systems. For further details see the Equivalent Qualifications section in the Introduction.

229

What is Involved?

As an optometrist you would be responsible for caring for people's sight. Your job would include testing sight, examining eyes and giving advice on visual problems. This may involve prescribing and fitting spectacles or contact lenses or it may mean referring the patient to their GP if you find a problem involving disease or damage to the eye. You would start by talking to the client to establish the reason for their visit, noting any history of problems or illnesses and whether they drive or play sport. You would then use a series of tests to examine the eyes and determine whether there are problems you can deal with or more serious issues in need of referral for medical treatment.

Opportunities for Training

To become an optometrist, you would need to pass the General Optical Council professional qualifying examination. This has two distinct parts:

• BSc Optometry (sometimes Ophthalmic Optics), a broadly based scientific degree combining theory with clinical work. The theoretical side includes anatomy and physiology, optics, optometry, pharmacology and the use of drugs, recognition of ocular abnormalities; the practical covers dispensing practice and management and professional studies.

• A pre-registration year of work supervised by a registered optometrist. At the end of this year you must take part II of the professional qualifying exam, which combines practical and oral assessment of the skills needed to manage patients and practise safely as an independent optometrist. After this is completed, you are eligible to register with the General Optical Council and become a member of the College of Optometrists.

Requirements

There are only eight British universities offering a first degree in optometry and there is a high demand for places. Most universities require two sciences at A level/AVCE/Advanced Higher, three Higher or equivalent qualifications, some specifying biology as one of them; chemistry, maths and physics are other particularly useful subjects. It is advisable to check entry requirements with the individual institutions. Before applying, you should spend some time on a work experience or work-shadowing placement with a qualified optometrist.

Kind of Person

Optometry involves combining expert knowledge with good communication skills, patience and precision to achieve the best possible care for your clients' eyes. You need to be able to understand a complex and precise science and have sufficient mathematical aptitude to make the accurate measurements and calculations needed. The instruments used are delicate and you would need manual dexterity to use them correctly. As there are constant developments in this field, you would need to keep yourself up to date. You would be dealing with people from all walks of life, some of them worried about their sight or the prospect of wearing glasses or lenses. If you intend to work in private practice, you would also need good business sense and management skills. An interest in fashion and colour is helpful.

B road Outlook

With more than half the UK population having a diagnosed visual defect, there is no shortage of work for the nation's 8,500 registered optometrists. Most work in general practice on their own, in partnership for a small independent firm or in one of the big high street chains. Excellent prospects for self-employment attract many people to the profession. There are also opportunities to work in hospitals alongside eye specialists and their teams. Some optometrists become specialists themselves in a particular field or else assist with eye tests and prescriptions following operations or other medical treatment. There are also chances for research and teaching.

R elated Occupations

You may be interested in other professions concerned with maintaining or correcting people's vision, such as dispensing optician or orthoptist. You might also consider other medical related professions, such as speech and language therapist or radiographer.

I mpact

Most optometrists in private practice work a 37.5-hour week, although in some of the large practices you may have to work on a rota system in which days off vary. Saturdays are often busy in high street practices. If you set yourself up in practice you would have to work long and unsocial hours, at least to start with, in order to establish yourself. In the NHS, you would work a 35-hour week, although you may be on call at evenings and weekends. There is considerable scope for part-time work.

E arnings Potential

Salaries for trainee optometrists in their pre-registration year tend to be very modest but, once qualified, you can expect to earn at least £20,000 to £25,000, rising as you become more experienced. Your earnings potential can be much higher if you set yourself up as an independent optometrist. Hospital eye service salaries are graded and start at around £13,000 for a newly qualified optometrist, rising to around £50,000 with experience.

F urther Information

College of Optometrists, London WC2N 5NG
Website: www.college-optometrists.org

Association of Optometrists, London SE1 0HL
Website: www.assoc-optometrists.org

The General Optical Council, London W1N 2DJ Website: www.optical.org

Alternative/equivalent entrance requirements can include: ILC, IB, EB, NC/ND and many other similar international systems. For further details see the Equivalent Qualifications section in the Introduction.

What is Involved?

As an orthoptist, you would carry out detailed eye testing, using advanced equipment, to diagnose the causes of your patients' eye problems. You could measure the extent of long or short vision, of misalignment of the eyes, astigmatism, loss of vision and detect glaucoma and other eye diseases. You would refer patients where necessary to doctors for further assessment, treatment or surgery. Then you would give your patients advice on suitable treatment and monitor their progress. This may involve exercises to 're-educate' the eye muscles in cases of lazy eyes or after strokes. You may be involved in helping patients with their recovery after operation.

You could also be involved with assessing the vision of older patients who have been affected by illness, injury or a stroke or of children, who are likely to be the majority of your patients, and who may have difficulty in explaining their difficulties. For example, you would use a computerised field analyser to find out where the patient is experiencing a blind spot. Each working day is likely to be different. As well as conducting clinics for outpatients, you would accompany consultants on ward rounds in hospitals. You could also work in private practice.

Opportunities for Training

You would need to study for a degree in orthoptics approved by the Orthoptists Board of the Health Professions Council. These are available at three universities in the UK: Glasgow Caledonian, Liverpool and Sheffield. The degrees are of three-year duration, leading to BSc or BMedSci (orthoptics) qualifications. The first year covers general anatomy and physiology. It gives an understanding of the normal visual system as well as introducing optics and orthoptics. In years two and three, the investigation and management of disorders of vision are taught. In addition, you would learn about ophthalmology and pathology so that you can recognise disorders and diseases of the eye. You would be given practical experience with clinical placements in all three years of your course.

Requirements

To take a degree in orthoptics you would need three A level/AVCE/Advanced Higher, four Higher or equivalent qualifications, including at least one science subject, preferably biology but physics or maths would be very helpful, together with five GCSE/S Grade passes A-C/1-3, which should include English, maths, and physics or dual science. It is advisable to arrange a visit to your local orthoptic department to see what the work involves before applying for a place.

Kind of Person

You would need a keen interest in biology, maths and physics, as well as having good interpersonal skills to deal with the wide range of people you would meet in this work. Some of your patients may be hard to communicate with because they are elderly or young children, so you would need to be patient and creative both in your explanations and to capture their attention.

Much of the testing involves skilful measuring and the use of precision instruments. You would be expected to keep accurate records on your patients so you would have to be well organised. As well as working as part of a team, you would also need to be able to work responsibly on your own.

B road Outlook

Most orthoptists work in hospitals with ophthalmic departments and mainly for the NHS, although there are opportunities to work in private hospitals, in private practice, in teaching hospital trusts and special schools, as well as in the community, or to conduct research at a university. Orthoptists only treat patients referred to them by a doctor or other qualified practitioner so cannot seek work directly with individual members of the public.

R elated Occupations

You may be interested in other related professions such as dispensing optician or optometrist. Alternatively, you might like to consider another profession in the medical field, such as radiographer, podiatrist, speech and language therapist or physiotherapist.

I mpact

Most orthoptists work normal hours from Monday to Friday. Your social and family life would therefore be far less disturbed than that of other health professionals working in hospitals, who have to deal with emergencies and patient care on a 24-hour basis.

E arnings Potential

NHS salaries start at about £15,500, rising to around £32,000 if you were head of a large department. Rates of pay may be different in private hospitals.

F urther Information

British Orthoptic Society, London WC1H 9HX
Website: www.orthoptics.org.uk

General Optical Council, London W1N 2DJ Website: www.optical.org

The Health Professions Council, London SE11 4BU
Website: www.hpcuk.org

Alternative/equivalent entrance requirements can include: ILC, IB, EB, NC/ND and many other similar international systems. For further details see the Equivalent Qualifications section in the Introduction.

233

What is Involved?

As an osteopath, you would be working as a practitioner in complementary medicine. Your skill would reside in your sensitivity of touch, which you would use to locate the source of problems presented by patients, and the manipulative skills of your hands as you apply the treatments. You would look for such things as tissue tension or variations in the movement of joints as indicators of underlying dysfunction. Using your hands to correct joint and tissue abnormalities, you would make it easier for a patient's body to function normally and use its own recuperative powers more effectively. Beyond diagnosing and treating the structural and mechanical problems of the body, you would look at each patient's diet, lifestyle and mental well being to restore the state of balance within their total bodily function.

You would start by listening to a patient's account of their problem and observing the way they stand, walk, and move. You would then use your hands to discover the underlying causes of pain. Sometimes you may make use of x-rays as well. On finding the source of the problem, you would ascertain that it could benefit from osteopathy and you would carry out treatment using a variety of manipulative techniques. You may need to refer the patient to their doctor or another healthcare professional if you feel the problem is not suitable for osteopathy.

Opportunities for Training

In order to practise as an osteopath you must be registered with the General Osteopathic Council, which means that you must have trained at an accredited osteopathic school. Courses vary from four to five years full-time or five years on a mixed-mode basis. There is also an 18-month course open only to medical practitioners.

All of these osteopathic courses offer BSc or BSc Honours degree programmes. You would learn basic medical sciences, including anatomy, physiology and pathology, in addition to osteopathic philosophy, concepts and techniques.

Requirements

While they may vary slightly between each school, the usual minimum entry requirements are three good A level/AVCE/Advanced Higher, four Higher or equivalent passes, two of which should be chemistry and biology, together with five GCSE/S Grade passes A-C/1-3, including English and maths.

Osteopathy is not limited to school leavers. In fact, many practitioners choose osteopathy as a second career later in life.

Kind of Person

You would need excellent communication skills, especially in terms of listening to your patients, teasing out details of their problem and explaining your diagnosis. Having gathered the relevant information, you would need to be able to take a logical problem solving approach in order to assess the facts and decide on a course of action. You would need a caring attitude, with the ability to put nervous or shy patients at ease.

You should be in good health, with a high level of manual dexterity; osteopathy requires skill and technique rather than muscle power, with men and women having equal success as practitioners. To be self-employed or working for a small practice, you would need good organisational and business skills.

B road Outlook

Over five million people a year seek osteopathic treatment and demand is increasing. With most people feeling that they stand a better chance of obtaining relief for back pain outside conventional medicine, osteopathy is a growing profession.

Each patient may require more than one treatment and it may be that some patients choose to come back once or twice a year to ensure that a problem does not recur.

R elated Occupations

You may be interested in other professions in the field of complementary medicine such as chiropractor or reflexologist. Alternatively, you might consider a therapy-based profession in the medical field such as physiotherapist or occupational therapist.

I mpact

As a newly graduated osteopath, you would have a number of possible areas of practice to consider: set up on your own; join an established practice; work within the NHS; or join a multidisciplinary practice. As with all professions, you should reckon on it taking two to three years to become established and develop a full practice with the financial return that goes with it. Whilst London may appear to offer the greatest opportunity, it also has the largest number of practitioners and the most expensive premises. Setting up your practice further afield, where your premises would cost less and your services should be in greater demand, could make a lot of sense.

E arnings Potential

Since most osteopaths are self-employed, your income could vary considerably and would be determined by your reputation and the hours you are prepared to work. The average charge is between £20 and £50 per session. You would need to meet a number of professional costs, including the retention fee for the professional body and medical malpractice costs. Other business costs may include rental of your clinic, heating, lighting and any equipment plus wages for a receptionist or administrative staff.

F urther Information

Osteopathic Information Service, General Osteopathic Council, London SE1 3LU Website: www.osteopathy.org.uk

Alternative/equivalent entrance requirements can include: ILC, IB, EB, NC/ND and many other similar international systems. For further details see the Equivalent Qualifications section in the Introduction.

What is Involved?

As a patent agent, you would have a particular expertise in intellectual property rights, encompassing patents, industrial designs, design rights and related copyright areas. You would work in the patent department of a large industrial organisation, in a private firm of patent agents or in a government department. A patent is a right granted to inventors or companies, in return for disclosure of an invention, to stop other people using that invention for a certain period of time (maximum 20 years). In order to secure a patent, a full description of the invention needs to be filed with the Patent Office and you would develop special skills in the long and complex process of securing, maintaining and enforcing patent rights.

Patent agency is becoming an increasingly Europe-wide profession and you would be likely to have considerable contact with the European Patent Office in Munich.

Opportunities for Training

While it is possible to represent clients without being registered, you would normally obtain a post as a technical assistant to a patent agent, either in a firm of agents or in an industrial patent department, and study for the examinations leading to entry on the Register of Patent Agents. Foundation papers are usually taken after about a year in the profession, followed by the advanced papers two or three years later. There are three-month full-time courses at Queen Mary & Westfield College, London and Manchester University, to which many employers send their trainees, giving exemption from all the foundation papers. Not giving an exemption, but providing valuable skills training, is a new four-week full-time course run by the Chartered Institute of Patent Agents.

Most patent agents also become European patent attorneys, taking an examination similar to the advanced patent paper. You must be on the list of qualified practitioners if you wish to act before the European Patent Office. It is also possible to qualify as a patent agent while working as a solicitor in a legal practice with an intellectual property department.

Requirements

You would usually need a science, technology or engineering degree, together with advanced writing skills, the ability to acquire legal skills and a reading knowledge of French and German.

Kind of Person

You would need to be a mixture of scientist, lawyer and linguist, with a reasonable level of skill in each of these areas. You must be able to write clearly and unambiguously and you would need a logical, analytical mind, combined with attention to detail and keen powers of recall. You may become heavily involved in litigation in the courts of the UK and other countries and would need personal qualities similar to those required by a solicitor or barrister/advocate. See our separate articles covering these occupations.

B road Outlook

Career development opportunities are generally good and do not always end simply by being a partner in a firm of patent agents or the head of a patents department. Some patent agents move to executive or management positions, while others move abroad, particularly to English speaking countries or to multinational companies who work in English. Some choose to take UK solicitor qualifications as well or even become US attorneys.

You could concentrate on patent work or broaden your scope to work across the whole intellectual property field. Similarly, you might specialise in securing or enforcing intellectual property rights for your clients or employers, or you might branch into related areas such as licensing and contract arrangements based on such rights.

R elated Occupations

You might also consider: patent examiner, solicitor, barrister/advocate, chemist, biochemist, pharmacologist, biotechnologist, physicist or chartered engineer for example.

I mpact

You would always be working to meet specific deadlines and the work itself can be very mentally and intellectually demanding. Standard office times would usually apply but the Internet makes work away from base increasingly viable, both within and outside normal hours. You could be involved in considerable travel, especially within Europe.

E arnings Potential

For industry and private practice, the starting salary for a science graduate would be about £15,000 to £20,000, with a progression through to between £35,000 and £45,000 on full qualification as a patent attorney. Beyond this, pay would depend on experience and promotion but could rise to over £50,000.

F urther Information

The Chartered Institute of Patent Agents, London WC1V 7PZ
Website: www.cipa.org.uk/

Alternative/equivalent entrance requirements can include: ILC, IB, EB, NC/ND and many other similar international systems. For further details see the Equivalent Qualifications section in the Introduction.

What is Involved?

As a patent examiner, you would be a civil servant employed by the Patent Office to examine new patent claims before accepting them as valid for official registration. The patent system provides a stimulus to invention by granting innovators a monopoly (extendible up to 20 years in the UK) for the manufacture and sale of patented inventions. In exchange, the innovator discloses the nature of the invention, allowing others to build upon the discovery and avoiding duplication of research effort.

Your job would be to investigate each application to ascertain that the invention is clearly described and you would conduct a search through UK and foreign patent specifications to ascertain that the invention is truly novel. You would write a report of your initial search results and would use this to determine with the applicant or their agent whether to proceed to the second stage of substantive examination and detailed investigation of the claims made for the invention. Finally, the application would either proceed to grant of a patent or would be refused. If refused, the applicant may appeal to the courts.

Opportunities for Training

You would be assigned to an experienced examiner for a period of training, usually 12 months, during which you would gain experience in all aspects of patent law and the various skills required of an examiner. You would receive training in the Patent Office IT systems and in French and German because many documents searched by examiners are published in these languages. To enable you to keep abreast of the latest developments, you would be encouraged to visit laboratories, factories and exhibitions and to participate in seminars.

Requirements

You would need a degree in a mathematical, engineering or scientific subject. Suitable disciplines would include electrical/electronic, telecommunications, mechanical, civil or chemical engineering, physics, organic chemistry, chemistry, biotechnology, computer science and mathematics. See our separate articles on these subjects for details of degree entry requirements.

Kind of Person

You would need sound scientific and technical knowledge and the ability to exercise this knowledge within the concepts of patent law. You should be prepared for a mixture of the legal, the scientific, the technological and the commercial. You would also need excellent analytical and critical skills, coupled with the ability to express an argument cogently, both on paper and orally. To appreciate the level of innovation in patent applications, you would need a flexible and creative approach to problem solving. The work increasingly involves the use of computers, so you would need good IT skills.

Broad Outlook

The Patent Office regularly recruits between 20 and 40 engineers/scientists from university or industry. The programme is normally advertised from late

238

autumn with the closing date for applications in early February. Interviews are held during March and April with successful candidates starting in September. Restricted discipline recruitment schemes may also be held at different times of the year. You may register your interest with the Patent Office in order to receive an application form for the next recruitment scheme.

The overwhelming majority of examiners complete their careers within the Patent Office, but there are opportunities for training in general management and for gaining experience in other areas of government. There is also the possibility of transferring to the European Patent Office in The Hague or Munich, especially if your German and French are strong.

R elated Occupations

You might also consider: electrical/electronic, telecommunications, mechanical, civil or chemical engineer, physicist, chemist, biotechnologist, mathematician or patent agent.

Experience of patent examining work is regarded as qualifying for corporate membership of the Institution of Mechanical Engineers or the Institution of Electrical Engineers.

I mpact

You would usually work a five-day week from Monday to Friday and you would enjoy the normal benefits of the civil service, with a progressive salary scale, promotion prospects and excellent pension fund. The work itself can be very mentally and intellectually demanding. There would be deadlines to meet and you would have to be sure that your decisions on the validity of a patent could not later prove to be incorrect.

E arnings Potential

All jobs in the Patent Office fall into pay spans. You would start as an associate patent examiner in span B2 and could expect to spend two to four years at this level, depending on your individual progress. Your actual salary and annual pay rise would be negotiated on a performance-related basis. On promotion to patent examiner, you would progress to span C1 and would normally remain at this level for about six to nine years before becoming a senior patent examiner in pay span C2. Any further promotion – to assistant director (span D1) and on to the senior civil service grades of deputy director, divisional director and director – would be competitive, requiring a vacancy to occur at the higher grade.

F urther Information

The Patent Office, Newport, S Wales NP10 8QQ
Website: www.patent.gov.uk/about/employment/index.htm

Alternative/equivalent entrance requirements can include: ILC, IB, EB, NC/ND and many other similar international systems. For further details see the Equivalent Qualifications section in the Introduction.

What is Involved?

As a PE teacher or instructor, you would be fulfilling a very specialised role in a school, in the armed services or in many other community activities including health clubs and fitness centres. Your job would be to help people to develop all-round physical fitness, coordination of hand and eye, awareness of the need for exercise, to develop their strength and endurance, to improve their performance in sports generally and to maintain healthy lifestyles.

In a school your job would, in the main, be performed outside the classroom in the gymnasium, sports hall or on the playing fields. You must become aware of the special demands which physical education poses in terms of commitment and dedication, especially, as often happens, when PE staff are responsible for the running of the school's major games, with often very demanding fixture commitments.

In the armed forces, either as an officer or a non-commissioned instructor, yours would be a very specialised function. Royal Marine instructors develop and supervise PT in training centres and commando units. The Army Physical Training Corps operates on similar lines, whereas the RAF equivalent also embraces specialist training in parachuting, leadership, outdoor pursuits and survival techniques.

Opportunities for Training

See our separate article 'Teacher' for details of routes to qualification. You could specialise in PE on the BEd route or you could take a degree in a sports-related subject and follow it with the PGCE. PE is one of the main exceptions to the broad rule that the BEd route is for people who want to specialise in primary education. A sports-related degree could also incorporate specific coaching awards as part of your qualification. You should check prospectuses for details.

In the armed forces, the Royal Air Force recruits people specifically as physical training instructors and physical education officers but the Army and Royal Navy normally appoint PE specialists internally.

Requirements

For entry to teacher training or to a sports-related degree, you would normally need two or three A level/AVCE/Advanced Higher, three or four Higher or equivalent passes, together with a good spread of GCSE/S Grade passes at A-C/1-3 or equivalent, including English, maths and a science.

You would need to be very fit and many courses would look for evidence of sporting achievement.

Kind of Person

You would need to be enthusiastic about sport and all manner of physical activity. You would be expected to comply with the code of conduct set down by the governing body of any sport with which you are involved and you should try to establish professional standards of behaviour. You should be able to motivate and inspire people and would need to be patient with those

240

who are slow to learn or who do not share your passion for sporting activity. Good organisational and communication skills would be essential.

B road Outlook

With more and more people becoming aware of the value of exercise and sporting participation, opportunities in the exercise and health club sector are steadily increasing. In education, there is a good balance of supply and demand for specialist PE teachers.

R elated Occupations

You might also wish to consider: leisure services manager, sports administrator, professional sportsperson or sports coach.

I mpact

As a PE teacher, you would be spared most of the daily round of marking and administration but you may be expected to organise and lead a great number of out-of-school activities. You could be involved during the holidays with school trips or visits, such as skiing, water-sports and outdoor adventure activities. In the armed services, you would have to be available for duty at any time and could be called upon to organise or participate in particularly demanding exercises or operations.

E arnings Potential

There are several incentive schemes at present to attract more people into teacher training. Check the websites below for the latest information. Salary scales for qualified teachers start at around £16,000 to £17,000 and can rise to £30,000. Headteachers can earn anything from £33,000 to £80,000 a year depending on the size of the school. In the armed services, you would be paid on the normal scale for your force, with the starting point determined by your age and qualifications.

F urther Information

Teacher Training Agency, London SW1E 5TT
Website: www.canteach.gov.uk

General Teaching Council for Scotland, Edinburgh EH12 6UT
Website: www.gtcs.org.uk

The Physical Education Association of the United Kingdom,
Reading RG1 5AQ Website: www.pea.uk.com

SPRITO employment, learning and skills portal for sports and recreation
Website: www.sprito-els.org.uk

Armed Services Websites: www.rafcareers.com www.army.mod.uk
www.royal-navy.mod.uk www.royal-marines.mod.uk

Alternative/equivalent entrance requirements can include: ILC, IB, EB, NC/ND and many other similar international systems. For further details see the Equivalent Qualifications section in the Introduction.

Petroleum Engineer

What is Involved?

As a petroleum engineer, you would be working in a specialised field of mining engineering concerned with exploration to find reservoirs of oil and gas in the earth. Once the exploration team has located a suitable source of oil and gas, you would determine how to set about the process of extraction. This would mean that you would liaise with other experts, such as geologists, to decide on the best method of drilling, bearing in mind the overall geography and geology of the area and particularly the types of rock involved. You would also need to consider the likely costs of extracting the optimum quantity from the reservoir. This process is likely to involve you in using computer technology to simulate the extraction process and so decide on the most appropriate equipment and processes needed.

Production, the process of getting the oil out of the ground, would be your specialist area as a petroleum engineer but you would be part of a team of engineers of every sort involved in designing, building, maintaining and running the complex structures and equipment on land or at sea.

Back in the research and development laboratories, you might work with scientists and chemical and mechanical engineers to improve products, create new ones, find new ways to extract oil and make the petroleum industry as environmentally friendly as possible.

Opportunities for Training

You should study for a degree at university, possibly focusing on the Centre for Petroleum Studies at Imperial College in London, which has strong links with the industry. Some other universities, such as Nottingham, would allow you to specialise in petroleum engineering as part of their degree in mining engineering. It is also possible to study petroleum engineering as a postgraduate course once you have completed a relevant first degree. In order to become a chartered engineer, you would need to complete an approved four-year MEng course or a three-year BEng degree course plus at least an extra year of postgraduate study. See our separate article on engineering qualifications.

Requirements

You are likely to need A level/Advanced Higher, Higher or equivalent qualifications to study at Imperial College or Nottingham, including at least two subjects from maths, physics and chemistry. If not actually required, then they will be strongly preferred by these universities.

Kind of Person

You would need a strong interest in maths, science and technology and should enjoy solving problems. Your work would involve you in using sophisticated computer technology, not only to model the possible drilling options but also to sift through the mass of complex information than needs to be considered. You would be working as a member of a small team, some of whom would have different specialised knowledge. You would need to communicate clearly with other team members and also to take account of their views. At times you may need to be flexible and to modify your proposals to fit in with other people's ideas.

B road Outlook

This is a specialised field of work but there are good job opportunities as there are only a limited number of qualified graduates. There is likely to be a continued demand for oil and gas, which means that there will always be a need for petroleum engineers to discover new petroleum sources on land or under the sea and to optimise the extraction process. It is important to be realistic about your chances of a career in the oil industry. In any one year, the opportunities are limited and they go to the people with the best qualifications and personal qualities for the work.

Engineers can be found in managerial, technical and non-technical roles in all parts of the petroleum business. Most oil companies operate throughout the world and every area of the industry offers a wide choice of jobs for engineers.

R elated Occupations

You might also consider: mining, biochemical, chemical, nuclear, energy or manufacturing engineer. Alternatively, you may prefer to consider: metallurgist, materials scientist, geologist or oceanographer.

I mpact

You are likely to spend a great deal of your time monitoring drilling production on locations as far afield as the North Sea or Alaska. This might involve you working in difficult, dirty or dangerous conditions, perhaps on an oilrig at sea or in arctic or desert conditions. You would, therefore, be expected to travel extensively as part of your job and this could have an impact on your family and social life.

E arnings Potential

You are likely to be well paid, starting on around £18,000 as a recent graduate. This should rise quite quickly as you gain in experience and achieve chartered status. There are good opportunities to move into management and the business side of the industry. Earnings can be very high in these areas.

F urther Information

Institute of Petroleum, London, WG1 7AR. Website: www.petroleum.co.uk

The Institution of Mining and Metallurgy, Doncaster, DN1 2DY
Website: www.imm.org.uk

The Engineering and Technology Board, London, WC2R 3ER
Website: www.engc.org.uk

The Engineering Careers Information Service.
Website: www.enginuity.org.uk

Alternative/equivalent entrance requirements can include: ILC, IB, EB, NC/ND and many other similar international systems. For further details see the Equivalent Qualifications section in the Introduction.

What is Involved?

Your job as a pharmacist would involve working with drugs and medicines. You would either prepare and dispense medicines or you would work in researching and developing medicinal products. The majority of pharmacists work in the community, usually in a pharmacy. This means that you would work directly with the public, preparing and dispensing medicines according to doctors' prescriptions and also offering advice. Alternatively, you may work in a hospital dispensing drugs, medicines and other preparations such as special feeding solutions or diagnostic materials. Some pharmacists choose to work in industry and become involved in the manufacture of drugs.

The role of the pharmacist is likely to change in the coming years. In September 2000, the government unveiled 'Pharmacy in the Future', a national plan for the development of pharmacy, which shows quite clearly that the role of the pharmacist in managing medicines and providing advice will increase, whereas the role in supply will reduce, with this being undertaken by technical staff and e-pharmacies. Out of hours services will be extended, for example, and patients will be referred to local pharmacies by NHS Direct.

Opportunities for Training

In order to work in a hospital or in the retail trade you must be registered with the Royal Pharmaceutical Society. This means that you will have to undertake a four-year Master of Pharmacy degree at a school of pharmacy, which includes some clinical experience as well as the theoretical study of pharmaceutics and pharmacology. There is also a five-year sandwich course, which includes blocks of practical training. At the end of your degree, you would need to complete one year of pre-registration training and then pass the Society's registration exam.

Requirements

For the degree in pharmacy, you would need three good A level/AVCE/ Advanced Higher, four Higher or equivalent qualifications, one of which must be chemistry. Most universities would want or prefer your other subjects to be chosen from maths, biology and physics.

Kind of Person

You would need a strong interest in science and in medicine, with a logical mind and a methodical approach to your work. Accuracy would be very important, as you would be handling potentially dangerous medicines, and you would need good concentration and organisational ability. In addition, you would have to enjoy dealing with people. You may be working with customers or patients, acting as a link between them and the doctor, and this could involve explaining how their prescribed drugs should be administered and detailing possible side effects. If you choose to work in industry, you would be working as part of a team involved in painstaking research and production processes.

Broad Outlook

The changing nature of community pharmacy (see above) makes it difficult

244

to be specific about future prospects. There should be attractive opportunities for qualified pharmacists to work in the 500 new one-stop primary care centres or to operate needle exchange services but traditional community outlets are suffering from growing competition from supermarkets. However, opportunities currently abound in both hospital and industrial pharmacy.

R elated Occupations

You might consider another profession in a scientific or medical field, such as doctor, dentist, pharmacologist, research biologist, biochemist or chemist.

I mpact

Whether you work in a pharmacy, a hospital or in a laboratory, you would be working in clean and sometimes sterile conditions. Hygiene is always important and you may need to wear protective clothing. Pharmacists are among the most accessible healthcare professionals because the public do not need to make an appointment to see them and many shops are open extended hours. You may therefore have to work unsocial hours, which could mean working on a rota or shift system, including evening and weekend cover. Industrial pharmacists usually work regular hours, Monday to Friday.

E arnings Potential

Present salaries for pharmacy graduates during their pre-registration year range from about £12,500 to £16,000. Although NHS starting salaries are at the lower end of this scale, some hospitals offer low-cost on-site accommodation with other mostly young staff and some have lively on-site social clubs. Newly qualified pharmacist salaries range from about £18,000 to £27,000, depending on the area of work. Hospital pharmacist salaries are higher for staff participating in the on-call service. Salaries in the NHS increase as you progress through the grades, so after a few years of qualification salaries tend to be similar in both hospital and community. The top NHS pharmacist salary is currently approximately £52,000. Such amounts can also be gained by having regional management responsibility in community pharmacy or a senior management post in industry.

F urther Information

The Royal Pharmaceutical Society of Great Britain, London SE1 7JN
Website: www.rpsgb.org.uk

The Association of the British Pharmaceutical Industry, London SW1A 2DY
Website: www.abpi.org.uk

The National Pharmaceutical Association, St Albans AL1 3NP
Website: www.askyourpharmacist.co.uk

Alternative/equivalent entrance requirements can include: ILC, IB, EB, NC/ND and many other similar international systems. For further details see the Equivalent Qualifications section in the Introduction.

What is Involved?

As a pharmacologist, you would be involved in the discovery and evaluation of new pharmaceutical drugs and associated treatments needed to arrest or cure human and animal diseases. Your work may be based in a hospital or in a laboratory or office within a pharmaceutical company. Having isolated or synthesised a promising bioactive substance, you would conduct experiments to discover its effectiveness, side-effects and safe dosages.

Later you would work with other medical professionals, pharmacists and doctors, to carry our clinical trials on human beings or animals, when it is considered safe to do so. Most of the life-saving drugs used every day by doctors or vets have been tested out in this way and include thousands of different substances, including antibiotics, anti-malarial and chemotherapy drugs used in cancer treatments.

But still millions of lives are lost each year and the search continues for drugs which will be effective against AIDS, CJD, Alzheimer's and Parkinson's diseases. Pharmacologists will be faced with these challenges for a long time to come, although recent advances in genetic engineering are having a significant impact on the rate of progress in these areas.

Opportunities for Training

You would need a degree in pharmacology, which could focus on pharmacology alone or combine it with another subject, such as biochemistry, immunology, toxicology or cell biology. You might start by reading another subject, such as biomedical sciences or medicine itself, and then decide to specialise in pharmacology during your course. There are some sandwich courses available, which allow you to gain practical experience whilst studying. However you organise it, your degree in pharmacology should cover topics such as the causes of disease, the normal functioning of the body, how drugs work and their development.

Requirements

To gain admission to a degree course in pharmacology, you would need three A level/Advanced Higher, Higher or equivalent passes, usually including chemistry and two from biology, physics or maths. You would also need a good spread of GCSE/S Grade passes at A-C/1-3.

Kind of Person

You would need a keen interest and proven ability in chemical and biological research, particularly in scientific and medical discovery. Whilst you would probably have the opportunity to follow your own interests, you would also be working as part of a closely-knit team.

You would report your findings/experimental results at weekly or monthly meetings, so good verbal and written communication skills would be essential. You would need considerable determination to overcome many of the difficulties likely to arise in this work.

New drugs frequently exhibit side effects and it can take months or even years to monitor the effects on patients in clinical trials. It is here that you would work most closely with pharmacists and other health professionals, in order to avoid making serious and sometimes irreversible mistakes.

B road Outlook

'There are still many diseases we need to find treatments and cures for, such as AIDS, cancer, cystic fibrosis, malaria. Pharmacologists are going to be busy for a long time,' say the British Pharmacological Society.

Pharmacology graduates often enter the pharmaceutical industry; others enter careers including teaching, the scientific or other branches of the civil service, business and publishing. The degree is a good starting point for several positions in pharmaceuticals, such as marketing, medical information and product registration, as well as research.

R elated Occupations

You might be interested in other medical careers, such as pharmacist, medicinal chemist or doctor. Alternatively, you might consider other scientific careers such as clinical biochemist, forensic scientist, chemical analyst or research chemist/biologist.

I mpact

You are likely to work normal hours from Monday to Friday. However, you may need to be prepared to work into the evenings researching a specialist topic or to meet deadlines. There would always be a need to keep up with this rapidly advancing subject and some of your private time in the evening and at weekends would doubtless be spent reading relevant professional journals and scientific publications.

E arnings Potential

Working in the commercial world, you are likely to have a starting salary of about £20,000 and this could rise to over £40,000 as you gain experience and managerial responsibilities.

F urther Information

British Pharmacological Society, London EC1V 2PT Website: www.bps.ac.uk

Alternative/equivalent entrance requirements can include: ILC, IB, EB, NC/ND and many other similar international systems. For further details see the Equivalent Qualifications section in the Introduction.

What is Involved?

As a professional photographer, you would most likely specialise in one particular area of work, such as fashion, newspaper, medical or high street photography. 'Photographer' tends to be a blanket term covering several different occupations in which the common factor is that you would be using a camera to record specialist information. The exact nature of your work, not to mention your work environment, would depend very much on your specialism and would determine the subject matter of the photographs being taken. As a medical photographer, for example, you would be likely to work in a hospital; as a newspaper photographer, you would work largely on location, going out to record newsworthy events; as a high street photographer, you would take portraits in a studio but would also go out to cover weddings or to take school photographs. The work would generally involve selecting the right location, setting up the lighting and choosing the appropriate cameras, film and lenses. It is, however, important to decide as early as possible which specialisation interests you most and to develop your career within that specialist area.

Opportunities for Training

Training can be formal or informal, depending on your specialist area. As a medical or newspaper photographer, for example, you would have to take relevant college degree higher national diploma (HND) courses and sit examinations. On the other hand, your training as an advertising or fashion photographer could be entirely on-the-job, starting with odd jobs in the studio such as messenger work or coffee making. Colleges offer a range of courses in photography every bit as varied as the range of specialisms in the work itself. You should check course information very carefully before making a commitment and you must be aware that there is no guaranteed route to suitable employment from the majority of courses. At the higher end of qualification levels, the Professional Qualifying Examination (PQE) of the British Institute of Professional Photography seems to enjoy a good reputation among employers. The PQE can be combined with degree or higher national diploma qualifications and is beginning to break down the traditional resistance of many employers to photography graduates.

Requirements

Whether you are applying for a job or a college course, a good portfolio is essential to prove your interest and motivation. It is likely to be the main discussion point of your interview. The subject matter should reflect the specialist professional area for which you are applying, so you should avoid such things as holiday snaps, sunsets and family photographs. A dozen or so well-presented prints or transparencies should be enough at this stage. To become a trainee medical photographer, you would normally need around four GCSE/S Grade passes at A-C/1-3, including English, maths and a science. The basic requirement for the press photographer training scheme is five GCSE/S grades (A-C/1-3), including English, or a further education course in photography.

Kind of Person

Most professional photographers are self-employed and you would need a high level of self-confidence, allied to exceptional talent and driving ambition, to survive in such fiercely competitive areas as advertising or fashion photography. Even in a high street studio, you would need good business skills and the ability to communicate effectively. While you need a good eye for colour and composition, qualities such as punctuality, patience and reliability are also important. You should have some interest in digital imaging technology and the use of computers, as photography is rapidly changing to accommodate these developments. As a medical photographer, you would need knowledge of anatomy and physiology.

B road Outlook

Some areas of photography are exceptionally competitive and overcrowded. It is particularly hard to find an opening in fashion, advertising or press photography and vacancies are rarely advertised. Starting as an assistant and gradually building up a network of personal contacts is often the only way to proceed. Once you are established in the profession, a combination of talent and perseverance can open the door to lucrative contracts. If you crave the security of a structured career path, medical photography may be the route to pursue.

R elated Occupations

You may wish to consider: TV and film camera operator, graphic designer, illustrator, journalist or multimedia specialist.

I mpact

The impact of the work on your lifestyle would depend on your specialisation. In press and fashion, you could expect to work long and irregular hours. High street photographers are often busiest at weekends, covering weddings and christenings. Medical and industrial photographers would keep much more regular hours.

E arnings Potential

This would vary enormously especially, depending mainly on how hard you are prepared to work as a freelance and how good your pictures are. As a rough guide, an assistant photographer could expect to earn in the region of £10,000 to £12,000 and a local press photographer around £25,000. Successful photographers in fashion, advertising or working for the national press can earn considerably more.

F urther Information

British Institute of Professional Photography (BIPP), Ware, SG12 9HN
Website: www.bipp.com

Photo Imaging National Training Organisation, Thornton Heath, CR7 7JG
Website: www.photoimagingnto.org

Alternative/equivalent entrance requirements can include: ILC, IB, EB, NC/ND and many other similar international systems. For further details see the Equivalent Qualifications section in the Introduction.

What is Involved?

As a physicist, you would be looking at the nature of matter and of energy. Your work could cover areas such as light, sound, heat, electricity, magnetism, the planets and the forces of gravity and atomic bonding. You could become involved with atomic physics, electronics, computing the uses of laser optics or quantum physics. Your work could form the basis for much of present and future technology.

Current work in nanotechnology, for example, is predicted to transform our lives over the next two decades to a far greater extent than silicon microelectronics did in the 20th century. One application of this technology – nanotubes – can behave like metals or semiconductors, can conduct electricity better than copper, can transmit heat better than diamonds and rank among the strongest materials known, yet they are just a few nanometres across.

Opportunities for Training

If you wish to work as a professional physicist, you should look for a four-year first degree leading to MSci or MPhys. This would provide for study of physics in greater depth than a three-year BSc and should not be confused with postgraduate MSc courses Most universities offer the option of switching from BSc to MSci/MPhys and vice versa but you should check prospectuses carefully before applying.

Requirements

Entry to most degree courses requires two to three A level/Advanced Higher, three to five Higher or equivalent qualifications, together with a good platform of GCSE/S Grade passes at A-C/1-3. Since there is a shortage of applicants, grade requirements in some universities are not high but all departments would be looking for good grades in physics and maths. For postgraduate study, you would usually need a first degree passed with first or upper second class honours.

Kind of Person

You would need to have a very strong interest in physics and you should be able to handle the numerical and theoretical aspects of the subject. You should enjoy the practical laboratory work that you do at school, as you are likely to be involved with analysing and monitoring experimental work in a laboratory. You would need good attention to detail and accuracy in taking measurements and readings. You are likely to use powerful computers to help you with the analysis of results, so you would need a high standard of IT skill.

There are likely to be rapid developments in your field and you would need to keep up to date with these and with new technology as it is developed. You would need to enjoy a challenge and have a logical and creative approach to problem solving.

In addition to your scientific interest and ability, you are also likely to need good communication skills. You would probably be working as part of a team and may need to instruct technicians who are helping you as well as keeping other team members up to date with your work. In addition, you may need to explain your work to others who do not share your academic and scientific background.

B road Outlook

There is a serious shortage of qualified physicists and there is a broad range of career opportunities. Jobs are likely to be available within industries as diverse as transport and aerospace, telecommunications, medicine and health, meteorology or building. You might research issues at the frontiers of knowledge or you could tackle problems arising from the application of physics in industrial or engineering environments. Alternatively, you might move into broadcasting, scientific journalism, law or high finance.

R elated Occupations

You might also consider: computer scientist, systems analyst or telecommunications, electrical, electronic or mechanical engineer.

I mpact

You would mainly work normal office hours from Monday to Friday, although you might occasionally need to work overtime to meet a tight deadline. In addition, you may have to spend some out of work time studying and reading to keep up to date with your subject. You may need to travel to conferences and meetings and could have to move in order to find a suitable job.

E arnings Potential

Salaries for new graduates are extremely variable, averaging around £17,500. This is what you might expect if you join the civil service as a researcher, enter the computing sector or take up a post as a teacher. You would earn rather less as a post-doctoral researcher in a university and considerably more if you develop your career in the financial sector.

F urther Information

The Institute of Physics, London W1B 1NT Website: www.iop.org

Alternative/equivalent entrance requirements can include: ILC, IB, EB, NC/ND and many other similar international systems. For further details see the Equivalent Qualifications section in the Introduction.

What is Involved?

As a physiotherapist, you would use movement, exercise, electrotherapy, manipulation and massage to treat pain, injury and damage to the body and to enhance the well being of the body. In addition, you would have to take into account any psychological, social and cultural factors that would affect your patients' ability to help themselves.

You may work in hospitals or in the community, rehabilitating sick or injured individuals, or helping the elderly or disabled to live as independently as possible. Alternatively, you may work as a specialist sports physiotherapist, repairing and trying to prevent injuries as well as helping people maintain levels of fitness.

Opportunities for Training

For membership of the Society and state registration as a physiotherapist you would need to take a three- or four-year course leading to an honours degree. The course is a mixture of theory and practical work, with a good deal of time spent working with qualified physiotherapists on placement in a clinical setting. You would at times find yourself training alongside other healthcare professionals, which is good experience for the workplace. Your clinical experience should cover areas such as outpatients, intensive care, rehabilitation, care of the older person, mental illness and work in the community. The academic side would include topics such as anatomy, pathology and psychology. In addition, you would learn the practical skills required in the workplace.

Requirements

You would need three A level/AVCE/Advanced Higher, four or five Higher or equivalent qualifications, at least one of which must be a science, together with at least five GCSE/S Grade passes A-C/1-3 including maths, English and two science subjects. Some physiotherapy schools specify biology and could have other admission requirements, which you must research before making an application.

Competition for places is high. Many physiotherapy schools interview applicants, looking for genuine interest in physiotherapy, work experience involving caring for others and the experience of having watched a physiotherapist at work.

Kind of Person

You would have to establish a relationship with a wide range of people, most of whom would be ill, frightened or in pain. You would need to maintain a cheerful and positive outlook in order to reassure them and then encourage them to help themselves. At times, it would be necessary to be firm to make the patient persevere with difficult or uncomfortable exercises. Patience and tact are also needed, as progress made by patients can be very slow.

As well as getting on well with people, you should be able to give clear instructions so that the patient understands what each exercise requires. At the same time, you must be able to work alongside others as part of a team. You should be well organised and able to maintain detailed records of each patient.

B road Outlook

Employment prospects have improved in recent years and demand looks set to remain strong. The vast majority of currently practising physiotherapists – some 39,000 – work in the NHS, but just over 10% work in private practice, with a further 4% active in the private sector.

Having completed a period of junior rotations in the NHS, you could choose to stay in the service and progress to the senior grades, move into private practice or specialise in the private sector in areas such as health farms, occupational health or sport.

R elated Occupations

You may be interested in other therapy-based professions in the medical field, such as occupational therapist, radiographer or speech and language therapist.

I mpact

NHS physiotherapists work a 36-hour week, which can include some unsocial or on-call hours. Physiotherapists in the sport and leisure sector often have to work during evenings and at weekends.

E arnings Potential

A newly qualified NHS physiotherapist would earn around £17,000 in 2002/3, rising to over £34,000 for a district superintendent. Salaries in the private sector are often linked to NHS levels but may be higher; salaries in NHS trust hospitals are also sometimes higher than those set nationally.

F urther Information

The Chartered Society of Physiotherapy, London WC1R 4ED
Website: www.csp.org.uk

Alternative/equivalent entrance requirements can include: ILC, IB, EB, NC/ND and many other similar international systems. For further details see the Equivalent Qualifications section in the Introduction.

What is Involved?

Podiatrist is the internationally recognised name for a specialist who cares for feet and chiropodists are in the process of changing their title to match. As a podiatrist, you would be responsible for maintaining feet and the lower leg in a healthy condition; you would be qualified to diagnose, advise on and treat problems; you would have the chance to work in a number of different environments – hospitals, clinics and in people's homes, for example – and with a range of different people.

There are four main areas of work:

• **General clinics,** the starting point for many newly qualified podiatrists. The job involves assessing, evaluating and advising on foot care for a wide range of patients. You listen to a history of the patient's health and hear about any foot problems; you then examine the foot, possibly using specialised equipment, and discuss possible treatments with the patient.

• **Biomechanics,** concerning the very complex structure and function of the foot. Podiatrists working in this area are concerned to preserve this mechanism, restore it when it is damaged and ensure that it is capable of working at its maximum capacity. One of the main areas is orthotics or specially designed insoles, fitted inside shoes to help solve structural problems such as fallen arches or to correct problems with children's feet.

• **High Risk,** concerned with patients who have an underlying illness or condition that puts their lower limbs and/or feet at high risk of damage. Examples include problems with circulation or people who have lost the feeling in their feet or lower limbs.

• **Surgery,** involving routine surgical procedures such as treating in-growing toenails or cutting away soft tissue problems. such as corns and callouses. This may involve the use of local anaesthetics, ultrasonics or freezing techniques. Some podiatrists opt for further study to enable them to work on more invasive surgery.

Opportunities for Training

To practise in the NHS, you must be state registered, which means that you must take a recognised degree course. These courses, offered at some 13 universities in the UK, take three or four years to complete on a full-time basis. They are modular in structure, comprising a mixture of theoretical and clinical modules, although the exact format and method of teaching varies between institutions. The theoretical subjects covered during the course include dermatology, anatomy, physiology, pharmacology, biomechanics and pathology as well as local anaesthesia and surgery.

Requirements

You would need two A level/AVCE/Advanced Higher, three Higher or equivalent qualifications, one of which should be a science subject, although some universities accept PE as an alternative. You should also have at least five GCSE/S Grade passes at A-C/1-3, including English Language and two sciences. It is best to check direct with the university admissions office in each case to be sure of specific requirements.

K ind of Person

Many podiatrists are self-employed and for this you need to have a good business sense, organisational skills and the ability to inspire confidence in your clients. Communication skills are important both in dealing with patients and with co-ordinating with other professionals. In addition, you need to have a keen scientific interest and would need to keep up to date with new developments and techniques.

Some podiatry courses offer access courses for students who do not have the necessary science background or post-graduate courses for students with a relevant first degree. With only a limited number of places available to read podiatry, admissions tutors look for evidence that you understand what is involved. Work shadowing of a podiatrist is a very good idea and usually quite easy to arrange.

B road Outlook

There are good opportunities for work in this area, including private practice and some areas of specialisation. Podiatrists often start their career in the NHS, where they encounter a broad range of problems and patients, before deciding to set up in private practice or to specialise.

R elated Occupations

You might also consider: doctor, physiotherapist, occupational therapist, radiographer, speech and language therapist or nurse.

I mpact

In the NHS, podiatrists usually work a 36-hour week. However, in private practice, where the potential for earning is higher, the hours worked are likely to be longer and more unsocial, especially in the early days of establishing your business.

E arnings Potential

Starting salaries in the NHS are usually about £15,500 and can rise to £34,000. Earnings in the private sector are likely to be higher than this.

F urther Information

The Society of Chiropodists and Podiatrists, London SE1 3LY.
Website: www.feetforlife.org

Alternative/equivalent entrance requirements can include: ILC, IB, EB, NC/ND and many other similar international systems. For further details see the Equivalent Qualifications section in the Introduction.

What is Involved?

As a police officer, you would serve the local community by working to protect people and property against crime, detecting offenders and taking a lead in dealing with emergencies. You would start your career, after initial training, as a uniformed constable on the beat. This may be on foot or in a patrol car. You must be prepared to deal with whatever comes along, from attending scenes of accidents, searching for missing people and responding to emergency calls, to making arrests, sorting out street fights, taking statements and attending large public gatherings. The work can mean being outside in all weathers, sometimes in unpleasant and potentially dangerous situations. You would also be involved in some office and court-related work, including preparing reports and taking statements, escorting prisoners and giving evidence. You may find it useful to join a voluntary cadet scheme if there is one in your area.

Opportunities for Training

You would be on a two-year probationary period when you start. You might spend a few weeks with your local force before attending a 15- to 18-week residential training course at one of the national police training centres, where you would learn about self-defence, legal systems and how to treat people fairly. You would also have to cope with some fairly arduous physical activities.

Following this, you would spend a few weeks on the beat at a local police station under the supervision of an experienced tutor-constable. After a short spell of further training, you should be ready to go out on patrol on your own. You would attend further training courses throughout your career and would have the chance to gain experience of specialist sections such as traffic, criminal investigation and dog handling.

Requirements

You must be at least 18 years old, in excellent health and physically fit and you would have to pass the Police Initial Recruitment Test. You must be a British citizen, a Commonwealth citizen with unrestricted right of residence in the UK or a citizen of the Irish Republic.

There are no height restrictions and no specific educational requirements but you must have good eyesight, including normal colour vision. Glasses or contact lenses may be acceptable but you must have reasonable unaided vision.

Kind of Person

Police work is tough on the body, taxing on the brain, draining on emotion and makes demands of your whole life. You would need to be socially aware, self-disciplined and without prejudice, mature and honest. You would be called on to make instant decisions and may face hostility and danger, so courage and self-confidence are very important qualities. You need to be able to stay calm yet able to weigh up a situation quickly. A sense of humour and a degree of flexibility are advantages. It is particularly important that you have good communication skills and can be assertive but courteous in your contact with the general public.

B road Outlook

There are many more applicants than there are vacancies at present, which means that competition is fierce and standards are high. The role of the police force and the problems it faces are ever changing, as politicians grapple with increasing demands for more funding for the service in order to combat new and continuing difficulties in society.

All promotion is on merit and you may be recommended for your first promotion – to sergeant – after about five years. The police service is under constant scrutiny to ensure that senior posts are allocated fairly in relation to gender and race.

R elated Occupations

You may consider other branches of the police service, including British Transport, UK Atomic Energy and the Ministry of Defence police. Other options might include: fire officer, prison officer, army, navy and air force personnel, security officer, health and safety inspector.

I mpact

As with all the emergency services, your hours of work would often be determined by the circumstances prevailing and you would regularly have to work over weekends and holidays.

Because the police force is locally organised, you are likely in your first few years of service to be based either in the area of your choice or your own home area. Later, promotion may depend upon your willingness to move area and be relocated on a regular basis.

E arnings Potential

You could expect just over £17,000 when you start, rising to around £20,000 when you have finished initial training and approximately £27,000 if you remain as a constable. Sergeants can earn up to £30,000 and Inspectors up to £40,000. Uniform is provided and occasionally help with accommodation or subsidised police housing.

F urther Information

The best starting point is the Police website at: www.policecouldyou.co.uk

You may access the websites of individual forces through: www.police.uk

Some forces will not accept an application if you are also applying to another force, so do check that out before going ahead.

Alternative/equivalent entrance requirements can include: ILC, IB, EB, NC/ND and many other similar international systems. For further details see the Equivalent Qualifications section in the Introduction.

What is Involved?

Working as a probation officer in England or Wales, you would be supervising offenders in the community and engaging with the victims of serious violent crimes. A lot of your time would be spent trying to help offenders change their behaviour by identifying and challenging what causes them to offend. In Scotland, similar work is carried out by criminal justice social workers as part of local authority social services.

You might be attached to a crown court, involved in drawing up pre-sentence reports to help determine the best way to deal with offenders, providing details about their personalities, the circumstances of crimes, the likelihood of re-offending and the level of risk posed to the public. You might be involved with supervising community rehabilitation or punishment; or on drug treatment and testing orders, trying to break the link between drug addiction and offending, or you could work with prisoners before and after their release from prison.

Opportunities for Training

Probation officer training in England and Wales centres on the Diploma in Probation Studies (DipPS), a two-year programme combining an undergraduate degree with an NVQ level 4 in community justice. You would normally be working as a trainee probation officer in one of the 42 local service areas making up the National Probation Service. Your training is likely to include about three days a week working under supervision, with two days studying areas such as social science and criminology, criminal behaviour and mental illness.

In Scotland, the Diploma in Social Work (DipSW) is the recognised qualification for probation work.

Requirements

You cannot qualify as a probation officer until you are at least 22 years old; this means that you have to be at least 20 to be accepted for the DipPS.

In England and Wales, if you are under 21 you would need two or three A level/AVCE passes, together with three GCSE passes at A-C. If you are over 21 but under 25, you would need five GCSE passes A-C; if you are over 25, the academic requirements can be waived but you would be assessed for your ability to cope with the DipPS. See our separate article on 'Social Worker' for Scottish entry requirements for the DipSW. Competition for training places is fierce and it is virtually essential to show experience of voluntary or other work in a field related to helping people in difficulty.

Kind of Person

You would have to deal with offenders, some of whom could be aggressive, violent, distressed or withdrawn. You would need to gain trust and develop a constructive relationship with people from a variety of backgrounds and with a number of problems. Your work would include listening to their stories, resolving conflicts and finding ways to move forward. This would need good

258

communication skills, together with patience, authority and persuasive power. You would be involved with researching and writing reports and letters so written communication would be important. You must be able to speak convincingly in court. You would be working as part of a team and handling a lot of confidential and sensitive information about people, so your integrity would be essential.

B road Outlook

There is stiff competition for trainee posts, with 14,000 applicants in 2000 for a mere 250 places. Once through the training programme, you would find that opportunities are plentiful. If you want promotion, you may have to move into a management role, although many probation officers prefer to remain at practitioner level.

R elated Occupations

You might also consider: social worker, teacher, psychologist, prison officer, police officer or youth and community worker.

I mpact

Your working week would be around 40 hours but you would often be able to arrange your own working hours to some extent, and this could involve something quite different from the nine to five routine. You might need to provide cover at night and at weekends, working on a rota basis, but you would probably be given time off to compensate. You might have to move around the UK to find a suitable job. At times you would be expected to deal with stressful situations, which you could not simply leave in the office and not think about again until the next morning.

E arnings Potential

You could expect to be paid around £13,000 to £14,000 whilst you are training. Salaries for qualified Probation Officers start at around £18,000, rising to £40,000 and beyond.

F urther Information

The Home Office National Probation Directorate, London SW1P 9AT
Website: www.homeoffice.gov.uk

National Association of Probation Officers, London, SW11 1HT.
Website: www.napo.org.uk

Scottish Social Services Council, Dundee DD1 4NY
Website: www.ccetsw.org.uk (temporary site)

Alternative/equivalent entrance requirements can include: ILC, IB, EB, NC/ND and many other similar international systems. For further details see the Equivalent Qualifications section in the Introduction.

What is Involved?

In most professional sports, you would be required to focus single-mindedly on your training, fitness and performance levels, shutting out most other demands on your time and energy. Every aspect of your life, diet, sleep, social relaxation and psychological strength would need to be subordinated to or controlled by the demands of your sport, and your career would become in many ways your principal way of life. A career as a professional sportsperson is frequently short, often ending by 35, especially in physical contact or physically demanding sports, and is vulnerable to termination through injury or loss of form. Dedication of vast amounts of time to training and preparation puts stress on both body and mind which you would need to learn to control. The ability to work with others in teams is increasingly vital, not just in team sports, but in individualised sports where agents, trainers, dietitians, psychologists and physiotherapists are likely to be constant assistants and companions.

Opportunities for Training

An academic qualification is not necessary but is increasingly considered a sensible insurance against the unpredictable pitfalls in a sportsperson's life. Many sports bodies attempt to synchronise sporting participation and development of a career with educational or vocational training and, wherever possible, it is important to achieve whatever academic levels are within reach and do not clash impossibly with sporting demands. Preparation for a future role as coach, manager or administrator is a route followed by many sports performers to guarantee an effective career path.

It is vital to realise that, in most money-making sports, ability would be recognised at an increasingly early age, with footballers as young as nine encouraged into academies and schools of excellence by premiership clubs, cricketers absorbed into colts teams by county cricket clubs, rugby players enrolled in apprentice schemes and training set-ups by rugby premiership sides, and other sports having their own schemes for identifying and exploiting talent. Even if you are an outstanding school player, it is highly unlikely that at 17 or 18 you are going to be able to break into a major sports scene.

Requirements

There are no formal entrance qualifications to professional sport but it is sensible not to neglect your education and to take the opportunity to go on to higher education if appropriate. You could often continue to take part in your sport at university, national or even Commonwealth or Olympic levels. Because of the extremely young age of entry, your parents would need to be supportive in both care and financing, though sponsorship might be available in some sports.

Kind of Person

Commitment, talent and a competitive streak seem common to all professional sportspeople. The resilience to overcome disappointment, defeat or injury is essential, along with an ability to adjust to the demands of travel, practice and performance. You would need total dedication to practising and improving your sport, maintaining your fitness at a peak level and monitoring your diet.

B road Outlook

There are huge sums of money involved in major sports like soccer, rugby, snooker, boxing and tennis, but these are relatively few in number and it is easy to be misled by appearances. It is certain that sport will continue to attract and entertain huge sections of society in the coming decades, but that may be accompanied by a spreading and thinning of the rewards. The participation of women, especially where there is a growth in their involvement in sports like tennis and golf, should open more doors to them in the future.

R elated Occupations

You might also consider: sports coach, PE teacher/instructor, physiotherapist, chiropractor, osteopath, leisure services manager, sports development officer, media sports reporter, television or radio commentator or analyst or sports shop owner.

I mpact

As indicated above, the full impact on your life is likely to be all-consuming and intense, taking over many aspects of it. Practice, training, travel away from home in the UK and abroad can all create pressure on family and social life.

E arnings Potential

It is impossible to specify, given the great range of sports. The greater the popularity of the sport and the higher the level attained, the greater the rewards you can achieve. In addition to salaried team players, earnings would include appearance money, fees, advertising and endorsements. For those in less popular sports, a supporting job is often necessary.

F urther Information

SPRITO, London NW1 2HD Website: www.sprito-els.org.uk

Sports Coach UK, Leeds LS6 3BJ Website: www.sportscoachuk.org

The UK Sports Council, London, WC1N 1ST Website: www.uksport.gov.uk

Alternative/equivalent entrance requirements can include: ILC, IB, EB, NC/ND and many other similar international systems. For further details see the Equivalent Qualifications section in the Introduction.

What is Involved?

As a psychologist, you would study the processes and nature of the human mind in order to understand how people behave, how they react to stimuli or circumstances and how they interact in small or large groups. You would use scientific methods to gather information and try to measure what constitutes normal or abnormal behaviour. You would be concerned not just with understanding human behaviour but also with using this understanding to help people and to bring about change.

There are six main specialisms for professional psychologists:

Clinical psychologists work with people with mental or physical health problems – which might include anxiety and depression, serious and enduring mental illness, adjustment to physical illness, neurological disorders, addictive behaviours, childhood behaviour disorders or personal and family relationships;

Counselling psychologists help people manage difficult life events such as bereavement, past and present relationships and working with mental health issues and disorders;

Educational psychologists are concerned with children's learning and development, working primarily in schools with teachers and parents;

Forensic psychologists undertake their work in the criminal and civil justice field, working with academic institutions, prison services, the National Health Service, probation services and social services;

Health psychologists are concerned with the application of psychological methods to the study of behaviour relevant to health, illness and health care. For example, why and when people seek professional advice about their health, how patients and health care professionals interact or how patients adapt to illness;

Occupational psychologists are concerned with the performance of people at work and in training, how organisations function and how individuals and small groups behave at work.

Opportunities for Training

To become a chartered psychologist, you must have a degree in psychology or equivalent qualification accredited by the British Psychological Society. Your degree would usually offer a broad introduction to the subject but, if you wish to work as professional psychologist, you would normally undertake postgraduate study in one of the six specialist areas.

Requirements

University admissions requirements for a degree in psychology are usually two or three A level/Advanced Higher, three or four Higher or equivalent qualifications, together with a good spread of GCSE/S Grade passes A-C/1-3, including English and maths. There is no need to take psychology as a pre-university subject, although you should be able to demonstrate that you have an understanding of what is involved. Entry is competitive and you should research the exact requirements of each course that interests you.

K ind of Person

You would have to work with a wide range of people. Depending on what type of psychologist you become, you could find yourself dealing with children or adults with learning difficulties, patients with brain damage or disease, prisoners or people at work. You would need good communication skills and an ability to mix with people. In addition, you should have keen investigative skills and should be sufficiently numerate to understand statistical methods.

B road Outlook

Employment prospects in most areas of psychology are good, especially for educational and clinical psychologists. There are opportunities to work for a number of different organisations, for the government and in private practice, although you may have to move several times to develop your career. It has been calculated that only 15 to 20% of psychology graduates end up working as professional psychologists.

R elated Occupations

You may be particularly interested in other professions concerned with helping people, such as careers/personal adviser, speech and language therapist, teacher, human resources manager, probation officer or social worker.

I mpact

This is very dependent on the type of psychology that you choose to pursue as a career. An occupational psychologist working with companies in industry and commerce would usually work normal office hours; an educational psychologist dealing mainly with schoolchildren would be busiest during term time. On the other hand, a forensic psychologist may be called out to collaborate with the police at unsocial hours.

E arnings Potential

Again this varies considerably between the different branches of psychology.

As a clinical psychologist working in the National Health Service, you would start at about £16,500 and could earn up to £60,000. As an educational psychologist, you would start at about £21,000, rising to around £40,000. As an occupational psychologist, you might generally start at around £14,000 but this could rise to over £100,000 with experience and with fees negotiated for consultancy work.

F urther Information

The British Psychological Society (BPS), Leicester LE1 7DR
Website: www.bps.org.uk

Alternative/equivalent entrance requirements can include: ILC, IB, EB, NC/ND and many other similar international systems. For further details see the Equivalent Qualifications section in the Introduction.

263

What is Involved?

As a public relations (PR) officer, you would specialise in the business of looking after the reputation of your clients, making a planned and sustained effort to establish goodwill and mutual understanding between them and the public. Your clients might include a business, a profession, a government department, a public service or an organisation concerned with health, culture or education. You would aim to find out the concerns and expectations of a client's customers, employees, suppliers, investors or other audience and feed these back to the management.

A large organisation might have its own in-house PR department, whilst smaller organisations would use an independent PR consultancy. You could find yourself organising receptions, entertaining clients at sporting events or gauging public reaction to a government initiative. At its best, PR helps an organisation to see its own role more clearly and helps it to react effectively to public perception of its performance.

Opportunities for Training

There are a number of routes into PR. You might enter the profession after working in another area, such as journalism, law, advertising or any industry of which you have experience. If you are looking to go into PR as your first job, you would almost certainly need a relevant qualification and work experience.

It is not essential but you could consider a first degree course specifically in public relations, approved by the Institute of Public Relations (IPR). Alternatively, you could take a postgraduate course. Once you have a job in PR, you could work towards IPR or CAM (Communication, Advertising and Marketing Education Foundation) professional qualifications.

Requirements

To gain admission to a degree course, you would need two or three A level/AVCE/Advanced Higher, three or four Higher or equivalent qualifications, together with a good spread of GCSE/S Grade passes at A-C/1-3. The minimum requirement for the CAM exams is five GCSE/S Grade passes at A-C/1-3, including maths and English but the vast majority of new entrants are graduates. Relevant work experience would be essential.

Kind of Person

Exceptionally good 'people' skills are needed here. You would need to be able to communicate and to remember that this is a two-way process. You would need flexibility to cope with a variety of projects at the same time, together with thorough attention to detail. The ability to get on with a variety of people and work with others as part of a team would be essential.

You would have to be assertive and determined, able to cope with pressure and tight deadlines and to make your point in discussions without alienating people. You would also need to be very well organised, with good IT and literacy skills. You would probably be expected to give presentations.

B road Outlook

PR has a glamorous image and entry has become very competitive. It is now one of the top three most popular career choices for graduates. The PR industry in the UK is the most highly developed in Europe with an annual turnover of an estimated £1 to £2 billion and good growth potential. Talent is still in great demand and, once you have been accepted by a consultancy, you could progress to become a manager and then a director or start your own consultancy.

There is no standard promotion pattern in PR but, on successful completion of an initial training programme, you might expect to spend one to two years as a junior account executive, two or three years as an account executive and two to three years as a senior account executive or account manager before moving to associate or account director. You might need to seek promotion by moving companies.

Over half of all people employed in PR work in-house for large companies, local authorities, government departments, professional bodies and charities.

R elated Occupations

You might also consider: journalist, solicitor, advertising copywriter, marketing executive, market researcher or events manager.

I mpact

You would be mainly office based and work normal office hours. However, when necessary you would be expected to work longer hours to meet deadlines. Depending on the nature of the work, you could find yourself travelling around the country or abroad on promotional tours or attending conferences. You might have to give presentations or organise functions in the evening or at weekends.

E arnings Potential

Salaries vary according to type of employer but a new PR consultant could expect to earn between £19,000 and £22,000; a manager £30,000 to £60,000 plus. You could earn considerably more as a director.

F urther Information

The Institute of Public Relations, London EC1V 0PR
Website: www.ipr.org.uk

CAM Foundation, Maidenhead SL6 9QH
Website: www.camfoundation.com

Public Relations Consultants Association, London SW1P 1JH
Website: www.prca.org.uk

Scottish Public Relations Consultants Association, Edinburgh EH6 6RA
Website: www.harrisoncowley.com

Alternative/equivalent entrance requirements can include: ILC, IB, EB, NC/ND and many other similar international systems. For further details see the Equivalent Qualifications section in the Introduction.

What is Involved?

As a quantity surveying technician, you would work under the overall supervision of a quantity surveyor, builder, architect or civil engineer on the costing and management of all types of building work. This could involve you in office work or in travelling out to building sites. In the office you might be concerned with studying plans or drawings and costing all the items of labour and materials that would be needed. In this way you would be concerned to draw up estimates of the costs of the projected work in a Bill of Quantities. You might also be involved in the conversion of these measurements into the actual quantities of materials that the construction workers would need.

When you are out on site, you might be involved with valuing work done and in progress, so that necessary payments can be made to contractors or suppliers. You could also be concerned with discussing the cost implications of alterations to the work required by the client or forced by a change of circumstances.

Opportunities for Training

It is normal for most entrants to take a higher national certificate/diploma (HNC/D) or a National/Scottish Vocational Qualification (N/SVQ) to level four. With either of these, you would be eligible for technical membership of the Royal Institution of Chartered Surveyors (RICS) and could follow a two-year period of structured training leading to the assessment of technical competence. Many of the larger employers would encourage technical surveyors to take further training courses and qualifications. It would also be possible to take a further bridging course and to become a chartered quantity surveyor through this route.

Requirements

To follow the HNC/D route, you are likely to need at least one A level/AVCE/Advanced Higher, two Higher or equivalent qualifications, together with a minimum of four GCSE/S Grade passes A-C/1-3, including English, maths and a science subject. There are no set entry requirements for the N/SVQ route, although individual employers or training providers may set their own standards.

Kind of Person

You would need to have a methodical approach to your work and to be very accurate with a sharp eye for detail. You could find yourself handling complex measuring equipment, which would require some degree of technical knowledge. You would need to be confident in using maths and operating computers. You would be expected to liaise with a wide range of different people, clients, chartered surveyors/senior management, architects and also construction workers on the sites.

You might need to explain your points of view to clients, persuading them to accept your opinion. You could be negotiating with contractors about the

266

amount of materials required for a job. Alternatively, you might find yourself encouraging the workforce to complete a particular job more quickly. You would need to be confident and articulate in both written and verbal communication.

B road Outlook

Employment prospects for quantity surveying technicians are generally good at the moment. The situation is slightly dependent on the state of the building economy in general but there are usually reasonable opportunities for qualified staff. There is a wide range of different employers who might want to use your expertise, ranging from private or large public companies to local or central government projects. You should be able to find work throughout the country and, if you are interested, there is often work abroad. There is also the option of continuing your studies to become a fully qualified chartered surveyor.

R elated Occupations

You might also consider: estate agent, architectural technologist, town planner or construction manger.

I mpact

If you were involved with working in an office you could expect to work regular office hours. However, you might also need to be on site and then the hours would probably be longer, particularly in the summer when there are more daylight hours. On site you would need to be prepared to get dirty and to wear protective clothing. To achieve promotion, you might need to move around the country.

E arnings Potential

As a school leaver studying part-time, you could expect to earn around £11,000, rising to around £15,000 once you have qualified. As you gain experience, you could expect your salary to rise accordingly. There is a difference in salary depending on where you work and also on how great the demand is for quantity surveying technicians in your particular area.

F urther Information

The Royal Institution of Chartered Surveyors (RICS), Coventry CV4 8JE
Website: www.rics.org.uk

Alternative/equivalent entrance requirements can include: ILC, IB, EB, NC/ND and many other similar international systems. For further details see the Equivalent Qualifications section in the Introduction.

What is Involved?

As a quantity surveyor you would be concerned with the financial and contractual aspects of construction projects. You would be involved at all stages of the project and would usually be appointed by the architect or engineer who has designed the construction. You would be acting as the financial overseer of a particular project, translating the plans into detailed costs. This would involve working out the timings of each process and the materials needed.

You might advise on alterations to the initial designs; you could be involved in obtaining funding for a particular project; you might be asked to draw up a feasibility study of a project and advise on how to reduce the risks involved. During the construction phase you are likely to be responsible for making sure that the contractors keep to the specification and to the quoted price.

Opportunities for Training

You would need to take a degree course approved by the Royal Institute of Chartered Surveyors (RICS), followed by the RICS Assessment of Professional Competence (APC). This involves two years of structured, practical training with an employer, ending with an RICS professional assessment.

There are some four-year sandwich courses available, which include a year spent working in a quantity surveying practice. This year can count towards your required training period, provided that it has been approved in advance by the RICS. The Architects and Surveyors Institute also offers examinations related to Quantity Surveyors; most members of this Institute work in the public sector.

Requirements

For a degree course, the minimum stated requirements are at least three A level/AVCE/Advanced Higher, four Higher or equivalent qualifications, together with five GCSE/S Grade passes at A-C/1-3. These should usually include English and maths.

Kind of Person

To be a successful quantity surveyor you would need to be a practical person with a logical and methodical approach to problem solving. You would need a high standard of numeracy, together with the ability to analyse the content of complicated documents. A good understanding both of construction techniques and technology and of the relevant laws and health and safety requirements would be essential.

You should have good communications skills as you could be required to express your views and opinions both verbally and on paper. You are also likely to be involved in negotiating with a wide variety of people. This means that you would have to listen to the points of view of others as well as expressing your own opinion. In addition, you are likely to be working as a member of a team, which may require you to motivate and lead people on site. Finally, you would have to be familiar with specific computer programmes.

B road Outlook

There are three main areas in which you could find employment: private practice; with a large building or civil engineering contractor or with local and central government. There is demand in each of these areas and there are also opportunities to work abroad on both long- and short-term contracts. There are increasing chances to work in Europe with some of the large consultancies and contractors, although you must have the relevant language skills.

R elated Occupations

You might consider another specialism as a surveyor or perhaps another profession allied to the building industry, such as architect, town planner, housing manger or civil engineer.

I mpact

You are likely to spend the majority of your time indoors, working regular office hours. You would also have to spend at least some time on site and you may have to start early or finish late to match the daylight hours usually worked by site contractors.

You could be out in all weathers, sometimes exposed to wet, cold and muddy conditions. Buildings under construction are likely to be dirty and potentially dangerous places. You would need to wear protective clothing at times and be prepared to climb ladders or scaffolding.

E arnings Potential

When you first start working you could expect to earn between £14,000 and £18,000. If you start working for a large contractor, you could earn more as you may get paid for working site hours. Your salary could easily rise to £30,000 and beyond with experience.

F urther Information

Royal Institution of Chartered Surveyors, Coventry CV4 8JE
Website: www.rics.org.uk

Architecture and Surveying Institute, Chippenham SN15 3WD
Website: www.asi.org.uk

Alternative/equivalent entrance requirements can include: ILC, IB, EB, NC/ND and many other similar international systems. For further details see the Equivalent Qualifications section in the Introduction.

269

What is Involved?

There are two types of radiography: diagnostic and therapeutic. As a diagnostic radiographer, you would produce and interpret high quality images of the body to diagnose injury and disease; as a therapeutic radiographer, you would plan and deliver prescribed treatment using X-radiation and other radioactive sources. Your work as a diagnostic radiographer would normally encompass a wide range of different imaging investigations, such as ultrasound, magnetic resonance imaging and x-rays, although you might later specialise in one particular area.

You would provide a service for most departments within a hospital, including Accident and Emergency, outpatients, operating theatres and wards. Therapeutic radiographers work closely with doctors, nurses, physicists and other members of the oncology team to treat patients with cancer. You would use ionising radiation (mostly high-energy X-rays) to deliver an accurate dose of radiation to the tumour/cancer whilst minimising the dose received by the surrounding tissues. The work would often involve the care of the cancer patient from the initial referral clinic stage, where pre-treatment information is given, through the planning process and treatment to the post-treatment review (follow-up) stages.

Opportunities for Training

You would need to complete a qualifying radiography course at honours degree level. In England and Wales, these courses are three years full-time whereas in Scotland and Northern Ireland they are normally four years full-time. You would usually spend equal amounts of time in your university and in hospital departments. Alternatively, you could qualify as a therapeutic radiographer at postgraduate level if you have a relevant first degree or another professional healthcare qualification. Qualifying courses in diagnostic radiography are currently offered at 24 higher education institutions in the UK and in therapeutic radiography at 17.

Requirements

Entry requirements vary between universities but you would usually need at least two A level/AVCE/Advanced Higher, three Higher or equivalent qualifications, together with three GCSE/S Grade passes A-C/1-3, ideally including maths and a science subject. A visit to a radiography department or radiotherapy centre is advisable before applying. You must be at least 17 to start a degree course in either diagnostic or therapy radiography, and mature students are especially welcome.

Kind of Person

Both diagnostic and therapeutic radiographers need good interpersonal skills to deal with patients of all types and ages, many of whom require reassurance and counselling as well as an explanation of the radiographic procedure with which they are being examined or treated. You would also need to be able to communicate well with the other professionals in the healthcare team to ensure that the most appropriate treatment is given to each patient. You must be confident about working with complex high-technology equipment and would need to give great attention to detail while remaining flexible enough to treat each patient as an individual case. The continuing development of radiographic techniques and treatments means that you would be constantly learning new skills. You would need to be able to think quickly and to be prepared to make decisions yourself.

B road Outlook

The NHS employs most radiographers, although there are also opportunities to work within the armed forces and in the private sector. Within the NHS there is a career structure that gives the opportunity to take on management responsibilities or specialist skills. This means that you could develop a wide range of transferable skills that would equip you for management at all levels within the NHS, industry or higher education.

There is currently a worldwide shortage of both diagnostic and therapeutic radiographers and the UK qualification is normally transferable to most overseas countries. State registration is the important factor for your career development, indicating that you meet the high ethical standards required, have achieved educational and professional excellence and are committed to duty of care.

R elated Occupations

You might also consider: doctor, nurse, medical physicist, biomedical scientist, occupational therapist, physiotherapist or photographer.

I mpact

It is normal to work a 35-hour week but, for diagnostic radiographers, this would include night and weekend shifts for emergency cover. Allowances are given for this flexible working. Therapeutic radiographers work more regular hours, seeing patients by appointment in a radiotherapy or oncology centre, although pressure to reduce waiting lists can involve overtime working. Exposure to x-rays can be dangerous and there is always a need to meet strict health and safety requirements.

E arnings Potential

As a newly qualified NHS radiographer, you could expect to earn about £15,500, rising to around £24,000 for a senior post. A consultant grade radiographer in the NHS can earn nearly £50,000.

F urther Information

The Society of Radiographers, London SE1 2EW Website: www.sor.org

The British Institute of Radiology, London W1N 4AT
Website: www.bir.org.uk

Alternative/equivalent entrance requirements can include: ILC, IB, EB, NC/ND and many other similar international systems. For further details see the Equivalent Qualifications section in the Introduction.

What is Involved?

Biology is the study of living organisms of all types. As a research biologist you might choose to work with plants, animals or micro-organisms.or ecology. A relatively new and expanding area of biology is biotechnology, which combines biology with technical developments such as genetic engineering.

Working as a research biologist, you would be at the cutting edge of your chosen specialised area, trying to discover new information and identify solutions to specific problems. In addition to working in universities in a pure research role, there are opportunities to work in food research institutions, in medicine-related areas or in such industries as pharmaceuticals or food production and brewing.

Opportunities for Training

To become a research biologist, you would need a good degree in biologywhich is recognised by the Institute of Biology. Most universities have relevant three- or four-year courses, offering biology as a single subject or in combination with a range of other subjects. There are also sandwich courses available which allow you to spend some time working in industry whilst you are studying. Some employers and large companies might sponsor you. Most research biologists would carry out postgraduate study and go on to take a PhD.

Requirements

Degree entry requirements vary between universities. Most would specify biology at A level/Advanced Higher/Higher or equivalent and some would also want chemistry at a similar standard. The minimum requirements are normally stated as two A level/AVCE/Advanced Higher, three Higher or equivalent qualifications, together with GCSE/S Grade passes A-C/1-3 in five subjects. Sometimes maths and English are specified.

To be accepted for postgraduate study leading to a career in research, you would normally need a degree passed with first or upper second class honours.

Kind of Person

As a research biologist you would need to have a deep interest in your subject and to be prepared to continue your academic study for many years. You would be working at the forefront of your specialised area of biology and as such could be moving the subject forward. In order to do this you would need an enquiring mind and an imaginative and creative approach to problem solving. If you do not find practical laboratory work interesting at the moment, this would probably not be the career for you. You would be expected to show accuracy and precision in recording your experimental results.

You are likely to be part of a team of scientists and to be involved with discussing your ideas and findings with other scientists. In addition, you may be expected to explain your research or developments in your field to others who do not have the same scientific background as you. You would almost certainly need to use computer technology both for your research and to communicate with other in the field.

B road Outlook

There are opportunities for laboratory-based researchers in both the private and public sectors. Some researchers move away from pure research into technical marketing and information services or take on management roles. Even if you choose to work in a laboratory, you are unlikely to be working alone and may have support staff and technicians to manage. You may have to move around the country in order to develop your career.

R elated Occupations

You may be interested in other careers based in the field of biology, such as microbiologist, forensic scientist or conservation officer. Alternatively, a career based in another science might appeal to you, including biochemist or pharmacologist.

I mpact

You are likely to be working regular office hours for five days a week most of the time. However, there may be occasions when you are under pressure to meet deadlines and would have to work late. You may need to read or write papers or journal articles in your free time. If you choose to work in an environment that is attached to a university, you may find yourself involved in some sort of lecturing role as well as being a researcher. In addition, you would be expected to travel to conferences and to other laboratories to keep up to date with your subject

E arnings Potential

As a research biologist assistant, you are likely to earn in the region of £13,000 when you first graduate. Senior researchers can achieve salaries of £50,000 or beyond. Larger salaries could be attainable in some large manufacturing or industrial companies.

F urther Information

The Institute of Biology, London SW7 2DZ Website: www.iob.org

Alternative/equivalent entrance requirements can include: ILC, IB, EB, NC/ND and many other similar international systems. For further details see the Equivalent Qualifications section in the Introduction.

Research Chemist

What is Involved?

As a research chemist, you would deal with the nature of atomic and molecular substances, their properties, chemical bonding and interaction. You might work in industry – in pharmaceuticals, foodstuffs, agriculture, oil and chemical manufacture or polymers, for example – or you might choose to stay within a university environment and carry out research that is primarily academic but could have major commercial potential. Increasingly, universities and their staff are patenting and licensing their discoveries – which can significantly increase their available revenues.

Opportunities for Training

You would need a good degree recognised by the Royal Society of Chemistry. Most universities offer suitable courses and it is often possible to take chemistry as a single subject or to combine it with another subject for a joint honours degree. A full-time degree course would take three or four years to complete. Some organisations will sponsor you to take a degree in chemistry in return for your commitment to work for the company when you graduate. This may involve working for them in the holidays, which can provide valuable practical experience. Having a PhD can be a great asset in a research career, so you would need to be prepared for further post-graduate study. This can be expensive but some companies might be prepared to help fund your studies.

Requirements

Competition for places on chemistry degree courses is not generally very fierce, so you may find that you are not required to obtain exceptionally high grades at A level/Advanced Higher, Higher or equivalent. However, you are likely to be asked for a good grade in chemistry at this level and some universities would want a second science at A level/Advanced Higher, Higher or equivalent level. In some cases this would be specified as maths or physics. It is best to check directly with the admissions tutors of universities that you are considering. At some universities, applicants without the appropriate science A level/Advanced Higher, Higher or equivalent qualifications may be able to take a foundation year before starting the chemistry course.

Kind of Person

As a chemical researcher you would need to have a very keen interest in your subject and an enquiring mind, constantly asking why reactions occur and examining the effects of chemical changes. You would be expected to keep yourself up to date with overall developments in the field and to show an analytic and logical approach to problem solving.

Accuracy and precision would be very important in making observations and in recording data. At times you would need to persevere in order to solve a particular problem and to be technically imaginative in your thinking. You would also need to work with other people as part of a research team and to be able to explain your ideas, theories and discoveries to others who may not be as expert as you.

274

B road Outlook

There are excellent job prospects if you are well qualified. This is, however, an academically competitive field and you would always be under pressure to complete work on time and to publish your results in regular departmental reports or in learned papers. You may find that you will need to study further, perhaps taking a PhD in order to gain recognition and promotion. Many researchers move onto the sales, administration or management areas of their companies.

R elated Occupations

You may be interested in other careers in the field of chemistry, such as chemical analyst, pharmacologist, biochemist, or chemistry technician. Alternatively, you might like to think about another scientific career such as metallurgist, research biologist or forensic scientist.

I mpact

You are likely to be working regular office hours on weekdays most of the time. You should be prepared to travel for conferences and other meetings. Your work would always involve reading journals and other papers outside your normal work hours to keep up to date in your own field. At times, when you are making especially good progress or are under pressure to find a solution to a problem, you may need to work extra hours to meet deadlines.

If you choose to work in a university, carrying out research, you are likely to be involved in some sort of supervision of laboratory work and even to lecture to undergraduates at times.

E arnings Potential

You are likely to earn in the region of £13,000 to £20,000 when you first start as a chemical research assistant. This could rise to £50,000 and beyond, with larger salaries available for senior staff in some large manufacturing companies.

F urther Information

The Royal Society of Chemistry, London W1V 0BN Website: www.rsc.org

Society of Chemical Industry, London SW1X 8PS Website: www.soci.org

Alternative/equivalent entrance requirements can include: ILC, IB, EB, NC/ND and many other similar international systems. For further details see the Equivalent Qualifications section in the Introduction.

What is Involved?

As a residential social worker, you would be responsible for looking after long- or short-stay residents in a particular home or hostel. You are likely to find yourself caring for children, elderly people or adults with physical disabilities, mental health or behavioural problems. Your job would be to help clients come to terms with their problems and, if possible, to become independent.

You could find yourself teaching, giving one-to-one counselling sessions, running group therapy classes and, at times, offering basic support such as help with dressing or feeding. You are likely to be involved with supervising the daily routine of the home and also with providing educational and recreational activities as appropriate. Other duties might include attending meetings and writing reports, dealing with staffing issues and checking the budget. You may not be resident yourself but you would usually be expected to sleep in for a certain number of nights on a rota basis.

Opportunities for Training

There are many possible training routes, depending to a certain extent on whether you want to achieve the professional qualification for social workers: the Diploma in Social Work (DipSW). You can study for this full-time, part-time or by distance learning, and you can follow a postgraduate course if you want to take a degree first. Indeed, you might choose to use some initial work experience in a home or hostel to gain a place as a mature student on a course leading to a degree or DipSW. Full-time diploma courses usually last two or three years; part-time and distance-learning courses vary enormously, according to the circumstances of participants.

Please note that a new degree in social work will be introduced in England from autumn 2003. This new degree will eventually replace the DipSW. Other arrangements will apply in Scotland, Northern Ireland and Wales. During the phasing out period, DipSW courses will continue to run and will continue to be recognised as valid social work qualifications. For further information about the new degree, visit: www.doh.gov.uk/swqualification

Requirements

For a degree course, you would need at least two A level/AVCE/Advanced Higher, three Higher or equivalent passes, together with five GCSE/S Grade passes at A-C/1-3. You would need similar qualifications to enter a DipSW course below the age of 21; although you may be able to gain admission over the age of 21 without formal examination passes.

Kind of Person

You would need to be extremely flexible and adaptable, showing great patience and tact in building relationships with residents. You would be involved with helping them to realise their potential and try to regain control of their lives. This can make your work environment quite tense and stressful, so you would need to be emotionally stable and resilient in order to cope. You are likely to be motivated by a desire to help people to make more of themselves and to be content with sometimes very slow progress towards that goal. You would need to be a good listener who can accept a wide variety of people without judgement. Your job would involve working with a number of other people as part of a team.

B road Outlook

There is strong demand for qualified residential social workers. Most homes or hostels are run by local authorities, voluntary organisations or the private sector. There are opportunities to specialise in a particular field and it may be possible to move into other fields of social work, depending on your experience and qualifications. In order to gain promotion, you would need to get as much experience as possible, perhaps transferring from the public or voluntary sector to the private.

R elated Occupations

You might consider: field social worker, care assistant, nurse, probation officer or youth and community worker.

I mpact

Spending some nights sleeping in, often in self-contained accommodation attached to the unit, including weekend and holiday period shifts, can severely disrupt your family and social life.

E arnings Potential

Salaries for residential social workers vary according to the type and size of home and the level of responsibility involved. You are likely to start on a salary of around £13,000, depending on your qualifications and experience, rising to around £25,000. It is possible to earn more than this if you gain promotion and become a team leader or manager.

F urther Information

Social Work Careers Website: www.socialworkcareers.co.uk

The General Social Care Council (England) Website: www.gscc.org.uk

The Scottish Social Services Council Website: www.ccetsw.org.uk (temporary site)

The Care Council for Wales Website: www.ccwales.org.uk

The Northern Ireland Social Care Council Website: www.ccetsw.org.uk (temporary site)

National Institute for Social Work, London WC1H 9SS
Website: www.nisw.org.uk

The British Association of Social Workers, Birmingham B5 6RD
Website: www.basw.org.uk

Alternative/equivalent entrance requirements can include: ILC, IB, EB, NC/ND and many other similar international systems. For further details see the Equivalent Qualifications section in the Introduction.

What is Involved?

As a restaurant manager, you could work in locations from small exclusive dining establishments or wine bars to fast food outlets, mass-appeal eating-houses, hotels, clubs and branches of major chain organisations. As well as having a working knowledge of food and wine, you would need to meet the expectations of your customers and ensure that they return in the future.

If you work for a national chain organisation, you would have to fit in with company menu policies; in other areas, your chef or catering manager would be responsible for selecting the items on the menu but you would have an overview. You would have overall responsibility for cleanliness and hygiene, health and safety, air pollution and compliance with by-laws together with recruitment, training and staff motivation.

Budgetary control would normally be an important part of your job, including ordering supplies, publicising the business, paying staff, banking each day's takings and investing for future development.

Opportunities for Training

There are many possible avenues for training. You could start as a chef or food service assistant, for example, and work your way through progressive levels of National or Scottish Vocational Qualifications (N/SVQ). You might at the same time study part-time or by distance learning for the professional qualifications of the Hotel and Catering International Management Association (HCIMA).

You could take a national diploma course at a local college or you could continue into higher education for a degree or higher national diploma (HND) in a subject such as hospitality or catering. At this level, you may secure a place on a management training scheme run by one of the large hotel or restaurant groups.

Another possible training route would be to join a Modern Apprenticeship (Skillseeker in Scotland) training programme.

Requirements

Experience, motivation and commitment would generally count for much more than examination success. Depending on the training route you choose, you could enter the restaurant industry with no examination passes at all, with GCSE/S Grade passes at A-C/1-3, with A level/AVCE/Advanced Higher, Higher or equivalent qualifications, with a degree or HND. You should research options carefully and talk them through with your careers or personal adviser.

Kind of Person

You would need a bright, extrovert personality and the ability to communicate well with everyone you meet. You should by nature be customer-orientated and service-focused, with a solid base of common sense and a resistance to pressure and stress, together with a sense of humour and tact, business flair and administrative thoroughness. Crises can often occur in the heat of a busy kitchen and you would need to be able to think quickly and act decisively to solve problems, while maintaining an atmosphere of unhurried and unflappable professionalism in the dining area. You should have a reasonable standard of numeracy to cope with the financial side of the business and sufficient IT skills to use specialist software packages for restaurants.

B road Outlook

Employment opportunities tend to be very good, in line with the huge increase in recent years in restaurant numbers in the UK. Many people gain experience for a few years with a large organisation before setting up their own business, perhaps with a specialist theme or in a carefully chosen location.

R elated Occupations

You might also consider: hotel or catering manager, publican or chef.

I mpact

Demands on your personal time would be substantial, with long hours, split shifts and late working, including evenings, weekends and public holidays. Indeed, the better you are at your job, the longer into the night your clients might want to stay. Your working hours would start long before the first customers arrive and finish after the last ones leave. Clearly your social and family life would be affected to such an extent that everything else would have to revolve around your work.

E arnings Potential

The range of remuneration is wide. As a junior trainee, you might start at around £8,000 to £16,000, rising with experience to between £20,000 and £23,000. A senior manager in a large restaurant could earn in excess of £40,000. If you set up your own restaurant, your income would depend entirely on your own ability to establish a profitable business.

F urther Information

Hotel and Catering International Management Association, London SW17 7HN Website: www.hcima.org.uk

Hospitality Training Foundation, London W5 5DB Website: www.htf.org.uk

Springboard, London WC2H 8LP Website: www.springboarduk.org.uk

The Hotel and Catering Training Company Website: www.hctc2.co.uk

Alternative/equivalent entrance requirements can include: ILC, IB, EB, NC/ND and many other similar international systems. For further details see the Equivalent Qualifications section in the Introduction.

What is Involved?

Your role as a retail manager would depend very much on the type of retailing in which you were involved. You could be selling goods and services on-line, in a retail park, shopping mall or high street; you might work in a supermarket, a large department store or a specialist boutique. If you were the manager of a large department store, you might have a large team of assistant managers dealing with, for example, individual departments, customer services, finance, buying and human resources.

In a smaller organisation, you might take on many of these functions yourself. The basic principles would remain the same: to maximise profits by setting and reaching sales targets, persuading customers to choose your outlet and training and getting the best out of all members of staff. You would expect to spend some of your time on the shop floor, to see how customers are reacting to your latest range of products and to check that customers are being properly handled by staff. You would attend meetings with your staff and deal with administrative matters in your office.

Opportunities for Training

You could work your way to the top through sheer hard work and talent. However, more emphasis is now being placed on qualifications. Many large stores and chains have their own training schemes, for both graduates and non-graduates, and the competition for places on these schemes can be fierce. Diploma courses in retail management are available at different levels for candidates with GCSEs/S grades, A levels/Advanced Highers/Highers or equivalent qualifications. Universities and other institutions of higher education offer relevant degree and higher national diploma courses.

Requirements

While there are no precise educational requirements laid down for entry into retail management, employers are increasingly looking for staff who have reached a certain educational level or have completed a period of training. Graduates are generally offered places on fast-track management schemes.

The actual subject of your degree would not be crucial, since the training would cover all the necessary topics, but subjects allied to retailing, including business studies, would obviously be helpful. For entry into other relevant marketing, retail management, and other degree courses you would need two A level/AVCE/Advanced Higher, three to four Higher or equivalent qualifications.

Kind of Person

You would need an outgoing personality, together with excellent communication skills, both spoken and written, since you would be dealing with a wide variety of people, including staff, suppliers and customers. Quick thinking and problem solving ability would also be necessary in a busy environment where many different things are happening at once. Physical and mental stamina would be important, as the hours could be long, and as manager you would be expected to be on hand to deal with anything that cropped up. A smart appearance would be necessary. You should be numerate and have a good eye for business.

B road Outlook

The retail industry employs more than 10% of the national workforce, and there are always vacancies to be filled. Entry into management schemes can be competitive but promotion can come quite quickly if you show determination and flair. There are plenty of opportunities, particularly with the diversification taking place within the industry, and there are new initiatives emerging for managers with originality and successful business acumen. Some managers gain promotion to the board of their company, while others may choose to go into allied occupations such as marketing or management consultancy. You could even be head-hunted by a competitor.

R elated Occupations

You might also like to consider: advertising account executive, buying executive, hospitality/hotel manager, management consultant, marketing manager, office manager, operational researcher, personnel (human resources) manager or public relations officer.

I mpact

Retail management can be a demanding occupation and store opening hours are becoming ever longer (even 24 hours). While you would not be expected to be present all the time, you would probably have to work some evenings and certainly some weekends.

E arnings Potential

Pay scales vary enormously, depending on the size and scope of the organisation, and the amount of responsibility undertaken. Trainee managers in multiple stores could start at anything from £14,000 to £18,000 but a top manager in a large organisation could earn well over £50,000. There would also be other benefits offered by larger employers, such as bonuses, commission, enhanced pension scheme, staff discount and good social facilities.

F urther Information

British Institute of Retailing, London W1X 9DA Website: www.bir.co.uk

British Shops and Stores Association, Middleton Cheney OX17 2TN Website: www.di-net.co.uk

Alternative/equivalent entrance requirements can include: ILC, IB, EB, NC/ND and many other similar international systems. For further details see the Equivalent Qualifications section in the Introduction.

What is Involved?

As an officer in the RAF, you would be part of the service which guards the airspace of the UK and other areas for which Britain has responsibilities, including its operations under NATO. You would be responsible for leading and managing other non- commissioned personnel on bases at home and overseas, either in an active role in flying or in any of the numerous support services on which pilots depend. RAF aircraft are divided into three groups: fast jets, multi-engine and helicopters. If you were a pilot, you would specialise in one of these and would devote most of your time to flying duties.

Apart from pilots, officers in the RAF are employed in a variety of specialised areas, including: navigators who plan routes and guide pilots; fighter controllers who use radar to direct pilots in action; air traffic controllers who provide pilots with flight information and help them take off and land safely; intelligence officers who interpret photographic and other images from reconnaissance aircraft; engineers who keep aircraft in operation; RAF Regiment officers who defend airfields and other installations; administrators, physical training personnel, training officers, police officers, lawyers, chaplains, doctors, dentists and nurses.

Opportunities for Training

You would complete a six-month initiation course as a new officer, which includes academic and practical exercises designed to reveal and develop your leadership skills and other important aptitudes. Once commissioned, you would proceed to the specialist training of your choice. For pilots, you would be selected for training on fast jets, multi-engine planes or helicopters on the basis of your performance after a short period of initial training and flying with an instructor. Your full training programme would last around three years.

Requirements

For basic entry, you must have at least two A level/AVCE/Advanced Higher, three Higher or equivalent qualifications, together with five GCSE/S Grade passes at A-C/1-3 including English and maths. You must also meet RAF nationality and residence requirements, be at least 17.5 years old and pass a series of selection tests – including aptitude and initiative tests, interviews and a medical – held at the RAF College at Cranwell. Many posts – but not all – have rigorous eyesight requirements.

If you want to go to university first, you will find that graduates are welcome in all branches of the service, particularly if your degree is in a technological or other relevant discipline. Currently about 40% of applicants are graduates.

You can seek financial support through a sixth form scholarship or sponsorship at university. A Flying Scholarship could provide some free flying training.

Kind of Person

You must be confident and capable as a leader, able to work in a team but also able to stand apart and make decisions, often very quickly. You must be physically fit and prepared to accept responsibility for both personnel and very expensive equipment. Good communication skills are vital.

Each branch of the RAF requires its own mix of personal qualities: thinking and reacting quickly for a pilot or air traffic controller; working logically for an engineer, for example. Most branches need officers with a keen interest in the operation of advanced technical equipment.

B road Outlook

Provided you complete your training programmes successfully and serve satisfactorily, promotion can be expected. However, promotion beyond flight lieutenant to squadron leader and above depends upon merit and performance. It is very competitive and dependent on vacancies. As an officer with a Permanent Commission, you would normally serve until you are 38 or for 16 years from the age of 21; a Short Service Commission is usually 12 years for a pilot or navigator and considerably less for ground-based work.

R elated Occupations

You may also consider: RAF airman/woman, Royal Navy officer, Royal Marines officer, Army officer, civil airline pilot, air traffic controller, aircraft engineer.

I mpact

You would have to be available for duty 24 hours a day, 7 days a week, but for much of the time you would work normal office hours from Monday to Friday, extended occasionally into weekends. During operations and in emergency situations, you would be expected to work whatever hours the circumstances demand. This and overseas commitments could take you away from family and friends, often for extended periods of time.

There is special provision for female officers who become pregnant either to seek early release from their commission or to take maternity leave before resuming their commission.

E arnings Potential

A pilot officer earns approximately £19,000, a flying officer about £25,000, while a squadron leader receives over £40,000 and a wing commander over £56,000. Aircrew receive flying pay in addition to their basic salary and there are generous allowances for living and travel expenses, generally in line with what is paid in the other defence services.

F urther Information

School and university careers and liaison service or local Armed Forces Careers Office. Website: www.rafcareers.com

Alternative/equivalent entrance requirements can include: ILC, IB, EB, NC/ND and many other similar international systems. For further details see the Equivalent Qualifications section in the Introduction.

What is Involved?

As a young naval officer, you would have a management responsibility for people and for state-of-the-art equipment. Eventually you might find yourself in command of a warship, flying a Lynx helicopter, supervising the safe operation of a submarine nuclear propulsion plant or providing emergency medical care. You would be trained as a specialist to perform key operational roles, working together with the Royal Marines to carry out vital work in ships, submarines, aircraft, naval air stations and shore establishments. Officer specialisms include warfare, aviation, diving, Royal Marines, hydrographic surveying, meteorology, engineering, supply and training management. Then there are medical and dental officers, nurses and chaplains. Closely linked to the Royal Navy, the Royal Marines are a specialist amphibious commando force able to operate at very short notice in a variety of terrains, often under considerable threat.

Opportunities for Training

Initial training is at Britannia Royal Naval College, Dartmouth, which is like a university, specialising in leadership, professional training and higher education across a broad range of subjects. Your general training would include an introduction to seamanship and naval warfare, plus technical subjects such as marine engineering and weapons and sensors; naval studies would add an understanding of modern naval technology, strategy and associated background subjects; leadership training would give you practical experience and assessment and you would have a period of sea training. Nurse officers train at the Royal Naval Hospitals at Portsmouth and Plymouth, although they also spend some time at Dartmouth.

Requirements

With two A level/AVCE/Advanced Higher, three Higher or equivalent passes, you could join direct as an officer, starting as a midshipman and rising to sub-lieutenant after two years. If you are studying maths and science subjects, you could apply to read for an engineering degree. Seventy-five per cent of officers enter as graduates or obtain degrees during training. You would have to go through a rigorous selection process known as the Admiralty Interview Board (AIB). This gives both you and the navy a chance to assess whether a career in the Royal Navy is right for you. The main aim of the AIB is to assess your potential. It lasts two-and-a-half days and takes place at HMS Sultan, a Naval base near Gosport in Hampshire. You must be at least 17 and 1.57 metres tall. There are nationality and residence requirements as well as strict eyesight standards. You must also be male if you want to fly strike aircraft, serve in submarines or join the Royal Marines.

Kind of Person

Life on board ship and in submarines requires very particular qualities of officers. You must be able to live and work under the pressures of confined space with large numbers of other people. This requires broadmindedness and high levels of self-discipline. As an officer responsible for the men and women under your command, you need good management, communication and interpersonal skills. You need to be quick thinking and resourceful, able to show initiative in sudden events which may be of a 'life or death nature' in the event of combat. Long spells working away from home require qualities of self-sufficiency and drive to get on with the job. An interest in science and technology is important in many areas of work. The hard physical nature of the commando training of the Royal Marines requires a very special level of fitness, stamina and determination.

B road Outlook

Opportunities for promotion are good and all officers have an equal opportunity to demonstrate their future potential within a highly structured system. You should be able to expect a new appointment every two or three years. Serving in the Royal Marines offers the opportunity to be on instant alert to serve as a first response service anywhere in the world where trouble may flare up.

R elated Occupations

You may consider: army officer, merchant navy officer, RAF officer, air traffic controller.

I mpact

You would be working in an environment where much is expected of you and where you would be on call 24 hours a day. On exercise and operational duty, shifts and hours can be long and demanding, both physically and mentally. Communal living in often cramped conditions away from families for various periods of time requires a calm outlook on life and a high level of tolerance. You must be prepared to serve anywhere in the world.

All officers join on an initial twelve-year commission (Royal Marines eight years), although there are options to leave early in certain cases.

E arnings Potential

Sub-lieutenants receive approximately £13,000 to £25,000, rising to £29,000 to £34,000 for lieutenants. Salaries rise significantly on further promotion and officers receive additional allowances for such things as flying, serving in submarines and being at sea.

F urther Information

Look up local Armed Forces Careers Offices in the telephone directory.
Website: http://www.royal-navy.mod.uk/

Alternative/equivalent entrance requirements can include: ILC, IB, EB, NC/ND and many other similar international systems. For further details see the Equivalent Qualifications section in the Introduction.

What is Involved?

As a rural practice surveyor, you would be involved in offering advice on a range of aspects of countryside management and development. You might undertake the sale or purchase of rural holdings, value land, property and livestock and organise auctions; you might issue shooting or fishing permits or advise on leisure activities such as golf courses, outward-bound activities or tourist accommodation; you might be involved with managing an estate or large farming enterprise.

You could be employed as a consultant offering advice to farmers or landowners on such things as buildings, livestock, and investment in machinery or other possible uses for farmland. You could become involved with insurance, tax or compensation issues. Another area that is becoming increasingly important is that of conservation and the environment. As these examples show, this can be a very varied job, concerned with a full range of countryside issues.

Opportunities for Training

There are several possible routes to qualification, including distance learning, taking an accredited degree or following a relevant postgraduate course. Whatever academic route you follow, you can work towards chartered membership of the Royal Institution of Chartered Surveyors (RICS) by completing a period of structured practical training with an employer, ending with the RICS Assessment of Professional Competence. Alternatively, you can work in a similar way towards corporate membership of the Architecture and Surveying Institute.

Requirements

For entry to a degree course you are likely to be asked for two or three A level/ AVCE/Advanced Higher, three or four Higher or equivalent qualifications, together with supporting GCSE/S Grade passes at A-C/1-3, including English and maths. Some courses will accept more practical qualifications in place of the above.

Kind of Person

You would need to have a good basic understanding of the countryside and of rural matters. In addition to your agricultural interests, you should have a sound knowledge of the law and of financial matters. You could be involved with such things as valuations, managing accounting systems and budgeting, so you would need to be numerate. You should enjoy solving problems and applying your knowledge to find practical and logical solutions.

You could find yourself working for or with a wide range of different people and you would need to be able to communicate with them all clearly and with authority. You would need to enjoy being part of a rural community and out in the countryside in all weathers. You are likely to be walking some distance and clambering around buildings, which means that you would need to be reasonably fit and agile.

B road Outlook

There are a number of different areas of employment for rural practice surveyors. You might work in the public sector for a local authority or a government department, such as the Ministry of Defence or the Department for the Environment, Food and Rural Affairs. You might equally find work with a major rural charity such as the Royal Society for the Protection of Birds or the National Trust. However, the major area of employment is the private sector, where you might be employed directly by an estate or large farm, indirectly by a group of smaller properties or within the rural department of a firm of general practice surveyors. There is increasingly work involving conservation issues and the diversification of use of rural land.

R elated Occupations

You might also consider: farm or horticultural manager, landscape architect, town and country planner, conservation officer or land, hydrographic, building or quantity surveyor.

I mpact

This is certainly not a Monday to Friday, nine to five job. The hours would depend greatly on the season and the consequent demands of the countryside. You would be working outside in all sorts of weather and at times likely to get wet, cold and muddy. You would need to spend a lot of time talking to farmers and other rural clients, listening to their problems and worries. You may be expected to travel quite long distances to get to your work.

E arnings Potential

Traditionally, this is not the best-paid branch of surveying, the compensation being that it offers an attractive lifestyle if you enjoy the country life. If you enter the profession as a graduate, you could expect to start on £10,000 to £12,000 and this is likely to rise to around £20,000 and beyond when you achieve full professional status. Sometimes you may be offered accommodation as part of the payment package.

F urther Information

Royal Institution of Chartered Surveyors, Coventry CV4 8JE
Website www.rics.org.uk

College of Estate Management, Reading RG6 6AW
Website: www.cem.ac.uk

Architecture and Surveying Institute, Chippenham SN15 3WD
Website: www.asi.org.uk

Alternative/equivalent entrance requirements can include: ILC, IB, EB, NC/ND and many other similar international systems. For further details see the Equivalent Qualifications section in the Introduction.

287

What is Involved?

As a member of a sales team (you might also be known as a sales representative or sales manager), you would be involved in selling products or services and ensuring that your clients are fully aware of your organisation's presence in the market place. You would usually be responsible for a range of products or services and might travel widely to meet customers and establish good relationships with them. Your work could include dealing with enquiries regarding specifications or prices, helping to solve any problems of supply or quality, seeking advice on technical issues and reporting any information on competitor activities to your sales and marketing colleagues.

You would usually work within a framework laid down by your head office marketing and sales department, who would generate enquiries from potential buyers by means of advertising, sales literature, the Internet and press and television announcements. You would normally have to meet revenue targets and generate new business in addition to maintaining relationships with existing customers.

Opportunities for Training

Many companies operate their own in-house courses for trainee sales staff, usually covering product knowledge, sales techniques and company sales policy. There are also relevant part- and full-time courses available at colleges and training centres and by distance learning, while bodies such as the Institute of Sales and Marketing Management, the Managing and Marketing Sales Association and the Institute of Professional Sales offer qualifications linked to grades of membership.

Increasingly, degree courses are available covering sales and related aspects of business management. These could provide a sound foundation for a future career in sales, although graduate opportunities are usually open to students of any discipline. You might need a degree in, say, IT or engineering for some specific technical sales areas.

Requirements

While there are no specific entry requirements for a career in sales management, employers often recruit graduates and people with experience in relevant fields. You would generally enhance your prospects with a broad platform of GCSE/S Grade passes at A-C/1-3, including maths and English, and would have even greater choice – including degree course entry – with A level/AVCE/Advanced Higher, Higher or equivalent qualifications.

Kind of Person

You should have a confident, outgoing personality, a readiness to make new contacts, sensitivity to others and the ability to listen carefully to comments or requests. You would need to believe in your own products or services and to know enough about your clients to be able to suggest the right products to meet their needs.

You would have to be persuasive in explaining the special features of your

288

products or services, aware of competition in the marketplace, efficient in handling orders and well organised in keeping appointments and maintaining your records. You would usually be expected to dress smartly. Other qualities needed would include numeracy, the ability to cope with rejection, patience to deal with awkward customers and the energy to keep going all day long.

B road Outlook

There is usually no shortage of sales executive opportunities anywhere in the UK. Promotion would normally depend on your track record to date and could lead to regional or national sales manager posts and eventually to a position as sales or export director. You may find that you need to move fairly regularly to other companies or parts of the country if you want to progress more rapidly, broaden your experience or take on more responsibility.

R elated Occupations

You might also consider: buying executive, marketing manager, advertising executive, retail manager or public relations officer.

I mpact

You would work under a great deal of pressure to meet targets and you might be expected to travel widely. Deadlines could intrude on your family and social life, and your customers would expect you to place them top in your priorities. In some jobs, you could spend days or even weeks away from home and you might have to write up your reports and prepare presentations in the evening or at weekends.

E arnings Potential

There are no set pay scales but you might expect to start on around £16,000 as a graduate trainee. This could rise to well above £50,000 for a sales manager. It is essential to check the full remuneration package before you join a company, as your earnings might be linked with commission, bonuses, a car or car allowance and travelling and accommodation expenses. Salaries in specialised areas such as pharmaceuticals, chemicals and technological equipment tend to produce higher rewards.

F urther Information

Institute of Sales and Marketing Management, St Albans AL3 4ET
Website: www.ismm.co.uk

Institute of Professional Sales, Maidenhead SL6 9QH
Website: www.iops.co.uk

Management and Marketing Sales Association, Cheshire CW11 3GE
Website: www.mamsasbp.com

Alternative/equivalent entrance requirements can include: ILC, IB, EB, NC/ND and many other similar international systems. For further details see the Equivalent Qualifications section in the Introduction.

What is Involved?

It is now generally accepted that the term Personal Assistant (PA) refers to a job involving more than the basic secretarial duties of typing letters, answering the telephone and dealing with routine administration. If you were a PA, your main role would be to act as a close support to a manager or executive, handling the day-to-day running of an office to allow them to make the most efficient use of their time.

Your work could involve dealing with correspondence and other communications, organising meetings, liaising with other departments, companies or customers, and sometimes even acting on behalf of the manager. With experience, you could become an office manager, often with your own administrative team.

Opportunities for Training

There is no single training route but employers would be looking for good keyboard skills and computer literacy, sometimes with shorthand. Specific training for a particular company would normally be carried out in-house, usually after you have completed a one- or two-year college course in office skills and management.

There are also university-level diploma and degree courses in secretarial studies and administration, together with some courses specifically designed for graduates. If you have the right level of training and experience, you would have the option of becoming a member of the Institute of Qualified Private Secretaries.

Requirements

While there are generally no specific educational requirements laid down for becoming a PA, employers would expect a high level of numeracy and proficiency and accuracy in written English.

Entry to secretarial courses usually requires a minimum of some GCSE/S Grade subjects, while others look for A level/AVCE/Advanced Higher, Higher or equivalent qualifications. If you are thinking of going to university, you might consider undertaking a course in secretarial and office skills first – it would never be wasted and you need never be unemployed.

Kind of Person

You would need to be very well organised, with an eye for detail and with excellent communication skills, both spoken and written. You should be tactful and discreet, possessing a talent for getting on well with people of all kinds. You would need to be a real team member, able to work both with and for other people, sometimes taking decisions and sometimes implementing the decisions of others. A smart appearance would be important, since you would probably be involved in dealing with customers or other visitors to your organisation.

B road Outlook

With the increased use of computers in office administration, the role of the PA has changed, with less call for the traditional shorthand/typist but increased scope for well-qualified and ambitious administrators. There will always be opportunities for such people to make their mark, and a good PA can often make the transition to management. You may decide to specialise in a particular area of work, such as medicine or law, or you might set up your own businesses, such as a secretarial or recruitment agency. Traditionally, the role of the PA has been undertaken almost exclusively by women; now more men are coming forward.

R elated Occupations

You might like also to consider: civil service administrator, hospitality/ hotel manager, office manager, personnel/human resources manager, public relations officer, medical secretary, farm secretery or secretary linguist.

I mpact

You would probably work usual office hours, though with increased responsibility and seniority might come the need to stay later at particular times of the year or travel to business meetings. Depending upon the amount of responsibility you were given, and/or the personality of your particular boss, you might need deep reserves of tact and diplomacy because you would have extensive access to confidential information.

E arnings Potential

Pay scales would vary widely, according to the size of the organisation and the seniority of your position. In general, salaries range from about £15,000 to £22,000 but top jobs in prestigious companies in London can command over £30,000.

F urther Information

Consult your local education authority for lists of local courses.

Institute of Qualified Private Secretaries, Maidenhead SL6 1RR
Website: www.iqps.org

Alternative/equivalent entrance requirements can include: ILC, IB, EB, NC/ND and many other similar international systems. For further details see the Equivalent Qualifications section in the Introduction.

What is Involved?

As a secretary linguist (or bilingual/trilingual secretary), you would be able to offer practical speaking and writing skills in one or more foreign languages in addition to the full range of secretarial skills. The exact nature of your job would vary considerably from one employer to another but could include anything from word processing in your different languages, translating correspondence and making phone calls abroad to receiving and entertaining overseas visitors, making foreign travel arrangements and keeping up to date with the political or commercial climate in relevant countries.

You may receive occasional requests for translating or interpreting but it should be clear that you are not a specialist in either of these fields. (See our separate articles on these occupations.) You would normally be based in an office and should have access to keyboards, software packages and reference materials specific to the languages you would be using.

Opportunities for Training

You could develop your secretarial and language skills in many different ways but would probably wish to gain a recognised qualification from one of the major awarding bodies, such as Edexcel, OCR, the London Chamber of Commerce and Industry (LCCI) or the Scottish Qualifications Authority (SQA). Your course should include English language skills, word processing and commercial applications of your chosen languages. There may also be specialist in-house training provided by your employer.

Requirements

You would need to be fluent in writing and speaking the languages you offer, and it would be a distinct advantage to have a sound understanding of the cultural, economic and social situation in the countries where your languages are spoken. Depending on the level you are aiming at, you may need A level/AVCE/Advanced Higher, Higher or equivalent passes in one or more languages and you could find a degree valuable. However, experience of travelling or living overseas and using foreign languages on a regular basis could count for as much as examination success. Whatever your linguistic background, you would need a high-level secretarial qualification.

Kind of Person

You would need excellent communication skills and the confidence to enter into multilingual conversations on the telephone or in face-to-face meetings. You should have a keen interest in keeping your language skills up to date and a willingness to learn specialist vocabulary. Attention to detail, advanced IT skills and good organisational ability would all be important.

You should be able to get on with people easily, especially if your work involves welcoming foreign visitors to your organisation and making them feel at ease. A willingness to travel would quite likely be part of your interest in using languages and could enhance your employment opportunities.

B road Outlook

With accelerating globalisation and the continuing development of the European Union, demand is healthy for people with genuine bilingual or trilingual ability (as opposed to a superficial smattering of language awareness). Most opportunities relate to the major European languages, especially French, German and Spanish, but there are also openings for specialists in Russian, Arabic, Japanese, Chinese and Eastern European languages.

A career as a secretary linguist presents above-average openings for late start, career break, flexitime, temping and freelance initiatives. There are also many job opportunities abroad, including the option of working as an English language specialist in a country where you can communicate easily in the local language.

R elated Occupations

You might also consider: teacher, translator, interpreter or another specialist role such as farm, medical or legal secretary.

I mpact

Many posts would involve a normal business week from Monday to Friday, but you could have to work unsocial hours if you need to be in regular contact with people in other time zones or if you are looking after overseas visitors. You may be expected to travel abroad as part of your job.

E arnings Potential

Levels of pay would vary considerably from one job to another, depending on the location and your ability and experience, but you could expect a salary higher than the normal secretarial rate, perhaps between £14,000 and £19,000, with additional allowances for out-of-hours working and overseas travel.

F urther Information

The Institute of Qualified Private Secretaries, Berkshire SL6 1RR
Website: www.iqps.org

The Languages National Training Organisation
Website: www.languagesnto.org.uk

Edexcel, London WC1H 0HH Website: www.edexcel.org.uk

OCR, Cambridge CB2 1GG Website: www.ocr.org.uk

The Scottish Qualifications Authority, Glasgow G2 7NQ
Website: www.sqa.org.uk

The London Chamber of Commerce and Industry
Website: www.lccieb.com

Alternative/equivalent entrance requirements can include: ILC, IB, EB, NC/ND and many other similar international systems. For further details see the Equivalent Qualifications section in the Introduction.

What is Involved?

As a shipbroker, your role would be to facilitate the business of international bulk shipping by bringing together ship owners with vessels to fill and charterers with cargoes to transport by sea. You would also be involved with the purchase and sale of very large ships such as bulk carriers, container vessels, oil tankers and specialist ships. The main centre of international shipbroking operations is the Baltic Exchange in London, with some 50% of all tanker broking and up to 40% of dry bulk chartering carried out by about 5,000 shipbrokers working in around 700 shipbroking companies (there are 20,000 shipbrokers worldwide).

Other major shipping markets are found in Tokyo, Singapore, Shanghai, Hong Kong and New York as well as in European centres like Hamburg, Copenhagen and Oslo. Your work would include making presentations to potential clients, negotiating the main terms of a contract or sale, providing your clients with market intelligence and advice, entering tonnage into the company's database, checking the technical nature of a cargo and building up your own personal contacts throughout the world of shipping. Good relationships are vital if you wish to succeed.

Opportunities for Training

While there are no specific qualifications required, you might wish to apply for membership of the Institute of Chartered Shipbrokers (ICS) and to undertake one of their diploma courses, which can be taken by correspondence course or day release. These courses cover maritime law, international shipping and trade, economics and bulk transport. The Baltic Exchange also runs regular training courses on many aspects of the shipbroking business.

Many new recruits are graduates entering shipbroking after completing a degree in maritime business, although any academic subject would be acceptable.

Requirements

There is no required shipbroking qualification but you would gain much relevant background information from a shipping business degree at Cardiff Business School, Southampton University, Liverpool University, City University Business School, Greenwich Maritime Institute or the Warsash Maritime Centre.

Kind of Person

You should be prepared to take a high level of responsibility, to mix well socially, to express views clearly and logically in both written and oral format, to have well-honed negotiating skills with a flair for maintaining contacts. Your intellectual credentials would be tested in the tenacity required to push through deals. Physical demands can also be high, with long hours, a global timescale, frequent exhausting travel, 24-hour availability in times of urgency and an extremely competitive global arena.

The highest levels of reliability, accuracy and integrity are essential. The motto of the Baltic Exchange – 'Our Word Our Bond' – symbolises the importance of ethics in trading. Members need to rely on each other and, in turn, on their principals for many contracts verbally expressed and only subsequently confirmed in writing. You would need good IT skills to cope with the sophisticated online information system at the Exchange.

B road Outlook

There is some competition from other shipping centres but the London market is growing steadily as world trade expands. This process may be affected by fluctuations in the global economy, but the dominance of sea over air transport (nine times greater) is unlikely to be basically altered.

The Baltic Exchange is becoming increasingly computerised and brokers acting for ship owners can place shipping information, including the technical details of ships, directly online. However, negotiation is still handled completely by the brokers personally, since this is too complex to be automated by computer. Every ship, port and cargo is different.

R elated Occupations

You might also consider: logistics manager, freight forwarder, stockbroker, insurance underwriter or marketing manager.

I mpact

The global market ensures that shipbroking services spread over 24 hours a day, seven days a week. Periods of frenzied activity occur regularly when there is a need to find employment for a fleet and, as a broker, you would wish to prove the value for money of your services to the ship owners and charterers. Typically, your day could start early in the morning, in time to catch the important far eastern markets, or could go on late into the night for the USA. You would be working by telephone, fax, email and mobile for much of the time and might need to make frequent trips abroad.

E arnings Potential

Medium to high levels of pay can be expected, with a starting salary of around £25,000, rising to £40,000–£60,000 for an experienced shipbroker. In good years, bonuses can easily double these figures.

F urther Information

The Institute of Chartered Shipbrokers, London EC3A 6EJ
Website: www.ics.org.uk

The Baltic Exchange, London EC3A 8BH
Website: www.balticexchange.co.uk

British International Freight Association, Middlesex TW13 7EP
Website: www.bifa.org

The Institute of Logistics & Transport, Corby NN17 4AX
Website: www.iolt.org.uk

Alternative/equivalent entrance requirements can include: ILC, IB, EB, NC/ND and many other similar international systems. For further details see the Equivalent Qualifications section in the Introduction.

What is Involved?

Social work covers many different areas of society, including services for children, older people, people with mental health problems, physical or learning disabilities, those who experience homelessness and those whose lives are affected by HIV and AIDS, drugs and alcohol. Some social workers work in youth and criminal justice services or in adoption and fostering. You might specialise in any of these areas and your job as a social worker would involve activities such as assessing and interviewing clients, organising packages of care and support, providing counselling and advice, writing court reports, attending court cases and liaising with psychiatrists, doctors and other professionals.

Opportunities for Training

You would need to spend a minimum of two years in training to obtain the Diploma in Social Work (DipSW), although there are many possible routes to this qualification. You could, for example, study full-time, part-time or by distance learning, and you could follow a postgraduate course if you want to take a degree first. Full-time diploma courses usually last two or three years; part-time and distance-learning courses vary enormously, according to the circumstances of participants. On a typical training course, approximately half of your time would be spent at university or college and the remainder in the workplace under the supervision of a qualified and experienced social worker.

A new degree in social work will be introduced in England from autumn 2003, eventually replacing the DipSW. Other arrangements will apply in Scotland, Northern Ireland and Wales. During the phasing out period, DipSW courses will continue to run and will continue to be recognised as valid social work qualifications. For further information about the new degree, visit: www.doh.gov.uk/swqualification

Requirements

Mature applicants over 21 do not always need formal academic qualifications but the DipSW selection panel would expect you to demonstrate your ability to study at higher education level. If you have a degree or equivalent qualification, you would be eligible to apply to a postgraduate route. Mature applicants are welcomed and experience of life is an important attribute for social work.

If you are under 21 on the date a DipSW programme starts, you must have at least two A level/AVCE/Advanced Higher, three Higher or equivalent qualifications, together with five GCSE/S Grade passes A-C/1-3. All DipSW programmes would require you to have some relevant paid or voluntary social work experience. Certain types of criminal conviction could prevent you from meeting the entry requirements.

Kind of Person

You would need to be open minded and prepared to examine and even change your attitudes and possible prejudices. You may need to deal with racism and other forms of discrimination. You would certainly require personal qualities such as patience, determination and the ability to help people face painful and distressing problems. Social work can be both physically and emotionally stressful and not everyone can stand back from situations and assess them in an objective but caring way. Good practice would rely on the intellectual skills of analysis, reflection and adopting a critical perspective.

B road Outlook

There is a shortage of qualified social workers, which currently means that, especially in London and the southeast, newly qualified social workers do not have to wait longer than six months to get a position in the team they want. Progression is also good, offering social workers the chance to study for post-qualifying awards and move up into management positions. There has also been growth in self-employed social workers offering counselling or training services on a freelance basis.

R elated Occupations

You might also consider: probation officer, residential social worker, teacher, nurse, occupational therapist, psychologist, police officer, prison governor or youth and community worker.

I mpact

Most social workers are involved in a system providing cover 24 hours a day, seven days a week. This means that your hours are likely to be long and irregular. You may well be required to work a rota system or to be on call at times after your official hours of work, for which you may get extra pay. You may find yourself facing difficult situations, which can be unpleasant and at times dangerous. For example, you may need to call on someone with a history of violence or visit clients living in a squat.

E arnings Potential

Salaries vary considerably, depending on age, experience, the responsibilities involved and also the location. As a newly qualified social worker you could expect to earn £17,000 to £23,000. A senior social worker might earn around £26,000 and a director of social services around £70,000.

F urther Information

Social Work Careers Website: www.socialworkcareers.co.uk

The General Social Care Council (England) Website: www.gscc.org.uk

Scottish Social Services Council, Dundee DD1 4NY
Website: www.ccetsw.org.uk   (temporary site)

The Care Council for Wales Website: www.ccwales.org.uk

The Northern Ireland Social Care Council Website: www.ccetsw.org.uk (temporary site)

Alternative/equivalent entrance requirements can include: ILC, IB, EB, NC/ND and many other similar international systems. For further details see the Equivalent Qualifications section in the Introduction.

What is Involved?

Working as a software engineer, you would be responsible for creating the original programs needed to enable computers to carry out a very wide range of functions. Your programs (or software) could include complex automation control for industry, accounts packages for book keeping or sophisticated business management systems. You would work on the basis of specifications laid down and agreed with a client, usually via a systems analyst in your own company or organisation. You would often work on your own for small projects, or as a member of a team of software engineers for large projects. Having written the software, you would make sure it works properly, oversee its installation and test it out in its finished form. You could also write up installation instructions and user manuals and even run training courses for the client's staff.

Opportunities for Training

There are a great many computer-related courses available at universities and there are significant differences between them, so it is important to read prospectuses carefully. Some courses offer a mixture of options combining the study of software and hardware and you then choose to specialise in one of these at the end of the first year. It is also possible to combine software engineering with a range of other subjects, including electrical and electronic engineering or management. Most degree courses last three or four years and some include a sandwich element of industrial experience. There are also higher national diploma (HND) courses, which are generally a year shorter than corresponding degrees, and postgraduate courses.

When in employment, you would be able to work towards professional qualifications offered by bodies such as the British Computer Society, the Institute for the Management of Information Systems or the National Computing Centre.

Requirements

To gain admission to a relevant degree course, you would need two or three passes at A level/AVCE/Advanced Higher, Higher or equivalent, almost certainly including maths and perhaps physics too, together with at least five GCSE/S Grade passes A-C/1-3 to include English, maths and a science subject. For an HND, you should have at least one A level/AVCE/Advanced Higher, two Higher or equivalent passes.

A good first degree would normally be necessary for admission to a postgraduate course.

Kind of Person

You are likely to be interested in technology and computers and up to date with developments in this ever-changing field. You should be strong at maths, with a logical and practical approach to problem solving. In addition, you would have to listen to the requirements and ideas of others and to accommodate these in your plans. With tight deadlines to meet, this would require you to prioritise effectively.

B road Outlook

There are opportunities to work for a wide range of large companies with in-house computer systems, together with chances to work for computer manufacturers and specialist software companies. There are increasing prospects for experienced software engineers to become consultants and to work for themselves. The increased use of computer-based technology should ensure considerable demand for software engineers for the foreseeable future.

R elated Occupations

You might also consider training as an electrical, electronic, communications, biomedical, aeronautical or automotive engineer. Alternatively, you might like to work as a systems analyst or designer, webmaster or cybernetics specialist.

I mpact

Whilst your standard working week might well be within normal office hours and confined to weekdays, you are a likely to find yourself occasionally working at the weekends or in the evenings, in order to meet deadlines or to sort out some problem that has arisen unexpectedly. You would also find yourself reading about your subject out of work time to ensure that you are up to date with new developments. You may find that you have to travel clients' premises.

E arnings Potential

Software engineers are usually well paid and have the potential to be very well paid indeed. You could expect to start on a salary of around £16,000 when you first graduate and this should rise quite rapidly as you gain experience to well above £35,000 if you are reliable and can produce useful results.

F urther Information

The British Computer Society, Swindon SN1 1HJ Website: www.bcs.org.uk

The National Computing Centre, Manchester M1 7ED
Website: www.ncc.co.uk

The Institute for the Management of Information Systems,
Sidcup DA1 5HR Website: www.imis.org.uk

E-skills UK Ltd, London SW1 6DR Website: www.e-skills.com

Alternative/equivalent entrance requirements can include: ILC, IB, EB, NC/ND and many other similar international systems. For further details see the Equivalent Qualifications section in the Introduction.

What is Involved?

As a solicitor, your job would be to provide clients with skilled legal advice and representation, including representing them in court. You might, like most solicitors, work in a 'private practice' partnership or you might work as an employed solicitor for central or local government, the Crown Prosecution/Procurator Fiscal Service, the magistrates/district courts or a commercial or industrial organisation. Your work could be general in nature – wills, divorce settlements, property sales, criminal cases and compensation for injury – or you could become expert in, for example, company, criminal, taxation, European, international or environmental law.

You could concentrate on work with legally aided clients, who could not normally afford a solicitor's fees, or you could specialise in advising multi-national corporate clients on urgent, multi-million pound deals.

Opportunities for Training

The law is complex and your training as a solicitor would have to follow a set of rigorous rules. The quickest route to qualification is by means of a qualifying law degree. If you take a degree in a subject other than law, you would have to complete a one-year full-time (or two-year part-time) course leading to the Common Professional Examination (CPE) or the postgraduate Diploma in Law. After successful completion of your law degree, CPE or Diploma in Law, you would have to undertake a one-year (or two-year part-time) Legal Practice Course, before entering a two-year training contract with a firm of solicitors or other approved organisation (such as a local authority or the Crown Prosecution Service), gaining practical experience in a variety of areas of law. At this stage, you would be paid a salary and would be a trainee solicitor. It is important to arrange a training contract as early as possible: you can apply in the final year of your degree but should think carefully about which area of the law you wish to enter. An alternative route would be to train as a legal executive and use this as a stepping-stone to qualification as a solicitor. See our separate article on 'Legal Executive'.

In Scotland, you would need a degree in Scottish Law or a three-year pre-Diploma training contract, together with the 26-week Diploma in Legal Practice. You would follow this with a two-year training contract with a practising solicitor in Scotland, towards the end of which you would have to sit a Test of Professional Competence to determine whether you are a 'fit and proper person' to enter the profession.

Requirements

Competition for places to read law is strong and university admissions tutors expect high grades at A level/Advanced Higher, Higher or equivalent. No particular subjects are specified. Similarly, intense competition for places on the CPE and postgraduate diploma courses normally requires a good honours degree.

Kind of Person

You would need excellent written, verbal and interpersonal skills, together with the ability to read widely and take in considerable amounts of information. You would spend a lot of time interviewing clients in order to establish the facts of a case and form an opinion. Much of what you are told by clients would be confidential and they would need to be sure that it should remain so. You may be involved with complex financial issues, including company accounts and taxation, so a good standard of numeracy would be important.

B road Outlook

In private practice, prospects for promotion to partner/associate status are always available, depending on your ability to deal with clients and colleagues and to build up a reputation for success. Openings have increased in recent years for employed solicitors in the magistrates/district courts and in the Crown Prosecution/Procurator Fiscal services.

R elated Occupations

You might also consider: advocate/barrister, legal executive, legal accountant or justice's clerk.

I mpact

The training can be very expensive, especially if you choose not to take a law degree, leaving you with a large loan to repay when you start training. Most solicitors work normal office hours, although you may have to put in many additional hours to complete work on time. Sometimes you may be on call, in the evenings or at weekends, to deal with clients who have been taken to a police station. Legal aid work can be poorly paid and demanding but would give you valuable experience in dealing with a wide range of cases.

E arnings Potential

You would receive a salary during your training contract, with recommended rates in Scotland of £10,300 for the first year and £13,905 for the second year. Equivalent rates in England and Wales are slightly higher and start at over £14,000 in central London. Once qualified, salaries can vary enormously, from around £20,000 to £30,000 for a general assistant solicitor to £100,000 or more for a successful specialist in central London.

F urther Information

The Law Society, Worcestershire B98 OTD Website: www.lawsociety.org.uk

The Law Careers Advice Network Website: www.lcan.csu.ac.uk

The Law Society of Scotland, Edinburgh EH3 7YR
Website: www.lawscot.org.uk

Alternative/equivalent entrance requirements can include: ILC, IB, EB, NC/ND and many other similar international systems. For further details see the Equivalent Qualifications section in the Introduction.

What is Involved?

As a speech and language therapist (SLT), you would be a specialist in communication disorders. The ability to communicate is central to all that we do: to who we are, how we learn and how we relate to each other at home, at school and at work. Your aim would be to help the thousands of people who fail to access education, social, economic and career opportunities due to communication difficulties.

In your work, you would assess and diagnose the people under your care or who have been referred to you, developing a programme of care to maximize their communication potential. You would also work to support people with swallowing, eating and drinking difficulties. You would work directly with a person with communication difficulties but would also be involved in breaking down communication barriers by influencing and supporting other people in their communication environment.

You might work with: people who stammer or have hearing impairments; babies with cleft palates or cerebral palsy; children who need help in learning to understand language or putting words together; adults or children involved in road traffic accidents; and adults who have had strokes or other neurological disorders.

Opportunities for Training

You would need a professional certificate to practise as an SLT. This can be achieved via an approved three- or four-year first degree or a two-year postgraduate course following a suitable first degree. A degree in any discipline may be considered but subjects such as linguistics, psychology or physiology are most relevant.

You would study the normal development of language and production of speech sounds, as well as communication disorders. You would also cover aspects of psychology, particularly normal development, phonetics and linguistics, neurology, physiology and anatomy, together with acoustics and audiology (hearing), as problems in these areas can affect speech and language. The practical side of your training would involve at least 150 hours of clinical placement with a range of client groups (eg children with special needs or adults with acquired neurological disorders), in which you would work under the supervision of qualified colleagues.

Requirements

For entry to a degree, you would need two or three A level/Advanced Higher, three or four Higher or equivalent qualifications. Some courses require biology at A level/Advanced Higher/Higher and some request English at this level too. It is best to check with individual course providers because competition for places is keen and requirements are generally higher than the minimum. All courses interview candidates and usually ask about clinical observations. Before interview, therefore, you should seek to arrange a visit to your local speech and language therapy service.

Kind of Person

Good interpersonal skills are essential. It is important that you can communicate clearly and are able to listen and so gain the trust of your patients. You would need skills in observation, analysis and problem solving as you work with patients and clients. You would need a flexible and creative approach because what works with one patient would not necessarily work with another. You should also have an interest in both science and language. It is important to keep records for each patient and monitor their progress. This demands organisational skill and the ability to work independently, as well as to be part of a team.

B road Outlook

Once you are qualified, employment prospects are good, although there is more competition for posts in the London area. The majority of SLTs work for the NHS, although opportunities for private work are now growing. In the UK, approximately 2.5 million people have a communication disorder of some kind. Of these, 800,000 have a difficulty so severe that it is hard for anyone outside their immediate families to understand them.

R elated Occupations

You may be interested in other therapy-based professions in the medical field, such as occupational therapist, radiographer, physiotherapist or podiatrist. Alternatively, you might be interested in becoming a teacher or an educational or clinical psychologist.

I mpact

NHS SLTs work a 36-hour week, usually Monday to Friday, but you should be prepared to work extra hours occasionally. In private practice, the hours may be longer and can involve some unsocial hours, but the earnings are likely to be higher. You may be required to travel to different locations during your working day.

E arnings Potential

Newly qualified SLTs earn from £14,000 per year, rising to around £28,000 for a specialist therapist. If you are prepared to take on management responsibilities, higher salaries are possible. Salaries in the private sector are likely to be above these levels.

F urther Information

Royal College of Speech and Language Therapists, London SE1 1NX
Website: www.rcslt.org.uk

Alternative/equivalent entrance requirements can include: ILC, IB, EB, NC/ND and many other similar international systems. For further details see the Equivalent Qualifications section in the Introduction.

What is Involved?

As a sports coach, you would provide coaching on the techniques of a sport to players under your tuition, assisting them to learn their sport, to enhance their skills and get the most out of their efforts. You would monitor their technique and performance; help them reach top physical and mental condition; confer, if necessary, with other specialists such as dietitians, physiotherapists or sports psychologists; and explain how the abilities of the individual should relate to those of the team. All areas of sport are covered by coaches, and more opportunities occur at a wider age range than ever before.

Coaches in exercise and fitness can be found in such activities as keep fit, yoga, weight training, circuit training, aerobics, aquafit, step and line dancing, and other movement and fitness classes. They are likely to be employed by leisure centres or to be self-employed. More and more they are setting up their own clubs and classes. Holiday camps, outward bound centres, cruise ships, private hotels and even large business organisations now employ their own resident trainers. The armed forces, security services, probation and prison services also have instructors to train in fitness and, if appropriate, in self-defence.

Opportunities for Training

The national governing bodies (NGB) often provide part- or full-time courses in their own sports areas. For example, bodies such as the LTA (Lawn Tennis Association), the PGA (Professional Golfers Association) and the RYA (Royal Yachting Association) offer courses for coaches and provide official recognition and registration. There is some higher education provision with higher national diploma (HND) courses in leisure studies, and more especially degree courses in PE, movement studies, sports science or coaching. Colleges of further education often run community coaching award schemes, set up by the Central Council for Physical Recreation (CCPR).

Requirements

The National Coaching Foundation offers a substantial range of options to would-be coaches in all areas. For entry to teacher training or to a sports-related degree, you would normally need two or three A level/AVCE/Advanced Higher, three or four Higher or equivalent qualifications, together with a good spread of GCSE/S Grade passes A-C/1-3, including English, maths and a science for teacher training courses. HNDs would require one A level/AVCE/Advanced Higher, two Higher or equivalent qualifications. You would need to be very fit and many courses would look for evidence of sporting achievement.

Kind of Person

In addition to physical fitness, you would need good verbal communication skills, sensitivity to others, the capacity to mix praise and criticism in acceptable doses, powers of analysis, persistence, organisation and stamina. As a professional representative of your sport, you would usually be expected to set an example to others in terms of your behaviour, appearance and adherence to the code of conduct laid down by your governing body.

B road Outlook

The expanding leisure industry now employs 750,000 people in the UK and, with the attendant boom in both community and commercial leisure centres, prospects look good. Outdoor pursuits is another growth area. Opportunities are now widespread in soccer, cricket, rugby, mountaineering, horse-riding, martial arts, badminton, squash, ice-skating, golf, swimming, tennis and fitness generally. You would find, however, that this is a very competitive world and therefore somewhat uncertain at times.

R elated Occupations

You might also consider: PE teacher/instructor, professional sportsperson, youth worker, leisure services manager, teacher, physiotherapist, chiropractor or osteopath.

I mpact

This can be only slightly less involving than for the full-time sportsperson, but possibly without the same level of personal intensity. Nevertheless, it can involve working throughout the day, at weekends and, for indoor sports, during the evenings. This could be seen as one of the most sociable of career fields with the most unsocial of time schedules to meet the likely demands of clients.

E arnings Potential

Part-time rates fluctuate between £20 and £30 per hour. Experienced full-time coaches would expect to achieve £20,000 per annum or above, rising to much higher levels for those with successful track-records. Those in professional soccer or tennis would anticipate considerably higher financial rewards. Against this must be set the seasonal nature of much coaching.

F urther Information

Sports Coach UK, Leeds LS6 3BJ. Website: www.sportscoachuk.org

Central Council for Physical Recreation (CCPR), London, SW1 1DE. Website: www.ccpr.org.uk

Institute of Sport and Recreation Management (ISRM), Melton Mowbray, LE13 1XJ. Website: www.isrm.co.uk

The Physical Education Association of the United Kingdom, Reading RG1 5AQ. Website: www.pea.uk.com

SPRITO employment, learning and skills portal for sports and recreation Website: www.sprito-els.org.uk

Additionally, there are all the national sporting bodies to be consulted.

Alternative/equivalent entrance requirements can include: ILC, IB, EB, NC/ND and many other similar international systems. For further details see the Equivalent Qualifications section in the Introduction.

What is Involved?

As a stage manager, you would liaise with all the members of a theatrical production, including the producer, director, actors, theatre manager and sound, lighting, set and costume designers. You would be the practical co-ordinator, from the planning stage before the rehearsals to the taking down of the set. On tour, you would be in charge of organising travel and accommodation for the cast, and of booking rehearsal space and time. Whatever the production, you would work very closely with the director, helping to implement his or her ideas and stage directions, collecting props and arranging sound effects, relaying the director's ideas to the set designers and making sure that actors were in the right place at the right time for rehearsals. You would also make sure that safety procedures were being followed at all times. During the actual performances, you would be present at the side of the stage, overseeing the smooth running of the production. You would normally head a team including a deputy stage manager, one or more assistants and a number of stagehands, although you might combine all of these roles in a small touring company.

Opportunities for Training

Whilst it may be possible to join a repertory company without formal training, only a very small number of people now enter the profession in this way. The more usual route would be to take one of the many two-year diploma courses available at drama schools, or follow the option of a three-year degree course.

You may be able to work towards National/Scottish Vocational Qualifications (N/SVQs) in stage management organised by Metier.

Requirements

Many of the courses on offer would result in a qualification of a degree or higher national diploma (HND). For a degree course you would need two or three A level/AVCE/Advanced Higher, three or four Higher or equivalent qualifications, together with five GCSE/S Grade passes A-C/1-3. For entry to an HND course you would need a minimum of one A level/AVCE/Advanced Higher, two Higher or equivalent passes, together with four GCSE/S Grade passes A-C/1-3. Relevant work experience or involvement in school or other amateur productions would prove as important as academic qualifications when applying for a drama school place.

Kind of Person

As the essential link between all the different people in a theatre company, you would need excellent communication skills and the ability to remain calm when others around you talk of crisis. Tact and diplomacy would be valuable, together with good organisation, an eye for detail, and accuracy in keeping records. The job often calls for a blend of leadership and the willingness to work as part of a team, which would enable you to liaise with confidence between a wide variety of people, often in stressful situations. Practical ability would be useful, and you would need to be interested in both the artistic and technical sides of productions. Physical, emotional and mental stamina would be of prime importance, allied to a strong sense of determination.

B road Outlook

Employment prospects for graduates of technical courses at drama schools are extremely good, with surveys of recent graduates across the sector showing that virtually 100% achieve employment in the industry. Some people who train and work as stage managers choose to stay in stage management all their working lives, while others might move into administration or producing. Many cross from theatre to television, to trade shows or to the music industry. The skills needed are similar, whatever the area of work. Indeed, film and television producers often look for stage management experience when recruiting for new productions.

R elated Occupations

You might also consider: actor, assistant director (in the film industry) or director, producer, floor manager (television), events and conferences manager or public relations officer.

I mpact

You would inevitably be working long and unsocial hours, perhaps rehearsing a new production during the day and managing the current performance each evening. There could also be a good deal of travelling involved, either on tour or moving around from one contract to another. The lifestyle of a stage manager would not necessarily fit well with family or social commitments.

E arnings Potential

Pay rates vary greatly, according to the type of theatre and size and scope of production. The minimum starting wage for an assistant stage manager is likely to be between £250 and £300 a week. As a more experienced freelance stage manager, you could be paid £600 per week (£30,000 pa). In a permanent post, an experienced stage manager could achieve around £25,000 or more depending on the location.

F urther Information

Association of British Theatre Technicians, London SE1 3XT
Website: www.abtt.org.uk

National Council for Drama Training, London WC1H 9SS
Website: www.ncdt.co.uk

Stage Management Association, London SE1 3XT
Website: www.stagemanagementassociation.co.uk

Metier, Bradford BD5 0BQ Website: www.metier.org.uk

Alternative/equivalent entrance requirements can include: ILC, IB, EB, NC/ND and many other similar international systems. For further details see the Equivalent Qualifications section in the Introduction.

What is Involved?

Your role as a stockbroker would be to buy and sell securities on behalf of clients. Securities are bonds, stocks and shares, which are used by the government and companies when they wish to raise additional capital. Government bonds carry fixed rates of interest but company shares can fluctuate in value in accordance with the fortunes of the company and the shareholder can make a profit or loss on them. It would be very important to be aware of a company's performance, together with the economic trends of the whole stocks and shares market. You would advise clients whether to invest their money, to hold or to sell shares they already have. Your clients may be individuals, companies or institutions, such as those acting on behalf of pension funds.

Opportunities for Training

All firms employing stockbrokers must be members of the Stock Exchange and you would have to be listed as a 'registered person' with the Financial Services Authority. To achieve this, you must pass the examinations administered by the Securities Institute. You would normally be expected to study for the examinations at home, in your own time, but your employer would often organise an in-house training programme.

Requirements

While there are no formal educational requirements laid down for entry into stockbroking, it has become virtually an all-graduate profession. Any degree subject could be acceptable but subjects such as economics, business studies, maths, statistics and law would be particularly relevant. For entry to a degree course, you would need two or three A level/AVCE/Advanced Higher, three or four Higher or equivalent qualifications, together with a minimum of five GCSE/S Grade passes at A-C/1-3. You might consider a sandwich course, which would include a business placement. You may wish to continue your studies with a postgraduate Master of Business Administration (MBA) course before you apply for a post.

Kind of Person

You should be able to cope with pressure and stress, sufficiently confident to back your own judgment and willing to take risks once you have analysed all the relevant data. You would need a high standard of computer literacy, as all your dealings would work through the Stock Exchange computerised settlement system. Good communication skills would be very important, in order to present detailed information to clients, and honesty and integrity are vital, as you could be dealing with large amounts of other people's money.

Advanced numeracy skills and an understanding of what can affect share prices are also of great importance. Dealing rooms can be fraught and busy places, with an atmosphere of tension and excitement as the brokers try to do their best for their clients by buying and selling at the most advantageous prices.

B road Outlook

Competition for vacancies is very intense and you should gain as much relevant work experience as possible before you apply. Once appointed, you would normally develop your career by taking on more responsibility and increasing the value of the portfolio you manage. Opportunities for stockbrokers can occur in organisations such as banks and finance houses, as well as the established stockbroking firms.

If you are interested in working in finance but are not quite sure about stockbroking, it could be possible for you to enter a large banking organisation as a trainee, to experience different areas of work before deciding on your speciality. A good deal of work is based in London but there are increasing numbers of openings in other large cities.

R elated Occupations

You might also consider: accountant, actuary, market maker, banking executive, economist, financial adviser, insurance broker or investment analyst.

I mpact

Probably the most obvious effect this career would have on your life would be the high pressure and long hours that it would involve. Global markets may require unsocial hours of work and this would have to be taken into consideration, although it may be a matter of starting early and finishing late rather than working through the night.

It is also quite likely that you would have to take work home with you over the weekend. You would have to be prepared to dress smartly.

E arnings Potential

At the beginning of your career, you might earn £20,000 to £30,000 and progress over 15 to 20 years to £100,000 or more, depending on your performance and promotion. You would be exceptionally well paid if you are successful, with bonuses adding considerably to your basic salary.

F urther Information

The Securities Institute, London EC3R 8AJ
Website: www.securities-institute.org.uk

The London Stock Exchange, London EC2N 1HP
Website: www.londonstockexchange.com

The Financial Services Authority, London E14 5HS
Website: www.fsa.gov.uk

Alternative/equivalent entrance requirements can include: ILC, IB, EB, NC/ND and many other similar international systems. For further details see the Equivalent Qualifications section in the Introduction.

309

What is Involved?

Working as a structural engineer, you would be involved in a field closely related to civil engineering. You would be concerned with all aspects of the design and construction of structural frameworks, ranging from bridges, coastal defences, grandstands and airport hangars to the steel structures used in large buildings. In addition to the technical requirements of a particular project, you would be expected to consider environmental factors. The structures that you are creating could have a major impact on the surrounding countryside and local conditions may also influence the type of structure that would be viable and appropriate. You could find yourself involved with tackling problems involving pollution and infrastructure as well as selecting the most appropriate construction materials.

Opportunities for Training

There are relatively few universities offering specific degree courses in structural engineering. Sometimes the subject is combined with architectural studies or with civil engineering. There are also civil engineering courses on which you could choose to specialise in structural engineering after a year or two. In all cases, it would be important to make sure that you choose a course accredited by the Institution of Structural Engineers. Sandwich courses are available, giving you the opportunity to spend some time working in industry whilst studying.

In order to become a chartered engineer, responsible for research, design and development, you would need to spend at least four years in undergraduate study, followed by postgraduate study and supervised experience. The initial requirement can be achieved by taking a four-year degree course that leads directly to an MEng. Alternatively, you could take a three-year degree course leading to a BEng and follow this with a year of more specialised post-graduate study. To become an incorporated engineer, responsible more for the efficient day-to-day management of projects, you could take the BEng route and follow this with further study and on-the-job training.

Requirements

In order to be accepted for an MEng in structural engineering, you are likely to need three A level/AVCE/Advanced Higher, four Higher or equivalent qualifications, including maths and physics, together with at least five GCSE/S Grade passes at A-C/1-3. Entry requirements for the BEng are usually slightly lower but would still normally include maths and physics or engineering at A level/AVCE/Advanced Higher or Higher.

Kind of Person

Your job would be to solve structural problems in a sensible and practical way. For this you would need to enjoy using your technical knowledge, combined with sound common sense, to reach logical conclusions about the structures you are designing and constructing. You would need a rigorous approach to each project. Much of your work would involve using sophisticated computer technology to model structures and test different design solutions before going ahead with construction.

You would work in a team and would have to be reliable and efficient, able to take orders and carry them out without delay, to coordinate the work of others or to give presentations to clients. You would need to explain your ideas and plans clearly to others who often may not share your specialist knowledge.

B road Outlook

There are usually good opportunities for structural engineers in the UK and abroad, as UK qualifications are recognised in many overseas countries. The industry is sometimes dependent on the state of the economy, which determines how many new projects are likely to be started.

R elated Occupations

You might be interested in another branch of engineering, such as: civil, mechanical or marine engineer. Alternatively, you might consider: architect, town planner, naval architect, offshore engineer, surveyor or construction manager.

I mpact

You are likely to spend quite a lot of time working out of the office and on site, often out of doors in all kinds of weather. You might occasionally get dirty, wet and cold. When you are working on site you may be expected to work site hours, which can be longer than normal office hours, especially during the summer months. In addition, you may be expected to travel quite long distances within the UK and overseas, which could disrupt your social and family life.

E arnings Potential

As a new graduate, you would be likely to start earning around £15,000 but this can rise rapidly as you gain experience and work towards chartered or incorporated engineer status. The average annual earnings for experienced chartered engineers are around £45,000 and for incorporated engineers around £37,000.

F urther Information

The Institution of Structural Engineers, London SW1X 8BH
Website: www.istructe.org.uk

The Engineering Careers Information Service, Watford WD18 0JT
Website: www.enginuity.org.uk

The Engineering and Technology Board, London WC2R 3ER
Website: www.engc.org.uk

> *Alternative/equivalent entrance requirements can include: ILC, IB, EB, NC/ND and many other similar international systems. For further details see the Equivalent Qualifications section in the Introduction.*

311

What is Involved?

As a chartered surveyor you would be a specialist in understanding both the built and the natural environments, seeking to gauge the right balance between them, physically measuring them but also measuring their impact on people and business. The work may appear to revolve around building sites and mathematical calculations but the broader perspective is important.

You would find that a qualification in surveying can prepare you for many different jobs, ranging from valuing residential or commercial property, fine art or antiques, to exploring mineral deposits, reclaiming land from the sea, preserving historic buildings or managing environmentally sensitive land. In rural practice you could expect to deal with land, plant and livestock in addition to property; in planning and development, on the other hand, you might find yourself advising on issues such as the suitability of a new shopping precinct.

You could work in the private or public sector, based in an office for report-writing but more likely spending a lot of your time out of the office visiting sites, buildings, land and farms.

Opportunities for Training

The principal professional body is the Royal Institution of Chartered Surveyors (RICS), which offers many different routes to qualified status. You would most likely meet the academic requirement through a full- or part-time degree or diploma course in a relevant subject, although there are many other options, including postgraduate courses if your first degree is not approved.

On achieving the academic standard, you must complete at least two years structured on-the-job training in a surveyor's office (one year if you have already spent a year with a surveyor as part of a sandwich course) before attempting the Assessment of Professional Competence (APC). Whatever route you follow for the academic stage, it is successful completion of the APC which ultimately confers chartered status.

Requirements

You would normally need three A level/AVCE/Advanced Higher, four Higher or equivalent qualifications for admission to an approved degree course. Many students opt for a more vocational route after GCSE/S Grade, following a relevant national award, for example, before progressing to higher education. Course titles include construction, land management or the built environment.

Kind of Person

The RICS stresses that good communication skills, both written and oral, are necessary for negotiating agreements, making presentations and submitting reports to clients. It also indicates that an aptitude for maths and science can be helpful for the more technical sides of the job and that a logical, practical mind is important.

You would need to be a practical person with good observation skills and you would almost certainly require the ability to drive.

B road Outlook

The outlook is generally good for chartered surveyors but can vary depending on your area of specialisation. For example, opportunities for surveyors working in property management and valuation of buildings tend be linked to the state of the commercial and residential property market. Surveying is an international profession and there are opportunities to work abroad. Many chartered surveyors work for firms of estate agents and progress to become partners, although – depending on the size of the firm – it may be necessary to change job in order to progress. You could start your own firm.

R elated Occupations

You might also consider: estate agent, civil engineer, architect, town planner, building surveyor, quantity surveyor and rural practice surveyor.

I mpact

Surveyors tend to work normal office hours, although a considerable amount of that time can be spent out of the office. Depending on your specialisation, you may have to travel considerable distances. If you are involved in estate agency, you may have to work at weekends and in the evenings in order to carry out surveys. It may prove necessary to move several times to build the right experience for your career development.

E arnings Potential

The average graduate salary is £19,000, which would increase with experience and can rise to well over £50,000 a year. Salaries in the commercial fields tend to be greater than those in the public sector and surveyors working in cities earn more than their rural counterparts. Working in estate agency, you could earn bonuses depending on house sales and as a partner you would have a share of the profits.

F urther Information

Royal Institution of Chartered Surveyors (RICS), London, SW1P 3AD
Website: www.rics.org

Alternative/equivalent entrance requirements can include: ILC, IB, EB, NC/ND and many other similar international systems. For further details see the Equivalent Qualifications section in the Introduction.

What is Involved?

As a systems analyst, you would investigate problems related to the use of computers in business and other organisations. Having been called in to analyse a particular system, you would begin talking to the client to ensure that you understand exactly what is required. You would then prepare a feasibility study to see whether the organisation's present system can be adapted to meet the newly identified need. If it cannot be suitably modified, you would advise on a new system to overcome the problem. You may design the new system yourself or you may call in a software engineer to take your specification and turn it into a working solution. See our separate article on 'software engineer'.

Whoever designs the system, you would normally remain responsible for its successful implementation. You would have to cost the whole operation, draw up a detailed implementation plan, write relevant user manuals and set up staff training programmes.

Opportunities for Training

The computer industry is still developing at a rapid pace. Job titles and training routes are not always clearly defined and employers often focus more on experience and ability, frequently taking a fairly relaxed view of formal qualifications. A very large number of higher education courses can now provide the right sort of background but you would find that many people currently working in systems analysis have moved there after gaining experience in programming. They would not necessarily have a degree in computing, although most would have studied to degree or higher national diploma (HND) level. There are specialist postgraduate courses available for graduates of almost any discipline, while some employers provide their own analysis and design training.

You may be able, if you wish, to enter computer-related work straight from school or college, studying part-time for National/Scottish Vocational Qualifications through a Modern Apprenticeship (Skillseeker in Scotland).

When in employment, you would be able to work towards professional qualifications offered by bodies such as the British Computer Society, the Institute for the Management of Information Systems or the National Computing Centre.

Requirements

To gain admission to a degree course, you would normally need two or three A level/AVCE/Advanced Higher, four Higher or equivalent qualifications, which may include maths for courses such as software engineering or computer science. For HND entry, one A level/AVCE/Advanced Higher, two Higher or equivalent would be the usual minimum requirement.

You would need a good first degree to gain a place on a postgraduate course.

Kind of Person

You should have a considerable knowledge of information technology and be able to think logically and creatively in this field. You must enjoy solving IT problems and implementing solutions. You would need to be able to explain problems and solutions clearly to others, so both verbal and written communication skills are vital. You would also need to be adaptable and continue to learn and implement new technology.

B road Outlook

The huge expansion of the use of information systems in business and commerce has resulted in an increasing demand for systems analysts. You may be employed in the IT department of a large company, you may work for a company that manufactures IT hardware or software, or you may work as an agency or independent consultant. There are opportunities throughout the UK and in many countries overseas.

You could progress within your company to become a senior analyst or even run the entire computer-based side of the organisation. An increasing number of analysts are self-employed, working as consultants or moving from one short-term contract to another. You could enter IT training and also teaching in further and higher education institutions.

R elated Occupations

You might also consider: software engineer, multimedia programmer or webmaster.

I mpact

You would usually work a 37- to 40-hour week with weekends free. If deadlines have to be met, you may have to work at weekends or late into the evening. Travelling to clients and periods spent away from home would often be necessary, with an impact of your social and family life.

E arnings Potential

Salaries vary depending on experience and the size of the company but are in the region of £20,000 to £35,000, increasing as you gain experience and take on management responsibility for a team working on a variety of different projects.

F urther Information

The British Computer Society, Swindon SN1 1HJ Website: www.bcs.org.uk

The National Computing Centre, Manchester M1 7ED
Website: www.ncc.co.uk

The Institute for the Management of Information Systems, Sidcup DA1 5HR
Website: www.imis.org.uk

E-skills UK Ltd, London SW1 6DR Website: www.e-skills.com

Alternative/equivalent entrance requirements can include: ILC, IB, EB, NC/ND and many other similar international systems. For further details see the Equivalent Qualifications section in the Introduction.

What is Involved?

As a teacher, you would enable pupils to develop their abilities and aptitudes and fulfil their own individual potential. Much of a typical school day would be concerned with specific subjects but you would also have a pastoral role to play – helping your pupils with personal problems and supporting them when they are faced with difficult decisions. You would also have links with parents, in particular at parents' meetings, which are usually held in the evening. Preparation of lessons and marking would take up a good deal of your time. As a *nursery school teacher*, you would work with children aged three to five. As a *primary school teacher*, you would work with children within the five to eleven age range. You would usually be responsible for a single class of children, though there might also be scope for teaching a particular subject to different classes within the school. As a *secondary school teacher*, you would specialise in one or two subjects, which you would teach throughout the school to different age groups from 11 to 16/18.

Opportunities for Training

Recognised training is essential for teaching posts in maintained schools. You would need to undertake Initial Teacher Training (ITT) and obtain Qualified Teacher Status (QTS) in England and Wales, with a similar requirement for Scotland. Once trained, you must register with the relevant General Teaching Council for England, Scotland or Wales. There are several different routes and courses involved and you should do some careful research to determine which one would be the best for you. Most of the courses are full-time but there are opportunities for part-time and distance learning. Most of the routes take three or four years and involve spells of teaching practice in schools.

The two main routes to QTS are as follows:

• A first degree that includes a teaching qualification. Many of these courses are aimed at students who wish to work in primary schools, although there are others aimed at secondary school work.

• A first degree followed by a postgraduate certificate in education. The first degree should normally be in a National Curriculum subject. This route is more commonly taken by students who wish to work in secondary schools.

Routes are similar in Scotland but are not described in terms of ITT/QTS and courses are geared to the specific needs of the Scottish education system.

Requirements

The minimum requirements for ITT in England/Wales are two A level/AVCE or equivalent and three GCSE grades A-C or equivalent, including English and maths. (Some courses also require a science at GCSE Grade C or above).

In Scotland, you would need at least two Advanced Higher or three Higher, including English or equivalent, together with S Grades 1-3 in two other subjects, including maths at grade 1/2 or equivalent.

Kind of Person

You would need to enjoy working with children and young people and to be patient with those who find it difficult to learn. You also need to enjoy the subject or subjects that you are going to teach. Training may help you to handle difficult situations in the classroom but the enthusiasm for learning and helping others to learn must come from you. You would need to have very good communication skills, to be well organised, a good member of a team but confident enough to work on your own, and consistent and fair in your treatment of your pupils.

B road Outlook

There will always be a need for good teachers and there are often shortages, although the situation varies from subject to subject and area to area. With the expansion of nursery education, there may well be increased demand in this field.

Teachers can be promoted to posts of responsibility in academic, administrative and pastoral roles – as heads of department or year group, personal tutors, heads and deputy heads. Allowances can also be offered for additional responsibilities.

R elated Occupations

You might also consider: careers/personal adviser, educational psychologist, nursery nurse, social worker or youth worker.

I mpact

Teachers are held in great esteem by some and blamed by others for many of the ills of society. Your life would probably be affected by the need to take work home with you, although good organisation and use of time in the holidays should help to cut this down. The holidays (particularly in the summer) are a great asset, though they should not be regarded as completely free – much organisation and forward planning goes on, both in and out of school.

E arnings Potential

There are several incentive schemes at present to attract more people into teacher training. Check the websites below for the latest information. Salary scales for qualified teachers start at around £16,000 to £17,000 and can rise to £30,000. Headteachers can earn anything from £33,000 to £80,000 a year depending on the size of the school.

F urther Information

Teacher Training Agency, London SW1E 5TT Website: www.canteach.gov.uk

General Teaching Council for Scotland, Edinburgh EH12 6UT
Website: www.gtcs.org.uk

Department of Education, Bangor, Co Down BT19 7PR
Website: www.deni.gov.uk

Alternative/equivalent entrance requirements can include: ILC, IB, EB, NC/ND and many other similar international systems. For further details see the Equivalent Qualifications section in the Introduction.

What is Involved?

As a textile designer, you would be concerned with the design of a range of fabrics or textiles that would be used mainly for producing clothes, curtains, furnishing fabrics, carpets or wallpaper. You might work initially on paper but you are more likely to use a computer with a specialist software package allowing patterns and colours to be changed rapidly and the designs to be printed out in colour for consideration and approval by clients. You would then produce samples by weaving, knitting or screen printing, taking great care to ensure the right fabrics are used in each case.

Your work would be very much influenced by changing fashion and lifestyle trends. Clients need new ideas and colour schemes and furnishing fabrics change every year, so you must constantly think ahead and anticipate the current and future moods of manufacturers and buyers. You must also take account of the manufacturing processes involved, ensuring that your designs could actually be put into production without being prohibitively expensive and that you are not specifying unrealistic colours or yarns.

Opportunities for Training

You would need to have a formal training in textile design, usually via one of the specialist courses available at degree or higher national diploma (HND) level in universities and art schools throughout the UK. Some courses focus purely on design and artistic creativity, while others are more orientated towards the technology of manufacturing or the business of marketing. You must check prospectuses carefully when researching possible courses. You might decide to continue your studies to postgraduate level before you enter the labour market.

Requirements

The main entry requirement for study or employment is usually a portfolio of work. This might include samples of knitting, sewing, dyeing or weaving in addition to examples of your drawing skills. Talent and creativity are usually more highly regarded than examination success, although it is always helpful and sometimes essential to have a platform of GCSE/S Grade passes A-C/1-3 and A level/AVCE/Advanced Higher, Higher or equivalent studies, including an art related subject.

In England and Wales, you would normally complete a one- or two-year foundation course before progressing to a three-year art and design degree. In Scotland, the foundation course is the first year of a four-year degree. The HND route is normally a year shorter and may be more closely linked to manufacturing processes.

Kind of Person

To be a successful textile designer you would need to combine artistic creativity, drawing skills and an acute awareness of colour and texture with a good understanding of the technical side of the business. You should have a keen interest in fashion and may spend some time visiting exhibitions and fashion shows to spot trends and see what other designers are doing.

You must be able to communicate your ideas visually and verbally to clients or colleagues and may need to persuade buyers to accept your work. You would also have to be prepared to see some of your ideas rejected. You would need good IT skills, especially in using computer design packages, and an understanding of how developments in technology could enhance your design concepts. Poor colour vision could present serious problems.

B road Outlook

Textile design is a very competitive field. Even well established designers can go out of fashion and find that buyers lose interest in their work. However, the textile business is one of the largest in the world and there will always be a demand for creative and talented people. You could work for a large manufacturer or a smaller independent design house. You could set up your own business and might use an agent to market your collections to prospective buyers. British design training is valued abroad and you might choose to work overseas.

R elated Occupations

You might also consider: fashion, graphic or interior designer or photographer.

I mpact

This is a global industry which means that, as well as career opportunities abroad, you could find yourself having to travel fairly extensively in order to keep up to date with trends and to visit overseas fabric manufacturers. If you are employed by a large group, you would normally work office hours from nine to five, but could also work at trade shows, which could involve weekend and evening work. As a self-employed designer, you would often need to work very long hours, late into the evening and over weekends, to establish your business and meet the last-minute deadlines of clients.

E arnings Potential

Your pay would depend upon the nature of your employment, whether for a large or small company or self-employed. Junior designers working for a textile manufacturing company usually start at about £12,000, which would increase as they become experienced. Your earnings as a freelance designer would vary greatly, depending on your reputation. Paying commission to an agent would reduce your fee income but could help you establish a broad client base.

F urther Information

The Textile Institute, Manchester, M1 6FQ Website www.texi.org

Alternative/equivalent entrance requirements can include: ILC, IB, EB, NC/ND and many other similar international systems. For further details see the Equivalent Qualifications section in the Introduction.

What is Involved?

As a tour operator, you would organise the package holidays, leisure activities, tours, expeditions, cruises and coach trips on sale at travel agents. Details of these are publicised in sales brochures and advertisements, written about in newspapers and magazines and featured on radio and TV travel programmes. Working as a product manager for a tour operator, you might arrange expeditions by elephant or bicycle, journeys by Pullman train or cruise liner, flights by hot air balloon or Concorde. You might organise accommodation in anything from a chalet to a chateau. As a contract manager, you would negotiate availability and prices with the airlines, hotels, local transport companies, attraction owners and others involved in the package. In addition, it would be vital to check the quality of food, sanitation, beaches and entertainment, usually in liaison with your local representatives.

Opportunities for Training

There is no single route to a head office position as a tour operator but you should at some stage obtain the ABTA Tour Operators Certificate (ABTOC), which is generally accepted by the tour operating industry as a recognised commercial qualification. The ABTOC primary examination would cover the knowledge you should have within about one year of starting work, including locational geography, emergency procedures, legislation, ticketing and administration. The advanced examination would then take this level forward to encompass the wider range of skills and deeper knowledge required after two or more years' experience, such as providing complex holiday itineraries. You might also work towards National or Scottish Vocational Qualifications (N/SVQ) in Travel Services (Tour Operations). Alternatively, you could consider a degree or higher national diploma (HND) in travel and tourism, hospitality management or leisure and recreation. You should look for a course having close links with the travel industry.

Requirements

Experience is generally regarded as far more important than academic success. There are no specific entry requirements for the ABTOC or N/SVQ routes, although individual employers might look for GCSE/S Grade passes A-C/1-3, including English, maths, geography and modern languages. You would need at least two A level/AVCE/Advanced Higher, three Higher or equivalent qualifications for degree course entry, slightly less for the HND.

Kind of Person

You would need to combine very strong organisational and entrepreneurial qualities with the vision to put together holiday packages that appeal to the public, are competitively priced and demonstrate a concern for the overall comfort and enjoyment of customers. You should enjoy travelling, visiting resorts, making new contacts and establishing friendly and long-term relationships.

Your work would call for considerable attention to detail in such matters as the accuracy of descriptions in your promotional materials or exchange rate considerations and local taxes in determining precise costs. You would also need to write contracts to establish agreements and take out appropriate insurance cover. Marketing, business administration and finance and accountancy skills would all be important, especially an understanding of how to manage cash flow in what can be a highly seasonal business.

B road Outlook

Travel and tourism is a thriving, multi-billion pound industry. As long as people need to travel around the world, and continue to enjoy taking holidays and visiting different places, growth looks set to continue. There is no fixed career pattern for a tour operator but you could spend some time overseas as a resort representative, and even work your way up to being area manager for some exotic destination, before moving to a head office post and using your experience to devise packages, write brochures and negotiate contracts. There is usually intense competition for full-time appointments and you might need to build up your experience through a series of short-term, seasonal contracts.

R elated Occupations

You might also consider: tourist information assistant, travel agent, travel guide, events and conferences manager or marketing executive.

I mpact

While you might work fairly standard hours in a head office post, you would usually have experienced the complete absence of set hours for a resort representative. You would often have to sort out problems at any time of the day or night in such a post, and would be expected to work for as long as it takes to resolve the issues. Frequent travel and extended absence from home would normally be a significant feature of the work and could disrupt your family and social life.

E arnings Potential

If you start as a resort representative, you would probably receive a weekly wage of £100 to £150, with free or subsidised accommodation and commission on sales of local excursions. When you reach a position of experience, your salary should rise to around £16,000 to £18,000 and move well beyond these levels as you take on more responsibility.

F urther Information

TTC Training, Woking GU21 5AR Website: www.ttctraining.co.uk/

The Travel, Tourism and Events National Training Organisation, Surrey KT14 6DY Website: www.ttento.com

The Institute of Travel and Tourism, St. Albans AL1 3TJ
Website: www.itt.co.uk

Alternative/equivalent entrance requirements can include: ILC, IB, EB, NC/ND and many other similar international systems. For further details see the Equivalent Qualifications section in the Introduction.

What is Involved?

Working as a town planner, your job would be to balance the demand for new development and buildings with the diminishing amount of land available. You would be responsible for maintaining an attractive environment that can also sustain the demands of the population who live there. You would be involved with listening to the views of a number of interested parties, including conservationists, builders, farmers and residents, before advising on planning decisions. You would need to consider future developments and demands on amenities as well as the current situation, taking into account such factors as design features, waste and environmental management, transport, urban renewal and employment or recreation demands.

You would sometimes be implementing national planning policy at a local level, such as, for example, the current government preference for building on brownfield sites. You would use various sources of information, including surveys, public opinion and existing legislation, and could be involved with large-scale projects or with decisions on home extensions. You would almost certainly be required to use a wide range of skills in order to produce your reports. Much of the work is based in an office and involves the use of a computer but you would also be expected to make site visits.

Opportunities for Training

There are two main routes to gaining a qualification accredited by the Royal Town Planning Institute (RTPI). The undergraduate route would involve taking a four-year, full- or part-time, single or joint honours degree in town planning. There are also sandwich courses available, lasting five years with the extra year being spent on a work placement. The graduate route would involve taking a degree in another subject and following it with a postgraduate course in town planning. This is usually a two-year, full-time or three-year, part-time course. In either case, it is important to make sure that the course is accredited by the RTPI.

Requirements

For a first degree in town planning, you would need two or three subjects at A level/AVCE/Advanced Higher, three or four Higher or equivalent qualifications, together with at least three GCSE/S Grade passes at A-C/1-3. A few universities specify particular subjects but most are looking for a combination of arts and science subjects. Geography can be a useful subject to offer. The content of the courses can vary considerably, so it is important to study the prospectus carefully to make sure that the course on offer covers areas of interest to you. Work experience is a good idea because it gives you a chance to find out about the range of options available.

Kind of Person

You should be committed to achieving the best possible quality of life in your area without causing undue damage to the environment. You would need to communicate effectively with a wide range different people and to listen to

322

their views. Your job would involve writing clear reports in language that can be easily understood and you would at times be required to work under pressure to meet tight deadlines. You would have to speak at public meetings and would need to be persuasive or assertive if your audience is hostile. You would probably be responsible for managing other staff.

B road Outlook

This is a relatively small profession but one that is expanding. Most qualified planners work in the public sector at national, county council or local level, although there are opportunities to work in private practice, often working as a consultant offering planning advice to companies, organisations or individuals. There are also openings to work for multi-disciplinary firms, large building contractors and organisations such as national parks or water authorities.

R elated Occupations

You might also consider: civil engineer, architect, landscape architect, surveyor or cartographer.

I mpact

You may have to travel quite large distances to get to planning sites, or find that you have to move around the country in order to find the job you want or to gain promotion. Most planners who work for local authorities work a 37-hour week although you might be expected to attend planning meetings in the evenings.

E arnings Potential

There are no set pay scales and salaries vary in different parts of the country. However, as a newly qualified planner you could expect to earn between £13,000 and £19,000 a year; this could rise to £30,000 or more for a senior planning grades. Salaries in consultancies may be higher than this but would depend on the amount of work you can attract.

F urther Information

The Royal Town Planning Institute, London EC3R 8DL
Website www.rtpi.org.uk

Alternative/equivalent entrance requirements can include: ILC, IB, EB, NC/ND and many other similar international systems. For further details see the Equivalent Qualifications section in the Introduction.

What is Involved?

In order to carry out their roles efficiently and effectively, town planners need a great deal of help from planning support staff. In this type of work, you would probably specialise in one of three main areas:

• As a *planning administrator* you could be searching various types of land and property files and plans to gather information, or perhaps helping at reception or on a 'help desk' to provide members of the public with advice on a range of planning matters.

• As one of the *technical support staff* your work might include carrying out surveys, mapping and recording information, the establishment and maintenance of databases or the production of illustrations and other graphics for documents and exhibitions. One specialist growth area is the application of computer technology to a range of planning tasks.

• As a *planning enforcement officer* your job would be to ensure that development has permission and that any conditions attaching to the permission are complied with. The work would involve monitoring a variety of sources, gathering and presenting evidence, field investigation and dialogue with property owners and developers.

Opportunities for Training

The generally accepted training route for town planning support staff is to work towards the National/Scottish Vocational Qualification (N/SVQ) at Level 3 in Town Planning Support and the higher national certificate (HNC) in Land Administration (Planning). The N/SVQ has pathways designed to meet the needs of different types of support staff: everyone studies the same core units and then there is a choice depending on whether you are a planning administrator, enforcer or working on the technical side. You can study for the HNC part-time at a number of colleges and it normally takes two to four years to complete.

There is also a distance learning foundation course in planning. This provides the underpinning knowledge for the N/SVQ but could be of interest to anyone pursuing a career in town planning support.

With one of the qualifications outlined above and at least two years relevant experience, you could be elected to technical membership of the Royal Town Planning Institute.

Requirements

There are no absolute minimum entry qualifications needed to obtain a job in town planning support, although you would normally be expected as a new entrant to have good GCSE/S Grade passes A-C/1-3 in English, maths and other appropriate subjects. Relevant experience might be a more important factor for more mature candidates. There are usually specific entry requirements for formal training programmes at college.

Kind of Person

Your work would require you to be both accurate and neat in your presentation. You would need to be computer literate as you may need to use specialised software to produce graphical presentations and relevant statistics. You should also be reasonably confident at maths, as you may need to explain the statistics involved in a report. You would find yourself working as part of a team but you are also likely to be responsible for your own particular work. At times you may have to work under pressure to meet a deadline. You should be able to express yourself clearly both in your written reports and when speaking to the public. You may be involved with a number of different projects at one time, so would need to be well organised. Enforcement work in particular requires diplomacy and maturity.

B road Outlook

The majority of planning support staff work in local government. Others work in central government departments – including regional offices and regional development agencies – in National Park authorities, local development and regeneration organisations. Smaller numbers of planning support staff are employed in the offices of major developers and planning consultants.

There is a clear promotion route in local authority planning departments, although it may be necessary to move in order to gain promotion. You could use your qualifications and experience to progress to professional town planner status.

R elated Occupations

You might consider: architectural technologist, technical surveyor, chartered surveyor, town planner, estate agent, land agent or landscape architect.

I mpact

You are likely to be working a 37-hour week in an office, although there may be occasions when you are expected to work overtime in order to finish a project on time. Planning enforcement entails a lot of travelling to development sites and can involve confrontation with abusive and uncooperative people.

E arnings Potential

There is a pay scale for planning support staff and your entry point would depend on your age and qualifications. As a trainee you are likely to earn from £9,000 up to around £13,000. As a senior member of the planning support team you could earn £18,000 or more.

F urther Information

The Royal Town Planning Institute, London EC3R 8DL
Website: www.rtpi.org.uk

Alternative/equivalent entrance requirements can include: ILC, IB, EB, NC/ND and many other similar international systems. For further details see the Equivalent Qualifications section in the Introduction.

What is Involved?

As a trading standards officer, you would work within local government enforcing the law and regulations that govern goods and services which we buy, hire and sell. You would be championing the rights of the consumer by making sure that they were not being cheated, which could involve anything from checking the scales of a local trader to testing the claims made about a product by its manufacturer or importer.

You might take samples of pre-packed food to ensure that the correct weight is shown; you might check weighing machines, beer and spirit measures and labelling. Another important aspect would be identifying potential hazards or unsafe products.

Sometimes a case may involve action in the criminal court, requiring you to investigate possible criminal offences and attend as a witness or present cases in the Magistrates Court. Although you would have to write up reports in an office, you would also be out in the local community.

The exact nature of the work would vary according to your location. In a rural area, you might spend much time on animal health ensuring, for example, proper transport of livestock to market. As a city-based officer, you could be more concerned with street traders and problems of counterfeit goods. In a port, you might work with customs to vet imported goods.

Opportunities for Training

There are two ways of training to become a trading standards officer. If you obtain a three-year, full-time degree in consumer protection from an approved university, you can apply for a post as a trainee trading standards officer. It may be possible to seek support and sponsorship whilst studying.

When you have both the degree and a trainee post, you can progress to the Diploma in Trading Standards (DTS). The course is of 18 months duration and is the statutory qualification for trading standards officers. The second route is to apply to work as an enforcement officer or consumer adviser and study by correspondence course for the diploma in consumer affairs. You can then use the APEL (accreditation of prior learning and experience) scheme to progress to the DTS.

Requirements

Entry to an approved specialist degree would require two or three A level/AVCE/Advanced Higher, three Higher or equivalent qualifications, together with five GCSE/S Grade passes A-C/1-3. You could become an enforcement officer or consumer adviser with a degree in any other subject. Relevant experience would be an absolute requirement before you could take the DTS examinations.

Kind of Person

You would need to be firm but tactful, not easily intimidated. You would need a good memory for all the relevant legislation and the ability for assessing the key facts in each situation. It would be vital to have a very keenly observant eye for possible deviations from the law. You would need the confidence and integrity to stand up for your views and make some unpopular decisions. This could involve explaining your cases with precision and clarity in courts of law, so some public speaking experience could help. You would also need to be able to write clear reports.

B road Outlook

Trading standards officers are employed throughout the UK and there is a clear promotion structure, ie senior officer to section head, divisional officer and then to deputy or chief trading standards officer. Departments are usually small, however, so promotion often calls for mobility.

There are increasing controls and regulations and consumers are complaining more, so there is plenty of work available. Local authority budgets have, however, been reduced and finding a training place can be very difficult. You may choose to develop your career by moving into the private sector, where you might advise on quality control or consumer law in the food or retail sectors.

R elated Occupations

You might also consider: environmental health officer, police officer or health and safety officer.

I mpact

You would normally expect to work regular office hours but the process of deregulation means that shops and public houses now have longer opening hours and can trade seven days a week. You may have to follow up certain complaints or queries during these 'non-traditional' times.

E arnings Potential

The starting salary for a qualified trading standards officer would be about £21,000 to £25,000, although this varies depending on location (in London, for example, local authorities pay an extra allowance). You could progress to manager of a department at about £30,000 and eventually to a head of service on £50,000 to £70,000, depending on the size of the authority you worked for. In private practice, you could earn slightly more and receive various perks such as a company car.

F urther Information

Trading Standards Institute, Essex SS7 2BT
Website: www.tradingstandards.gov.uk

Local Government Careers, London EC1M 5LG
Website: www.lgcareers.com

Contact your local authority and ask to speak to the manager of the trading standards department.

Alternative/equivalent entrance requirements can include: ILC, IB, EB, NC/ND and many other similar international systems. For further details see the Equivalent Qualifications section in the Introduction.

What is Involved?

As a translator, you would be a highly skilled linguist specialising in the written word. You would normally translate into your mother tongue and would be required to produce authentic, idiomatic and accurate versions, which mirror the tone and levels of meaning of the originals. In literary areas, style and idiom would predominate, but most translation work is in commercial, legal, scientific or technical material, where accuracy and understanding are much more important. Your work may span a very broad spectrum, from medicine, tourism or engineering to law, politics or finance, and could include legal contracts, scientific articles, technical manuals, promotional brochures or business letters.

Opportunities for Training

You would normally be expected to study one or more foreign languages to degree level. It could be helpful if the course includes modules in translation or if you combine language studies with a subject such as business, law, computing or engineering. Almost all courses of this kind would give you the opportunity, which you should take, to spend at least a year abroad. You might then progress to a full- or part-time postgraduate diploma in translation. You may be expected to work towards the National/Scottish Vocational Qualifications (N/SVQ) level five in translating and you would usually need to join and pass the examinations of professional organisations such as the Institute of Linguists (IOL) and/or the Institute of Translation and Interpreting (ITI).

Requirements

For entry to a degree course, you would usually need two or three A levels/ Advanced Highers, three or four Highers or equivalent, including a good pass in at least one foreign language. You would need a good first degree for progression to a postgraduate course. The N/SVQ route does not require any formal academic qualifications and could prove attractive if you have advanced linguistic skills, cultural awareness or technical knowledge but do not want to go to university. You may, for example, have come to translating through a bilingual upbringing, residence abroad or regular contact with speakers of your second language. You would have to provide evidence of your ability by maintaining a detailed record of texts translated and building a portfolio of your best work.

Kind of Person

You must be able to write impeccably in your mother tongue, preferably in a variety of styles. An enquiring mind would be essential, with a particular interest in researching and understanding commercial or technical issues. In addition to your mastery of at least one foreign language, you must have a thorough knowledge of the institutions, culture, attitudes and practices in the countries where that language is spoken, normally acquired through residence there. You would need to be capable of working alone in front of a computer screen, armed with specialist dictionaries and reference books, working at speed to find the right words and phrases. Editing and IT skills would come together in the growing use of computerised translating programs, which produce fast but rough drafts for revision to an acceptable final standard.

B road Outlook

While some international organisations, government departments, multinational companies and aid agencies employ their own translating teams, around 80% of translators work on a full- or part-time basis for a specialist language company or translation bureau. French, German and Japanese are the most sought-after languages. It is possible, but far from easy, to start up as a freelance translator. The competition is intense and you would need to be very skilled, professional and businesslike to succeed. A lot of work is passed on by the recommendation of colleagues.

R elated Occupations

You might also consider: teacher, foreign correspondent, secretary linguist, interpreter, tourist operator or diplomat.

I mpact

You can choose your own hours if you are working from home, sending and receiving material by email. However, the work can be unpredictable and you may need to supplement your income with other activities, especially teaching. As a staff translator, you would be more likely to work normal office hours from Monday to Friday, with occasional overtime if a translation is needed urgently.

E arnings Potential

How much you earn could depend on your language combinations, your subject areas and your speed and reputation. You would normally quote a freelance rate based on every 1,000 words translated, ranging from around £70 per 1,000 words for French or German to double that for Chinese. Salaries for full-time employment range considerably, from around £17,000 for a young graduate to £50,000 or more for an experienced specialist.

F urther Information

Institute of Translation and Interpreting (ITI), London EC1V 1ND
Website: www.iti.org.uk

Languages National Training Organisation (LNTO), London WC2N 4LB
Website: www.languagesnto.org.uk

Institute of Linguists (IOL), London SE1 1UN Website: www.iol.org.uk

European Commission Recruitment Unit, B-1000 Brussels, Belgium
Website: www.europa.eu.int/en/

Alternative/equivalent entrance requirements can include: ILC, IB, EB, NC/ND and many other similar international systems. For further details see the Equivalent Qualifications section in the Introduction.

What is Involved?

As a travel agent, you would sell holidays on behalf of tour operators, together with air, ferry, train and coach tickets, hotel reservations, car hire services, tours and expeditions, theatre seats and insurance. You might work with the general travelling public or specialise in services for business customers and you would sometimes be asked to arrange complete itineraries.

Some travel agencies are independently owned and others are part of chains like Thomas Cook, Going Places or Thomsons, who market their own tours and package holidays as well as those of other tour operators. Most of the 7,300 travel agencies in the UK have high street, shop-front premises, where you would inform and negotiate with clients and check availability on computer systems before completing a sale.

Opportunities for Training

Most of the young people entering the travel industry each year join as participants in the Travel Training Programme operated by TTC Training, a subsidiary of the Association of British Travel Agents (ABTA). This is a two-year government-funded Modern Apprenticeship programme (Skillseekers in Scotland) giving you the chance to earn while you learn and take the first steps towards a career as a travel agent.

You would work towards National or Scottish Vocational Qualifications (N/SVQ) in Travel Services. TTC Training could also advise you on how to obtain the ABTA Travel Agents Certificate (ABTAC), the standard examination-based qualification for travel agents, accepted by large organisations and many independents as demonstration of the competence levels they expect from their frontline staff. Alternatively, you might consider a degree or higher national diploma (HND) in travel and tourism or a related subject.

Requirements

Experience is generally regarded as far more important than academic success. There are no specific entry requirements for the ABTAC or N/SVQ routes, although individual employers might look for GCSE/S Grade passes A-C/1-3, including English, maths, geography and modern languages. You would need at least two A level/AVCE/Advanced Higher, three Higher or equivalent qualifications for degree course entry, slightly less for the HND. For entry to the Travel Training Programme, you would need to be 16 to 24 years old. (Relevant AVCE/vocational Higher or equivalent: travel and tourism.)

Kind of Person

To be a successful travel agent, you would need to be a good communicator and come across as friendly and helpful. You would be selling holidays and travel-related products and would therefore need to be enthusiastic and a good salesperson. A retentive memory and a thorough knowledge of hotels, resorts and travel possibilities would be very helpful in building trust and retaining your clients, together with a good working knowledge of geography for discussing possible destinations.

You would have to be very efficient and organised, as you would often be dealing with more than one client at a time and it would be essential not to make mistakes with reservations and tickets. You would be dealing with prices and overall costs of holidays, so you would need to be numerate. You should also have good IT skills, as computers are always used for making bookings and finding up-to-date information. You should have a smart appearance and you should have the ability both to listen carefully and to make suitable travel suggestions.

B road Outlook

Travel and tourism is a thriving, multi-billion pound industry. As long as people need to travel around the world, and continue to enjoy taking holidays and visiting different places, growth looks set to continue. According to TTC Training, you could be managing your own travel shop by the time you are 25, although you would have to prove your worth in a very competitive market.

Travel agencies differ greatly in size and there maybe more scope for promotion to more senior positions in larger companies and chain stores. A growing number of travellers are using the Internet to make their own travel arrangements but many people continue to use travel agencies for their specialist knowledge and advice.

R elated Occupations

You might also consider: tour operator, leisure/recreation services manager, tourist guide, travel courier, resort representative or tourist information centre manager.

I mpact

You would normally work shop hours from Monday to Saturday, although you may have to work some evenings and Sundays as well in a busy shopping centre. You may find that you are required to go to resorts abroad for research purposes but this would usually be seen as an occasional perk of the job.

E arnings Potential

As a trainee on the Travel Training Programme, you would probably start on a modest training allowance, which should rise when you are qualified to around £15,000. You should also receive a discount on your own holidays and travel.

F urther Information

TTC Training, Woking GU21 5AR Website: www.ttctraining.co.uk/

The Travel, Tourism and Events National Training Organisation, Surrey KT14 6DY Website: www.ttento.com

The Institute of Travel and Tourism, St. Albans AL1 3TJ Website: www.itt.co.uk

Alternative/equivalent entrance requirements can include: ILC, IB, EB, NC/ND and many other similar international systems. For further details see the Equivalent Qualifications section in the Introduction.

TV/Film Camera Operator

CLCI: GAL

What is Involved?

As a camera operator in the TV/film industry, you would use different types of camera to record action on film, videotape or digital media. You might work on large- or small-scale productions in a studio; you might be part of an outside broadcast team covering sports fixtures or public ceremonies; or you might use special lightweight equipment in a small newsgathering team.

You would mostly be expected to follow instructions from a director, although you would usually be invited to contribute ideas for camera positions and shots during rehearsals. Depending on the budget and resources of the project on which you are working, you may be part of a team or you may have to operate sound and other equipment in addition to your main work with the camera.

Opportunities for Training

Getting started in this industry is far from straightforward. Experience is what counts but TV companies like the BBC no longer run in-house training schemes. Film and TV Freelance Training (ft2) provide apprentice-style technical courses for freelance entrants but you have to be over 18, based in London and unemployed to meet their entry criteria. What's more, competition for the few places they offer is fierce.

There may be limited training opportunities with Scottish Screen and CYFLE in Scotland and Wales respectively (some for Welsh speakers only). Beyond that are various college courses up to degree and postgraduate level but none of these formal qualifications is a guarantee of work. It is important to get practical experience in any way you can, even if it means initially working for nothing.

Requirements

While it is not essential, you would be able to build your experience by taking a degree in photography or film studies following successful completion of a foundation year in art and design with some specialisation in camera work. You should have a portfolio of photographs or film and you should be able to demonstrate a keen interest in film and television. It would help if you had A level/AVCE/Advanced Higher, Higher or equivalent qualifications and enough understanding of maths and physics to appreciate the technical aspects of film-making and broadcasting. You would need to be physically fit to be able to move equipment that is often heavy.

Kind of Person

In order to succeed in this kind of work you would need to be passionately interested in film photography and prepared to put up with short-term contracts, uncertainty of employment, lots of pressure and long working hours. You must be a team player, with a good eye for colour and composition. The work can be creative but also requires a high standard of technical awareness. Good eyesight and normal colour vision are essential, together with good hand/eye co-ordination. Some camera positions call for a head for heights!

332

B road Outlook

You would almost certainly work on a freelance basis, building up a network of personal contacts and establishing a reputation for certain types of work. Small independent production companies spring up on a regular basis, in addition to the established film and television organisations, usually offering new work opportunities but most often on short-term contracts.

R elated Occupations

You might wish to consider: photographer, production assistant, photojournalist or – with sufficient experience – film director.

I mpact

Initially, you can expect long hours, low wages and endless pressure. The early jobs are not likely to be very glamorous although later on they may well be. In the world of film and television, the hours always tend to be irregular, starting early, finishing late and often involving waiting around for hours on standby. If you work as a news camera operator, you may find yourself abroad, sometimes in potentially dangerous situations.

E arnings Potential

You could find yourself sometimes working for next to nothing, gaining experience and hoping that you will receive a retrospective payout if the film turns out to be a commercial success. At other times, you might be on a daily or weekly rate depending on the project. With training and experience, you could expect to earn about £30,000 a year.

F urther Information

Skillset – Sector Skills Council for the Audio Visual Industries, London W1D 3TH Website: www.skillset.org

FT2 – Film and TV Freelance Training, London W1R 5RA
Website: www.ft2.org.uk/recruit

CYFLE, Gwynedd LL55 1NS Website: www.cyfle-cyf.demon.co.uk

Scottish Screen, Glasgow G2 4QE Website: www.scottishscreen.com

Alternative/equivalent entrance requirements can include: ILC, IB, EB, NC/ND and many other similar international systems. For further details see the Equivalent Qualifications section in the Introduction.

What is Involved?

As a veterinary nurse, you would be involved in caring for animals before, during and after treatment by a veterinary surgeon. You could be required to carry out treatments such as administering drugs, taking x-rays and preparing animals for surgery. You may also offer advice to owners, for example on post-operative care.

You would be working mainly with domestic pets but could be required to cope with horses, farm animals or even zoo animals.

Your job would also include clerical and administrative work in a veterinary practice, such as keeping records, filing reports, answering the telephone and dealing with reception.

Opportunities for Training

You must have a qualification recognised by the Royal College for Veterinary Surgeons and, for most people, the Veterinary Nurse Scheme (VNS) is the established training route. It takes at least two years to complete and you must be currently working in a registered veterinary practice. During the programme, you would build up a portfolio recording your work and you would have to pass two sets of examinations. The course covers areas such as basic anatomy and physiology, animal welfare and first aid, diagnostic and surgical skills, anaesthesia, x-ray techniques and laboratory procedures. You would also learn about the care of animals, dietary requirements, pain assessment and handling techniques.

There is also a four-year degree in veterinary nursing, run by Middlesex University and the Royal Veterinary College in London. It covers the same topics as the VNS, together with elements of business and management, computing and communication skills and research methods. This route could particularly useful if you want to work as a practice manager or perhaps move into animal-related sales, marketing or product development.

Requirements

You must be at least 17 before you can start training for the VNS and you would need a minimum of five GCSE/S Grade passes A-C/1-3, including English and two of the following: a biological science, a physical science or maths. There is a pre-VNS course, available at college or by distance learning, if you do not have the required qualifications.

For the degree course in veterinary nursing, you would need the same GCSE/S Grades plus at least two A level/AVCE/Advanced Higher, four Higher or equivalent qualifications, including biology and preferably another science subject.

Kind of Person

You would need a genuine concern for animals and a wish to care for them. At the same time, you would need to take an unsentimental approach as, inevitably, you would be involved with putting animals down or with unsuccessful surgical procedures. The work is likely to be messy and unpleasant at times as it frequently involves clearing up after animals. In addition to handling a variety of animals, you would need to be able to communicate clearly and sympathetically with their owners. You would have to work as part of the team within the practice and you would need some office skills for keeping records and booking appointments.

B road Outlook

Most veterinary nurses work for vets in a private practice but there are opportunities to work for animal welfare organisations or in zoos. There are also jobs within veterinary hospitals, universities, breeding establishments, laboratories and research centres.

Some veterinary nurses work in pharmaceutical companies or for feed companies. In large veterinary practices, there may be chances for promotion to practice manager. You could develop your career by taking an advanced course, specialising perhaps in dermatology, medical or surgical nursing, which would enhance your promotion prospects.

R elated Occupations

You may be interested in other occupations working with animals, such as RSPCA inspector, zookeeper, dog trainer or groom.

I mpact

You may be involved in working long and unsocial hours, including evenings and weekends, perhaps on a shift basis. The work can be physically demanding and emotionally draining, not to mention smelly and unpleasant at times. You would wear a uniform and would add protective clothing when necessary. There may be opportunities for part-time work.

E arnings Potential

There are no set salary scales for veterinary nurses. However, pay can start at about £8,000 while you are training, rising to £14,000 and above when you are qualified. Some veterinary nurses are offered a share in the profits of the practice to compensate for a lower salary.

F urther Information

The British Veterinary Nursing Association, Harlow CM20 1XA
Website: www.bvna.org.uk

The Royal College of Veterinary Surgeons, London SW1P 2AF
Website: www.rcvs.org.uk

Alternative/equivalent entrance requirements can include: ILC, IB, EB, NC/ND and many other similar international systems. For further details see the Equivalent Qualifications section in the Introduction.

What is Involved?

As a veterinary surgeon, you would be concerned with the health and welfare of animals, including household pets, zoo animals, farm animals and horses. This may involve diagnosing and treating them when they are unwell or injured or advising on their living conditions and on steps that can be taken to ensure they stay in good health.

Vets also offer advice on such topics as breeding stock, any government or EU regulations regarding animals and vaccination programmes. Some vets are concerned with research and others work for government agencies ensuring that standards are maintained, particularly in animals destined to join the food chain.

Opportunities for Training

You would have to be registered with the Royal College of Veterinary Surgeons before you could practise veterinary surgery in the UK. This means that you must complete an approved degree in Veterinary Science. The degree usually takes five years, with some students opting to take an additional science subject for a year. At Cambridge it is a six-year course for everyone. The degree courses combine theory and practical work.

Requirements

There are only six universities in the UK offering a degree in Veterinary Science and you are restricted to a maximum of four applications. Competition for places is very intense and the grades required are high. Generally, universities are looking for 3 A levels or equivalent at grades AAB or above (340-360 points). All veterinary schools require chemistry at A level/Advanced Higher/Higher, some specify biology as well, while others want one or two subjects from maths, biology or physics as well as chemistry. Some universities will accept a third A level/Advanced Higher/Higher in a non-science subject if it is considered to be an academic subject. You also need English GCSE/S Grade A-C/1-3. Scottish applicants without Advanced Highers would need Highers of AAABB or equivalent, including chemistry at grade A. It is important to check with individual veterinary schools to be sure of their requirements.

All university veterinary schools insist that you show evidence of your interest and commitment by having gained experience of working in a veterinary practice and working with and handling animals including livestock. However, practical experience is not a substitute for academic qualifications.

Kind of Person

You would need a lot of determination to get onto the course in the first place: only about a third of applicants are successful. You then have to be dedicated and prepared to work hard throughout your training and when you start your career. As well as having top academic credentials and a good scientific understanding, you must have a real interest in animals. You also need to be unsentimental about them and prepared to face some hard decisions. Dealing with the owners is also very important: you must appear confident, in control and able to explain clearly both the problems and the treatments. You would need to be compassionate when dealing with a sick but much-loved family pet; at other times, when you find evidence of neglect for example, you would need to be firm and insist on correct standards of care. Handling large animals requires a reasonable level of physical fitness.

Most vets need to spend at least some time travelling to see their clients so you should be able to drive. You would be likely to work as part of a team whilst at the same time having to take decisions for yourself. You may also need to have good business skills to handle the business side of the practice.

B road Outlook

There is currently a decline in the need for large animal vets because of the problems with farming; however, there is an increased demand for horse vets and small animal vets who look after people's pets. Buying a share in an established practice can be an expensive commitment for a young vet.

R elated Occupations

In the medical field, you might consider training as a doctor, homoeopath, radiographer or physiotherapist.

I mpact

Every veterinary surgeon has an obligation to deal with emergencies in any species at any time. It is a 24-hour service, 365 days a year. Being a vet is not a job where it is possible to work regular hours as animals require attention at all times of the day and night. Conditions of work can be unpleasant, smelly, dirty and very physically demanding and can involve a great deal of travelling.

E arnings Potential

Once qualified, most vets start working in a general practice as a veterinary assistant. You could expect to earn about £15,000 at this stage and you might receive other benefits – accommodation, a car and fuel for example – worth up to another £10,000. Should you become a partner, your earnings would depend on the size and location of the practice but could be substantial. Vets working for the government earn from £25,000 upwards.

F urther Information

The Royal College of Veterinary Surgeons, London, SW1P 2AF
Website: www.rcvs.org.uk

Alternative/equivalent entrance requirements can include: ILC, IB, EB, NC/ND and many other similar international systems. For further details see the Equivalent Qualifications section in the Introduction.

What is Involved?

Your main tasks as a webmaster would be to set up, run and maintain websites for companies, organisations or individuals. The websites might be used for such purposes as publicity, marketing or buying and selling on the internet and you would need to start by discussing in some detail the precise needs of your client. At this stage, you would advise on what could be included on the website, including graphics, text and sound, together with the possibility of links to other sites. If the company or organisation has its own intranet (an internal version of the internet), you would discuss how this could best be linked to the web. You would be expected to advise on the cost of the project, and either design and program the website pages yourself or supervise others to do this. Once the design is agreed and the site is up and running, you would make sure that it is kept up to date and any problems are dealt with. You might work on a freelance basis as an independent consultant or you might be employed full-time by a large company or organisation.

Opportunities for Training

There is no single route to becoming a webmaster. Experience and talent can be as important as qualifications in this relatively new field; if you have experimented with web design as a hobby this could prove of benefit. There are, however, many relevant courses available at different levels of entry and you should look very closely to find out which would be the best one for you to follow. Training ranges from short courses offered by local colleges or commercial companies in web design, development and authorship to higher national diploma (HND) and degree courses with titles such as Interactive Multimedia Design or Media Technology. Once in employment, you could work towards a professional qualification awarded by an organisation such as the British Computer Society or the National Computing Centre. You could also find employment with training via a Modern Apprenticeship (Skillseeker in Scotland).

Requirements

While there is no educational requirement laid down for entry into the profession, and plenty of young people virtually teach themselves to design websites, many employers look favourably at the possession of certificates from some of the courses mentioned above. Some webmasters pursue courses based on art and design, while others choose more IT-oriented courses. Short courses usually need a minimum of GCSE/S Grade qualifications for entry, while A level/AVCE/Advanced Higher, Higher or equivalent passes are needed for HND and degree courses. A good portfolio of current artwork is a necessity for most art-based courses.

Kind of Person

You would clearly need to enjoy working with computers and to be skilled at programming. You must be prepared to update your skills and knowledge on a regular basis in order to keep pace with rapid technological change. A talent for design would also be very important, since websites need to have instant

338

appeal, in keeping with the image that your clients wish to project. Good communication skills would be necessary, both spoken and written, as you untangle your clients' needs and explain your proposed solutions. You should develop a good understanding of business and budgeting, and you must be able to deliver your work within tight deadlines.

B road Outlook

There is little job security in the IT sector. Some individuals rapidly amass fabulous fortunes while others are associated with equally spectacular failure. With the current expansion of the Internet, however, there is generally good demand for webmasters, and plenty of opportunities are on offer with a wide variety of clients. You might be employed full-time by an agency or consultancy, dealing with briefs from clients, or by a large company or organisation as a full-time webmaster or combining that responsibility with other tasks in the IT department. Once experienced, you might work on a freelance basis or set up your own consultancy.

R elated Occupations

You might also like to consider: computer games designer, database administrator, graphic designer or systems analyst.

I mpact

If you were employed full-time by a company or organisation you would probably work a normal five-day week, although there might be occasions when you would have to meet deadlines or deal with problems and, therefore, put in extra hours in the evening or over a weekend. As a freelance worker, you would almost certainly find yourself in this position from time to time.

E arnings Potential

Earnings can vary a great deal, depending on the terms of employment. A webmaster in full-time employment within a company might earn around £20,000 a year on starting, rising to more than £40,000. As a self-employed freelance webmaster, your earnings would depend on the number and size of your commissions.

F urther Information

British Computer Society, Swindon SN1 1HJ Website: www.bcs.org.uk

British Interactive Multimedia Association, Essex CM11 2PR
Website: www.bima.co.uk

e-skills UK Ltd, London SW1E 6DR Website: www.e-skills.com

The National Computing Centre, Manchester M1 7ED
Website: www.ncc.co.uk

Alternative/equivalent entrance requirements can include: ILC, IB, EB, NC/ND and many other similar international systems. For further details see the Equivalent Qualifications section in the Introduction.

What is Involved?

As a youth worker, you would work with young people aged between 11 and 25, particularly those aged between 13 and 19, to promote their personal and social development and enable them to have a voice, influence and place in their communities and society as a whole. Youth work is carried out in different situations and locations, using a range of approaches. You might, for example, operate from a youth club or centre, offering some activities for all young people in the area and some targeted at specific groups. You might be a detached or outreach youth worker, making contact with young people who do not use youth centres. You could work in a school or college, contributing in particular to PSHE (personal, social and health education), citizenship and study support programmes. You might be involved with young people who have been excluded from school, who persistently misuse drugs or alcohol, or who have been involved in crime.

You would often work with other services – such as social services, housing, leisure, and health – to develop and improve provision for young people. This kind of partnership work is becoming more common with the current introduction in England of the Connexions Service. Youth work is seen as being at the heart of Connexions, with youth workers having a particularly important role in reaching and supporting young people at risk. Support services for young people are also being strengthened in Scotland, Wales and Northern Ireland but are not following the Connexions model.

Opportunities for Training

There are many different ways of training to become a professionally qualified youth worker, normally building on part-time or voluntary experience. Qualifications vary considerably from one United Kingdom country to another and you should research local requirements carefully. The National Youth Agency is responsible for validating awards in England and Ireland but separate arrangements apply for Scotland and Wales. Since youth workers operate in a wide range of settings, courses at different institutions reflect different occupational needs and have a range of titles. There is a marked trend towards part-time, employment-based training, usually associated with a degree, diploma of higher education or postgraduate course.

Requirements

A degree course would normally require at least two A level/AVCE/Advanced Higher, three Higher or equivalent qualifications in any subject, together with five GCSE/S Grade passes at A-C/1-3. If you are a mature candidate with relevant experience, you may be admitted without meeting these academic requirements. For postgraduate study, any first degree subject could be acceptable.

Kind of Person

You would need to build relationships with young people based on trust and respect, offering them new experiences and challenges and encouraging them to think critically about their lives and values. You would encourage young people to take on greater responsibility for themselves and others and to work effectively as a team, judging when to stand back and when to intervene. This may mean letting them make mistakes but ensuring that they learn from them. You would use a range of interpersonal skills such as counselling, advocacy and group work. You could not be expected to be an expert on everything affecting young people but you should be aware of other local agencies and what they offer, and to recognise when you need to involve people with specialist skills and knowledge, while continuing to support the young person concerned.

B road Outlook

Youth work skills are in great demand and opportunities for qualified people are expanding. In addition to employment within local authority youth services, there are an increasing number of opportunities for employment in other settings. These include other local authority departments such as leisure, arts and housing, health authorities, youth justice teams, and a range of voluntary organisations. The introduction of the Connexions Service in England is leading to more posts for people with youth work skills

R elated Occupations

You might consider: social worker, probation officer, teacher, careers/personal adviser or education welfare officer.

I mpact

As a full-time worker, you would be contracted to work a set number of hours, usually 35 to 37 a week. Your contract would almost certainly specify evening and weekend sessions.

E arnings Potential

If you are in local authority employment, you would be paid on a three-level salary scale, with level one generally used as the starting grade and level three reserved for posts with substantial management, development or training responsibilities. Your starting point would be on a scale ranging from around £14,000 to £26,000.

F urther Information

National Youth Agency, Leicester LE1 6GD Website: www.nya.org.uk

Communities Scotland, Edinburgh EH12 5HE
Website: www.communitiesscotland.gov.uk

Wales Youth Agency, Caerphilly CF83 1BQ Website: www.wya.org.uk

Youth Council for Northern Ireland, Belfast BT8 4TA
Website: www.youthcouncil-ni.org.uk/

Connexions Website: www.connexions.gov.uk

Alternative/equivalent entrance requirements can include: ILC, IB, EB, NC/ND and many other similar international systems. For further details see the Equivalent Qualifications section in the Introduction.

Lack of space prevents us from giving a complete WORKBRIEF analysis of every possible career idea but we list below a selection of further occupational titles. Our top priority is to include here a majority of careers mentioned under 'Related Occupations' in the main section but not described in their own detailed chapters. In almost every case, we provide a careers library (CLCI) reference, a brief description of the work and at least one relevant website address.

Aircraft Maintenance Engineer – RAC/YAB

Aircraft maintenance engineers are technicians who inspect, maintain and repair civil and military aircraft. They may be mechanical engineers, specialising in airframes and engines, or avionics engineers concerned with electronic and electrical systems. Normal colour vision is essential.

Websites: www.lae.mcmail.com www.aerosociety.com www.srgcaa.co.uk www.rafcareers.com

Antiques Dealer

Antiques dealers buy and sell antique furniture or other artefacts, such as ceramics, clocks or ancient firearms. Numerous other specialisms exist, each one calling for individuals with detailed knowledge and experience. Central to the work are auctions and fairs, where dealers may sell or buy in stock, observe levels of buyer interest and develop their expertise. They often sell or buy for collectors and export to other countries. This is a relatively small field of employment and jobs are difficult to obtain, unless you have suitable connections with a firm of dealers.

Website: www.bada.org

Archaeological Illustrator/Surveyor – UM/FAH

Archaeological illustrators and surveyors are concerned with the specialised surveying of archaeological sites and with recording the layouts of structures and artefacts unearthed during excavations.

Website: www.aais.org.uk

Archivist – FAG

Archivists save and look after the records of the past. These may include official documents, newspaper cuttings, rare books, photographs, films, videos and tape recordings, and may be publicly or privately owned, in national or local collections. Archivists carry out research, indexing and cataloguing, and give help to scholars, research scientists and others seeking specialist information.

Website: www.archives.org.uk

Aromatherapist – JOD

Aromatherapists work in the field of alternative or complementary medicine, carrying out massage on patients' bodies with a range of aromatic oils, either to promote a sense of well-being or to treat specific medical conditions.

Website: www.int-fed-aromatherapy.co.uk

Art Restorer/Conservator – EZ

Art restoration involves the cleaning, repair and renovation of damaged works of art. It requires a scientific knowledge of materials used in the past, the processes of their deterioration and of modern materials which must be compatible with the originals. Antiques conservation calls for similar skills.

Websites: www.abpr.co.uk www.chnto.co.uk

Art Therapist – JOD

Art therapists work with individuals and groups experiencing a range of medical and emotional conditions, using artistic activities as an opportunity for expression and communication. You would need to achieve a diploma in art therapy, usually after completing a degree level course in art. You might work with paints of all kinds, canvasses, papers, pastels, clay, fabrics, collages, carving, sculpture or weaving materials, to allow clients to express and share their innermost thoughts and feelings.

Website: www.baat.org

Biomedical Scientist – JAX

Biomedical scientists (sometimes known as Medical Laboratory Scientific Officers) carry out tests on body fluids and tissues to support doctors in diagnosing disease and monitoring progress after treatment. You might specialise in an area such as haematology or histopathology or work in a multidisciplinary environment.

Website: www.ibms.org

Cell Biologist – QOD

This new science field breaks down the boundaries between cell biology, biochemistry, genetics and microbiology, focusing on the DNA making up genes. Cell biologists study cell structure and function, cell metabolism, molecular organisation, biochemical regulatory mechanisms, immunology, genetics, evolutionary patterns and mechanisms of reproduction.

Website: www.icmb.ed.ac.uk

Chef – IC

A person trained to cook food, usually in the kitchens of a restaurant, and to produce food to a high standard. Chefs may specialise in certain branches of cooking, such as French, Indian or Thai, or simply produce a wide range of menus of all kinds.

Website: www.hcima.org.uk

Civil Aviation – YAB

Civil aviation is a broad term, covering a range of career opportunities associated with air transport. These could include flying as a pilot or cabin crew, working in engineering maintenance and repair of aircraft or providing services for passengers within airports.

Website: www.caa.co.uk

Communications Engineering – RAL

Working in this field would usually require a basis of electronics engineering – but concentrating on communications by means of fibre optics, audio, broadcasting, television, radio, video, satellite and telephone systems. These are areas of high demand at present.

Website www.tia.org.uk

Computer Games Designer – CAV

The computer games industry is now of very great economic global importance, with a need for highly gifted and skilled computer programmers able to use multimedia and animation techniques and to create challenges for young people, in ever more imaginative and sophisticated ways.

Website: www.bcs.org.uk

Computer Engineer/Scientist – CAV

Computer engineers/scientists are involved in the design, development and manufacture of new computer hardware and its integration with suitable software. They work closely with electronic engineers and information technologists. Opportunities in the UK have been overshadowed by overseas competition in recent years – however, this field remains one of vital importance to the UK for the long-term future.

Website: www.bcs.org.uk www.iee.org.uk www.enginuity.org.uk

Computer-Aided Design – ROD

Working in the field of computer-aided design, you would use specialised computer software packages to produce 2-D or 3-D designs, 3-D computer models of proposed building structures or engineering products, engineering and architectural drawings, often with virtual reality features to allow people to explore a design on a 'walk through basis' before its final construction.

Website: www.bcs.org.uk

Conservationist (Nature) – WAR

Nature conservationists are concerned with the protection of plants and animals in the wild and with the wider impacts of herbicides, pesticides and pollutants on the environment as a whole. Some one hundred National Nature Reserves and thousands of sites of scientific interest require management by wardens and their assistants. Scientists – usually biologists, botanists, zoologists, and geographers – are employed as Assistant Regional Officers in researching and monitoring environmental issues.

Website: www.britishecologicalsociety.org

Conservator – FAE

Conservators are concerned with the conservation and restoration of historic objects such as ancient books, documents, oil paintings, water colours and paper decorations (eg Chinese wallpapers and silks), and work within museums, art galleries, ancient houses, properties of the

National Trust and the various national Heritage organisations, as well as in the private sector.

Website: www.ukic.org.uk

Cybernetics – QOZ
Cybernetics is the study and application of computerised feedback control systems, for example, in industrial production units or on aircraft. Thus, if the temperature of a chemical process rises above a set limit, a message to reduce the input of heat to the system is triggered. Heating is increased again if the temperature falls. Such processes are similar to those which occur in the human body.

Website: www.cybsoc.org

Dancer – GAF
Dancers communicate ideas visually, physically and musically in ballet, contemporary dance and in entertainment generally, working in films, television, pantomime, cabaret and sometimes in education.

Website: www.cdet.org.uk

Database Administrator – CAV
Database administrators manage and supervise the creation and installation of computer databases. Their services are required by central and local government, universities, schools, research establishments, libraries, accounting practices, industrial, banking and other commercial or financial groups.

Website: www.bcs.org.uk

Dental Hygienist – JAF
Dental hygienists work closely with dentists to clean and polish the teeth of patients – and thus help prevent dental decay. They try to educate people to take care of their gums and teeth, and often visit schools to check on the dental health of pupils.

Website: www.bdha.org.uk

Dental Nurse – JAF
A dental nurse is trained to assist a dentist in a dental surgery, ensuring that the dentist has the materials and instruments needed in treating patients at exactly the right moment. The nurse is responsible for the hygiene of the surgery and equipment.

Website: www.badn.org.uk

Education Welfare Officer – KEB
Education welfare officers or education social workers are employed by local authorities to investigate the problems of children whose education is being threatened by a wide range of social, behavioural, financial, transport, diet or health factors. They visit schools and identify the causes of problems, talk to the children and their families and devise solutions to overcome them.

Website: www.lgcareers.com

345

Energy Engineer – RAN

Energy engineers are concerned with the uses and economic combustion of fuels, with atomic energy and developments in the use of water, wind, tide and sun as sources of energy. They study the relative costs of producing energy in industry, comparing the economic advantages of using fuels such as coal, oil, natural gas, nuclear- or wind- generated electric power. They also look at methods to conserve energy and reduce heat loss from buildings.

Website: www.instenergy.org.uk

Estate Manager – UM

As an estate manager you would be qualified to manage estates, farms, amenity horticulture sites and forestry operations. You may at times be responsible for developing leisure and recreational facilities, such as fishing, shooting, golf and hill walking, and even to establish and market holiday accommodation for tourists. Estate managers usually have qualifications in farming/agriculture or in surveying. They need a sound understanding of costing, accounts and management. They were originally known as Factors in Scotland – but are nowadays usually described as rural practice surveyors. Land agents cover much of the same ground but often specialise in the valuation and sale of agricultural land, farm buildings and agricultural machinery.

Website: www.rics.org

Exhibition Designer – ET

Exhibition designers specialise in creating attractive display stands for major exhibitions. You would need to be able to work in a variety of styles, using a wide range of materials and specialist lighting effects.

Website: www.yourcreativefuture.org

Farm Secretary – CAT/WAB

A farm secretary works in an agricultural environment, helping employers to complete forms, keep accounts, monitor crop and milk production and calculate employees' wages. A farm secretary may work for one employer, be freelance or be sent out by an agency to a number of farms.

Website: www.iagsa.co.uk

Fashion Buyer – OP – see Buying Executive

Fashion buyers specialise in buying attractive garments for sale within fashion and dress shops or large retail store groups. They attend exhibitions where fashion houses show their latest collections to UK, European and International buyers. There is no guaranteed entry or single training route to this sort of work.

Website: www.cips.org

Fashion Journalist – FAC – see Journalist

Fashion is a subject which creates considerable interest from a clothes conscious market – and this calls for specialist journalists who are fully in touch with trends in fashion design. They need the ability to make value judgements in this very creative field and to write with professional authority, flair and insight. A degree in fashion design could provide a strong foundation but there is no guaranteed route into this relatively small career field.

Website: www.nctj.com

Film Director – GAL
Directors supervise and guide the actors and actresses taking part in plays, films and radio productions. They interpret the author's intentions and the stage, studio or outside effects and background scenes required.

Website: www.bfi.org.uk

Film Set Designer – ET – see Television/Theatre Set Designer
Website: www.bfi.org.uk

Fine Art Dealer
Art dealers display original paintings, sculptures and other works of art in their galleries for purchase by the public or by members of the art trade. They usually specialise in a particular type, field or period of painting, sculpture or ceramics. They attend art auctions or buy direct from the public and need to become expert in such areas as valuation, restoration and authentication.

Website: www.slad.org.uk

Fish Farmer – WAG
Fish farming is concerned with the healthy cultivation and harvesting of fish under scientifically controlled conditions, usually in specially constructed tanks. Fish such as salmon, trout, plaice and sole produced in this way are now available in shops and restaurants throughout the UK and mainland Europe. Much of the work is concerned with preventing disease, controlling temperature and oxygen levels and keeping water free from pollution.

Website: www.ifm.org.uk

Floor Manager (TV) – GAL
Floor managers perform similar functions to stage managers but work within television or film studios and co-ordinate camera crews. They make sure that the director's instructions are passed on, give cues to make sure things happen on time and ensure that actors are available and in position.

Website: www.skillset.org

Foreign Correspondent – FAC/GAL – see Journalist
Foreign correspondents are journalists who seek out news for television, radio, newspapers, magazines and news agencies. They may be based in one country or travel around the world whenever a major news event occurs. They would normally need considerable experience and proven track records within their home country before being selected for this type of work.

Website: www.nctj.com & www.bjtc.org.uk

Geneticist – QOD

A genetic scientist studies the ways in which animals and plants transmit their characteristics from generation to generation by means of their genes. Scientists also study how to carry out genetic modification of plants to improve their resistance to disease and to increase the yields of fruit or vegetables.

Website: www.genetics.org.uk & www.bshg.org.uk

Health Visitor – JAD

The health visitor is a trained nurse who visits people in their own homes, often when they have been ill or are recovering from an operation and need supportive medical help.

Website: www.msfcphva.org

Herbalist – JOD

As a medical herbalist you would be trained in the diagnosis of human diseases and their cure using a very wide range of plant extracts, often known from antiquity to have medicinal effects. You would undertake a training course leading to a degree in herbal medicine – also called phytotherapy – at one of a small number of universities. There is also a one-year course for qualified doctors at the School of Herbal Medicine.

Website: www.amfoundation.org/herbinfo.htm

Historical Researcher – FAG

Historical researchers are concerned with exploring historical records, books and relevant documents in establishing facts and in confirming or challenging existing historical theories, and are usually university based.

Website: www.history.ac.uk

Hospitality Manager – IB/IC

Hospitality management involves the management of hotels, restaurants and diverse leisure facilities, for example, receptions for company clients, wedding receptions, annual dinners, conventions, conferences, banqueting and holidays.

Website: www.htf.org.uk

Housing Manager – UH

Housing managers work for local authorities and housing associations to provide a service to tenants of rented properties, assessing their needs, allocating property and arranging transfers. They may also collect rents, inspect for damage and arrange repairs and redecoration.

Website: www.cih.org

Information Technology Specialist – CAV

Information technologists specialise in the use, modification and control of existing standard software to achieve the needs of organisations and to provide essential management information. IT systems are used in banks, stock exchanges, insurance companies, the Civil Service, Armed

Services, air traffic control, retail, manufacturing control and automation/ robotics. Financial packages can produce sales invoices and statements, tax and VAT statements, stock lists, for example. Many other types of IT software are widely available, requiring expert installation and training of personnel.

Website: www.bcs.org.uk

Jewellery Designer – EG

Jewellery designers design and produce a wide variety of jewellery, some hand-made, some mass-produced. These can include traditional pieces using precious metals and gems, cheaper costume jewellery using synthetic stones and less precious metals, and fashion accessories made from other materials. There is most scope for designers of less expensive items.

Website: www.bja.org.uk & www.artscouncil.org.uk

Land Agent – UM – see Estate Manager

Legal Accountant – CAT

Legal accountants are people employed to conduct financial work in the offices of lawyers.

Website: www.icaew.co.uk & www.icas.org.uk

Loss Adjuster – NAG

Loss adjusters are called in by insurance companies to examine large and complicated insurance claims and to establish fair settlements. They may be members of the Chartered Institute of Loss Adjusters or qualified in for example law, surveying, accountancy or engineering.

Website: www.cila.co.uk

Market Maker (Finance) – NAL

As a market maker, you would be one of a team of people dealing in a range of financial products. You would use your specialist knowledge to buy and sell commodities such as foreign exchange, equities, crude oil, metals, gold, vegetable oils, and grains. You would be dealing with buyers and sellers on a global scale – almost always in a fully computerised dealing room, by email or telephone rather than face to face with people on the floor of an exchange.

Website: www.securities-institute.org.uk

Mathematician – QOG

Mathematicians use their specialist skills in abstract and applied mathematical concepts to define, quantify and predict almost any situation connected with teaching, science, technology, business logistics, manufacturing, computing, economics and finance.

Website: www.ima.org.uk

Media Researcher – GAL – see Broadcasting Researcher

Medical Laboratory Scientific Officer – JAX – see Biomedical Scientist

Medical Secretary – CAT/CAL

Medical secretaries keep the medical records of patients and handle medical correspondence and filing. They may work in hospitals or private practices, for individual doctors/consultants or in health centres, and are trained in the use of medical terminology.

Website: www.amspar.co.uk

Method Study Officer – COD

Method study traditionally involved the analysis of clerical/administrative work, but nowadays is closely related to work study and can include the analysis of the production methods used in industry. It involves measuring time and the human effort put into tasks in the workplace and looks for improvements which can be made, especially in reducing delays, bottlenecks, quality rejection, frustration and component shortage.

Website: www.imgtserv.co.uk/imgtserv/

Mining Surveyor – UM

Mining surveyors explore and map mineral deposits and consider the feasibility of their safe and profitable extraction. You might survey for metal ores, coal, salt or building materials, and could also be made responsible for mine safety and for avoiding environmental damage. You could advise of the value of deposits, leasing of land or mines and on legal matters.

Website: www.imm.org.uk

Molecular Biologist – QOD

Molecular biologists specialise in the biology of protein structures, DNA and RNA and the large molecules which govern the functions of cells and are associated with genetic factors. This field is sometimes referred to as the 'new biology'.

Website: www.iob.org

Multimedia Programmer/Specialist – CAV

Multimedia programmers bring together a wide range of software, including the technologies of computer simulation, animation, illustration, sound, virtual reality, satellite communication, laser science, television production, telephone and microwave systems. This is a rapidly growing field affecting education, medicine, entertainment, leisure, science, engineering, technology, commerce, industry and government.

Website: www.skillset.org & www.e-skills.com

Music Therapist – JOD

Music therapists are usually trained musicians with a postgraduate qualification in music therapy. They work with people of all ages, using mainly improvised music as a form of self-expression for clients with a variety of mental health problems, communication disorders and serious physical illness.

Website: www.bsmt.org

Naturopath – JOD

This branch of alternative medicine is based on the belief that the human body is self-regulatory and capable of self-repair if given the right conditions. Treatment can consist of special diets or fasting, coupled with hydrotherapy and osteopathic techniques. Degree and postgraduate courses are available.

Website: www.naturopathy.org.uk

Nuclear Engineer – RAN

Nuclear engineers work on the production and use of nuclear fuels to generate electric power, and the design and construction, control and safety of nuclear reactors. Their field covers many other branches of engineering – mechanical, civil, electrical and electronic – but is adapted to the handling and control of highly dangerous radioactive materials.

Website: www.world-nuclear.org

Nursery Nurse – KEB

A nursery nurse cares for babies and young mainly healthy children, usually under eight years of age, working in hospitals, clinics, crèches, nurseries and schools. Nursery nurses talk to children, read to them, show interest in their activities and their play with other children, discuss their painting and art work, helping them to enjoy their nursery life and to become confident and well adjusted socially.

Website: www.cache.org.uk

Orthotist/Prosthetist – JOL

Orthotists fit surgical appliances to human beings to correct a wide range of physical disabilities or weaknesses. They fit plaster casts, leg and arm supports, surgical collars and finger splints. The majority work for manufacturing companies who supply the health service, but spend a great deal of time in health service hospitals with patients. Orthotists measure patients, take casts and write instructions for appliances to be manufactured to meet their individual requirements. They also train patients to use the appliances and check that they are working properly, leg appliances in particular.

Prosthetists measure and fit amputees who have lost mainly legs. A major part of their work involves people who have lost limbs in car accidents, in armed conflicts and so on. They must be able to deal with children, whose appliances will become too small as they grow.

Website: www.bapo.com

Pathologist – QOD

Pathologists study human and animal tissues and assess diseases which affect cell structures, often detecting clues to sickness and also the causes of death.

Website: www.pathologists.org.uk

Presenter – GAL

A television or radio presenter is someone who links together the different parts of broadcasting programmes, introducing correspondents and conducting interviews with selected people. Genuine flair and originality, charisma and a captivating personality are required. News presenters need skills in journalism and an excellent grasp of current affairs; other presenters require specialist knowledge, for example weather presenters need training at the Met office, while political/financial presenters need an up-to-date understanding of parliamentary and City developments. There is no formal route into this very competitive careers field.

Website: www.skillset.org.uk

Press/Information Officer – FAC/FAF

Information officers work in the Civil Service to inform and explain government legislation or policy. Press officers release this information to the media and often accompany ministers on official overseas visits, when they release information on negotiations or developments to journalists. Information/publicity officers also produce publicity materials in association with, for example, public relations and advertising agencies and arrange conferences, exhibitions and marketing campaigns to explain government policy. In industry, commerce and education, information officers are very closely associated with librarians and perform many of the same tasks of keeping their organisations aware of relevant information released in magazines, newspapers, on television, radio or in published books and reports of all kinds.

Website: www.ipr.org.uk www.nctj.com http://www.civil-service.gov.uk/jobs/

Prison Governor – MAD

A prison governor is in overall charge of a prison, responsible for prison staff, the inmates and for all of its services or activities. Governors liaise closely with the police, social services and Home Office and must control the activity of inmates, and ensure they are kept in secure but humane conditions.

Website: www.hmprisonservice.gov.uk & www.sps.gov.uk (Scotland)

Prison Officer – MAD

In day-to-day contact with prisoners, prison officers are responsible for all the arrangements for food, hygiene, accommodation and recreation. The main roles are security and the maintenance of discipline.

Website: www.hmprisonservice.gov.uk & www.modernprisonofficer.com (Scotland)

Production Assistant (Film/TV/Radio) – GAL/GAB

Production assistants work in television, radio and film production, providing administrative and secretarial support for the producer. This is a demanding job and first class secretarial skills are essential.

Website: www.skillset.org

Prosthetist – JOL – see Orthotist

Psychotherapist – KEL
As a psychotherapist you would be concerned with helping patients with psychological problems, such as depression, behavioural problems or eating disorders. You would usually encourage them to talk about their feelings, thoughts and worries and to get them to speak freely in group or one-to-one situations. This work is closely linked with that of clinical psychologists and psychoanalysts.

Website: www.bap-psychotherapy.org & www.bcp.org.uk

Radio/TV Producer – GAL
Producers are responsible for promoting theatrical, film and video productions, for selecting or commissioning plays or scripts, for hiring directors, actors, actresses and for ensuring money is available to pay bills.

Website: www.skillset.org & www.metier.org.uk

Recording Engineer – RAL
Recording engineering is a specialised branch of electronic/radio engineering. Recording engineers are mainly employed by broadcasting authorities and recording studios for programmes to be transmitted later, or sold on tape or disc. Vacancies are limited.

Website: www.skillset.org

Recruitment Consultant – KED
Recruitment consultants advertise for candidates needed to fill employment vacancies at many different levels, from executives or directors to temping, secretarial or technical roles. They also maintain databases of available candidates for high demand positions. Some specialise, for example, in IT, nursing/medical or office vacancies.

Website: www.rec.uk.com

Reflexologist – JOD
Reflexologists are complementary medicine practitioners, applying pressure to patients' feet and hands to treat a range of medical problems.

Website: www.aor.org.uk

Robotics – R
Robots have evolved over the last 50 years from mechanical devices operated remotely by humans. In the car industry, such robots have been used for some time in production lines, to perform the routine and repetitive mechanical tasks of mass assembly. From these beginnings, robots have developed rapidly through advances in microelectronic and computing technology. Robots can now 'see', sense, move and manipulate, executing complex and precise tasks at very high speeds. They have come a long way from the car assembly line and a recent development has been the application of robotics in the human body.

Website: www.bara.org.uk

RSPCA/SSPCA Inspector – WAL

RSPCA inspectors provide 24-hour cover for animals in need, carry out rescues, investigate cruelty complaints, bring perpetrators of cruelty to court, inspect animal establishments, give advice and administer first aid. Entry is extremely competitive.

Website: www.rspca.org.uk & www.scottishspca.org

Scriptwriter – FAC

Scriptwriters produce scripts to be used in TV, radio, film or theatrical productions or performances and indicate the settings and effects that should accompany them. They may adapt existing works or create new ones.

Website: www.skillset.org

Security Officer – MAG

Security officers protect people, money, property, documents and organisations from theft, industrial espionage, kidnapping for example – using modern electronic devices, special patrols and specially armoured vehicles. Over 200,000 people are employed in private security companies. They are usually adults with armed services, police, prison officer and fire services backgrounds – but experts in electronic security systems are now increasingly employed.

Website: www.ipsa.org.uk

Shorthand Writer – LAG

Shorthand writers work in Crown Courts, the House of Commons and the House of Lords, where they record proceedings in shorthand or by using stenography equipment (Civil courts use audio recording equipment). In Scotland, they work in the High Court, Court of Session and the Sheriff Court.

Website: www.courtservice.gov.uk & www.verbatim-reporters.co.uk

Statistician – QOJ

Statisticians work with a variety of quantitative data, organising and analysing it to produce information on which decisions can be made, for example in government, finance, market research, economics, production and insurance. The statistician uses specialised knowledge of probability theory to estimate the likelihood of future situations arising, as well as producing statistics of past events.

Website: www.rss.org.uk

Telecommunications Engineering – RAL

Telecommunications engineering deals with the communication of sound, vision and written information of all types by telephone, radio, television, satellite and cable, optical fibre, electronic mail, fax and teletext. It is at the forefront of modern technological advance. Development work is conducted by electronic engineers and computer scientists. Telecom engineers install, maintain and repair equipment.

Website: www.net-works.org.uk

Television/Theatre Set or Stage Designer – ET

As a stage designer you would work closely with a TV or film director to create the required costumes and sets for theatrical, film or television performances. You could produce drawings and also scale models of costumes and scenery for the production staff to work on. You would usually have a qualification (Degree/HND) from an art school in this field.

Website: www.metier.org.uk

Travel & Tourism Clerk – GAX

Travel agency clerks work at counters discussing holiday choices and checking availability of hotels and flights on their computers – which they also use to print out details and quotations. They spend a great deal of time on the telephone.

Website: www.ttctraining.co.uk/abtac.html

Work Study Officer – COD

Work Study involves the analysis of industrial or administrative work, measuring time and human effort put into tasks in the workplace and looking for improvements which can be made especially in reducing delays, bottlenecks, quality rejection, frustration and component shortage. Traditionally work study was confined to production processes but can now include the study of office work and is closely linked with method study.

Website: www.imgtserv.co.uk/imgtserv/

Zoo Keeper – WAM

Keepers look after animals in zoos, mucking out their living quarters, preparing their bedding, water and food. They work long hours – from early in the morning to late in the evening – much of the time out of doors, and the work is often physically demanding. They must keep public and animal safety in mind and be constantly alert to animal health, assisting vets when animals are treated.

Website: www.abwak.co.uk

Zoologist – QOD

Zoology is the scientific study of animals, their anatomy, physiology, ecology, evolution, breeding/embryology. Zoological research takes place in government and agricultural research centres, university departments, fishery research units, veterinary schools and agricultural colleges and has wide advantages for agriculture, conservation, fisheries and animal breeding.

Website: www.iob.org

If you have strong religious beliefs, you might wish to consider a career as a vicar, priest, rabbi, elder, imam or whatever is appropriate for your particular faith. Many different religions are practised in the United Kingdom and we cannot possibly do justice to them in a book of this kind. You are probably already an active member of a religious group and we suggest that you start by discussing your career aspirations with a local representative of your religion.

Each religion has its own training methods but most involve a period of college-based study in the United Kingdom or overseas. You can obtain further information by visiting relevant websites from the list below.

Baptist Church – Website: www.baptist.org.uk

Buddhism – Website: www.buddhism.org

Church of England – Website: www.cofe.anglican.org

Church of Ireland – Website: www.ireland.anglican.org

Church of Scotland – Website: www.churchofscotland.org.uk

Hinduism – Website: www.hindu.org

Islamic – Website: www.islamic.org.uk

Judaism – Website: www.jewish.co.uk

Methodist Church of Great Britain – Website: www.methodist.org.uk

Methodist Church of Ireland – Website: www.irishmethodist.org

Roman Catholic Church in England & Wales – Website: www.catholic-ew.org.uk

Roman Catholic Church In Ireland – Website: www.catholicireland.net

Roman Catholic Church in Scotland – Website: www.catholic-scotland.org.uk

Sikhism – Website: www.sikhs.org & www.sikhnet.com